Reading Negri

Series: Creative Marxism
Series Editor: Bill Martin

Reading Negri

Marxism in the Age of Empire

EDITED BY

Pierre Lamarche,
Max Rosenkrantz, and
David Sherman

OPEN COURT
Chicago and La Salle, Illinois

Volume 3 in the series Creative Marxism

To order books from Open Court, call 1-800-815-2280 or visit www.opencourtbooks.com.

Open Court Publishing Company is a division of Carus Publishing Company.

© 2011 by Carus Publishing Company

First printing 2011

Printed and bound in the United States of America.

Library of Congress Cataloging-in-Publication Data

Reading Negri: Marxism in the age of empire / edited by Pierre Lamarche, Max Rosenkrantz, and David Sherman.
        p. cm. — (Creative Marxism ; v. 3)
    Includes bibliographical references and index.
    ISBN 978-0-8126-9655-4 (trade paper : alk. paper)
    1. Negri, Antonio, 1933- 2. Political science—Italy—Philosophy.
I. Lamarche, Pierre. II. Rosenkrantz, Max, 1966- III. Sherman, David, 1958-
JC265.N4R43 2010
335.4092--dc22

                                                     2010042142

For Harry Cleaver, teacher and friend

Contents

Political Biography and Selected Bibliography of Antonio Negri

Antonio Negri was born in 1933 in Padua, Italy. His first forays into social and political activism date from his days as a philosophy student at Padua University where he first became involved with the student catholic activist organization *Gioventú Italiana di Azione Cattolica*. He was expelled from this group in 1954 as a result of a crackdown upon *Azione Cattolica's* spokesman, Mario Rossi, that was imposed by none other than Pope Pius XII. Shortly thereafter, Negri joined another leftist catholic group, *Intesa*, but resigned from that organization in 1958, frustrated by the meddling of the bishop of Padua in its affairs, particularly what the bishop viewed as its socialist tendencies. In 1956 Negri produced a dissertation on German historicism, which earned him a graduate degree in philosophy, and, after additional study at the Benedetto Croce Institute for Historical Studies, obtained in 1959 a professorship in the Philosophy of Law at Padua University.

Having abandoned the catholic activist organizations of his schooldays in the face of the conservative, reactionary culture of the Italian catholic church's hierarchy, Negri had begun to seek out new avenues to pursue the issues of social justice that would remain his lifelong concern. In the same year he obtained his professorship, he was also elected to the post of municipal councilman and he began to direct the journal of the Italian Socialist Party, on whose ticket he had run. However, in 1963—a watershed year for Negri—he left the Italian Socialist Party in reaction to its decision to enter into a political alliance with the Christian Democrats. During what has been called the "hot" summer of 1963, Negri organized reading groups on Marx's *Capital* among the city's industrial workers, many of whom were employed in the petrochemical industry. Around this time, moreover, Negri was involved in two revolutionary periodicals. The first, *Potere Operaio* ("Workers Power"), was of a more practical nature, as it addressed the workers and their political needs directly, while the second periodical, *Quaderni Rossi* ("Red Notebooks"), with offices in Turin, Milan, Rome, and Padua, addressed theoretical issues from the workers' perspective. Other theorists that were involved in founding *Quaderni Rossi* included Raniero Panzieri, Romano Alquati, Mario Tronti, and Sergio Bologna—all of whom, like Negri, would become associated with what would become the Autonomist Marxism movement. Other worker publications were founded between 1963 and 1967, as Negri continued to both engage in revolutionary political activities and teach at the University.

The years 1967–1973 saw an intensification of revolutionary political activity as student and worker struggles in Italy converged in a way that was unprecedented in Europe. During this period, it is clear that Negri's positions, as well as the positions of the political movement in general, were moving well to the left of the Italian Communist Party, which was increasingly taken to be reactionary. Groups such as *Lotta Continua* ("Struggle Continues"), *Avanguardia Operaia* ("Workers' Vanguard"), and *Movimento Studentesco* ("Student Movement") arose and shared a common view of Negri as one of their leading theoreticians. The differences between these groups and the Communist Party became especially clear in 1973, when the Communist Party formed an alliance with the Christian Democrats, who, along with the industrial unions, were seeking to extract givebacks from the workers while reducing health and safety precautions and increasing the speed of the production lines.

It was with the birth of "autonomous" worker committees in the factories during 1973 that *Autonomia* ("Autonomy") first arose. These committees, comprised of younger, more militant workers, responded not only to the particular fact that longstanding institutions such as the Communist Party and the industrial unions no longer represented their interests; they also responded to a more general distrust of institutions as such, regardless of where they stood on the ideological spectrum. It was around this time that Negri began to theorize the historical movement from "the mass worker" (i.e., the industrial worker producing consumer goods in the factory) to "the social worker," a movement that reflects the idea that capital was in the process of moving beyond the workplace and turning society itself into a factory of sorts in order to press the general population into the service of generating profits, and, ultimately, retaining social control for the elite. Negri's theory both reflected and influenced the more radical elements of society, as social groups not previously understood as part of the proletariat by classical Marxist theory—such as housewives, students, and environmentalists—came together with the industrial workers in social protest on the grounds that all were being instrumentalized by capital.

Padua itself was hit hard by the protests, and various acts of violence occurred. Criminally charged with inciting the protests, Negri fled to Paris, where he began teaching at the *École Normale*, then run by the French philosopher Louis Althusser, who was trying to make sense of Marxism in structuralist terms. (One of the courses Negri taught at the *École Normale* formed the basis for his book *Marx Beyond Marx: Lessons on the Grundrisse.*) Although Negri was cleared of the criminal charges in 1977, he continued to teach in France until 1979. On returning to Italy, however, and along with other prominent left-wing intellectuals linked to *Autonomia*, Negri was arrested on charges that were unspecified though allegedly in connection with the kidnapping and murder of the Italian industrialist Aldo Moro by the Red Brigades, a case that was then receiving international attention. Despite the fact that Negri had no known connection with the Red Brigades (and, indeed, although its top-down style was anathema to the principles of autonomism), he remained in jail for five years without going to trial.

In 1983, while still in jail, Negri ran for office in a national election and received enough votes on the national Radical Party ticket to lead it in Parliament. Under a then-existing law that provided prosecutorial immunity for members of Parliament, Negri was freed from jail. In September of that year, however, Negri was stripped of his parliamentary immunity, and he once again fled to Paris. From 1983 to 1997, he taught at the *Université de Paris VII* (St. Denis) and the *College Internationale de Philosophie*. Although a condition of his residence in France was that he refrain from engaging in political activities, Negri continued to write, to engage in productive collaborations with such French philosophers as Giles Deleuze, Félix Guattari, and Yann Moulier, and he founded the journal *Futur Antérieur*.

Negri returned to Italy in 1997, at which time he was arrested and jailed at Rebibbi Prison in Rome, where he continued to write. In 2000 Negri's book *Empire*, co-written with his student Michael Hardt, was published and received international acclaim. In the spring of 2003, Negri was released from jail. Since being released, he has continued to both write and speak publicly.

Selected Bibliography of Books in English by Antonio Negri

Commonwealth (with Michael Hardt), Harvard University Press, 2009.
Communists Like Us (with Felix Guattari), Autonomedia, 1990.
Empire (with Michael Hardt), Harvard University Press, 2000.

Goodbye Mr. Socialism: Antonio Negri in Conversation with Raf Valvola Scelsi (tr. Peter Thomas), Seven Stories Press, 2008.

Insurgencies: Constituent Power and the Modern State (tr. Maurizia Boscagli), University of Minnesota Press, 2009.

The Labor of Job: The Biblical Text as a Parable of Human Labor (tr. Matteo Mandarini), Duke University Press, 2009.

Labor of Dionysus: A Critique of the State Form (with Michael Hardt), University of Minnesota Press, 1994.

Marx Beyond Marx: Lessons on the Grundrisse, Autonomedia, 1991.

Multitude: War and Democracy in the Age of Empire (with Michael Hardt), Penguin Press, 2004.

Negri on Negri: In Conversation with Anne Dufourmentelle, Routledge, 2004.

The Political Descartes: Reason, Ideology, and the Bourgeois Project (tr. Matteo Mandarini), Verso, 2006.

The Politics of Subversion: A Manifesto for the Twenty-First Century, (tr. James Newell), Polity Press, 2005.

The Porcelain Workshop: For a New Grammar of Politics (tr. Noura Wedell), Semiotext(e), 2008.

In Praise of the Common: A Conversation on Philosophy and Politics (with Cesare Casarino), University of Minnesota Press, 2008.

Reflections on Empire (with contributions from Michael Hardt and Danilo Zolo, tr. Ed Emery), Polity Press, 2008.

Revolution Retrieved: Selected Writings on Marx, Keynes, Capitalist Crisis, and New Social Subjects, 1967–1983 (trs. Ed Emery and John Merrington), Red Notes, 1988.

The Savage Anomaly: The Power of Spinoza's Metaphysics and Politics (tr. Michael Hardt), University of Minnesota Press, 1991.

Time for Revolution (tr. Matteo Mandarini), Continuum, 2003.

Reading Negri: An Introduction[1]

PIERRE LAMARCHE, MAX ROSENKRANTZ, and DAVID SHERMAN

Published at the turn of the millennium, shortly after the explosive Seattle protests against the World Trade Organization, Antonio Negri and Michael Hardt's *Empire* has become one of the most widely discussed political works of our time. The book, influential and controversial by turns, has become a rallying point for many students, workers, and intellectuals who oppose the capitalist globalization processes of "the New World Order." For many other intellectuals and pundits, who span the full range of the political spectrum, however, it is the virtual embodiment of reckless theoretical speculation. In either case, although *Empire*, as well as its 2004 sequel, *Multitude*, have catapulted Negri and Hardt to international prominence, it must be recognized that, for Negri, these books are the culmination of roughly 40 years of intense theoretical and practical labors, which have their genesis in the 1950s Italian worker movement known as "autonomist Marxism."

Motivated by the belief that *Empire* and *Multitude* cannot be fully appreciated without an understanding of Negri's earlier work, as well as the autonomist Marxist movement that spawned it, all of which deserve attention in their own right, we seek in this collection to consider this larger body of work. Moreover, as anyone who is acquainted with this larger body of work fully knows, Negri is an expansive thinker whose work draws on such diverse figures as Machiavelli, Marx, Spinoza, Schumpeter, Keynes, Deleuze, and Foucault, all of whom, in varying degrees, find expression in the pages of this collection. And, lastly, because Negri is an important thinker whose larger body of work has not been sufficiently

[1] We would like to thank Elaine Englehardt and the office of the Vice President for Scholarship and Outreach at Utah Valley University for their generous support of this project, and UVU research assistant Jared Smith for his hard work in helping to prepare the final manuscript.

appreciated, in this collection we seek to bring his thought into a productive tension with other important critical thinkers and traditions in order
to better situate it. Thus, not only shall we consider Negri's theoretical
underpinnings in the Italian New left, as well as the influential Spinozist
and Marxist dimensions of this thought, but we shall also consider his relationship to various other thinkers and traditions, which include Georges
Bataille, the Frankfurt School, Donna Haraway, Rosalind Krauss, and
Michael Taussig. It is only in these ways that the depth and breadth of
Negri's work can be fully appreciated.

*   *   *

Two essays by Negri, "Marx on Cycle and Crisis" and "Crisis of the
Planner State: Communism and Revolutionary Organization," written in
1968 and 1971, provide much of the theoretical scaffolding for Negri's
subsequent work. And these essays, in turn, follow from the works of earlier autonomist Marxists, such as Raniero Panzieri and Mario Tronti, who,
beginning in the late 1950s, sought to come to grips with the crisis that
plagued the Italian labor movement—in fact, the international labor movement overall—in the aftermath of the Soviet Union's invasion of Hungary
and Khrushchev's revelations concerning the Stalinist era.

In its end run on orthodox Marxism, autonomist Marxism has continuously returned for sustenance to the writings of Marx himself, as is
evident in the earliest works of Panzieri and Tronti, who contend that to
revivify Marxism, both theoretically and practically, it is necessary to begin
not from the abstract standpoint of the theoretician but from the concrete
standpoint of the working class's struggles in the factory. In terms of practice, this constitutes the rejection of a working class politics predicated on
a manufactured identity between workers and the so-called "organic intellectuals" of a vanguard party, who dispense directives in their name from
above: worker control, Panzieri asserts, "must emerge and make itself
concrete within the reality of the working class, expressing its revolutionary autonomy."[2] Correlatively, in terms of theory, this constitutes the
rejection of an approach that starts from concerns that are ideological
rather than politico-economic, the notion being that if it is preoccupied
with ideology, theory, even when purportedly in the service of the working class, implicitly assumes the perspective of capital. Panzieri therefore
seeks "to restore Marxism to its natural terrain, which is that of perma-

    [2] Quoted in Steve Wright, *Storming Heaven: Class Composition and Struggle in Italian
Autonomist Marxism*, London: Pluto Press 2002, 19.

nent critique,"[3] but instead of privileging "ideology critique"—as did the critical theorists and, closer to home, the Gramscians—he argued that critique should follow determinately from the mass action of workers in their struggles from below. This approach is exemplified by his critique of technological rationality. In "Surplus Value and Planning: Notes on the Reading of *Capital*," Panzieri breaks from the conventional Marxist view (most forcefully articulated by Lenin) that state economic planning is antithetical to the proper functioning of capitalism, and argues instead that such planning had become an indispensable aspect of it. "The development of capitalist planning is something closely related to that of the capitalist use of machines,"[4] Panzieri argues, and he sees this development as a rearguard action by the state in defense of corporate profits. Moreover, the increasingly technological rationalization of the production process, he asserts, must be understood as a historically specific reaction by capital to working class struggles, which is what necessitated the greater levels of planning.[5]

So, too, in "Social Capital" Tronti affirms that capital has permeated all aspects of life, but, again, rather than look at the matter ideologically, and thus from the perspective of capital, he looks at it economically (i.e., as a moment within the unfolding relations of production that underlie capitalist development) and from the perspective of the working class.[6] Returning to volume II of *Capital*, he begins by building on the distinction that Marx had made between the "direct process of the production of capital" and "the total process of capital reproduction"—that is, between the process of value creation during work and the processes of consumption and reproduction of capital itself. Tronti contends that as capitalism develops the socialization of its consumption and reproduction processes becomes increasingly necessary, which calls forth a reconstituted form of social organization: society, in its very essence, becomes capitalistic. And, at this stage of capitalist development, as he maintains elsewhere, "the social relation becomes a moment of the relation of production [and] the whole of society becomes an articulation of production; in other words, the whole of society exists as a function of the factory and the factory extends its exclusive domination over the whole of society."[7] In this way,

---

[3] Raniero Panzieri, *La crisi del movimento operaio: Scritti interventi lettere, 1956–1960*, Milan: Lampugnani Nigri 1973, 47, quoted in Steve Wright, *Storming Heaven: Class Composition and Struggle in Italian Autonomist Marxism*, Ibid., 16.
[4] Quoted in Steve Wright, *Storming Heaven*, Ibid., 44.
[5] See Harry Cleaver, *Reading Capital Politically*, Leeds: Antitheses 2000, 65–66.
[6] Mario Tronti, "Social Capital," *Telos* no. 17, Fall 1973, 98–121. "Social Capital" is a chapter in Tronti's *Operai e capitale*, Turin: Einaudi 1971, whose chapters constitute discrete essays.
[7] Mario Tronti, "La fabbrica e la societa," in *Operai e capitale*, 51, quoted in Steve Wright, *Storming Heaven*, Ibid., 38–39.

the social totality itself becomes a factory of sorts, a "social factory" (which testifies to the socialization of exploitation), and, therefore, both the capitalist class and working classes must be comprehended in aggregate terms. Thus, according to Tronti, the "collective capitalist," produced by the new form of social organization, functions with respect to "social capital" rather than the capital of any particular capitalist—or, for that matter, the collective capital of individual capitalists—for its aim is nothing less than the socialization of capitalist production itself. And, with this argument, Tronti is in a position to make what is arguably autonomist Marxism's most fundamental claim: notwithstanding the self-understanding of individual capitalists, as a form of social organization, capitalism is less about the drive for profits than for social control based upon the imposition of work.

With the concept of the social factory, in which "there is a social surplus-labor which is taken from the working class and which ends up socializing the very existence of surplus value,"[8] Tronti is saying from an economic perspective what critical theorists such as Adorno and Horkheimer are saying from a cultural one with their concept of "the culture industry." Yet, while both perspectives assert that under late capitalism there is a push to colonize every nook and cranny of leisure time to reproduce capitalist relations, their assessments of this phenomenon differ. When Tronti asserts that "any attempt to assume the general interest, every temptation to stop at the level of social science, will only serve to better inscribe the working class within the development of capital,"[9] he is indirectly critiquing Adorno and Horkheimer, who, by seeing the burgeoning working class in sociopsychological terms, unwittingly adopt the perspective of capital. "From labor's viewpoint," Tronti declares, "the integral control of the social process becomes all the more possible as capital becomes social capital,"[10] for capital's move to generalize the work relation within society by harnessing the non-work time of workers and non-workers alike gives rise to a corresponding generalization of the struggle against it. Seemingly disparate segments of society, whether waged or unwaged and whether galvanized around universal matters relating to the socialization of capital (the consumer and environmental movements) or particular ones (movements by minorities, women, and students), increasingly come to see themselves in class terms. For Tronti and other autonomist Marxists, however, this burgeoning working class is not powerless, subordinate, and increasingly indistinguishable, as Adorno and Horkheimer depict it, but rather powerful by virtue of its role within the functioning of capitalism, insubordinate by virtue of its recognition that

---

[8] Mario Tronti, "Social Capital," 101.
[9] Ibid., 120.
[10] Ibid., 119.

capital's imperatives are not its own, and increasingly differentiated and autonomous—both as a general class with respect to capital and as particular groups that comprise this general class, who in pursuing their own interests also pursue the general class interest by challenging the prerogatives of capital. In sum, then, while Adorno and Horkheimer see the cultural sphere (what Tronti following Marx calls "the processes of consumption and the reproduction of capital") as simply mirroring the valorization processes that occur in the workplace, Tronti and those who follow him see the social factory as comprised of groups that are engaged in autonomous, self-valorizing activities, which have the consequence of leading to further capitalist crises.

It is within this framework, in which "the total process of capital reproduction" figures no less than the "direct process of the production of capital," that Negri's earlier works on economic crises must be understood. In "Marx on Cycle and Crisis," he attacks the notion that economic crises are deviations from a more fundamental underlying tendency toward equilibrium within market economies and argues, instead, that such crises, mystified by economists of all stripes (including Marxist political economists), *are* the fundamental underlying tendency, and that they are so for reasons that are essentially political in nature. According to Negri, in the aftermath of the economic breakdown of the 1920s and 1930s, it was recognized that economic crises result from the various dualisms that underlie the economic process (i.e., wages and profits, supply and demand, consumption and production) which do not reconcile of their own accord, as if by some "invisible hand," but rather have to be regulated. Development, it was thought, could perform this regulatory function, and, as the only alternative to crisis, it would have to be the new form of the business cycle. But what most political economists failed to see, Negri asserts, was not only that these dualisms could not be smoothly regulated through development, but that economic crises are actually the spur to development and thus productive of profit. Two exceptions were Keynes and Schumpeter, and it was Schumpeter, in particular, who, with his idea of "creative destruction," recognized that the developmental process is really an open-ended one in which "innovation is a healthy force, provoking crisis, and thereby reactivating the economic process, over and against the action of antagonistic forces bent on the destruction of profit."[11] Still, given their proclivities, what even Keynes and Schumpeter could not see was that these antagonistic forces bent on destroying profits were not wholly internal to the economic process—for example, they did not issue solely from competition amongst capitalists—but instead were attributable to the working

---

[11] Antonio Negri, "Marx on Cycle and Crisis," in *Revolution Retrieved*, London: Red Notes 1988, 55.

class, whose struggles for higher wages, less work, and better working conditions, more generally, tend to undermine profits, induce the reconstitution of the production process, and thus place the foundation upon which future profits might be derived on a sounder footing. Moreover, Negri contends, "capital itself, in its collective form, is not only obliged to accept the fact that the working class determines development, but may also be forced, within certain limits, to solicit this kind of working class response to its control over development, to guarantee the conditions whereby the cycle can be regulated."[12]

Put more starkly, according to Negri, political economists regularly fetishize capitalism's underlying economic processes by failing to see that, above all, capitalism is based upon a set of social relations grounded in class exploitation, and that the ebb and flow of this exploitation, i.e., the relative *political* power of these classes at any point in time (as evidenced by the amount of surplus value appropriated from the working classes) is what determines the rate of profit and, consequently, the contours of future development. As a result, development must not be viewed in neutral terms, or, worse, in terms that would make it appear to be beneficial to the working class; rather, it must be viewed as a restructuring of power relations, or, to be more precise, as capital's attempt to regain greater control in response to crises brought about by working class attacks. And the ways in which capital regains control, as Panzieri and Tronti had respectively asserted, is through the increased use of machinery against the working class (i.e., "technological development") and the increased socialization of the conflict. Over the long run, however, both responses exacerbate certain antagonistic tendencies that underlie capitalist relations. Following Marx's analysis, Negri points out that the substitution of machinery for labor in response to any given crisis may well reestablish profits, but over the long run, as a general response to crises, it diminishes the sole source of value on which capital can draw, and thus causes a lowering of the rate of profit. (And, insofar as capitalism is about structuring society on the basis of work it, undercuts its own *raison d'etre*.) So, too, building on Tronti's extension and transformation of Marx, Negri contends that progressively drawing in the broader society "ends up revolutionizing social stratification (or, to define it more correctly, the political class composition) and laying the groundwork for a deepening, an extension and radicalization of the class antagonism."[13] Profit thus "becomes dependent only on the political functions of capital [which] strips itself back to basics, and attempts to restructure itself by heightening the level of its own political nature."[14]

---

[12] Ibid., 69
[13] Ibid.
[14] Ibid., 72.

A scant three years later, however, Negri was forced to retheorize the political nature of capital by virtue of its fundamental restructuring in response to the economic crisis of the early 1970s. The "planner state," based upon the theories of Keynes, had been the political form of capital for roughly three decades, and had more or less effectively managed crises, according to Negri, by bringing the worker struggles that produced them, and thus the "creative destruction" that spurred development, into a larger economic plan, which, crucially, included wage increases that reflected increases in productivity. But the increased socialization of capital had increased the pressures imposed on capital by the waged and unwaged alike during the turbulent 1960s, which ruptured the "wage-productivity deal" at the heart of this politico-economic model. The planner state for managing crises was, therefore, itself thrown into an insuperable crisis.

In "Crisis of the Planner State: Communism and Revolutionary Organization," Negri, establishing the framework for arguments that he and Hardt will build on almost 30 years later in *Empire*, says that "the sequence state-plan-enterprise is overthrown, becomes reversed. Whereas the state previously fulfilled a hegemonic role, representing and guaranteeing equivalence of all the factors in the movement of production-reproduction, the collapse of equivalence now makes the function of the state subordinate to that of the big enterprise."[15] And this leads, in turn, to the predominance of multinational corporations, which means that "at the level of the world-market, the 'crisis-state' thus also represents a crisis of 'national-states' in relation to the multinational enterprise as the dominant form of capitalist command."[16] The "collapse of equivalence" that sets this train of events into motion obliquely refers to the fact "that money no longer . . . merely "mediat[es] exchange between labour and capital" but is instead utilized by capital as a tool of unbridled domination.[17] This phenomenon itself, however, is only symptomatic of an underlying breakdown in the Marxian "law of value," which, for Negri, based upon his interpretation of the *Grundrisse* (Marx's 1857 economic notebooks), means that the working-class insurgencies that had induced technological development had done so to such a degree that the labor theory of value, the heart of Marx's analysis of capital, was increasingly irrelevant:[18] "Capital . . .

[15] Antonio Negri, "Crisis of the Planner-State: Communism and Revolutionary Organization," in *Revolution Retrieved*, London: Red Notes 1988, 121.

[16] Ibid., 122.

[17] Ibid., 102.

[18] See Harry Cleaver, "Work, Value and Domination: On the Continuing relevance of the Marxian Labor Theory of Value in the Crisis of the Keynesian Planner State," http://www.eco.utexas.edu/facstaff/Cleaver/offenegri.html.

becomes more and more dissociated from a purely value definition and operates more and more in a context of relations of force."[19] In sum, then, there is a social recomposition of labor, which, by virtue of the decline of the nation-state, increasingly takes place on a global level (hence a move from the social factory to the "global factory"[20]), and which, by virtue of a change in the "organic composition of capital," increasingly is for the end of social control rather than wealth creation (given the advanced technological state of production).

On the flip-side of the equation—and, again, in a fashion that anticipates *Empire*—Negri argues that labor, now coterminous with the global factory, increasingly becomes indifferentiable because it increasingly becomes a mere adjunct to technology, which is comprised of the value appropriated from the working class during previous economic cycles. And, this "ending of any qualitative differentiation within social labor as a whole,"[21] he says, engenders "an increasingly compact and unified 'social individual'."[22] For Negri, this is the impetus for a new revolutionary strategy, one that moves beyond the workerist struggle over wages that marked a differentiated labor force (when the "law of value" still held sway) to one over reappropriating the means of production, which is required for ending capitalist social control.

* * *

Our volume begins with a selection of three papers that situate Negri's work vis à vis his own theoretical basis in the Italian New Left movement, and that explore the relationship between his revolutionary project and those of the Frankfurt School theorists and of Georges Bataille—theoretical connections which have not yet been explored in secondary literature on Negri's work.

Upon his arrest in 1979, Antonio Negri was widely denounced as a *cattivo maestro* (wicked teacher). In "*Cattivi Maestri*: Some Reflections on the Legacy of Guido Bianchini, Luciano Ferrari Bravo and Primo Moroni," Steve Wright opens our volume with a *tour de force* examination of the writings of these three other Italian communists (two of whom were also imprisoned as part of the '7 April case'), whose work still remains little known in the English-speaking world. The first of these, Luciano Ferrari Bravo, was a close associate of Negri who would go on to develop his own

---

[19] Antonio Negri, "Crisis of the Planner-State," Ibid., 127.
[20] Ibid., 123.
[21] Ibid., 117.
[22] Ibid., 103.

distinctive understandings of the relationship between state and class conflict. The second, Guido Bianchini, likewise worked at the University of Padova and in the extraparliamentary group *Potere Operaio*, where he would chart a unique exploration of the shifting trajectories within class composition. The third, Primo Moroni, participated in a series of influential journals (from *Primo Maggio* to *Derive Approdi*), while running a bookshop that became a central cultural hub for Milan's radical left. Each would prove influential in their own way, helping to form the sensibilities of successive generations of Italian leftists. Examined together, their efforts to understand the possibilities for radical social change provide important insights into the richness of postwar Italian radical thought. By examining the contributions of these central but lesser known figures within the Italian New Left movement, Wright offers a sweeping and fascinating account of the activist and intellectual milieu within which Negri truly cut his teeth, allowing us to situate his theoretical underpinnings and subsequent development much more clearly and fully. Indeed, Wright's paper confirms his status as the foremost historian of the Italian New Left in the English-speaking world today.

Pierre Lamarche begins his paper, "Selling a Revolution: Negri, Bataille, and the Arcana of Production," by noting the emphasis that Negri and his collaborators place on analyzing the project of transcending capital/Empire in terms of the liberation of productive force from the limitations imposed on it within the regime of wage labor that is central to capitalist production. Consistent with a central aspect of both Marx's analysis of capital and the Autonomist movement, Negri emphasizes the fact that the revolutionary social transformation that he and his collaborators are attempting to theorize involves freeing "work"—as creative, imaginative, productive life activity—from the strictures of "work"—as imposed wage labor—hence liberating the vast potential of social productivity.

Lamarche also notes the fact that Negri and his collaborators, particularly in the recent works with Hardt, identify a qualitative transition in the labor process, and argue that "immaterial labor" producing knowledge, information, affects, etc., while currently still a tendency, will become hegemonic in the postmodern age of Empire, in the same way that Marx argued that socialized, industrial wage labor was a tendency that would attain hegemony in modern, capitalist nations. Although Marx associated the transformation to socialized labor with the privileged revolutionary status of the industrial proletariat, Lamarche notes that Hardt and Negri explicitly reject assigning a privileged political status to immaterial labor in the recent *Multitude*. Instead, the privileged bearer of transformative force is "the poor," and those who struggle in poverty. Since, in the postmodern age of Empire, the poor everywhere are central to cycles of production and accumulation that they are, nonetheless, excluded from in both private and public realms, their productive force always aims at accumulation that is neither private, nor public, but rather *in common*, as Hardt and Negri hearken to the old notion of "the commons" to try to signal a mode of social accumulation and distribution that transcends the limitations of capital/Empire's public/private model.

Lamarche argues that Hardt and Negri privilege "the poor" rather than immaterial laborers as the *topos* of that production in common which can carry us beyond Empire because the transformation to immaterial labor alone is insufficient to explode the commodity form, and hence the imposition of wage labor, that is central to capitalist production. It is only production in common that can truly disrupt the constant reimposition of the commodity form on the products of labor, material or immaterial, and hence that can facilitate a real social transformation beyond capital/Empire.

Ultimately, Lamarche argues that this emphasis on modes of social production in Negri's work, while providing valuable contributions to progressive analysis of that area, requires a corrective in order to avoid two dangerous traps, namely that of equating people with productive force and life with work, and of commodifying human life and experience as nothing more than so many things ("subjectivities," "affects," etc.) that we produce. Lamarche argues that such a corrective can be located in the work of Georges Bataille, who would criticize Negri's work as remaining within the bounds of limited economy, and hence as fixated on circuits of production and accumulation, ignoring the excessiveness characteristic of contemporary circuits of global production, both material and immaterial, and hence the need to liberate not "work" or productive force, but rather people *from* work, and to refuse the identification of life with work—an identification tantamount to equating people with slaves.

Lamarche thus seeks to engage Negri's work in a productive dialogue with another—on his view, underappreciated—theorist of progressive social transformation, bringing together two figures the relationship between whom has not yet been analyzed. In the late 1920s and early 30s, Bataille sought a conception of revolutionary transformation that could function as an alternative to fascism and Soviet state capitalism, and later to the status quo of Western market capitalism. That alternative had to offer something substantive to ordinary working class people—a selling point—in the same way that fascism had promised real change for people suffering under the conditions of economic and political instability and crisis between the wars. So too, Negri and Guattari forcefully argue in their 1985 *Communists Like Us* that communism in the postmodern age must offer a real hope of substantive change to ordinary people who are "swing-voters" between capitalist and progressive paths. Lamarche ultimately argues that selling Negri's revolution today—making it meaningful and attractive to ordinary people—requires a Bataillean correction to his and his collaborator's trajectory, which tends towards commodifying life and experience, and equating life with work.

David Sherman begins "Metapolitics Now: Negri, Critical Theory, Praxis" by scrutinizing the notions of production, labor, and value in *Empire* and *Multitude* in order to clarify the conceptual scaffolding of what he takes to be "the primacy of the political" in Negri's thought. Building on Negri's 1989 book *The Politics of Subversion*, Sherman argues that Negri tends to absolutize one of autonomist Marxism's earliest and most crucial insights, namely, that as a system capitalism is concerned at least as much with structuring the social totality through the imposition of work as it is with the generation of profits, which has the effect of generalizing these notions, and thus causing them to lose their descriptive power. As a result, despite many important theoretical insights, Negri not only tends to obscure the mechanics of how capitalism actually unfolds, but he also tends to put out of play the sort of emancipatory dynamics inherent in Marx's analysis of capitalism. As the successors to capital and the working class, Empire and the multitude, Sherman contends, are indeterminate totalities, and it is only by virtue of Negri's reference to Deleuze's postmodern ontology, rather than capitalism's inherent contradictions, that there is reason for historical optimism.

In their argument for the primacy of politics over economics, Negri and Hardt's position in *Empire* and *Multitude*, according to Sherman, is reminiscent of the position that was taken by the first generation of the Frankfurt School. Although acknowledging certain crucial differences, Sherman argues that Friedrich Pollock's prognoses concerning state capitalism are a forerunner of what he calls Negri and Hardt's empire capitalism. Accordingly, although the pessimism of Adorno and Horkheimer, which was based on Pollock's work, stands in sharp contrast to Negri and Hardt's optimism, and state capitalism manifested a centralized model that stands in sharp contrast to Empire's decentralized one, both systems ultimately facilitate a process of centralized political integration that culminates in a totalitarian authority that supplants all economic considerations. As a corrective to these totalizing models, Sherman points to Franz Neumann's *Behemoth*, which, in the process of balancing political and economic considerations, offers finely detailed empirical analyses that can serve as the basis for political praxis.

Sherman's underlying concern, then, is that by moving to "the primacy of the political," Negri and Hardt paradoxically undermine, instead of facilitate, the theoretical bases for political action. In this respect, he agrees with Ernesto Laclau's depiction of Empire as "metapolitical," but as against Laclau, who jettisons all class analyses in favor of a putatively "radical democratic politics" based on discourse, he sides with Negri and

Hardt, who, he asserts, rightfully retain a class analysis that goes beyond the unduly restricted notion of "the working class." Ultimately, because it moves them beyond a Deleuzian ontology that flattens important insights, Sherman applauds what he takes to be the crucial philosophical move in *Multitude*, namely, the rejection of the conceptual coupling "identity-difference" in favor of "commonality-singularity." Yet, he argues, one further move is needed, a move to "commonality-particularity," which opens up the basis for dialectically informed political determinations that would, in turn, lead the way to more determinate forms of praxis.

Sherman's article, which sees Negri's theory of value as the basis of his political theory, opens on to the next section of our collection, which includes three important articles that deal directly with Negri's theory of value. Melinda Cooper's "Marx Beyond Marx: Creating a World Outside and Beyond Measure" is the most sympathetic of the three papers on Negri's writings on Marx's value theory. Like Caffentzis, Cooper takes up Negri's attempt to discern an ambiguity in Marx's discussion of labor. One strand—found in Capital—makes the notion of measure in terms of time central: The law of value depends on a radical separation of necessary and surplus labor and the measurability of both. The other strand—found in the "Fragment on Machines"—posits a conception of labor that is beyond measure. Cooper argues, in support of Negri, that it is this latter conception that is appropriate to the postmodern world. Given that labor is no longer measurable, the refusal of work loses pride of place in the self-activity of revolutionary subjects. Rather, the central task of anticapitalist forces is to unleash these productive energies and create a world "beyond measure."

Cooper reads Negri as holding that Marx's value theory presupposes both temporal and spatial measurability. The real subsumption of society—a condition in which "capital has subjugated all conditions of social production to itself"—collapses the distinction between necessary and surplus labor. Since the significance of the theory of value construed as a theory of temporal measure depends upon the distinction, this collapse undermines that construal. Similarly the theory of value as a theory of spatial measure depends upon the centrality of nation states and the related division between first, second, and third worlds. In the smooth space of Empire geopolitics has become spatially immeasurable. Finally, Negri's contention that capitalist development is now characterized by a perpetual state of crisis poses a further problem for measurability. Periods of equilibrium cannot be distinguished from periods of disequilibrium; correlatively it becomes harder to distinguish resistance from recuperation.

The collapse of the theory of value construed as a theory of measure points to a challenge: a reconceptualization of time "beyond measure". To move beyond Marx, Negri turns to Lucretius and his concept of the clinamen. The clinamen allows Negri to posit a constitutive theory of time, one that breaks with the Hegelian (and Marxian) notion of time as measure and negation. This constitutive theory of time is required to supplement the constitutive theory of power Negri finds in Spinoza.

George Caffentzis's "Immeasurable Value? An Essay on Marx's Legacy" is a thorough and forceful attack on Negri's critique of Marx's value theory and the use to which he puts it. Caffentzis points out that Negri attempts to use the theory of value as a criterion to distinguish Marx's useful writings from the useless ones. For Negri, those texts that depend on the theory of value ought to be discarded. Caffentzis shows that the criterion evolves over time. Negri begins by rejecting those texts which involve any commitment to value theory whatsoever, but later, in works written collaboratively with Michael Hardt, rejects only those that depend on the theory of value-as-measure.

Caffentzis rejects the Hardt-Negri criterion on two grounds. First, he argues that they have simply not made the case that labor time—and hence value—is not measurable. Second, he points out that the notion of subsumption upon which they base their argument that value is no longer measurable itself depends upon the measurability of value. Caffentzis concludes that the full range of Marx's texts remain useful for understanding and opposing capitalism.

Max Rosenkrantz's "*Empire*, Imperialism and Value: Negri on Capitalist Sovereignty" is both a criticism and a defense of Negri's analysis of the present manifestation of capitalist sovereignty, which he designates 'Empire'. Rosenkrantz defends Negri's view of the form of sovereignty, while attacking his view of its content.

According to Negri (in collaboration with Michael Hardt) there is a single form of sovereignty: Empire. This view requires abandoning the theory of imperialism associated with Lenin, and still widely embraced on the left today. That theory places the nation-state at the center of analysis, rather than class as Negri does. Rosenkrantz defends *Empire* against the theory of imperialism, arguing that the latter has failed to provide convincing evidence for the centrality of the nation state in world politics.

Turning to critique, Rosenkrantz takes up Negri's rejection of Marx's theory of value. Negri argues that the theory of value has been overturned by the "real subsumption" of society. As has already been noted, for Negri, the real subsumption of society makes it impossible to distinguish life from work, and thus it is impossible to measure work-time. Negri thus rejects the quantitative aspect of Marx's value theory. Rosenkrantz argues that this rejection is neither theoretically nor empirically well founded. Further, abandoning the quantitative dimension of Marx's value theory leaves Negri with a vacuous notion of capitalist exploitation.

The positive appropriation of the figure of Spinoza on the part of left materialists is not something that was invented by Negri, or Deleuze for that matter. Nor did it first emerge in France in the 1960s, but rather began at least as far back as Plekhanov in the first decades of the twentieth century. Michael Goddard reminds us, though, of the widespread turn to Spinoza, particularly in France, during the crises that emerged in Marxist thought in the 1960s. Spinoza's revival during this time period has every-thing to do with the transition to a postmodern paradigm that emerged then, and hence the belief that it was now necessary to go beyond Marx as the horizon of materialist theory, and to construct a "post-Marxist" mate-rialism for the new age. Reflecting this context, Michael Goddard notes throughout his paper "From the *Multitudo* to the Multitude: The Place of Spinoza in the Political Philosophy of Antonio Negri" that Negri's reading of Spinoza is not exegetical, but rather an active engagement with Spinoza's texts, aimed in particular at interpreting Spinoza's thought in such a way as to make it relevant to contemporary political conditions, and useful for contemporary political struggle. For Goddard, this opens up the question of what characterizes Negri's particular turn to Spinoza in the context of this wider appropriation of his thought during the transition to post-Marxism.

Goddard traces Negri's analysis of Spinoza's transitions from pantheism to materialism, and from ontology to politics—from being, through modal existence, to politics. Since Negri's reading associates Spinoza's modal plane with politics and Spinoza's single substance with ontology, this pas-sage is accomplished, on Negri's view, in Book III of the *Ethics*, where Negri argues that the body and its affects become foundational, rather than substance. This reading ultimately yields Negri's interpretation of Spinoza's distinction between *potentia* (the constitutive power of the mul-titude) and *potestas* (the constituted power which aims to order and con-trol *potentia*). Within this distinction we find the key to the Spinozian dimension of Negri's thought, namely Spinoza's "affirmative understand-ing of the multitude as constituent power," which Negri utilizes "as an alternative model of power whose realization is perhaps only now possi-ble," as Goddard notes.

Goddard's detailed analysis of the ways in which the multitude and the categories of constitutive versus constituted power are taken up in the work of Negri allows him to elaborate Negri's conception of the multitude from the side of its Spinozian origin, rather than as the postmodern, post-Marxist articulation of the revolutionary subject, as, for example, Lamarche does, thus bringing a fuller dimension of understanding to the concept.

Those rejecting the general notion of a shift to postmodernity, and the concomitant necessity of moving beyond Marx's analysis of modern capi-tal to a post-Marxist analysis of postmodern capital, will also reject Negri's work in general, and his appropriation of Spinoza's thought in particular, as we see in turning to our next paper.

Negri argued that Spinoza presents us with a "savage anomaly" to the standard arc of modern political theory. Whereas Hobbes, Locke, Rousseau, and Hegel all saw the central problem of political theory as the question of the relationship between the 'people' and an external, governing, 'sovereign' force, Spinoza, on Negri's view, understands sovereignty as the immanent, self-organization of the populace. In "How Savage was Spinoza?: Spinoza and the Economic Life of Seventeenth-Century Holland," George Caffentzis presents us with a fascinating analysis of Spinoza's life, and his relationship to contemporary Dutch economic and political institutions and to the intellectual and technological developments of the day. He ultimately concludes that Negri's reading of Spinoza as anomalous and exceptional is incorrect.

Caffentzis maps some of the same territory as Goddard by sketching the main arcs and theses of Negri's reading of Spinoza. However, his interest is not in understanding what prompted Negri's particular appropriation of Spinoza's thought, but rather in challenging the core of that appropriation. Caffentzis argues that Negri's attempt to make Spinoza relevant to contemporary political struggle confuses both Spinoza's work and the nature of the contemporary struggles Negri alleges he is relevant to. Caffentzis notes how deeply implicated Spinoza was in the bourgeois economy of Holland, and, using biographical and historical information, teases out an alternative to Negri's Spinoza. While agreeing with Negri that Spinoza offers a radical alternative to Hobbesian or Renaissance models of sovereignty, Caffentzis ultimately rejects any claim that Spinoza's model somehow places him outside the sphere of bourgeois political economy. Was Spinoza an anomaly? Yes, on Caffentzis's view, but only in the sense of being a rather peculiar, perhaps exceptional, strand of the richly variegated, modern, bourgeois political theory.

Taken together, Goddard's and Caffentzis's papers offer intriguing, and competing visions of Negri's appropriation of Spinoza; one that accepts the post-Marxist underpinnings of the reading—and hence the value and relevancy of that appropriation—and one that rejects them.

The "monstrosity" that Hardt and Negri associate with Merleau-Ponty's thinking of "flesh" and with Haraway's cyborg fable, that Negri associates with the political dimensions of Spinoza's thought in general, that Massumi associates with Deleuze and Guattari's project of analyzing postmodern desiring machines in *Capitalism and Schizophrenia*, and that has thus affected Negri's theoretical development so powerfully for the past quarter century, links the final two papers in this volume. In trying to help conceive of new ways for humanity to live and work together, in trying to facilitate a real social transformation, part of the project entails trying to think of an entirely new social body that one might call, for want of a better word, a, or maybe *the* multitude. This new social body, wherein the "irreducible singularities" comprising it will work through the task of creating new ways of living and working together, is, as truly "new," necessarily also *monstrous*. Monstrosity itself is creative, imaginative, and productive of being—productive of new social bodies through which passages from capital and Empire may be negotiated.

Bryan Kubarycz's paper "Idiotic Square: Empire and Its Double" examines the work of Negri and Hardt from the perspective of two disciplines which appear, from a strictly analytic perspective, as extraneous to the philosophical, political, or economic issues raised in *Empire*—art history and anthropology. Kubarycz's turn to these particular fields, along with their attendant methods, is motivated by a desire to investigate *Empire* in terms of the companion values of insight and originality.

Kubarycz argues that Negri and Hardt's work analyzes modern aesthetic experience in terms of a categorically imposed act of sublimation. They see this drive as intrinsic to the fundamental logic of global capitalism, as well as its continual development. The moment of pure insight, liberated of all positive political content, appears in Negri and Hardt as the constitutive moment of empire. The work of art historians Rosalind Krauss and Hal Foster shows how the very object of this aesthetic experience and disinterested judgment is never original but in fact always a reconstituted object, a fabrication staged at the site of a loss. Thus the ostensibly politically neutral object emerges as the consummate vehicle of ideology. The original revelation of essence and destiny which Negri and Hardt find so central to the ideology of globalism appears in this light as the effect of powerful acts of repression which function to naturalize a simulacrum. In particular, the critique of the avant-garde found in Krauss and Foster allow for a discussion of the extent to which Empire's own theoretical insights are motivated by theatricality, a category traditionally understood as theory's other.

Kubarycz's turn to anthropology is similarly motivated, since this complicity between theory and practice, or philosophy and theatre, is a topic much under discussion within contemporary anthropology. The work of Michael Taussig, in particular, sheds an uncanny light on the counter-empire formulated by Negri and Hardt. When viewed in terms of radical mimesis, which for Taussig no longer means imitation of an original but rather the performance of pure difference, the idealized field of social meanings is suddenly dissipated. In place of an official culture grounded upon the classical economic concepts of value, equivalence, and accumulation, there emerges instead a shocking desublimated material vision of empire centered around singular instances of extravagance, hybridity and disaffection. Kubarycz thus uses Taussig's work to help to determine the extent to which Empire escapes or participates within the production of value, which is to say the obscene staging of value's monstrous conception.

In "Things to Come: Monstrosity and Futurity", Steven De Caroli and Margret Grebowicz take up two important themes in Negri's reading of Spinoza: omens and monsters. Omens portend the future; not a future that in some sense is, though not here yet, but one that can be brought about. Monsters are significant because they are disruptions in the natural order. They thus show that the natural order is not immutable as it is often taken to be. In short, what is often taken to be natural is in fact not natural at all. Drawing in the first instance on the precursory work of Spinoza, and introducing critical interventions on the part of Derrida, Lyotard, and Donna Haraway, De Caroli and Grebowicz apply this discussion to the field of reproductive technologies and the changes in the body—possibly emancipatory, possibly not—they promise to bring about.

De Caroli and Grebowicz's sweeping, rich, and creative work closes this volume, and brings Negri into touch with some of the foremost figures of postmodern theory by examining his and Hardt's attempt to theorize a new and hence monstrous social body—a body *to come*—in the light of contemporary thought concerning the enormously complex and difficult issue of "the body" itself, and of nature, and futurity.

* * *

Despite the varied approaches of the papers that comprise this collection, there is one point on which they are all, at least implicitly, in agreement: Negri is a radical thinker who wants to help think and develop new and different ways of living and working together. He recognizes the fact that a meaningful alternative to the status quo must be made viable, and the proposals that he makes toward this end are audacious in that they break from a not insubstantial number of leftist shibboleths, not the least of which is that the migration of political sovereignty from the welfare state to Empire is a bad thing. Most important of all, however, Negri brings an unbridled optimism to his theoretical project, one inspired by a tremendous faith in, and hope for, ordinary people, whose power to transform the world in positive ways he has never doubted. To be sure, this combination of theoretical audacity and unbridled optimism can be exasperating, even for progressive theorists, and not without good reason. Nevertheless, Negri's theoretically intransigent hopefulness, his refusal to deviate from the perspective of ordinary people in the face of a political reality that works hard to bury all hope, may well be, as he says of the event that thrusts us into a better future at the end of *Multitude, "the real political act of love."*

PART I

Reading Negri: Contexts and Connections

1

Cattivi Maestri: Some Reflections on the Legacy of Guido Bianchini, Luciano Ferrari Bravo, and Primo Moroni

STEVE WRIGHT

You were like one who, traveling by night, Carries the torch behind—no help to him—But he makes those who follow him the wiser.[1]

Upon his arrest in 1979, Antonio Negri was widely denounced as a "wicked teacher" who had led younger people astray through incitement to revolution. This chapter examines the work of three other so-called *cattivi maestri*—two of whom were also arrested as part of the "7 April case"—whose writings still remain little known in the English-speaking world: Guido Bianchini (1926–1998), Luciano Ferrari Bravo (1940–2000), and Primo Moroni (1936–1998).

What makes these three men of interest? For one thing, like Negri himself, each was a significant participant within the decade-long "creeping May" that did so much to change the face of Italian society after 1968. Each also made important contributions to the crafting and diffusion of radical viewpoints during the years in question. Bianchini collaborated with Negri at both the University of Padua and in the extraparliamentary group Potere Operaio (PO), while developing his own unique exploration of contemporary class composition. A specialist in political theory who addressed the relationship between state and class conflict, Ferrari Bravo would for his part spend many years in prison for no reason other than his close intellectual and personal bond with Negri. And if the hand of repression did not touch his person directly in the same way, Moroni—a key

---

[1] These lines of Dante (1987) were read by Ferruccio Gambino (2000) at Luciano Ferrari Bravo's funeral. I would like to thank Ferruccio, along with Volker, Devi Sacchetto, Patrick Cuninghame, and Brett Neilson for providing some hard-to-find materials used in the writing of this essay. Unless otherwise noted, all translations—and mistakes—are my own. Thanks too to Alberto Toscano for last-minute help with a particularly curly quote, Hobo for corrections, and Sergio Bologna for his critical comments.

actor in a series of Italian radical cultural institutions—would nonetheless play a central role in supporting militants caught up in the state's repression of mass dissent during the seventies and eighties.

Important in their own right for what they accomplished as political militants and researchers, each is remembered within Italy's "movement" for another reason: their part in helping to form the sensibilities of individuals from younger, up-and-coming generations. Looked at from another perspective, it is evident how for each in turn, a politics of "place" was fundamental for who they were and what they did. Examined together, therefore, the efforts of Bianchini, Ferrari Bravo, and Moroni to understand and actualize the possibilities for social change can provide important insights into the richness of postwar Italian revolutionary politics.

That the "7 April case"—and the broader state repression of which it was part—remains a sore point within contemporary Italy was borne out once again as recently as 2003, after the leftist publishing house Manifestolibri produced a short book on Ferrari Bravo's life and work, penned by his longtime friend Antonio Negri. When student activists in Padua petitioned for the book to be launched in the main lecture theatre of the faculty where Ferrari Bravo (along with Negri and Bianchini) had worked, permission was denied ("for reasons of public order," according to one report in a local Indymedia site).[2] In the end, the event went ahead successfully, not unlike the local launch eighteen months before of a posthumous collection of Ferrari Bravo's writings, attended by more than two thousand individuals (Milanesi 2001).

But why the label "wicked teacher"? After all, the many accounts available of Bianchini, Ferrari Bravi, and Moroni attest to the dignity and integrity of their commitment to fundamental social change as a process within which "the free development of each is the condition for the free development of all." Is the term's use merely a matter of irony? In his introduction to some of Negri's writings from the seventies, Timothy Murphy (2005, xvi) reminds us that the term can be translated into English as "both 'bad teacher' and 'evil genius'." Negri himself helps to answer the question in his book about Ferrari Bravo, which opens with an "Apologia del cattivo maestro." In tracing the meaning and use of the term, it is inevitable that he refer to Socrates, charged by the authorities not only with failure to respect the gods, but also with "corrupting the youth" of Athens. Socrates, Negri tells us, was driven in part by indignation: in his case, "indignation against those who hate reason and man" (sic). Indignation—"hatred towards him who injures another . . . who has

---

[2] See IMC liviano 2003. Negri's previous visit to the university in 2001 had seen property damage by a fascist group, and fears of a repeat incident may have been played a part in the decision (Il Mattino di Padova 2003).

done evil to another," in the words of Negri's beloved Spinoza (1883)—is thus one of the distinguishing characteristics of the so-called "wicked teacher." While "good teachers" such as Plato look with admiration to the powers that be, *cattivi maestri* are compelled, by "the intensity of their critical will" and their thirst "to transform the real," to question the presuppositions that undergird authority. Today, more than ever, Negri concludes, "indignation—or, as was said of Socrates, the corruption of youth—is our moral ideal" (2003, 11, 10, 15).

Guido Bianchini: "State and Party are Past Participles"

A key figure in the development of workers' self-organization within Italy's North-East, Guido Bianchini's long political life saw him at different stages collaborate closely with—but also strongly dissent from—other, more famous *operaisti*. Working with Negri and Ferrari Bravo within local workerist circles of the sixties, by the beginning of the following decade Bianchini would spell out at some length his own particular views on the opportunities facing the emerging social subjects of the time.

Born in Verona in 1926, Bianchini participated at an early age in the Resistance. Joining the Italian Socialist Party (PSI), he was active in a variety of labor movement organizations during the fifties, above all as a union organizer.[3] The early sixties found him part of a circle of Socialist dissidents—alongside Negri, Ferrari Bravo and Mario Isneghi—who then published the journal *Il Progresso Veneto*. Developing links with the national network around *Quaderni Rossi*, the Venetian group established a lively if ultimately contradictory place for itself within the local left. PSI members who sought a privileged audience amongst Communist party (PCI) workers, who criticized in print the electoral process and who sought to encourage workplace organizing outside official union structures, the circle of *Il Progresso Veneto* was never destined to last long within Socialist party ranks. Looking back on the experience many years later, Bianchini would recall the group as "believing, as intellectuals, that a journal could be a political organizer in its own right, as a surrogate for the weaknesses or evasions of a political organization proper" (quoted in Isnenghi 1980, 229). Having burnt their bridges with the PSI (although some, including Bianchini, briefly held membership in the breakaway PSIUP formed in 1964), many of the former editors of *Il Progresso Veneto* now set about building "a political organization proper," in the form of the regional grouping Potere Operaio veneto-emiliano (POv-e) (Wright

---

[3] According to Zagato (2001, 2), Bianchini was also for a period a PSI municipal councilor in Monselice.

2002, Chapters 3–4). In this project too, Negri argues, Bianchini played a central role: "without him, Potere Operaio would never have got off the ground" (2003, 27).

Lauso Zagato has offered a vivid account of Bianchini—"my personal '*cattivo maestro*'"(2001, 2)—from this period. Along with other workerists such as Romano Alquati and Romolo Gobbi, Bianchini seemed to possess quite "different DNA" to those leftists that the young Zagato had previously met. With a particular talent for discussing one-on-one and in small groups, Bianchini was central in weaving together the network of workplace militants that POv-e helped construct in that decade:

> he was absolutely always for the mass line. . . . He had an extraordinary capacity to speak in any environment, in any crowd or any part of Northern Italy. In the South his accent would have given him away instantly, but at a strike anywhere in the North [*in pianura padana*] where they heard Guido's Veneto or Veneto-Lombardy tones, everyone would shut up and listen, because they were convinced that this was someone from a nearby factory. He had an extraordinary capacity to produce social struggle, to live it, to organise it. (Zagato 2001, 5)

Zagato (2001, 5) recalls that Bianchini rarely spoke at the biggest political gatherings, to the point where some in Potere Operaio risked not knowing "his importance, [mistaking] him for a sympathiser from a previous generation." All the same, it is Bianchini's interventions at a few crucial large meetings, no less than his teaching style and writings, which a number of his associates readily recall. Ferruccio Gambino, for example, has emphasized the significance of one speech that Bianchini made to a national conference of student and far left groupings in 1968. Arguing that a push for equal wage rises for all proffered a vital key to the process of class recomposition, Bianchini's words would be met with incomprehension from many outside his immediate circle. Within the year, however, similar demands would resound across the workplaces, large and small, of Italy's North and Centre:

> How had Guido come to anticipate the seismic wave that would shake the Italy of 1968? To my mind, through tireless grassroots work—together with Licia De Marco and a few other comrades—between Padua, Ferrara, Bologna and Modena, amongst workers whom two decades of intimidations had left extremely wary: leaflets, interventions, snippets of verbal assent [*mozziconi di frasi di consenso*], knowing looks. These were their sonar and their radar, apparently much more humble than the syntheses attempted by others, in reality much more ambitious and noble, because they indicated and demonstrated the possibility of a shift in Italian society, one which until that moment had been whispered more than proclaimed.

If that shift then took place, we owe it also to Guido Bianchini. (Gambino 1999, 163)

In the process of this mass work, Bianchini played an important role in rethinking radical political practices in the region. Bianchini's unique contribution to *operaismo* lay in identifying a distinctive class composition in the Veneto. Rather than the "rational demographic composition" presupposed by historical materialism, this revolved around a factory worker "rooted in [both] the agricultural world and in the industrial world, still living in the fields of the 'Bassa Padana' or in a little village."[4] In the mid to late sixties, the "political organisation proper" that Bianchini helped to build in Italy's North-East was very different from the Leninist model then popular in far left circles. Rather than a goal of centralization, it worked "to organise spaces for the enlargement and diffusion of struggles, to link class strata separated by the bosses' policy." If Bianchini held a keen interest in *Socialisme ou Barbarie* and similar experiences,[5] the inspiration for his approach was less ideological than practical: "It was this that workers demanded":

> The tendencies to centralise decisions or to elaborate tactical and strategic lines particular to the party-form were defeated in those years first of all because of their ineffectiveness . . . the only effective process was a subterranean, directly working class generalisation of struggles. (Bianchini and Pergola 1980)

And in such situations, the "external" militants sallying forth to support factory conflicts were often given a lesson in humility, discovering on several occasions that the workers they had come to leaflet about goings-on at FIAT's gigantic Mirafiori plant—the flagship of Italy's mass worker—knew more than they did about events there, thanks "to the information that they had received in the consignments of parts shipped from Turin" (Bianchini and Pergola 1980). Indeed, in a later essay written for a journal edited by the designers Ennio Chiggio and Paolo Deganello, Bianchini

---

[4] Personal communication from Sergio Bologna, 3 January 2007. Bologna adds that this positioning between agriculture and industry, which in the Veneto of that time was also bound up with the petrochemical cycle, may help explain the particular approach to environmental issues developed by Bianchini and certain other *operaisti* in the region (for example, Augusto Finzi).

[5] A website dedicated to the memory of Cornelius Castoriadis contains this message from Bianchini (1997): "Without him we would have been different. We came out of the gloom and incomprehension of the present state of things only after having read 'Socialisme ou barbarie'. Since then the world has changed greatly, but this change, in part, is thanks to him. At the very least we owe him the fact that a high quality debate was possible, capable of drawing out [*sviscerare*] the miseries of the European left's politics."

(1974) would return to this question of the place of information within workplace regimes and conflicts, as part of his rereading of the restructuring then underway in response to the turmoil at FIAT and elsewhere since the Hot Autumn.

"Understanding, explaining, finding agreement: the true toil of humans lies in these" (Bianchini 1989). Imbued with what Ferrari Bravo (1998, 326) later called a passion "to decipher and change the world" from below, Bianchini was a great admirer of Romano Alquati, one of the figures who first helped to define *operaismo* as a distinctive Marxist tendency committed to reading—and changing—the workplace from "the workers' point of view." When Alquati's essays of the sixties on FIAT were published by Feltrinelli as part of its Materiali Marxisti series, it was due in no small part to Bianchini's editorial work. In the words of Negri (2000, 7),

> Bianchini knew very well how hard it was to lay hands on Alquati's writings. It was something I'd attempted for years: it was infuriating, trying to put Alquati's things in order and make them readable, only to be insulted for my efforts. But Bianchini, poor thing, truly adored him . . . .

The title of Bianchini's own collection of writings, *On the Union and Other Essays*, echoed that of Alquati's Feltrinelli anthology. If these were written in a typically cool and detached manner, the illustrations which accompany them—covers of revolutionary journals and texts (from *Neue Rheinische Zeitung* to *Potere Operaio* and *Lavoro Zero*), and images of acts of mass defiance (from the toppling of the Vendome column, to the decapitation of Stalin's giant statue during the Hungarian Revolution of 1956)—leave no doubt as to the iconoclastic spirit that moved Bianchini's pen. Introducing the book, Negri (1990, xi) argues that

> Bianchini's analysis displays its originality above all in this way: when rational research and ethical transparency fuse, they produce a project. What does project mean in this case? It means finding in the real—in the new real that analysis has uncovered, and that the ethical instance traverses—the tendency of transformation. A tendency of transformation that is animated by subjects, by social figures that emerge in the process of defining themselves and becoming active [*che vengono man mano definendosi e diventando attive*]. All of Bianchini's analyses conclude with the definition of subjects.

While one reading of his work might suggest that Bianchini was at bottom no more than a sophisticated factoryist, other writings—for example, a brief but poignant obituary for Felix Guattari (Bianchini 1992)—indicate that Bianchini was open to perspectives that celebrated the emergence of new subjects. Indeed, pondering the crisis that emerged within Potere Operaio in 1971, leading to the group's eventual collapse, Bianchini would ask

if one could still speak of a unitary subject as the reference point of the revolutionary process, or whether one must not rather take account of the
multiplication of subjects that exalted their 'differences'? (Bianchini and
Pergola 1980)

In a similar fashion, Alisa Del Re (2000) remembers Bianchini's objections
to viewpoints that privileged one layer over the rest within a given class
composition:

> according to an old '70s model . . . the factory worker used to lead the
> process of capitalist development along with the revolutionary process.
> Today it is difficult to individuate a subject of such import. Guido
> Bianchini, who is unfortunately dead too, would have said that this kind of
> individuation could only bring about a model of the revolution resembling
> an upside-down pyramid, in the sense of the Winter Palace, some rather old
> attempt at proposing once again the dictatorship of the proletariat and
> Leninist models.

In this sense, Bianchini's distinctiveness as a workerist tactician emerged
most strongly after the failure of Potere Operaio, which he abandoned in
the early seventies: due amongst other things, he latter attested, to the
problematic relationship within the organization between leaders and
other members. With the group's collapse, many in Potere Operaio soon
entered the new autonomist movement, even as others chose the
Communist party—or, in a different form of the autonomy of the political, the nascent armed groups. Bianchini's orientation then, in his own
words, stood in "ideological contrast" to Negri's engagement with
Autonomia, leading instead towards the unions (Comitato 7 aprile and
Collegio di difesa 1979, 79, 82).[6] Active (until his expulsion towards
decade's end) in the local branch of the university staff union, Bianchini
would spend much of the seventies pursuing what he later called the
"search for a dialectical relation between the new subjectivities and the historic organisations" of the labor movement:

> Once the historic phase of the groups had finished, [we] considered it more
> useful, within the new social dimensions of conflict, to develop the contra-
> dictions that the capitalist response to the crisis produced upon class com-
> position, seeking to open channels of communication in the first place with
> the union which, more than the parties, had shown itself to be permeable
> by the new realities. (Bianchini and Pergola 1980)

---

[6] Judge Calogero, who headed the 7 April prosecution in Padua, had a different reading of this: according to him, Bianchini's disagreements with Negri about the terrain, form,
and goals of class struggle were simply a subterfuge designed to deflect "possible accusations
of membership in Autonomia Operaia" (quoted in Ferrajoli 1983, 190).

One of the key pieces reprinted in *On the Union and Other Essays* is a document of early 1970, not long after POv-e merged with circles elsewhere on the peninsula to form the Italy-wide incarnation of Potere Operaio. Bianchini's piece was circulated in the aftermath of PO's first national conference, a gathering which in its own way already foretold the future of the group, as the considered analysis of class composition came to be overshadowed by the proclamation that "the working class dictatorship, the conquest of the State, is the fundamental goal upon which we move" (Potere Operaio 1970; Berardi 1998, 111–22). Significantly, Bianchini's own short contribution to the proceedings included this pithy warning:

> It is not possible to develop a discourse on organisation, repeating ad nauseum discourses on determinate types of objectives that no one contests, while lacking the patience—and probably even the intellectual stature—to ponder for a moment whether the bosses in the meantime might not, perchance, have changed their own techniques of responding to the behaviours of the working class. (Bianchini 1970a)

The focus of Bianchini's document was upon Potere Operaio's work in PCI-led Emilia-Romagna, a region soon to become famous (along with the traditionally Catholic Veneto, which saw a rather different encounter between industrialization and urbanization) as a key component of the so-called "Third Italy," an emblematic example of flexible specialization in practice. In the process, it would be held up—above all in the English-speaking world of the eighties—as testimony to how relations of trust between management and employees, and between nominally "competing" firms, can overcome (or at least minimize) both the contradictions inherent in the effort bargain, and the increasing vagaries of the modern marketplace. The distinctive features of the "red" version of the Third Italy were all identified in Bianchini's analysis of Emilia: the prevalence of smaller firms, the role of the regional Communist party and cooperative movement in providing social consensus, and the integration between local manufacturing and agricultural cycles. At the same time, it was argued that this "Emilian model" was less than independent from the production cycles of Italy's leading manufacturing and petrochemical concerns. Indeed, the article continued, it was this very integration with large companies that explained the "anomalous" prevalence of small-scale production in the region. In their struggles against a "socialist" regime of accumulation overseen by the Communist party, workers in Emilia-Romagna were striking a blow against "development" itself, as well as undermining the PCI's attempt to build a new national agenda based upon social peace in "its" home bases.

The version of Bianchini's essay reprinted in his book—and that trans-lated for an English-language anthology from the seventies (Red Notes 1978)—breaks off rather suddenly with a discussion of the political wage, and how workers' struggles must step beyond the factory to confront the cost of living. Bianchini's original document, however, continues for a number of pages, pages which point both to the partial convergence of his thought with the post-Hot Autumn shift in Potere Operaio's focus, but also to an important degree of diffidence towards the latter. For example, there is some agreement with others in the group that the unofficial work-place committees thrown up in 1968 and 1969 can no longer afford to work in isolation—must, indeed become subject to "the discipline" of "an overarching autonomous working class organisation." But there is also an acute sense of the tensions involved in this turn that rejects any Leninist reading of the problem:

> Going beyond factoryism and at the same time starting from the factories, real-ising an intervention in the factories in order to carry the workers outside the factories: the contradiction is here, in recognising the limits of past interven-tion precisely when this intervention is bearing fruit. The difficulty that com-rades face is not simply psychological: it is real. (Bianchini 1970b, 9, 13, 11)

Finally, there is a strong sentiment that approaches to organization ham-mered out in Turin or Porto Marghera would only fail if applied in a sim-plistic way to places—such as Emilia-Romagna—where the local class composition was of a different stamp. If a common thread could indeed be found, it lay in the need for a working class that *organized* itself against work (and so against its own condition as proletariat):

> Working-class estrangement from any socialist project must be measured in the concrete of struggles, and in the identification of specific objectives that express the working class interest. Only the organisational process can trans-form estrangement into the material refusal of work. (Bianchini 1970b, 13)

Around the time that this document was first drafted, Bianchini began working in the University of Padua, developing course materials and con-ducting research. In April 1979 he was arrested together with Negri, Ferrari Bravo, and a number of other work colleagues from the "red" Institute of Political Science. While Negri faced different warrants, Bianchini and seven others would be charged by Judge Pietro Calogero with unspecified crimes within the ranks of Potere Operaio and then Autonomia, associations apparently established

> to subvert by violence the constituted order of the State by means of pro-paganda and incitement to practice so-called mass illegality and of various

forms of violence and armed struggle (proletarian searches and expropria-
tions; arson and damage to public and private property; robberies and kid-
nappings; beatings and woundings; attacks on prisons, barracks, the offices
of parties and associations, and so-called dens of the black economy) by
means of training in the use of arms, munitions, explosives and incendiary
devices, and finally by means of recourse to acts of illegality, violence and
armed attack against some of the objectives specified above. (Comitato 7
aprile and Collegio di difesa 1979, 4; slightly modified translation based
upon Murphy 2005, xii)

Bianchini would be released some months afterward, rearrested, then
released again in September with all charges dropped. In France for much
of the early eighties, he mixed with a variety of new circles, including dissidents from Eastern Europe, becoming involved in Amnesty International's
prisoner support work, before finally returning to Italy once again.

Explaining in detail his decision to set Bianchini free, Judge Giovanni
Palombarini noted in passing that accusations that the defendant ran cadre
schools for Potere Operaio in the halls of the university were unfounded,
and if anything testimony rather to the fact that

Bianchini's lessons—for their originality and cultural wealth, to which not
a few witnesses had attested, alongside the accused's analysis of various
sectors of the labour market—were considered in PO an important
moment for the formation of the organisation's militants. (in Comitato 7
aprile and Collegio di difesa 1979, 127)

A few weeks before his first arrest, Bianchini spoke with Mario Isnenghi
about their work together more than fifteen years earlier with *Il Progresso
Veneto*. According to Isnenghi (1980, 230), Bianchini waxed ironic about
his role "in forming pieces of the ruling class through the numerous re-
entries into the apparatuses of the historic left and local government."
Claudio Greppi (2000, 9) provides a somewhat more positive take in his
account of how the present day political class in the city of Ferrara was
largely shaped through its encounter with Bianchini, who had "creamed
off" the best militants for Potere Operaio and left behind only "the village
idiot" for the Communist party. In Greppi's telling, it is Bianchini's role as
a mentor that comes to the fore, his ability "to gather around himself hundreds of Ferrara's young people . . . a certain generation inevitably passed
under his wing." In a similar way, Zagato (2001, 2) emphasizes Bianchini's
maieutic method of challenging others to look within themselves in order
to grapple with the issues that they faced. Ferrari Bravo (1998, 327) suggests that Bianchini evoked the experience of Socrates in another sense, for
he too was "a man of the city, in perpetual motion, known everywhere,
always open to discussion."

To date, much of Bianchini's work has not received the wider attention that it deserves. According to Zagato (2001, 6), *On the Union and Other Essays* was published "at least ten years too early, when the matters it addresses had lost their importance . . . we'll have to wait until they return to the fore in order to appreciate his work in all its brilliance." Zagato adds that other valuable writings by Bianchini remain to be recovered, including work on "precarious labour in the university and some reflections on the immaterial." Fortunately, some of Bianchini's most insightful observations are accessible as shorter texts published in the Ferrara-based review *Antigone*, which Bianchini had helped to found. For example, there is a fascinating reflection on the difference between "creating (that is, producing)" and "communicating (that is, exchanging)." In that piece, Bianchini goes on to argue that "precisely for this reason, it will be necessary for producers to know how to create interstices of non-communication, of interruptors designed for escaping from control and from prescriptions" (Bianchini 1990b). Like all his other writings, these short essays for *Antigone* are infused with that sense of commitment of which Negri had written, for which "the informational chaos of the present" stands as proof of nothing more than "the absence of a hierarchy of values, of the disjuncture [*scissione*] between ethical and rational values" (Bianchini 1995). Bianchini, known to quip that state and party were no more than "past participles,"[7] had no hesitation in rejecting such a disjuncture. Or as Ferrari Bravo (1998, 327) would emphasize when speaking at his friend's funeral, for Bianchini "a knowledge that does not grip your whole life is worth little or nothing."

Luciano Ferrari Bravo: "Looking the Gorgon in the Face"

The early years of classical *operaismo* were ones in which the initial hypotheses advanced by the likes of Mario Tronti and Romano Alquati came to be fleshed out—more rarely, amended—through further research conducted by a broader network of exponents. These findings were often presented in essay form, in journals such as *Classe Operaia* and *Contropiano*. After the upsurge of 1968, texts collectively penned by movement groupings became increasingly common; even so, the individually-signed essay remained as a favored vehicle for the presentation of *operaista* theoretical enquiry. Now, however, such essays were as likely to be collected together in a book, organized around some common theme. The most prestigious series of workerist anthologies was the Feltrinelli col-

---

[7] In Italian, *stato* is the past participle of the verb essere, *partito* the past participle of the verb partire.

umn entitled *Materiali Marxisti*, edited first by Antonio Negri and Sergio Bologna, and then by the "Collettivo di Scienze politiche di Padova." After Negri, the most prominent author of essays in the Feltrinelli series was Luciano Ferrari Bravo, who contributed chapters to many of the volumes published: on imperialism, on class struggle in the interwar period, on underdevelopment in Italy's south, as well as the translation of Benjamin Coriat's influential book *l'Atelier et le chronométre*. "Chapters" may not be the right choice of words, however: as Adelino Zanini (2001, 103) points out, Ferrari Bravo's introduction to the imperialism volume is itself "a book within the book," and the other pieces are far from slight (the "essay" on the south, for example, is nearly 120 pages long).

For all the apparent diversity of topics, there is a constant focus to Ferrari Bravo's work, which centers in each case upon "the state-form" of the capital relation: above all, the task of grasping "the political system, the specificities of the mechanisms of power from a working class point of view" when confronted by the vagaries of the accumulation cycle and social conflict. According to Sergio Bologna (2001, 11),

> In forty years of reflection upon the theme of the state-form, Luciano Ferrari Bravo remained faithful to an interpretative methodology that closely entwined processes of governance and transformations within class composition.

A native of Venice, Ferrari Bravo's life was intimately bound up with that city and its surrounds. Youthful summers in Lido, university teaching in Padua and Preganziol, political activity in Venice's industrial port of Marghera: these localities were all touchstones across the years. As cosmopolitan as the rest of his generation—Negri (2003, 112) suggests that Ferrari Bravo's holiday destination of choice was New York—he was by all accounts most comfortable in Italy's North-East, even as that region underwent extraordinary and distinctive social and economic change after the Second World War. Forced after April 1979 to endure a circuit of prisons up and down the length of the peninsula, Ferrari Bravo's relief upon returning to the Veneto is evident in this letter to his friend Sergio Bianchi:

> Yes, you read right! I'm in Venice, beloved city of my birth. The atmosphere is still the same—filtered through the bars and the walls. An air humid to the core, Levantine, full of carnal humours. Somewhat languid, but also rich in intelligence, albeit an intelligence lacking any metaphysical angst. (Quoted in Bianchi 2000, 112)

Antonio Negri's "Ritratto di un cattivo maestro" provides the most detailed biographical portrait extant. In the late fifties, Ferrari Bravo had left the "refined intellectual society" (Negri 2003, 26) of Lido (where he had rubbed shoulders with likes of Hugo Pratt and Tinto Brass) to study law in Padua, where he took up residence in the house of Francesco Tolin, brother-in-law of Bianchini. Indeed, in Negri's account, it was amongst the "circuit of crazies" convened in Tolin's tobacconist shop that the young Ferrari Bravo was "re-educated":

> It was there that we began to discuss politics and so develop a relentless analysis of *Capital*, confronting it with the experiences of social and factory analysis that we had begun to undertake. (Negri 2003, 31)

When Negri assumed the chair of State Doctrine, Ferrari Bravo was employed as his assistant. Sergio Bologna (2001, 35), who taught and researched alongside both men during the seventies, wrote in these terms about their friendship when introducing a collection of Ferrari Bravo's essays:

> As the writings reproduced here testify, we can truly say that from the end of the sixties until the end, Negri was the principal dialectical reference of Luciano Ferrari Bravo's theoretical activity, and that the friendship between them, while within two very different existences, was indissolubly linked for forty years.

Like Bianchini, Ferrari Bravo played a leading role in the development of Potere Operaio veneto-emiliano's workplace networks. Summoned before a judge in 1983 after four years of "preventive detention," Ferrari Bravo (1983, 221) recalled the daily routine of "external" militants at Porto Marghera during the late sixties:

> It meant, for those like me who lived in Padua, getting up at 3, 4 in the morning so as to be outside the factory gates by 5, to catch the first shift that entered at 6, and to remain there until the day workers had entered. It meant returning to Padua, to work in the faculty, and then in the late afternoon, a meeting to discuss the reception of the leaflets that we had distributed about the factory situation and so on.

The origins of this involvement in the industrial complex of Porto Marghera lay much earlier in the decade. Ferrari Bravo had been amongst those who had organized a *Capital* reading group in the Dorsoduro quarter of Venice in the early sixties, and by the middle of the decade he was in contact with a rising generation of local workplace activists at Petrochimico and neighboring workplaces soon destined to lead industrial disputes of national import (Perna 1980). As one of them, the late Augusto Finzi, remembered in a recent documentary film on the Porto Marghera workers,

Around 1965–66 Bruno Massa introduced me to his friends, whom he called 'the friends from Padua'. He introduced me to Guido Bianchini, Toni Negri, Ferrari Bravo. I'd already come across them distributing leaflets outside the factories, but I hadn't made contact with them because they were described as foreign agents and provocateurs. I met Massimo Cacciari and others who were following with great attention these industrial transformations then underway, and who began to elaborate their initial political proposals . . . I learned what it meant to hold a picket, to draw up demands, I learned about alternatives to piecework, the meaning of information and professionality. All things that I knew of in a nominal sense, but the meaning of which no-one, no organisation nor party nor union, had taught me. (Pellarin 2004)

In 1970 Ferrari Bravo decided to take a break from such intense political activity, in order to focus upon family commitments and research. Intended as a short interlude, this hiatus ultimately stretched into the second half of the decade. During these years, he consolidated his reputation as a fine teacher (Bologna 2001, 17, 35). Alisa del Re (2000) remembers Ferrari Bravo both for his part in collective intellectual enterprises, and for his ability "to listen, appreciate and also address forms of thought *in fieri*." On the other hand, the widespread if mistaken perception of Ferrari Bravo as simply Negri's right hand man—which would carry such a heavy price after 7 April 1979—could sometimes exact a toll even in the years before. In a wide-ranging interview on *operaismo* and the *operaisti*, Claudio Greppi (2000, 9) tells of

once meeting Luciano coming out of a lesson, and he asked, 'Why do I have to waste my time explaining Toni's books?' He was a wreck after two hours of interpreting the thoughts of the great master. Basically this was ideology, rather than the critique of ideologies.

Finally, the early to mid seventies saw the appearance of some of Ferrari Bravo's most important pieces of writing. These included his account of the postwar state's efforts to plan Italy's so-called "Southern question" (Ferrari Bravo 1972)—to my knowledge, one of the few essays by Ferrari Bravo that have been translated (in part) into English (Ferrari Bravo 1974a)—and a critical review of current Marxist debates upon the meaning of imperialism, as well as one of his most intriguing writings, an invited talk prepared for a conference of industrial designers (Ferrari Bravo 1974b).

Ferrari Bravo, it seems, had several nicknames bestowed upon him by other *operaisti*, one of the less obscure being "the American" (Negri 2003, 17). Such "Americanism" was of course an emblematic feature of workerism, from Mario Tronti's celebration of a working class that struggled *because of* the absence of socialist ideologies (and ideologues), through to *Primo Maggio*'s rediscovery of the IWW, via the cross-Atlantic connections that Ferruccio Gambino spearheaded with the likes of Martin Glaberman.[8] Not surprisingly, then, Ferrari Bravo's first sustained essay on the state concerns Roosevelt's New Deal, published as part of the collection *Operai e Stato*. This volume brought together papers presented at a 1967 conference which coincided with Negri's promotion to full professor. An overview of important workers' struggles in Europe and the United States during the first third of the twentieth century, as well as a critique of capital's response to these in the shadow of 1917, *Operai e Stato* was a fundamental statement of perspectives from those workerists aiming to carve out their own territory, beyond the confines of the official left and labor movement. Within this project, Ferrari Bravo's piece on the United States played a pivotal role, even if subsequent attention has tended to focus instead upon the contributions of Negri (on Keynes and the state) and Bologna (on the German council movement and the IWW). Carefully researched, it examined the processes that led the US state of the thirties to seek a privileged interlocutor able to manage "the labor factor" within a new cycle of accumulation. The understanding with the unions that emerges at this point will later serve, *mutatis mutandis*, as a key plank of the social compact that served to underpin the so-called "trente glorieuses" throughout so much of the West after World War Two (Guinan 2002). Along the way, Ferrari Bravo was not adverse to throwing out the occasional *marxisant* aphorism:

> [the American] exception has the same sense as every exception in the capitalist mode of production: it is either suppressed, or else it imposes itself as a general rule, with the force of a natural law . . . . As always, it is in the moment of crisis that the essential foundations of the old order are revealed. (Ferrari Bravo 1967, 41, 57)

The theses outlined in the discussion of the New Deal were soon brought to bear on Italy's postwar government intervention within the country's South. Once again, Ferrari Bravo would interpret state policy as one fundamentally reactive to stimuli from below. Whether in the overt form of struggles, or more obtusely as labor mobility, the popular pressure was "to translate hunger for land into hunger for income, thus revealing their inner nature." And as with the New Deal, so too in Italy "it is the crisis that reveals the fundamental lines of a process" (Ferrari Bravo 1974, 149, 172). As

---

[8] In this sense Sergio Bologna (2003, 99) is correct to point to the absence, in my own discussion of *operaismo*'s history, of Gambino's role during the sixties in promoting "the intensification of the relations with the American Left."

Negri (2003, 52) notes in his commentary on *Stato e sottosviluppo. Il caso del Mezzogiorno italiano,* Ferrari Bravo's line of argument challenged mainstream left assumptions about "underdevelopment," while finding further evidence of the workerist understanding of capital's state-form as a relationship that must be renegotiated with each new class composition: "Struggles break the old institutions, which must be invented anew."

Ferrari Bravo's scholarship has been much commented upon, both in posthumous recollections and during his lifetime. In a typically waspish introduction to the translated excerpt from Ferrari Bravo's study of "The Industrialization of the South," Paul Piccone (1974, 5) explains that "the staggering amount of documentation has been cut to a bare minimum," before adding:

> It should be remembered, however, that what in the English translation appear as unsubstantiated claims were originally nailed down by an army of footnotes useful only to superspecialists.

Equally of note is Ferrari Bravo's style as an essayist. Bologna (2001, 10) argues that his writings—for example, in his discussion of the American union movement's role in institutionalizing class conflict within the New Deal—managed to avoid leftist moralism, even if Ferrari Bravo's purpose in setting pen to paper was "not academic research," but rather "the construction of a political thought." Calm, methodical and reasoned, combining rigor and commitment, there is a fluidity and understatement to his prose that stands in stark contrast to the offerings of more demagogic authors:

> The formal structure of his writings can deceive the reader. They present themselves as a review, a commentary accompanying a bibliography, with the authors in discussion to the fore, never himself. His thought seems camouflaged: it appears briefly, then disappears again. Only a unitary view across his scientific work, and the perception of the recurring themes that cross a thirty-year arc of time, can give the measure of how his thought was one of substance rather than of momentary whim [*d'occasione*], as he loved to demonstrate. Certainly this formal structure, as with his comparative approach, had a great didactic efficacy, a great propaedeutic value that confirmed his vocation for teaching. (Bologna 2001, 21)

As mentioned earlier, one of the most striking essays in Ferrari Bravo's anthology first appeared in a 1974 issue of the Padua-based journal *Quaderni di Progetto,* alongside Bianchini's discussion of "Technology and class organisation." "Utopia and Project: Their Possibility and Relationship" opens with a brief overview of utopian socialism, the particular class compositions which nurtured it, and the understandings of knowledge and knowledge work which it generated. These circumstances are contrasted with the nineteen seventies, by which time design has been subsumed to capitalist social relations, and those engaged in design work no less subject to the tendency towards proletarianization than other sections of the workforce (Ferrari Bravo 1974b). As Negri (2003, 72–73) comments, this text was produced at a point of time when Ferrari Bravo, like many of the *operaisti*, had begun to turn his attention towards "new intellectual subjectivities that must, and perhaps can, place themselves within the class front."

Perhaps the most important of Ferrari Bravo's essays from this period is his 1974 introduction to a collection of contemporary Marxist pieces debating the nature of imperialism, written by the likes of James O'Connor, Martin Nicolaus, Stephen Hymer, and Ernest Mandel. In his long and sustained overview of the debate's evolution, Ferrari Bravo's introduction manages to be broad ranging in its sweep, while remaining taut in its argument. Lenin's classic text on the subject, to which many Marxists continued to pay formal obeisance, was found wanting on a number of scores. The most damning of these for Ferrari Bravo lay in its limited (and limiting) understanding of class composition, which confined itself to explicating the notion of a "labor aristocracy." In any case, he continued—following the line of argument set out in *Operai e stato*—the nature of capitalist development (in other words, class struggle) had changed precisely because of the October revolution and capital's attempts to contain its repercussions. As a consequence, Ferrari Bravo (1974c, 85) concluded, Lenin's pamphlet, "unlike many of the writings of the classics (Lenin included), [is] a product of its time." In this sense, Sergio Bologna (2001, 13) has likened Ferrari Bravo's approach to Lenin in this moment to that of Negri, in that both displayed an often "severe critique" of the theories expounded by "the founding fathers of communism," "where these seemed obsolete or misleading," alongside "respect, identification, admiration for their practices." Consistent with reflections then being developed by other workerists, such as some of the editors of the journal *Primo Maggio*, Ferrari Bravo locates the seeds of a contemporary reading of international capital (and thus imperialism) in Marx's work on money in a global context. Provocatively, he ends his discussion by attempting to draw out the useful aspects of Arrighi Emmanuel's third-worldist analysis of unequal exchange. If Emmanuel's work represents "one step forwards, two steps back," the advance lies in the latter's recognition of the wage "no longer as a biological and ethical-historical fact, but as the fact of an irreducible political subjectivity" (Ferrari Bravo 1974c, 132).

While Ferrari Bravo had remained a particular kind of Leninist in the years immediately after his departure from Potere Operaio, something had changed by the middle of the seventies. According to Negri (2003, 77),

If one could describe Luciano's philosophical position in this period (note that this was much earlier—two years at least—than 1977), you could say that his philosopher of that time was Guy Debord.

Thus, when Ferrari Bravo resumed a direct political engagement in the second half of the seventies, he was drawn, like Primo Moroni, to the task of constructing "service" structures able to sustain the wider movement's development. In Ferrari Bravo's case, these included the launching of the radio station Radio Sherwood, as well as work in the legal defense organization Soccorso Rosso. In both instances, the focus was primarily local: within the Veneto, and first and foremost in Padua. But this was to be a new local context, with different players on the scene than before. In particular, involvement in Sherwood and Soccorso Rosso brought contact with a younger generation of political militants, many of them from the dominant autonomist grouping in the region, the Collettivi Politici Veneti (CPV) (Wright 2005). While his own political outlook and culture was quite different from the CPV, which had sprung in large part from the old Padua branch of Potere Operaio, Ferrari Bravo (1984, 193–201) was an occasional interlocutor for the group as it navigated its way through the shifting alignments within the national autonomist movement. In the months before his arrest, he was also involved in the launch of a regional journal, which sought to bring together a range of viewpoints from the revolutionary left in the Veneto—even if the relative weight of the CPV again gave a distinctive stamp to the whole enterprise. As Bologna (2001, 18) summed up Ferrari Bravo's circumstances at this point,

> 'Where' to be he had already chosen, but 'how' to be in the movement or in the organised groups of Autonomia Operaia was not so evident—an unresolved contradiction that would cost him dear.

Upon his arrest, Ferrari Bravo initially faced not only the charges brought against Bianchini, but also a warrant for "armed insurrection against the powers of the State" as an alleged member of the Brigate Rosse leadership. Negri (2003, Chapter 3) recalls him as a central figure in the 7 April defense campaign, bringing his legal training and contacts forcefully to bear. Negri also remembers Ferrari Bravo as a central inspiration for two important collective documents written in prison: "Do You Remember Revolution" (L. Castellano et al. 1983), and a proposal in favour of "disassociation" (Baletta et al. 1982) aimed at distancing its authors both from those who continued to advocate armed struggle, and from those detainees who turned state evidence [*pentiti*]. According to Negri (2003, 90), this latter statement represented the recognition, on the part of 51 imprisoned comrades, of *the end of the armed struggle*, of its dangerousness and craziness by that point (1982). Informing on others [*delazione*] was called infamy in that document. Disassociation was defined as a declaration of an exit from the movement of armed struggle *without any admission* and thus without any type of participation in the regime's trials and repression.

More than five years after his arrest, Ferrari Bravo was finally released, "due to lack of evidence." If much of the time spent in prison had involved a seemingly interminable wait for trial, punctuated by regular transfers to different prisons, there had also been moments of terror, such as when police and paramilitary forces beat detainees, regardless or not of their involvement, following a revolt in the Trani "super prison" (Comitati Autonomi Operai 1980). At the same time, prison life further consolidated Ferrari Bravo's ties with younger comrades politicized during the seventies: a generation, he once wrote, "not my own, yet whose destiny I long ago accepted to share" (Ferrari Bravo 1984, 200). As Sergio Bianchi (2001, 109) put it in his eulogy,

> I am always asked why Luciano, unlike others of his generation, spontaneously and with aplomb, shared his daily life, and therefore his feelings, with youths half his age, who by cultural formation were certainly unable to sustain a very profitable intellectual exchange with him. I'm convinced that the answer lies in his acute sensitivity in grasping a fragility intrinsic to [*connaturata*] our generation.

The last fifteen years of Ferrari Bravo's life were spent teaching once again at the University of Padua. He published nothing for the first decade after his release, only to produce a flurry of essays thereafter. From an overview of the varied nuances assigned to the categories labor and general intellect by the journals *Luogo Comune* and *Futur Anterieur* (Ferrari Bravo 1996a) to a incisive review of *Homo Sacer* (Ferrari Bravo 1996b), from the analysis of how the Italian state-form had addressed social conflict in recent years to an exploration of the problems posed for states by so-called "globalization," there is "a strong unity and internal coherence" (Bologna 2001, 20) in Ferrari Bravo's final offerings. Amongst other things, a number of the subsequent criticisms of the post-workerist reading of "immaterial labor," as of Agamben's "bare life," are already anticipated here. Binding them all together is this argument, highlighted by another of Ferrari Bravo's close friends, the Swiss economist Christian Marazzi (2001b):

> If we want to look the Gorgon in the face, without it paralysing us; if we want to continue to hope—given that certainly there is no God that can

save us—. . . it is to the body we must look, to the resistance and to the 'power' [*potenza*] that bodies know how to express, even in the most hidden recesses of the social bond, to the subjugating pressure of power. (Ferrari Bravo 1996b, 284)

Primo Moroni: "Socializing Knowledge Without Founding Power"

Sergio Bianchi (1998, 51) once called Primo Moroni, more than an archivist, "the richest walking human historical archive that the movement had at its disposal." For the novelist Giuseppe Genna (2001), "Primo Moroni died, and with him an entire universe." If developments within Italy's North-East were integral to the identities of Bianchini and Ferrari Bravo, Moroni's political and intellectual history was inseparable from that of postwar Milan, a city which for many years could vie for the title of Italy's cultural capital. This history was likewise bound up with the need to understand—and to facilitate—the process of class recomposition. Thus what Moroni (1997b) once identified as the "two key words" for deciphering the mid seventies in Italy—"recomposition and territory"—also sum up his own research agenda. Indeed, Moroni's description of the flows within the political geography of Milan's first generation of social centers lays bare his method for thinking about how best to respond to capital's attempts to subordinate labor through the twin weapons of restructuring and withdrawal (Holloway 1995):

The problem at once became that of following capital on its terrain. Interpreting its strategies and its lines of 'flight' from the great industrial concentrations. In some way fragmenting as it moved across the territory, finding conflict under another form, occupying the spaces that were left void. (Moroni 1997b)

In mapping the particular use of such spaces within Milan from the seventies to the nineties, Moroni (1996c) developed an understanding of class recomposition not in terms of "unity" or the hegemony of a particular layer, but instead of the development, in the midst of modernity's "relapse," of "collective intelligences" able to "socialise knowledges rather than powers" (Decoder 1989).

Moroni recounted chapters from his life story on a number of occasions (Moroni 1983, 1993a, 1996a). Influenced by the many Communist party members who frequented his parents' Milan trattoria, he joined the PCI in 1953. Abandoning school at an early age, Moroni held a variety of manual jobs before entering the hospitality trade, where he ultimately became a senior chef in a leading restaurant. Drawn to dancing as a social activity, he competed in a variety of national tournaments—even winning, he later told Cesare Bermani, a European-level competition in Holland (Moroni 1983). Moroni's skills as a dancer also brought status within his neighborhood peer group, offering a means through which he and his friends could meet young women. Contact with the rich clients he encountered while working in restaurants encouraged a taste for the good things in life, even as he was aware that the latter—along with dancing itself—drew disapproving glances from many in his local party section (Moroni 1996a). Ever restless, Moroni moved from a stint as a private investigator to work during the sixties in the publishing industry, where he climbed to a senior management position, complete with Maserati. After a brief period as a nightclub proprietor, Moroni finally found his vocation, opening with his then partner the bookstore that would make his name in the world of Italian revolutionary politics.

If Moroni's written legacy is extensive,[9] it is for the cultural institutions that he helped to sustain, beginning with the Calusca bookshop, that Moroni is best remembered. Founded in 1971, Calusca was housed in a number of successive shopfronts in the Porta Ticinese quarter of Milan, closing for a period in the mid eighties before reopening in its current premises within the Cox 18 social centre (http://www.cox18.org/). Run for many years with his first wife Sabina and with Renato Varani—another important figure in the development of Italian radical publishing—Calusca soon established itself as a crucial hub for the movement in Milan and beyond. While material circulated within the space from across the spectrum of the Italian left, Calusca was intended to be a home above all for those marginalized by the largest of the country's far left formations (the so-called *triplice* of Avanguardia Operaia, Lotta Continua, and Il Manifesto). If the early seventies in Italy were a "golden age of ultra-Leninism" (Bologna 1974), the most creative political projects at that time were those that emanated from what Moroni (in Cevro-Vukovic 1976, 33) once called "the non-organised, the *cani sciolti*, this indefinable area that stretches from the bordighists to the proto-situationists, the councillists, to the internationalists, the anarchists, to the anarcho-communists, the libertarian communists." Influenced in part by workerist thought—chiefly the exploration of class composition, which drew him to the circle that would produce the journal *Primo Maggio* (Wright 2002, Ch. 8)—it was with "this indefinable area" that Moroni most strongly identified (Bianchi 1999, 53). Another side of the bookshop was the space given to counter-

---

[9] An exhaustive bibliography of Moroni's words in print can be found in Libreria Calusca (n.d.).

cultural politics, such as the journal *Re Nudo,* which likewise shared the left libertarians' and autonomists' hostility towards the *triplice* (Moroni 1996b, 26; Bertante 2005). Finally, Calusca was then also important in Lombardy as a reference point for local teachers committed to developing a new curriculum worthy of the post-1968 social climate, and Moroni (1993a) was proud of the fact that, at its height in the late seventies and early eighties, this Centro di documentazione scuola claimed a bigger membership than Milan's leftwing teachers' union.

Wherever it was housed, Calusca provided a space in which one could happily be lost for hours browsing all manner of revolutionary texts. Perched at the counter of Calusca, Moroni became famed as someone with his finger on the pulse of radical politics in Milan and its hinterland. Nor did he feel the need to travel far in the process; Laura Corradi (1999, 167) recalls him saying, "In the end, everyone passes here at Calusca . . . I never need to move myself." While some were in awe of his capacity to read the cultural shifts within the Italian movement, Moroni himself was happy to share his secret. As he explained in one interview (Moroni 1993a),

> Whoever today undertakes an overarching political project has in reality one goal: mixing with the world in all its components, socialising to the maximum the knowledges of which they are bearers. When in the seventies, I worked in Calusca, everyone thought that I was very intelligent because I knew a ton of things. In reality I was simply the collector of more than two hundred intelligences that frequented the bookshop: so, when I spoke, I knew more, but only because there were many separate things that I continued to elaborate along common coordinates.

Corradi (1999, 167) also remembers Moroni's attentiveness in a different sense, in his preparedness to spend time with younger comrades, discussing everything from politics and music to personal problems:

> he had a special magnetic charm . . . a great willingness to listen to you, to understand what you needed to read, to suggest the right books for you, but above all to engage you in discussions as an equal. Whereas many older comrades acted superior, he didn't put on airs, even when he became famous . . . .

Moroni acknowledged the influence of a number of mentors in his own political development. During the seventies he drew close to Sergio Bologna, a central figure in the *operaismo* of the sixties who after the early years of Potere Operaio chose a different political course to that of Negri or Ferrari Bravo, while still collaborating with them on a number of publishing projects at the University of Padua. Together, Bologna and Moroni worked on the journal *Primo Maggio*, which during the seventies was the focal point for important reflections on contemporary class composition and struggle, as well as assessments of past cycles of mass efforts to subvert the capital relation (Wright 2002, Ch. 8). Twenty years later they were still collaborating in a number of initiatives, including the *Libera Università di Milano e il suo Hinterland* (LUMHI), which aimed to explore "knowledges" and "the transmission of knowledges" through a series of projects that ranged from the relationship between Nazism and the working class (Bologna 1996), to the particular forms of self-employment arising at the century's turn (Bologna and Fumagalli 1997).[10] According to Sergio Bianchi, Bologna was "the person that Primo had always taken as his principal theoretical reference point, respecting the acuteness of his analysis married to a singular rigour in exposition." For his part, Bologna remembers Moroni as "a master in networking,"[11] possessing "a sensitivity, a curiosity and a passion for culture that I have found in few people" (Bologna 2001, 5).

As a libertarian communist, Moroni felt a fundamental gulf between his values and practice and those of the PCI, an institution he had left in 1963. Reviewing the postwar political maneuverings attempted by various components of the US state, Moroni (1992b, 41) was contemptuous of the Communist party leadership's inability to defend its own interests, let alone those of its constituents in the working class: "The PCI, as usual, understood nothing and contributed to disseminating disasters without obtaining any recompense." On the other hand, he always made a point of indicating those figures within the Communist party who, back in the fifties, had nurtured his curiosity, and "had transformed me into a communist, and almost an intellectual" (Moroni 1996a). Moroni retained a strong affection and respect for party activist and writer Mario Spinella, while the lessons of Rossana Rossanda—for a time pivotal to the cultural activities of Milan's PCI Federation—would remain with him decades later. Perhaps even more importantly, however, was the "cultural deprovincialization" (Moroni 1983) that Rossanda brought in her wake: for example, the notion that it was legitimate to enjoy a host of books and films frowned upon by other party leaders. In her own practice, Rossanda also legitimated Moroni's (1996a) sense that "the good life" should be accessible to all, not just the rich clients he had met in the hospitality industry: "from the sixties onwards, I'd thought that this rigid communist theory of the party, that consumer goods had to be

---

[10] The LUMHI project has been revived in recent years—details are available from www.lumhi.net

[11] Personal communication from Sergio Bologna, 3 January 2007.

renounced, was crap." Forced to choose between party hacks who looked down on workers desirous of a refrigerator rather than an ice-box, and Rossanda in her twin set and pearls, Moroni had no doubt as to who was the "correct communist."

In the PCI of the fifties, Moroni also found other, less publicly noted mentors, such as partisans latterly involved in the Volante Rossa armed group (Bermani 1977). These militants were reticent to discuss their activities, saying only "We'll tell you when you're older, not now, these are complicated things" (Moroni 1983). In sum, Moroni's (1983) account of his time in the Communist party paints a complex picture of a young man attempting to establish his own identity in the face of conflicting pressures and desires, satisfied neither by the official party culture promulgated by Togliatti and his associates, nor by that *sotto voce* (Montaldi 1971) that whispered of a Resistance still unfulfilled. Yet, as he recalled many years later, the former members of Volante Rosse whom he met awakened in him

> the passion to recount history from the point of view of those who had made political choices: not only according to the apparatuses, but being on the side of those who act each day, with their motivations. (Moroni 1999, 26)

Thus, unlike those who assumed that all the youngsters in the forefront of the factory-based Hot Autumn had sprung from nowhere, Moroni (1983) argued that in many workplaces, older Communist workers

> while marginalised from the party, transmitted memory . . . they worked within the class, even annulling their own rigorous leninist and stalinist identity, in the name of the overarching unity of the struggle.

Looking back on the period, Moroni pointed to his encounter with such militants, as well as particular events like the mass clashes in Genoa of July 1960, as important moments in his transition to becoming an "extremist." Ever the raconteur, he also advanced his own explanation as to why the protagonists of Genoa had gone down in history as *i giovani delle magliette a righe*:

> I took part in July '60, we went to Genoa, our political commissars and section secretaries had said, 'the Social Movement[12] is holding a congress at Genoa, the city that won the Resistance gold medal, it's intolerable, it's the Tambroni government, we have to go there and stop them'. So we left at night with these old Milanese factory communists, we went to Genoa and

---

[12] Movimento Sociale Italiano (MSI), the neofascist party upon whose parliamentary support the Tambroni government relied.

we raised hell . . . The matter of the striped T-shirts was that it was hot as blazes [*un caldo della madonna*], being July, and at the port they only sold these fucking T-shirts, with red or blue stripes, and so we all bought them . . . . (Moroni 1996a)

Given his fascination with the art of conversation, it is not surprising that Moroni placed great store in oral history as a means of sharing subversive experiences. Sergio Bianchi (1998, 52) tells us that Danilo Montaldi's *Militanti politici di base* was one of Moroni's favorite books, and in his own writing and interviews Moroni spoke of the importance of working with oral historians involved in *Primo Maggio* and the Istituto Ernesto De Martino. Placing the lived experiences of those "at the base" at the centre of any serious approach to social history, he once suggested that the best way to make sense of the radical left's fortunes in the crucial decade of the seventies was

> to arm yourself with a tape recorder and then get individual militants to recount—for hours if need be—their subjective history, their perception of the world, their relations with institutions, their understanding of the polit-ical context. And then, when you've finished, to reorganise all this immense material of subjective experience into a great synthesis which can be achieved only by supplementing this with documents, and through a deep-ened reading of the overall context. (Moroni 1999, 32–33)

Having learned so much from others, Moroni delighted in sharing knowledge and conversation in turn with those new to revolutionary pol-itics. One of his greatest intuitions with younger people concerned the punk circles that multiplied in Milan during the eighties (Philopat 2006). Finding it difficult at first to understand their culture, he was determined to avoid the path of "the sociologists [who] study them like insects in order to catalogue them in their taxonomies" (Moroni 1997b). Instead, he became fascinated with the way in which Italian punks inverted the nihilism commonly associated with the phrase "No Future": rather than a cry of despair, this became an injunction to "invent the present" (Moroni 1996, 41–42; Bianchi 1998, 55). Bringing a new infusion of energy and creativity into a number of local social centers (Wright 2000), some of Milan's punks also began to use space at Calusca for their activities. Along the way, as Raf Scelsi (2000, 7) remembered, there took place "a slow process of trying to understand ourselves and the older ones who came from the movements of the sixties and seventies, for which the point of mediation was Moroni." While many of the older generation were less than open to such an encounter, Moroni saw great possibilities in the likes of Scelsi, whose associates would go on to establish the cyberpunk journal *Decoder*—one of the most innovative of Italy's alternative publications in the late eighties and early nineties—and later the publishing house ShaKe, dedicated to Moroni's injunction "to seek to decodify the present" (Voce 2005).

The great bulk of Moroni's writings were produced after the defeats of the late seventies and early eighties. As he later recounted, the suicides, drug-induced deaths, and state repression that followed the movement of 1977 slowly destroyed the social fabric that had defined his work in and around Calusca. Much of what Moroni wrote in these years, therefore, was an attempt both to make sense of what had happened, and to share those reflections with a younger generation. For example, one of his earliest pieces of historical excavation concerned a collective in Milan's Barona neighborhood, some of whose members had been accused of politically-motivated murder. In trying to uncover the collective's development in the seventies, Moroni laid bare the circumstances within which the complex movement of autonomia diffusa emerged as one response of young working class people to the profound changes then reshaping Italian society. The article had a more obvious, immediately political objective as well, which was to challenge the state's reduction of all such experiences to no more than preludes to, or recruiting grounds for, the rise of the armed groups that tried to impose their own understandings of revolutionary practice upon the movement as a whole (Farnetti and Moroni 1984).

Involvement in prisoner support inevitably drew Moroni into the most dramatic polemic within the Italian radical left of the eighties: that over the stance of "disassociation" launched by Negri, Ferrari Bravo, and others. There is still, to my knowledge, no detailed reconstruction of the debates surrounding the experiences of such prison politics in Italy during this period. Matters are only furthered confused by legislation later passed in the Italian parliament which, while talking of "disassociation," offered sentence reduction to those who renounced their political past (Portelli 1985; Ruggiero 1993). What is clear is that for Moroni and his closest associates of the time, the term "disassociation" carried very different connotations to those advanced by Negri. Speaking in the early nineties, Moroni argued that

> For a long time there was a linguistic problem. We had always said that the *pentito* in reality did not exist: the true *pentito* for us was the *dissociato*, who, faced with the State, recognised that they had been mistaken and sought a reduction in sentence by virtue of the fact that they had renounced their own identity and past history. The *pentito* officially recognised as such by the judges and media was instead the classic figure of the informer—or if you like, of the traitor (Moroni 1993a; cf. Moroni 1990).

At the centre of Moroni's efforts to compile an *aide de mémoire* to the sixties and seventies is the anthology on postwar politics that he assembled with autonomist poet and novelist Nanni Balestrini. First published in 1988, and reprinted a number of times since then, *L'orda d'oro* stands as an indispensable resource for anyone who wants to understand what the book's subtitle calls "the great revolutionary and creative, political and existential wave of 1968 to 1977." Beyond the impressive collection of original texts brought together in the volume—from Danilo Montaldi's account of the 1960 Genoa clashes, to debates on the "mao-dadaist" aspects of the 1977 movement; from insights into the apparent hegemony of the mass worker at the beginning of the seventies, to the challenges thrown up by Italy's powerful feminist movement—*L'orda d'oro* offers a wealth of reflective pieces by the likes of Negri, Oreste Scalzone, Lucia Martini, Paolo Virno, Lanfranco Caminiti, and Sergio Bianchi. What holds the book together, however, is the sometimes understated but always powerful narrative provided by its editors. In a preface to a 1997 edition of the book, Moroni (1997c, 6) wrote that, unlike some interpretations of *Sessantotto*,

> We have tried instead to underline how the movements of the seventies made an enormous effort to elaborate an alternative conception of modernity, a conception that profoundly opposed the postwar model of consumer capitalism, and ultimately the intrinsic and formidable efficiency of the fordist-taylorist hierarchical model . . . . The movement therefore as the mirror 'reversal' of the dominant paradigm, as the radical and irreducible expression of the maturity reached by the capital-labour conflict.

One of Moroni's strongest intuitions about the development of radical movements concerned the connection between self-defined political revolt and that more diffuse, existential unrest that has repeatedly manifested itself over the last century and more in the form of "countercultures." Sensitive to developments in the worlds of literature, film, and music, Moroni (1993a) emphasized the barometric function of "underground" creative expression: "countercultures really have this extraordinary historical function, that of anticipating successive, more political movements." In many ways, he believed, the story of postwar social revolt in Italy (and not only there) could be read as the relationship between these two projects:

> the ten years preceding '68 were ten years of the enormous accumulation of knowledges with apparently normal daily behaviours, if you exclude the visibility of the hippies and the beats. Yet in course was a social laboratory of the accumulation of knowledges that put everything up for discussion. (Moroni 1993a)

For a brief time, the political and counter-cultural facets of social revolt came together, until their profoundly different understandings of "the present state of things," and how to subvert them, drew them apart again. If the early seventies would see the party-builders of the New Left fend off and marginalize the *frikkettoni*, the latter would have their revenge by the middle of the decade, when the question of how "to change life" led increasing numbers of young militants to abandon membership of the *triplice* in favour of the garb of "metropolitan indians" (Mariani 1987). In a similar fashion, Moroni would argue that the richest period in the history of the social centers movement occurred during the late eighties and early nineties, precisely when the "politicos" and cultural enthusiasts were able to find some mutual accommodation. Writing somewhat later, however, Moroni (1997b) would note that if the number of those "frequenting" the social centers "had grown impressively . . . the management collectives had remained largely the same for the past seven-eight years":

> The error underlying this was probably the separation of musical and cultural activities [*programmazione*] from the course of attempted political recomposition.

In his research, Moroni (1989) was drawn again and again not only to the "movement of '77," but also the crucial two years that preceded it, as the crisis of the *triplice* created space for the emergence of new collective intelligences keen to explore both political and existential subversion. As well as the "proletarian youth circles" captured so vividly in Nanni Balestrini's novel *The Unseen*, these years saw the expansion of both "diffuse" autonomist collectives outside the groups of Autonomia organizzata and "creative" forces on its borders (Wright 2005). Alongside his careful mapping of Milan's radical left in that period, Moroni showed a particular appreciation for the journal *A/traverso*, closely linked to the experience of Radio Alice in Bologna (Moroni 2004; Berardi and Guarneri 2002; Day and Wright 2005). As he put it in a conversation with Sandrone Dazieri,

> When the movement is diversified, distributed and complex, a minor sensor can become the synthesis of a disquiet that is subterranean but shared and extensive, and in need of visibility. If the subjects that produce it are in turn pervaded by that disquiet, their publication can become its direct expression. So *A/traverso*, which sold very few copies when it first came out, ended up being stolen [*andare a ruba*] because it was the expression of a real mutation. I think that *A/traverso* was a brilliant cross between political movements and the underground practice of 'situations': a fusion between experiences of existential revolt, counter-cultures, critical Marxism and some intelligent things emerging in the French cultural and philo-

sophical scene (think of the work of Deleuze and Guattari). (Moroni 1996b, 32)

After the difficult times that followed the defeat of Italy's decade-long "creeping May," the nineties proved to be full of new projects for Moroni. If anything, the eviction of the Leoncavallo and Cox 18 social centers at the end of the eighties inspired a new wave of occupations, driven forward by young activists radicalized through the so-called Pantera university movement of 1990 (Portelli 1997). Calusca—renamed "Calusca City Lights," in honor of the San Francisco bookshop cofounded by beat poet Lawrence Ferlinghetti—reopened in the reoccupied Cox 18, once again holding regular book launches, debates, and presentations (Associazione Calusca City Lights 1996). In the face of Dazieri's description of the state of play in Italy in the mid nineties as one of "a rich panorama of small publishing houses, self-managed centers, computer networks and movement radios," Moroni (1996b, 44) responded as follows:

> It's true! Indeed it's almost surprising, above all for the revival of activity by grassroots publishers—and the multiplication of infoshops in the social centres is very interesting. Something is emerging that is close to the idea of a circuit, but all this has little to do with what I consider underground or counter-culture. The counter-culture, a term I continue to prefer to underground, is a network of production, a way of conceiving not only communication but also the world, an existential practice and a model that is in continuous and disquieted research: almost always a paradigm that is the inverse of the dominant one.

For all his guarded judgment on that front, Moroni was quietly optimistic about certain developments around him. Beyond Calusca, Moroni's periodic fieldwork for the AASTER research consultancy (led by his old friend Aldo Bonomi, with whom he had earlier collaborated in the journal *Controinformazione*) offered another rich source of material for reflection on the warp and woof of Italy's changing social fabric. The crisis of legitimacy that gripped many of the institutions of the First Republic at the beginning of the nineties, as Italy's formal constitution strove to catch up with realignments within its material constitution, generated both opportunities and dangers. For one thing, as the first issue of *DeriveApprodi* proclaimed on its front cover in 1992, "It is possible to think that a long period of the destruction of collective intelligences is beginning to come to an end, and that a new perception of the present is emerging in the metropoles." As for the dangers, some of these were sketched out in a short article that Moroni contributed to this *"numero zero"* of the new journal. Addressing "The Adventure of the Transition," his piece focussed upon the reshaping of class and space in Milan as a consequence of fordism's crisis. Prominent amongst these was the growth of seemingly anomalous figures (like the "second generation" self-employed workers then being researched by Sergio Bologna (1992)) and the marked lengthening of the working day, all swirling together in

> A vast process of self-valorisation and de-salarisation that, instead of producing social cooperation outside the hierarchical domination of the enterprise (as some would have wished), produces new egoisms and separate, intolerant individualities. This is, in substance, the triumph of the ideology of labour and of self-entrepreneurship. (Moroni 1992, 45)

These themes were taken up at greater length in a long essay by Moroni published in the first issue of *Vis-à-Vis*, another important journal founded in part by survivors of the earlier autonomist movement. Here he set himself the task of understanding the success of Italy's "new social right" (first and foremost, the Lega Nord) in winning support within proletarian communities of the country's north. A number of processes, he argued, had intertwined: the destruction of the old working class strongholds of the sixties and seventies through industrial restructuring, the flight of younger people towards work in the tertiary sector or even in self-employment, and the traditional left's inability or unwillingness "to comprehend the political-cultural characteristics of post-fordist labour" (Moroni 1993b, 48), much less represent them within the political system. All in all, workers were once again "without allies," as the *operaisti* had proclaimed (with a rather different emphasis!) back in the sixties. One of Moroni's greatest fears was that for all its resurgence in the nineties, Italy's antagonistic left still lacked the conceptual tools that could enable it to confront this new present, and would instead choose either to take refuge in formulaic restatements of past truths, or else close itself into the political and cultural ghettoes within which the social centers had eked out their existence in the eighties. Perhaps this concern helps to explain some of the controversies of Moroni's final years: for example, his involvement in debates that marked the growing divisions within the social centers movement after 1993 (Moroni et al. 1995; Wright 1995). At the same time, it also helps to explain the Deleuze quote that Moroni chose to close the penultimate paragraph of his essay on the "new social right":

> The great and only error lies in thinking that a line of flight consists in fleeing from life; the flight into the imaginary, or into art. On the contrary, to flee is to produce the real, to create life, to find a weapon. (quoted in http://www.pluralist.dk/aestetik/sta004.htm)

And Now?

Interviewed for the book *Futuro Anteriore* (Borio et al. 2002), the writer Valerio Evangelisti was asked if there were any important authors he wished to cite as helpful guides in making sense of "the present state of things." After mentioning, amongst others, Moroni and his work on the Lega Nord, Evangelisti (2000, 21) turned the question around. The point, he argued, was not so much one of "evoking good or bad teachers," but instead "of creating, by ourselves, the identities of a collective teacher— and seeing that we live in this society here, of trying to understand it."

For anyone keen to contribute to the constitution of such collective intelligences, there is much to be learned from the efforts of Guido Bianchini, Luciano Ferrari Bravo, and Primo Moroni, even as there is much to be criticized and surpassed. For example, one useful avenue to be explored is Ferrari Bravo's insistence that, in an age when "the same series of facts offer different and 'untranslatable' readings" (2001b, 358), the adequacy of our explanatory frameworks can only tested in terms of their ability "to provide meaning to the prospect of liberation from oppression and exploitation" (2000, 344). For his part, Bianchini offers the challenge of looking beyond the grand pronouncements of the world's political class, learning instead how to engage with those seemingly ephemeral signs in neighborhood and workplace that, on occasion, may point to fundamental realignments towards class recomposition. And finally, reflecting upon the efforts of the Milan social centre with which he was long associated, Moroni argues against those who would keep separate the threads of political and existential revolt:

> Certainly we have never had any illusions about changing the world through words or through ideology. Only by 'dirtying ourselves' with 'the real' can we understand it and, perhaps, begin to change it. (quoted in Bianchi 1998, 54)

References

Associazione Calusca City Lights 1996. "La Calusca in Cox 18 degli anni novanta," in Consorzio Aaster et al., *Centri sociali: geografie del desiderio*, Milan: ShaKe.

Balestrini, N. and P. Moroni, eds., 1997. *L'orda d'oro*, second edition, Milan: Feltrinelli.

Baletta, G. et al. 1982. "Una generazione politica detenuta," *Frigidaire: Autocritica della guerriglia*, February 1983.

Berardi, F. 1998. *La nefasta utopia di Potere operaio*, Rome: Castelvecchi.

Berardi, F. and E. Guarneri, eds., 2002. *Alice é il diavolo. Storia di una radio sovversiva*, Milan: ShaKe.

Bermani, C. 1977. "La volante rossa," *Primo Maggio* 9.

Bertante, A. 2005. *Re Nudo: Underground e rivoluzione nelle pagine di una rivista.* Rimini: NdA Press.

Bianchi, S. 1998. "Mescolando il riso alle lacrime: In memoria di Primo Moroni," *DeriveApprodi* 16, Summer.

———. 2001. "Pantera rosa," *DeriveApprodi* 20, Spring-Summer.

Bianchini, G. 1970a. "Compagno di Ferrara," in *Linea di Massa 4. Potere Operaio: Convegno nazionale di organizzazione Firenze 9-10-11 gennaio.*

———. 1970b. "Materiale di analisi sulla situazione emiliana e proposte politico-organizzative di Potere Operaio," manuscript.

———. 1974. "Tecnologia e organizzazione di classe," *Quaderni di Progetto* 1.

———. 1989. "Perché Antigone," *Antigone* 1.

———. 1990a. *Sul sindacato e altri scritti*, Padua: Edizioni Quaderni del Progetto.

———. 1990b. "Lo spettro di Antigone si aggira tra di noi," *Antigone* 3.

———. 1992. "Epicedio per un compagno di strada," *Zeronetwork* 2, September.

———. 1993. "Do You Remember '68," *Zeronetwork* 8, February.

———. 1997. "Contenu du Registre en-ligne—Guido Bianchini', http://ccastor.club.fr/registre.htm, accessed 19 June 2005.

Bianchini, G. and M. Pergola 1980. "Prefazione," *Potere Operaio 1967–1969*, Padua: Edizioni cooperativa libreria calusca.

Bologna, S. 1974. "Rapporto società-fabbrica come categoria storica," *Primo Maggio* 2.

———. 1992. "Problematiche del lavoro autonomo in Italia (I)," *Altreragioni* 1, June.

———. 1996. *Nazismo e classe operaia 1933–1993*, second edition, Rome: Manifestolibri.

———. 2001. "Prefazione," in L. Ferrari-Bravo, *Dal fordismo alla globalizzazione. Cristalli di tempo politico*, Rome: Manifestolibri.

———. 2003. "A Review of *Storming Heaven. Class Composition and Struggle in Italian Autonomist Marxism* by Steve Wright," *Strategies* 16, no. 2, November, translated by Arianna Bove.

Bologna S. and A. Fumagalli, eds., 1997. *Il lavoro autonomo di seconda generazione. Scenari del postfordismo in Italia,* Milan: Feltrinelli.

Borio, G., F. Pozzi and G. Roggero 2002. *Futuro anteriore. Dai 'Quaderni Rossi' ai movimenti globali: ricchezze e limiti dell'operaismo italiano*, Rome: Derive Approdi.

Castellano, L., et al. 1983. "Do You Remember Revolution?," in A. Negri (1988).

Cevro-Vukovic, E. 1976. *Vivere a sinistra.* Rome: Arcana.

Comitati Autonomi Operai 1980. "The Revolt at Trani Prison," in A. Negri (1988).

Comitato 7 aprile and Collegio di difesa, eds., 1979. *Processo all'Autonomia*, Cosenza: Lerici.

Corradi, L.1999. "In ricordo di Primo Moroni," *Altreragioni* 8.

Dante 1987. *Purgatorio*, Canto XXII, 67–69, translated by James Finn Cotter, http://www.italianstudies.org/comedy/Purgatorio22.htm, accessed 1 May 2005.

Day, R. and S. Wright 2005. "Go Ask Alice: Some Thoughts Concerning the Place of Mobile Communication within Italian Radical Politics and Contemporary Social Movements," presented to the Rutgers Workshop on Mobile Communication and the Network Society, Rutgers University, 21 May.

Dazieri, S., ed. 1996. *Italia overground: mappe e reti della cultura alternativa*, Rome: Castelvecchi.

Decoder 1989. "Intervista a Primo Moroni," *Decoder* 4.

Del Re, A. 2000. "Intervista a Alisa Del Re," 26 July, from the CD-ROM accompanying G. Borio, F. Pozzi and G. Roggero (2002), translated by Arianna Bove, http://www.generation-online.org/t/alisadelre.htm, accessed 11 November 2004.

Del Re, A., L. Ferrari-Bravo and F. Gambino 1998. "Un comunista fuori dai ranghi," *il manifesto*, 22 August.

Evangelista, V. 2000. "Intervista a Valerio Evangelisti," 18 March, from the CD-ROM accompanying G. Borio, F. Pozzi and G. Roggero (2002).

Farnetti, P. and P. Moroni 1984. "Collettivo Autonomo Barona: appunti per una storia impossibile," *Primo Maggio* 21, Spring.

Ferrajoli, L. 1983. "Il caso '7 Aprile': Lineamenti di un processo inquisitorio," *Dei delitti e delle pene* 1.

Ferrari-Bravo, L. 1972. "Il New Deal e il nuovo assetto delle istituzioni capitalistiche," now in *Dal fordismo alla globalizzazione. Cristalli di tempo politico.* Rome: Manifestolibri.

———. 1974a. "The Industrialization of the South," *International Journal of Sociology* 4, no 2–3, Summer-Fall.

———. 1974b. "Utopia e progetto," in Ferrari-Bravo (2001a).

———. 1974c. "Vecchie e nuove questioni nella teoria dell'imperialismo," in Ferrari-Bravo (2001a).

———. 1975. "Il ruolo dello Stato e delle istituzioni nella crisi," in Ferrari-Bravo (2001a).

———. 1983. "Interrogatorio," in Ferrari-Bravo (2001a)..

———. 1984. "Al dott. Giovanni Palombarini, giudice istruttore presso il tribunale di Padova," in Ferrari-Bravo (2001a).

———. 1996a. "Lavoro e Politica," in Ferrari-Bravo (2001a).

———. 1996b. "Homo Sacer," in Ferrari-Bravo (2001a).

———. 1997. "Americanismo e postfordismo," in Ferrari-Bravo (2001a).

———. 1998. "Compianto per Guido Bianchini," in Ferrari-Bravo (2001a).

———. 2000. "Sovranità," in Ferrari-Bravo (2001a).

———. 2001a. *Dal fordismo alla globalizzazione. Cristalli di tempo politico.* Rome: Manifestolibri.

———. 2001b. "Globalizzazione: Convergenza o integrazione?," in Ferrari-Bravo (2001a).

Ferrari Bravo, L. and A. Serafini 1972. *Stato e sottosviluppo: Il caso del Mezzogiorno.* Milan: Feltrinelli.

Gambino, F. 1991. Review of *Sul sindacato e altri scritti*, *Antigone* 4, October.

———. 1999. "Guido Bianchini lungo i gironi del movimento operaio," *Altrieragioni* 8.

———. 2000. "In Memoria di Luciano," manuscript.

————. 2001. "Lezioni di metodo," *il manifesto*, 4 July.

Genna, G. 2001. "Assalto a un tempo devastato e vile," http://www.libreriauni-versitaria.it/BIT/8887418225/Assalto_a_un_tempo_devastato_e_vile.htm, accessed 18 February 2004.

Greppi, C. 2000. "Intervista a Claudio Greppi," 23 September, from the CD-ROM accompanying G. Borio, F. Pozzi and G. Roggero (2002).

Guinan, J. 2002. "Empire," *Voice of the Turtle*, http://www.voiceoftheturtle.org/show_article.php?aid=211, accessed 1 October 2006.

Holloway, J. 1995. "Capital moves," *Capital and Class* 57, Autumn.

IMC liviano 2003. "univPD vietato incontro per paura degli anni 70," http://italy.indymedia.org/news/2003/04/249401.php, accessed 8 March 2005.

Isnenghi, M. 1980. "Fra partito e prepartito. Il 'Progresso Veneto' 1961–1963," *Classe* 17, June.

Libreria Calusca (n.d.) "Bibliografia di Primo Moroni," http://www.cox18.org/viewcalusca.php?step=primobiblio.php, accessed 7 June 2005.

Marazzi, C. 2001a. "Libri donati," *DeriveApprodi* 20, Spring-Summer.

————. 2001b. "Preambolo per il popolo di Seattle," *il manifesto*, 4 July.

Mariani, G. 1987. "Was Anybody More of an Indian than Kart Marx?: The 'Indiani Metropolitani' and the 1977 Movement," in C. Feest, ed., *Indians and Europe: An Interdisciplinary Collection of Essays*, Aachen: Rader Verlag.

Masi, E. 1999. "Saluto a Primo Moroni," *Altreragioni* 8.

Il Mattino di Padova 2003. "Preside Facolta' Padova Nega Aula Magna Per Libro Su Toni Negri," *Il Mattino di Padova* 5 April, web.tiscali.it/almanacco/sinis-traaprile2003.htm, accessed 8 March 2005.

Milanesi, E. 2001. "Faccia a faccia Toni Negri-Palombarini," *il manifesto* 11 July.

Montaldi, D. 1971. *Militanti politici di base*. Turin: Einaudi.

Moroni, G. 2001. "Schivo conferenziere," *DeriveApprodi* 20, Spring-Summer.

Moroni, P. (n.d.) "Introduzione all'edizione tedesca di *L'orda d'oro*," http://www.urla.com/consapevolezza/modules.php?name=Content&pa=showpage&pid=8, accessed 5 July 2004.

————. 1983. "Da 'Don Lisander' alla 'Calusca': l'Autobiografia di Primo Moroni," *Primo Maggio* 18, Autumn-Winter, http://www.inventati.org/apm/index.php?step=donlisander, accessed 5 July 2004.

————. 1989. "Intervista a Prima Moroni," in Federazione Milanese di Democrazia Proletaria, *Libro bianco sul Leoncavallo*, http://www.ecn.org/leoncavallo/storic/moroni.htm, accessed 5 July 2004.

————. 1990. "Primo Moroni Centro di documentazione Calusca Milano," in Cooperativa Editoriale Zero, eds., *La vostre menzogne la nostra lotta*, Milan: Collana Edizioni Rosse.

————. 1992a. "L'Avventura della Transizione," *DeriveApprodi* 0, July.

————. 1992b. "Quel ferrovecchio di 'Gladio'," in M. Cogliotore and S. Scarso, eds., *La notte dei gladiatori. Omissioni e silenzi della repubblica*. Padua: Calusca edizioni.

————. 1993a. "Ma l'amor mio non muore" in R. Giuffrida et al., eds., *Maledetti compagni, vi amerò. La sinistra antagonista nelle parole dei protagonisti degli ultimi vent'anni di conflitto*. Rome: Datanews, http://www.inventati.org/apm/index.php?step=malamor, accessed 5 July 2004.

———. 1993b. "Tra post-fordismo e nuova destra sociale," *Vis-à-Vis* 1.

———. 1994. "Origine dei centri sociali autogestiti a Milano: Appunti per una storia possibile," in F. Adinolfi et al. *Comunità virtuali: I centri sociali in Italia.* Rome: manifestolibri.

———. 1996a. "La sinistra antagonista nell'Italia dell'Ulivo," http://urla.com/consapevolezza/primo.html, accessed 26 March 2001.

———. 1996b. "Vita, morte e miracoli dell'underground: Intervista con Primo Moroni," in S. Dazieri (ed.) 1996) *Italia overground: mappe e reti della cultura alternativa.* Rome: Castelvecchi.

———. 1996c. "Un certo uso sociale del spazio urbano," in Consorzio Aaster et al., *Centri sociali: geografie del desiderio.* Milan: ShaKe.

———. 1997a. "Centri sociali e comunicazione," http://www.hackerart .org/media/amc/moroni.htm, accessed 15 June 2004.

———. 1997b. "Il cerchio e la saetta: I Centri sociali," http://urla.com/consapevolezza/moroni1.html, accessed 26 March 2001.

———. 1997c. "Prefazione alla nuova edizione," in N. Balestrini and P. Moroni, eds. (1977).

———. 1999. "Storia vissuta. Sinistra militante e storiografia," in P. Moroni and IG Rote Fabrik, eds., *Le parole e la lotta armata. Storie vissute e sinistra militante in Italia, Germania e Svizzera.* Milan: ShaKe.

———. 2004. "Un'altra via per le Indie. Intorno alle pratiche e alle culture del '77," in S. Bianchi and L. Caminiti, eds., *Settantasette. La rivoluzione che viene.* Second edition. Rome: Derive Approdi.

Moroni, P., D. Farina, P. Tripodi, eds., 1995. *Centri sociali: che impresa! Oltre il ghetto: un dibattito cruciale.* Rome: Castelvecchi.

Murphy, T. 2005. "Editor's Introduction: Books for Burning," in A. Negri, *Books for Burning: Between Civil War and Democracy in 1970s Italy,* London: Verso.

Negri, A. 1988. *Revolution Retrieved,* London: Red Notes.

———. 1990. "Prefazione," in G. Bianchini, *Sul sindacato e altri scritti.* Padua: Edizioni Quaderni del Progetto.

———. 2000. "Intervista a Toni Negri," 13 July, from the CD-ROM accompanying G. Borio, F. Pozzi and G. Roggero (2002).

———. 2003. *Luciano Ferrari Bravo: Ritratto di un cattivo maestro.* Rome: Manifestolibri.

Pellarin, M. 2004. *Porto Marghera: gli ultimi fuochi,* Venice: Controcampo Produzioni.

Perna, C. 1980. *Classe sindacato operaismo al Petrolchimico di Porto Marghera,* Rome: Editrice Sindacale Italiana.

Philopat, M. 2006. *Costretti di sanguinare,* Turin: Einaudi.

Piccone, P. 1974. "Introduction: The 'Southern Question' in Italian Sociology," *International Journal of Sociology* 4, no. 2–3, Summer-Fall.

Portelli, A. 1985. "Oral Testimony, the Law and the Making of History: the 'April 7' Murder Trials," *History Workshop Journal* 20, Autumn.

———. 1997. "Conversations with the Panther: The Italian Student Movement of 1990," in *Battle of Valle Giulia: Oral History and the Art of Dialogue.* Madison: University of Wisconsin Press.

Potere Operaio 1970. "Seconda relazione: Conquista dell'organizzazione e dittatura operaia," in *Linea di Massa 4. Potere Operaio: Convegno nazionale di organizzazione Firenze 9-10-11 gennaio 1970.*

Red Notes, eds.1978. *Italy 1977-8: "Living with an Earthquake,"* second edition, London: Red Notes.

Ruggiero, V. 1993. "Sentenced to normality: The Italian political refugees in Paris," *Crime, Law and Social Change* 10, no. 1, January.

Serafin, A. and L. Ferrari Bravo 1972. *Stato e sottosviluppo. Il caso del Mezzogiorno italiano,* Milan: Feltrinelli.

Spinoza, B. 1883. *The Ethics Part III,* translated by R.H.M. Elwes, http://www.yesselman.com/e3elwes.htm, accessed 13 December 2006.

Virno, P. 2001. "Negli anni del nostro scontento," *DeriveApprodi* 20, Spring-Summer.

Voce, L. 2005. "Generazione X: un colloquio con Marco Philopat sulle culture antagoniste," *L'Unità,* 3 January, http://www.shake.it/mel.html, accessed 14 December 2006.

Wright, S. 1995. "Confronting the Crisis of Fordism: The Italian Debates," *Reconstruction* 6.

———. 2000. "'A Love Born of Hate': Autonomist Rap in Italy," *Theory, Culture and Society* 17, no, 3, June.

———. 2002. *Storming Heaven: Class Composition and Struggle in Italian Autonomist Marxism,* London: Pluto Press.

———. 2005. "A Party of Autonomy?" in A. Mustapha and T. Murphy, eds., *The Philosophy of Antonio Negri: Resistance in Practice,* London: Pluto.

Wu Ming 2004. "The Seventies? What Seventies?" *Giap/digest 28,* 30 May 2005, http://www.wumingfoundation.com/english/giap/giapdigest28.htm#seventies, accessed 7 June 2005.

Zagato, L. 2001. "Intervista a Lauso Zagato," 1 November, from the CD-ROM accompanying G. Borio, F. Pozzi and G. Roggero (2002).

Zanini, A. 2001. "Meditatio vitae," *DeriveApprodi* 20, Spring-Summer.

2

Selling a Revolution: Negri, Bataille, and the Arcana of Production

PIERRE LAMARCHE

The proletariat pushes capital further than it's willing to go with certain processes, certain kinds of freedom of movement, or creation of desires. It doesn't respond to capital's creation of desire with asceticism. It says, "Let's actually make real the promises of desire, or push capital further than it can go."

I remember a lot of stifling discussions, "Well, you can never get people in the U.S. to do anything because they're all so comfortable, and you'll never get them to give up things." I remember thinking, Man, those in the U.S. are all so miserable; if you could just show them the joy of what a different life could be. I remember thinking about politics, rather than as an ascetic redistribution, as a collective project for the increase of joy.

MICHAEL HARDT, "The Collaborator and the Multitude: An Interview with Michael Hardt."

Negri and the Project of Liberating Productive Forces

In the first quote from his 2004 interview in *The Minnesota Review*, Michael Hardt is referring to a "Deleuze and Guattarian reading of Marx," one that accords with his and Toni Negri's analysis of the activity of the contemporary analog of Marx's proletariat—the "multitude"—within the postmodern constitution of global capital they call Empire. Like capital before it, Empire produces not simply material commodities, but also subjectivities, relationships, knowledges, and desires. Further, unlike capital, whose characteristic product was the material commodity, it is these immaterial products that characterize the tendency of production within Empire. In *Kairòs, Alma Venus, Multitudo*, Negri suggests that within Empire production has become "the production of subjectivity," and that the Spinozist multitude which bears the productive force of Empire "is an ensemble of constellations productive of subjectivity."[1] As Hardt remarks in the *Minnesota Review* interview, he and Negri believe that the point of a revolutionary movement that would transcend Empire's order is not to engage in an ascetic, moralistic critique of the creation of such subjectivities and desires, as part of the project of simply redistributing social wealth from an affluent class, now chastened for its greed and/or decadence (for the nature of its "subjectivity" and "desires"), to an impoverished class. It is, rather, to liberate the subjectivities and make good on the desires that are created within Empire, since "what is beautiful is the generation of subjectivity" through the activity of the irreducible singularities that constitute the multitude.[2]

The second quote, however, introduces a tension in Hardt's and Negri's recent collaborations, and in the work of Negri in general. Hardt's recollected interlocutors warn him that no one in the US is going to buy an ascetic redistribution of wealth anyway. They like their things too much, and want not only to keep the things that they have, but also to accumulate more stuff to boot. Hardt's response, however, clearly involves a normative judgment concerning at least some of the desires that are created within US capitalism.[3] Hardt feels that the "things" that Americans seem extremely resistant to give up are actually contributing to their misery, rather than gratifying them in any meaningful way. Obviously, Hardt is alluding to a consumerist culture that imposes the commodity form on our desires, cultivating a subjectivity rooted in the accumulation of commodities, and the tendency to accept the concomitant necessity of ceding greater and greater portions of one's life to wage labor. Capital, Empire, produce desires and subjectivities, and also devote enormous amounts of

---

[1] Antonio Negri, *Kairòs, Alma Venus, Multitudo* in *Time for Revolution*, Matteo Mandarini trans., London and New York: Continuum, 2003, 230. *Kairòs, Alma Venus, Multitudo* first appears in 2000, and post-dates *Empire*. Cf. Hardt and Negri, *Empire*, Cambridge, MA: Harvard University Press, 2000, e.g., p. 32: "The great industrial and financial powers thus produce not only commodities, but subjectivities."

[2] Ibid., 203. Obviously this celebration of the production and proliferation of "subjectivities" within Empire—influenced of course by the work of Foucault and Deleuze and Guattari—is also intended to short-circuit post-structuralist critiques of Marxist theories of social transformation, which argue that there is no subjective position outside of the apparatuses of power that could confront those apparatuses—all "subjectivity" is implicated within the very same power structure it seeks to subvert. This is not a problem, at least initially, for Hardt's and Negri's position. Just as Marx identified the subject that is created by capital with the subject that will transcend capital—the proletariat—Hardt and Negri do not look outside of Empire to locate the force that is capable of transforming itself into a political subjectivity that would transcend Empire, the force of the multitude.

[3] And while it might be argued that other cultures have resisted what Hardt is alluding to here to a greater extent than the United States has, we can probably extend this observation to include most of the so-called affluent nations, to lesser or greater extents.

energy to the task of imposing the commodity form on those desires—to the task of requiring that all desire aim at gratification by means of commodities, directing subjectivities to become, essentially, consumers. What Hardt is clearly suggesting is that if people could be shown the possibilities of a "different life"—i.e., a life beyond the commodity form, and the associated exigencies of wage-labor—they would gladly give up their attachment to those things that bind them to the endless regime of wage-labor and the commodity form, thus creating the conditions necessary for a "collective project" not of satisfying the desire to accumulate things, nor of ascetically redistributing wealth, but rather for the "increase of joy." Again, implicit within this telling remark is the recognition that the consumerist subjectivity that desires, essentially, the accumulation of commodities—material and immaterial—and that is generated within Empire is not, really, a "beautiful" thing.

As I've suggested, the same tension runs through much of Toni Negri's work over the past several decades. In a 1985 collaboration with Félix Guattari, the tension is, colorfully, articulated:

> Extermination or communism is the choice—but this communism must be more than just the sharing of wealth (who wants all this shit?)—it must inaugurate a whole new way of working together. Real communism consists in creating . . . activities in which people can develop themselves as they produce. . . .[4]

Marx emphasizes the centrality of the commodity form within capital in the famous first sentence of *Capital*: "The wealth of those societies in which the capitalist mode of production prevails, presents itself as 'an immense accumulation of commodities.'"[5] As such, any simple redistribution or sharing of "wealth" within capital amounts to nothing more than a redistribution of the means to acquire commodities that continues to bind us to the commodity form and to wage labor. Guattari and Negri ask with regard to this immense accumulation of commodities that *is* wealth under capital; "who wants all this shit" anyway? *All this shit* is nothing other than the pathetic accretions of our collective lives, and our thralldom to it only reinforces the perpetuation of our lives as wage laborers, and as members of what they later call the "pacified consuming classes."[6] Unfortunately, of course, the answer to Guattari and Negri's

---

[4] Félix Guattari and Toni Negri, *Communists Like Us*, Michael Ryan trans., New York: Semiotext(e), 1990, 13. Originally published in 1985 as *Nouvelles espaces de liberté*.

[5] Marx, *Capital v. 1*, Moore and Aveling trans., New York: International Publishers: New York, 1967, 35.

[6] Op. cit., n. 3, 22.

question appears to be, *we do*. Hardt's friends were right. We don't want to give up our hard-earned things, since they are the object of the only created desire that capital has actually made good on. To paraphrase a prescient observation of Horkheimer and Adorno's, it is the triumph of the generation and ordering of subjectivity and desire that takes place within Empire, that people feel compelled to buy and use things, even though they see through them.[7]

Perhaps this is one of the reasons why Negri's account of the project of a revolutionary transformation of society focuses on an analysis of modes of social production, and emphasizes to such a significant extent the liberation of productive capacities from the shackles of Capital/Empire, the creation of aforementioned "new ways of *working* together . . . activities in which people can develop themselves *as they produce*," allowing us to "tap into the potential of individual creative energies, previously suppressed" under capital's yoke.[8] The notion that the ways in which capital imposes order on the labor process ultimately serve to stifle the productive, creative capacities and potential of labor is, of course, not something that is invented by Negri. It was a notion that was central to Marx's own analysis of capital, and Negri emphasizes this in his reading of Marx's *Grundrisse*. There, in *Marx Beyond Marx*, Negri argues that, for Marx, the transition from capital to communism is characterized by the liberation of the productive forces of socialized, living labor from the strictures of "work," i.e.; of wage labor imposed and ordered by capital, which stifles the creativity and productivity of labor.[9] In *Empire* Hardt and Negri argue that the "multitude is the real productive force of our social world." Just as Marx had identified Capital as a "vampire" sucking the lifeblood and sapping the energy of proletarian social productivity, so too Empire parasitically feeds off of the productive force of the multitude. Hence, transcending Empire means getting the parasite off of the multitude's back, thus liberating its prodigious creative force.

---

[7] Cf. Horkheimer and Adorno, "The Culture Industry: Enlightenment as Mass Deception," *Dialectic of Enlightenment*, Cumming trans., New York: Continuum, 1988, 167.

[8] Ibid., 17. Emphasis added. This focus is consistent with Marx's approach as well, of course, and Negri and his collaborators also clearly want to emphasize the power and creativity of the working class, and the multitude in general, in opposition both to the view that the productive forces of society are driven by capital/empire—by the *entrepreneurs* and venture capitalists who are responsible for innovation and economic expansion—and to the view that the working class is politically passive, and incapable of exercising political force. It is the "genius" of the multitude that creates and produces, and their creativity sustains a parasitic Empire. Further, the multitude is fully capable of becoming a political subject, and effecting a real transformation of global society.

[9] Cf. Negri, *Marx Beyond Marx: Lessons on the Grundrisse*, Cleaver, Ryan, and Viano trans., Fleming ed., New York: Autonomia, 1991, "Lesson Eight: Communism and Transition."

In *Kairòs, Alma Venus, Multitudo,* Negri argues that, with the transition from modernity to postmodernity, Marx's notion of exploitation reduces, more and more, to a condition of "deflation; it is a thwarting and a reduction to measure" of the immeasurable value produced by the multitude.[10] Exploitation is no longer the extraction of surplus value, and hence the theft of the living labor, of the life, of the worker through the imposition of surplus labor; it is rather the thwarting of the immeasurable productivity of which the multitude is capable. The problem of exploitation via the imposition of wage labor (the attempt to impose measure on what is immeasurable) is no longer the fact that it involves the imposition of work with no return, and thus the theft of life-time; rather it is that exploitation stifles the creativity and productivity of work.

This emphasis on the liberation of productive forces is particularly evident in *Communists Like Us.* In a telling passage that demonstrates in embryonic form the trajectory of Negri's recent collaborations with Hardt, Negri and Guattari argue that

> Traditionally, the refusal of work, as an instance of struggle and as spontaneous action, has aimed at those structures which are obstacles to the real liberation of work. From now on, that struggle involves appropriating a new capital, that of a collective intelligence gained in freedom . . . This involves all projects of awakening and building towards liberation; in short, anything that helps reclaim mastery over work time, the essential component of life time. All the current catchwords of capitalist production invoke this same strategy: the revolutionary diffusion of information technologies among a new collective subjectivity. This is the new terrain of struggle, and it is not utopian to believe that consciousness itself is the "swing voter" deciding if capitalist or non-capitalist roads are taken.[11]

Here, the rallying cry of communists like Guattari and Negri is not the abolition of work, but it's "real liberation;" not the cessation of work time (which is the "essential component of life time"!), but the project of reclaiming mastery over it, in the interest of liberating suppressed "creative energies;"[12] in short, not the end of work, but the unleashing of its enormous potential, all with a view to selling the revolution to that swing voter between capitalist and non-capitalist roads who likes his things. The goal of this new, postmodern communism (the way to package and sell our revolution today) is to celebrate subjectivities and make good on desires, even if some of them seem intractably stamped with the commodity form, and hence anathema to any substantial social transformation.

---

[10] Op. cit., n. 1, 232–33.
[11] Op. cit., n. 3, 15–16.
[12] See n. 6.

Guattari and Negri would insist, of course, that the difference between those two, aforementioned roads is all important; that one road leads directly and irrevocably to *all this shit*—cheap consumer goods, mindless entertainment; things, amusements, and nothing more—while the other leads to an eruption of true, collective imagination and creativity that could carry us beyond the commodity form. Nonetheless, the emphasis on liberating work (imaginative, *productive* creativity) from work (imposed wage labor), rather than on freeing us from work to, say, "leisure" in the sense of the completely unproductive expenditure of time, remains.[13] The specter of a social transformation aiming at unproductive expenditure seems to haunt Negri's work, and so we should also note the moralism that lurks behind this emphasis on production (not to mention the, however understandable, contempt for *all this shit*). Negri wants to reassure swing-voters that we're all going to work hard and be even more productive after the revolution; no slacking off, for communists like us. After all, "work that is liberated, is liberation from work."[14]

Negri emphasizes the project of liberating productive forces—of liberating work—not without reason, of course. The argument that work will be more creative, imaginative, and *productive* once it is freed from the strictures of the capitalist labor process is a compelling one. Further, this emphasis focuses attention on the power of the multitude, not simply to resist imperial order, but also to effect real social transformation and, indeed, to *produce* a new regime of social life. Nonetheless, the emphasis on liberating work that we find in Negri and his collaborators' analysis of transformation risks a return of a kind of vulgar Marxist repressed, namely the identification of life with labor, of human beings with productive force. As such, while acknowledging the validity and importance of this aspect of their work, we must remind ourselves that the liberation of the productive force of the multitude that Negri et al. are attempting to theorize involves freeing not work but human beings from the strictures of waged-labor, and thus also freeing human beings from thralldom to the commodity form. It is not, essentially, work (even as, say, life activity) that must be freed from the straightjacket of wage-labor. It is the worker who must be freed from

---

[13] There are, of course, many ways in which leisure time can be expended in such a way as to facilitate productive processes, not the least of which is through the consumption of commodities which stimulates production. And Negri and Hardt would certainly add that, in the context of the tendency towards the hegemony of immaterial, intellectual labor within Empire, one might be hard pressed to locate a "leisure" activity that does not facilitate greater productivity through the nurturing and stimulation of our imaginative and creative capacities. What I have in mind here as an alternative to this emphasis on the liberation of productive forces as the goal of real social transformation is something like Bataille's notion of pure expenditure, as I will later discuss.

[14] Op. cit., n. 8, p. 165. My point, of course, is that work that is liberated is still *work*.

the necessity of selling herself for a wage in order to live. Once she is liberated from wage-labor her work becomes liberated *along with her*.

If the goal of revolution in our postmodern age of Empire is the liberation of "work" rather than people, then there seems a substantial risk that Žižek is correct in diagnosing the transformation being peddled by Hardt and Negri as amounting to little more than an "ongoing 'soft revolution'"—a revolution that changes the way that we work, but not the fact that life is, still, essentially, work. It's the revolution Žižek believes appeals to yuppies reading Deleuze on the Paris subway, who like their gadgets, latest software programs and lifestyle accoutrements, who are self-managed and creatively fulfilled on the job, and who want their subjectivity celebrated, and, moreover, their many, many desires made good on, whether that requires "liberated" work, or some other kind.[15]

From the Industrial Proletariat to The Poors

In the same *Minnesota Review* interview, Michael Hardt admits to a significant theoretical tension between the two collaborations with Toni Negri, *Empire* and *Multitude*, with regard to the central category of the multitude. Hardt confesses that he and Negri "use the term multitude in essentially two ways," ways that are "in contradiction with one another."[16] The multitude of *Empire* is Negri's Spinozist multitude—an "always-existing social force," or that *potentia* which constantly and everywhere resists the constraining order of *potestas*. In *Multitude*, the eponymous set of "irreducible singularities" is a "political project"—the not yet existing revolutionary subject that would effect a real social transformation in the contemporary postmodern age. One might think of these competing multitudes in the context of Marx's mid nineteenth century project of facilitating the transformation of the industrial proletariat into a political force. The industrial proletariat is the bearer of the tremendous productive force of socialized labor.[17] Within capitalism, this productive force is under the command, and in the service, of capital, spurring its development and expansion through its generation of "wealth." It is also a force of resistance against the imposition and constraints of waged labor, from the time of its

---

[15] See Slavoj Žižek, "The Ongoing 'Soft Revolution'," *Critical Inquiry* 30, Winter 2004, 292–323.

[16] "Toni and I use the term multitude in essentially two ways. . . . There's one notion of multitude that's always-already, and there's another that's not-yet." Michael Hardt, "The Collaborator and the Multitude: An Interview with Michael Hardt," *The Minnesota Review*, n.s., 2004, 61–62.

[17] See, e.g., "The bourgeoisie, during its rule of scarce one hundred years, has created more massive and more colossal productive forces than have all the preceding generations

emergence at the dawn of the industrial revolution out of the bloody process of primitive accumulation, to the revolutions of 1848, the year of the publication of the manifesto. The problem for Marx is how to facilitate a transformation of the industrial proletariat from the force that simultaneously drives and resists capitalist expansion (more the former than the latter for Marx, in the early and mid nineteenth century), to an *organized* political force capable not simply of sporadic acts of resistance, but of ultimately transcending capitalism and its limitations. In other words, how to facilitate a transition of the industrial proletariat from the agent of economic production that simultaneously engages in—again, sporadic, disjointed—resistance to capitalist command, to its organization as the subject of a political transformation that would transcend capitalism. Just as Marx and Engels set as their goal the realization of the potential of socialized labor through political organization and struggle aimed at overcoming capitalism, so too, Hardt and Negri set as their goal the transition of the multitude from an always-existing social force that, in *Empire*, has, through its activity, engendered a new imperial order and driven its expansion, to the organization of the multitude as a not-yet existing political force capable of transcending that same imperial order—the new global sovereignty called Empire.

This tension between the two different conceptions of the multitude, from *Empire* to *Multitude* is transparent. On the one hand, Hardt and Negri argue as follows:

> . . . the construction of Empire and its global networks is a *response* to the various struggles against the modern machines of power, and specifically to class struggle driven by the multitude's desire for liberation. The multitude called Empire into being.[18]

As I have just mentioned, here, in *Empire*, the multitude pre-exists Empire, and, through struggle, calls it into being. In the face of global resistance to the excesses associated with the development of the modern nation state—notably "nationalism, colonialism, and imperialism"—*potestas*, as that always-existing power which functions to order and constrain the *potentia* of the multitude, responds by shifting sovereign power away from the

---

together. Subjection of Nature's forces to man, machinery . . . railways, electric telegraphs, clearing of whole continents for cultivation . . .—what earlier century had even a presentiment that such productive forces slumbered in the lap of social labour?" "Manifesto of the Communist Party," *The Marx-Engels Reader*, Tucker, ed., 477. The bourgeoisie has accomplished the creation of the modern, industrial world by harnessing the extraordinary power of socialized labor, putting it to work towards the bourgeoisie's ends of capitalist expansion.

[18] Michael Hardt and Antonio Negri, *Empire*, Cambridge, MA: Harvard University Press, 2000, 43.

nation state and towards multinational apparatuses that operate in the name of "global justice," thus creating the new, global sovereignty identified with Empire.[19]

By contrast, in *Multitude* Hardt and Negri announce that:

This book will focus on the multitude, the living alternative that grows within Empire. . . .
. . . the multitude emerges from within the new imperial sovereignty and points beyond it. The multitude is working through Empire to create an alternative global society.[20]

Here, the multitude "emerges" from within Empire, and grows there, as its "living alternative." The living alternative to imperial sovereignty would be the multitude not merely in its guise as an always-existing social force that tests the boundaries of, presently, Empire, forcing it to develop and adapt (as it has always done *qua* Spinozist *potentia*) but the multitude *organized* as a political subject, whose goal is the transcendence of Empire and the creation of an "alternative global society"—the multitude as the political *project* to be, the creator of *commonwealth*.[21]

This distinction, and the coinciding issue of transition, points to yet another tension within Hardt's and Negri's thinking of the multitude. Marx believed that the transition from the proletariat as engine of capitalist development to political subject was possible because of the qualitative changes in the labor process that take place through the socialization of labor within modern, capitalist industry. For Marx, the industrial proletariat were, in spite of their small numbers, the privileged revolutionary class, precisely because of the transformation to socialized labor that takes place within capitalism, which opens up the possibility for organizing and mobilizing the power of socialized labor in the service of struggle against capitalism, rather than of capitalist expansion. Negri and Hardt explicitly refuse this maneuver, even though, as we have already seen, they identify a postmodern qualitative alteration in

---

[19] This analysis is consistent with one of the central aspects of the Italian New Left movement, namely its commitment to the notion that the working class is primary to the development of capital, i.e., that capital develops precisely in response to the force of working class struggle. On this view, capital is not a hegemonic power that imposes its will on a hapless working class. Rather, it is constantly on the defensive against the force of working class struggle. The fact that the working class has not yet transcended capital, that capital has, thus far, been flexible enough to adapt and maintain order over the working class, is irrelevant.

[20] Michael Hardt and Antonio Negri, *Multitude: War and Democracy in the Age of Empire*, New York: Penguin, 2004, xiii, xvii.

[21] Cf. "We need to investigate specifically how the multitude can become a *political subject* in the context of Empire." Ibid., 394. The multitude is the political subject *to be*.

the labor process that is just as significant as the transition to socialized labor that was central to the development of modern industry. Just as Marx had argued that socialized labor (i.e. industrial wage labor) was a tendency that would eventually attain economic hegemony as the *form* of all processes of production within capitalism, Hardt and Negri argue that, presently, *immaterial* labor—again, labor that produces knowledge, information, affects, desires, subjectivities—is a tendency that will attain the same sort of hegemony within Empire as industrial labor had within capitalism, i.e. they argue, à la Marx, that a qualitative change in the labor process will fundamentally alter all productive processes henceforth.

> In the final decades of the twentieth century, industrial labor lost its hegemony and in its stead emerged "immaterial labor," that is, labor that creates immaterial products, such as knowledge, information, communication, a relationship, or an emotional response.[22]

In an effort to head off a pervasive criticism of their theorization of the hegemony of immaterial labor in *Empire*, Hardt and Negri immediately clarify:

> When we say that immaterial labor is tending toward the hegemonic position we are not saying that most of the workers in the world today are producing primarily immaterial goods. . . . Our claim, rather, is that immaterial labor has become *hegemonic in qualitative terms* and has imposed a tendency on other forms of labor and society itself. Immaterial labor, in other words, is in the same position that industrial labor was 150 years ago, when it accounted for only a small fraction of global production and was concentrated in a small part of the world but nonetheless exerted hegemony over all other forms of production.[23]

Again though, whereas Marx identified the industrial proletariat as the privileged political subject on the basis of the hegemonic tendency of socialized, industrial labor, Hardt and Negri explicitly refuse to associate immaterial labor with a new, privileged, revolutionary force:

> . . . there is no political priority among the forms of labor: all forms of labor are today socially productive, they produce in common, and share too a common potential to resist the domination of capital. Think of it as the equal opportunity of resistance. This is not to

---

[22] Ibid., 108.
[23] Ibid., 109.

say . . . that industrial labor or the working class are not important but merely that they hold no political privilege with respect to other classes of labor within the multitude.[24]

Immaterial labor may have supplanted industrial labor as a tendency that will gain hegemony over all productive processes—as the paradigmatic form of "wealth" creation—but neither the industrial proletariat nor the new mass of "intellectual" laborers will be identified as a privileged political force in this postmodern age of Empire.

Indeed, if there is a privileged bearer of revolutionary force in Hardt's and Negri's work, it is not the mobile army of highly educated, linguistic and communicatively savvy, immaterial, 'high-tech' laborers in both affluent and 'developing' nations. Rather, it is the figure of "the poor," and those who suffer under poverty. For Hardt and Negri, "*the poor embody the ontological condition not only of resistance but also of productive life itself*"[25] precisely because they are the bearer of exclusion and indigence, and hence have become "enormously creative and powerful,"[26] as is demonstrated by the innumerable, exceptionally creative and productive techniques of survival they have developed.

In *Kairòs, Alma Venus, Multitudo*, Negri privileges the condition of poverty as the substratum of all social productivity that is *in common*, as opposed to productivity that is ordered under the regime of private accumulation, or of "public," state control and limitation. The poor are the "motor" both of "materialist ideology"[27] and of "democracy."[28] It is the poor who "render love real;" that love which is the "desire" and the "constitutive *praxis*" of the common. The condition of poverty is thus the privileged site of all resistance to the imposition of order—and thus limitation and exclusion—on the productivity of the multitude. Hence, the poor are the privileged bearers of the production of the common they are currently excluded from, since, within capital/Empire, the common production of social labor is immediately ordered into schemes of private and public accumulation. Ultimately, the "completely open possibility that is given in poverty shows itself as creative plenitude."[29]

---

[24] Ibid., 106–107.

[25] Ibid., 133, emphasis theirs.

[26] Ibid., 129.

[27] Op. cit., n. 1, 197.

[28] Ibid., 240.

[29] Ibid., 221. In making recourse to the notion of the `plenitude of poverty,' Hardt and Negri evoke central aspects of the work of figures such as Heidegger, Blanchot, and Bataille. A further connection here is to the tradition of Catholic Radicalism. Timothy Brennan has

Hardt and Negri elaborate this somewhat paradoxical notion in *Multitude*:

> . . . the production of the common always involves a surplus that cannot be expropriated by capital or captured in the regimentation of the global political body. . . . revolt arises only on the basis of wealth, that is, a surplus of intelligence, experience, knowledges, and desire. When we propose the poor as the paradigmatic subjective figure of labor today, it is not because the poor are empty and excluded from wealth but because they are included in the circuits of production and full of potential . . .

Since, as part of the tendency toward immaterial production, wealth is no longer an immense accumulation of material commodities, but rather the surplus products of intellectual labor that tend to resist capitalist expropriation and the imposition of the commodity form, the poor and impoverished have access to a surplus of "intelligence, experience, knowledges" that will nurture their own fecund creativity, guile, and ingenuity, which, as a result of their condition of exclusion from private accumulation or participation in public (state) control, always aim at the production of the common. This is the revolutionary "potential" of the poor, namely; the fact that their tremendous productive force is one that functions essentially in common.

So why this privileging of the figure of the poor as the *topos* of any real transformation, rather than the class category analogous to Marx's industrial proletariat, namely the immaterial laborer—the producer of information, knowledge, affect, subjectivities? Insofar as the products of the latter's labor seem well situated to resist the commodity form—open source software, free access to "knowledges" via the internet, etc.—it seems reasonable that the immaterial laborer would be the focal point of an attempt to theorize the liberation of productive force from the strictures of wage-labor and the commodity form. Hardt and Negri certainly acknowledge the necessity of theorizing ways to resist efforts to reimpose the commodity form on the products of immaterial labor in both *Empire* and *Multitude*, where they at least mention the attack on the open source movement, the, diabolical, project of patenting genetic information, and other analogous terrains of struggle vis à vis so-called intellectual property. Nonetheless, the answer to the question, "why not analyze immaterial labor as the bearer of a privileged revolutionary force?" appears obvious

---

noted Negri's early association with that tradition in "The Italian Ideology," *Debating Empire*; Balakrishnan ed., London and New York: Verso, 2003, 115. As I have indicated, it is to Bataille that I will turn to try to make sense of some of the paradoxes of Negri's thought, and to supply a useful addenda to Negri's and his collaborator's work.

enough. Negri and Hardt seem to have anticipated Žižek's dismissive charge of peddling little more than a soft revolution that transforms the way we work, but leaves fundamentally unopposed the necessity of imposed work. The yuppie on the Paris subway may already feel that their work has been liberated, their creativity and imagination set free, while remaining a wage laborer who satisfies his needs via commodities. So too for the entrepreneur in New York or Los Angeles who is busy transforming the latest subjectivity 'produced' by the multitude of the urban metropolis into a lucrative commercial enterprise, as has so spectacularly been accomplished in the past couple of decades with "hip-hop" and "skating" cultures, to name but two examples. Self-directed, self-managed, creatively fulfilling (highly paid) intellectual labor may constitute a real transformation for the immaterial laborer herself, regardless of the fact that the products of her work are immediately stamped with the commodity form, and regardless of the fact that such a transformation means little to the person cleaning the toilets in her Paris, or San Jose, or Bangalore research "campus."

This, of course, is not to suggest that the ascendance of immaterial labor has had no impact on the lives of those on the periphery of today's global, highly educated classes. The poor in both affluent and impoverished nations are making use of information and communications technologies to improve their lives in innumerable creative, imaginative, and effective ways. Beyond this though, Negri and his collaborators clearly realize that simply celebrating a transformation in the way that we work does nothing to facilitate a real social transformation, as long as work is still fundamentally ordered and imposed under capital/Empire by means of the wage and the continual reimposition of the commodity form on the products of immaterial labor. What is needed is a theorization of transformation that is rooted in *common* production regardless of the form of labor involved, and regardless of whatever hegemonic tendency is transforming the *way* that we work. The hegemonic tendency of immaterial labor is not, in itself, enough to carry us beyond Empire. It is only production *in common*, driven by the power of 'the poor,' that can slay the twin monsters of wage labor and the commodity form, and no real social transformation is possible except on the basis of such a transcendence.

From Immeasurable to Excessive Production

It is natural to refuse authority, and the refusal of authority is going on every day at all levels of society. And all of the various forms of modern and contemporary liberatory politics are at base a refusal of servitude, a refusal to accept as natural our subordination to rulers.[30]

> In the final analysis it is clear that a worker works in order to obtain the violent pleasures of coitus (in other words, he accumulates in order to spend). On the other hand, the conception according to which the worker must have coitus in order to provide for the future necessities of work is linked with the unconscious identification of worker with slave.[31]

Refusal—yes! But refusal is always only the beginning for Negri and his collaborators. In *Empire*, he and Hardt praise Melville's Bartleby as a "beautiful soul," but warn us that the sort of absolute refusal of servitude that Bartleby enacts "in itself is empty," a vain gesture that "leads only to a kind of social suicide."[32] We must refuse, but only in order to produce "a new social body" from the ruins of that which we refuse. Well and good, but does this refusal of authority that Hardt speaks of as "natural" include the refusal of that authority which identifies me, essentially, as the bearer of productive force, as a being the "essential component" of whose life time is "work time?"

In *Multitude*, Hardt and Negri take Bakhtin's *carnevalesque* and the related notion of polyphonic narrative as a model for the linguistic construction of the common by and through a multitude of singular voices—from out of the Babel of the multitude, the common will be articulated by means of a carnevalesque, polyphonic polylogue.[33] Again, well and good, but Hardt and Negri ignore another essential aspect of the carnevalesque in their brief excursus, namely its status as a complete suspension of all 'business-as-usual;' a condition of exorbitantly variegated *free play*, a mad cacophony of games and amusements, a pure *jouissance*—play to no end other than the joy of play, and thus also a sort of great refusal of any kind of work, liberated or not. The carnevelesque is not only a polyphony that speaks subjectivities and desires in common, it is also an 'immeasurable' time that resists any structuring or conditioning, a time without calendars or clocks, and thus, from the perspective of any schema of order, a disordered squandering of time, to no gain whatsoever—a time put utterly out of *production*. The carnevalesque is the scandal of *all* work.

---

[30] Michael Hardt, "Sovereignty, Multitudes, Absolute Democracy: A Discussion between Michael Hardt and Thomas L. Dumm about Hardt's and Negri's *Empire*" in *Empire's New Clothes*, Passavant and Dean eds., New York and London: Routledge, 2004, 167.

[31] Georges Bataille, "The Use Value of D.A.F. de Sade," in *Visions of Excess: Selected Writings, 1927–1939*, Stoekl ed., Minneapolis: University of Minnesota Press, 1985, 99.

[32] Op. cit., n. 16, 204.

[33] Cf. op. cit., n. 18, 208–11.

As we have just seen, Negri and Hardt celebrate the poor, again, for embodying "the ontological condition not only of resistance but also of productive life itself." The power, potential, creativity, and productivity of those who are impoverished is celebrated as the *topos* of that production in common to come—a transformation that will deliver the processes of production from Empire's fetters, producing not a vast accumulation of commodities to be privately accumulated and publicly redistributed, but a new way of living and working in common. Three times well and good, but again, Hardt and Negri overlook another kind of genius associated with those who are "impoverished" from the perspective of a culture bent on accumulation at all cost. When we consider the example of cultures that operate on the basis of a subsistence economy, we should recognize the particular genius of them in recognizing when it is no longer necessary to work. From the perspective of "developed" economies, subsistence economies are poor and impoverished. They also—displaying an intelligence beyond the grasp of "advanced" cultures—know when they have enough, and can devote their time to enjoying their lives, unproductively. So too with many of the relatively poor in affluent nations, whose genius in spending time enjoying their lives, their families, their communities, is idiotically misinterpreted as a lack of ambition to 'get ahead,' and 'improve themselves.'

Bataille argued that people accumulate in order to spend. Under capital, wage labor is required in order to accumulate, and so we sell ourselves in wage labor not in order to accumulate, but in order to spend, which is the end in itself. "On the other hand," Bataille writes, any conception according to which expense is not the end itself, but the means to work (in order to accumulate, in order to spend in the future, in order to work . . .) expresses an unconscious identification of worker with slave. Conceiving of accumulation, for example, as primary, on the part of either the capitalist who profits directly from accumulation or the workers who express their sovereignty by means of the accumulation of commodities, expresses, unconsciously, the identification of life with work, of worker with slave. Bataille is not saying that we should work to live and not live to work. That popular expression is far too flaccid, as is demonstrated by the fact that our extraordinarily affluent culture almost entirely ignores it, even as we nod agreement with the sentiment. Bataille, rather, expresses the forceful insight that is meekly gestured towards by the trite phrase 'work to live, don't live to work:' Living to work is, precisely, being a slave. Relating this insight to Negri's emphasis on production, could we then also think of the conception according to which expense is not the end itself, but the means to work, as an unconscious expression of the identification of ("essential") life time with work time, of human beings with labor power, of the multitude with the production of (creative, imaginative, desiring, productive) subjectivities?

Bataille also wanted to sell a revolution—a real social transformation. The Sade text dates from approximately 1930, and was composed in the context of the extraordinary transformations that were taking place in the aftermath of the First World War; of the social, political, and economic upheavals that were shattering the fragile foundations of European liberal democracy. Neither Liberal democracy nor Socialism in Western Europe had any answer for Mussolini, Hitler, and Franco. The radical transformation effected by the Soviets had led to the dead-end of Stalinism and Soviet state capitalism. In this context, some other alternative was imperative, one that, like fascism, offered real change for ordinary, working people. Bataille's proposal was something like a thoroughgoing, Sadean critique of all moralities of improvement, which spurn "base matter" and the satisfaction of base needs, and which require the individual to sacrifice the present for the vagaries of the future, or of the fatherland for that matter. Bataille read the Western morality of propriety and hygiene as fundamentally in the service of an ethos of work or 'service' which constituted an unconscious identification of human being with slave. Hence, Bataille sought to sell a revolution by means of liberating individuals from a morality that functions, at bottom, to keep them—clean, sober, and diligently—at work, or in ranks.

Later, in the context of the post World War II choice between state and private capitalism, Bataille again sought an alternative for working people, an alternative that did not identify people with slaves, regardless of how benevolent the master might appear. In his bafflingly under-appreciated *The Accursed Share*, Bataille distinguished between competing perspectives towards the processes of social production which he expressed through the distinction between "limited" and "general" economy. In *The Accursed Share*, Bataille argued for a movement away from the perspective of "limited" economies based upon a primal myth of scarcity, and aimed at accumulation at all cost (the necessity of capitalist expansion), towards the perspective of "general" economy that was founded upon a primal excess, and aimed at unproductive expenditure—at "leisure."[34] Our devotion to capitalist expansion is perpetuated by means of an ideology that entrances us with both a morality and ethos of work, and crucially a vision of scarcity and need in the face of the insane accumulation of things that characterizes affluent economies. This myth of scarcity and primacy of accumulation is central to "consumer" culture as well, since consumer culture *is* that culture whose wealth is identical to Marx's immense accumulation of commodities, and the function of the periodic *consumption* of those commodities is to reanimate the myth of primal scarcity and hence reani-

---

[34] And of course "leisure" is presently the site of a desperate attempt to commodify all life and experience, to reinscribe unproductive activity into the cycle of production by demanding that leisure time involve the consumption of commodities, from internet providers, to high-end hiking boots, to viagra.

mate the motivation to work and to accumulate. Consumption thus rein-
scribes the worker within the cycle of capitalist production and expansion
by reproducing her labor power *and* her motivation to sell her labor power
for a wage, hence consumption reinforces that ideology which unconsciously identifies her with slave. This is a very different logic from that
which sees excess as primary, and hence unproductive expenditure—the
simple enjoyment of life—as the end of life activity.

On Bataille's view, the ideology of limited economy must be overcome,
the excessive abundance that characterizes our production in common must
be recognized, the fact that we produce and accumulate too many things,
that too much of life is given over to "productive" activity (material or
immaterial—they're still *things*, and it's still *work*) must be acknowledged,
and hence life must be delivered back over to living—to the unproductive,
miraculous in Bataille's word, activity of enjoying a glass of wine, or the brilliance of the sun on a spring morning, to borrow two of his examples.[35] It
is solely on the basis of a transition to the perspective of general economy
and primal excess that we can escape the identification of life with work
(and the accumulation and periodic consumption of commodities), and
hence the identification of worker—ourselves—with slave. Hence, to return
to Negri's terms, could we not then read the prodigality of the productive
force of the multitude not solely in terms of its "immeasurability," but also,
indeed primarily in this postmodern age, in terms of its *excessiveness*?

And so, while acknowledging the positive aspects of Negri's emphasis
on the project of liberating productive forces, and privileging the productive force of the poor as the *topos* of a production in common aimed at
transcending Empire, I want to close by offering a correction inspired by
Bataille to a serious danger associated with this emphasis, namely, as I have
already mentioned, the danger of identifying life with labor, and human
beings with productive force.

Hardt and Negri are right. We must refuse the imposition of capitalist
or imperial order, in order to begin the task of producing a new social body,
and new ways of living and working together. But we must also, as part of
that project, refuse our identification with productive force—pursuing the
goal of a real social transformation that would not simply change the way
that we work, but end the identification of life with work, requires that. As
such, Negri and his collaborators must acknowledge that "work time" is
not the "essential component of life time." Human beings are not productive force. Life is not work, not even "liberated" work. "Subjectivities,"
"affects," etc. are not merely, not even primarily "produced," rather, they
are lived by the "irreducible singularities" that compose the multitude.
Emphasizing the fact that affects, desires, subjectivities etc. are "products"

---

[35] Bataille, *The Accursed Share*, v. *III*, Robert Hurley trans., New York: Zone Books,
1991, 199.

of Empire carries the danger of furthering the tendency to commodify all human life, experience, desire, etc.—a tendency anathema to Negri's et al's own goals. As such, we should recognize that what is beautiful is not the "generation of subjectivity," but the experience of that very subjectivity on the part of living, breathing human beings. What is beautiful is life, not production, and life is *not* equivalent to production, even in this age of the transition to immaterial labor. The multitude is not merely "an ensemble of constellations productive of subjectivity," it is also, and more essentially, the constellation of living subjectivities whose experiences and desires are not affects that are produced, but rather moments that are lived. Indeed, the "multitude" is not a constellation of "irreducible singularities"—a fully ontological term that functions precisely in opposition to Hardt's and Negri's intention, in reducing the human beings that form the multitude to a lumpen mass which "generates" subjectivity, but does not seem to live it. By refusing to reduce those irreducible singularities, Hardt and Negri, ironically, treat them as an abstract set of (productive) practices and activities, whose intersection constitutes the multitude—they are no longer human beings. The multitude expresses itself through its prodigious productivity, but it is not merely a force, or a "constellation," or a network of practices, that produces life—it is human beings living life. The multitude finds itself not only in the processes of social production, but also in leisure, in joy, in love, in Bataillean unproductive expenditure, and simply in its experience of the world produced in common, none of which can be reduced to "products," but are, simply, life.

In short then, we must refuse the notion that life, subjectivity, desire, affect, etc., are, essentially, produced rather than lived, as part of the general product of refusing the commodification of life. And while poverty may be the *topos* of production in common, poverty is not the primal exigency of social life, nor is production in common the end of revolutionary struggle. The excessiveness of our collective productivity grounds social life, the end of which is for all of us to live—to enjoy the moments of our lives. This refusal of the commodification of life, and of the perspective of Bataille's limited economy which leads us to identify life with work, is, on my view, absolutely necessary to the task of selling a revolution for the postmodern age—of imagining a truly new regime of social life and making it meaningful for ordinary people, like me.

---

[36] And let me simply add what should be obvious to most readers at this point; the impending destruction of our world through environmental degradation requires our collective recognition of not the immeasurability, but truly the excessiveness of current circuits of global production. Life on this planet depends on it. Addressing the tension between this impending disaster, and Bataille's project of opposing a primal myth of scarcity with a primal myth of excess, is a matter for another day. However, allow me to merely point out that it's the former that has gotten us to this point.

3

Metapolitics Now:
Negri, Critical Theory, Praxis

DAVID SHERMAN

As the ultimate successors of "Capital" and "the working class," Negri and Hardt's "Empire" and "the multitude" are the two axes on which they strive to come to grips with the consequences of the "postmodernization of the global economy."[1] This analogy conceals more than it reveals, however, for beneath superficial similarities the two sets of terms are structurally dissimilar. By virtue of the variegated postmodernizing processes that brought them into existence, Empire and the multitude are not simply capital and the working class raised to a global level.

A basic dissimilarity, one that is not overtly raised in this analogy, is the changed relation between capital and sovereign authority, and, in particular, how changes in the nature of capital's imperatives have actually changed the nature of sovereign authority itself. Unlike thinkers such as Chomsky, who view the American drive for global domination as the primary political feature of the present age,[2] Negri and Hardt do plainly hold that the current world order is characterized, first and foremost, by the migration of sovereignty from the national to global level: Empire, as the primary "political subject," is "the sovereign power that governs the world" (*Empire,* xi). Yet, crucially, although it supersedes all nation-states, Empire does not operate as an *über* nation-state but rather, in decisive respects, as the opposite of one. Although nation-states were based on the centralization of power and the imperial conquest of territories, Empire is based on a decentered and deterritorialized logic that, for the most part, mirrors the neoliberal capitalist globalization processes that in large part brought it into existence. So, too, unlike those thinkers who continue to

---

[1] Michael Hardt and Antonio Negri, *Empire,* Cambridge, MA: Harvard University Press, 2000, xiii.

[2] See, e.g., Noam Chomsky, *Hegemony or Survival: America's Quest for Global Dominance,* New York: Henry Holt and Co., 2003.

look to "the working class" (no matter how broadly defined) as the primary site of resistance to global capital, Negri and Hardt hold that the multitude is, in its very essence, a far more "open, inclusive concept," one "composed potentially of all the diverse figures of social production."[3] But, once again, although it supersedes all segments of the working class, the multitude does not operate as an *über* working class but rather, in decisive respects, as the opposite of one. "The working class," not to mention such modern concepts as "the masses" or "the people," all point toward a manufactured unity, while the multitude, although characterized as "a social subject," is "composed of a set of singularities" whose common stuff is flesh (*Multitude*, 192).

A more basic (albeit related) dissimilarity, the one that I would like to pursue here, does not concern the decentralized processes to which Empire and the multitude refer—decentralized processes that themselves differ in that Empire parasitically draws on these processes to extend its own sovereign imperatives while the multitude continues to be informed by the singularities that comprise it. Rather, the dissimilarity that I would like to pursue here involves the slide from "Capital," which previously used the sovereign in the pursuit of its interests, to "Empire," which is the sovereign—or, in other words, the slide from a "modern" politico-economic problematic to a purely political "postmodern" one. On the first page of *Empire*, Negri and Hardt concede that for many theorists the current sociohistorical situation evinces the ascendance of economics over sovereignty, but they rightfully reject this thesis:

> Many argue that the globalization of capitalist production and exchange means that economic relations have become more autonomous from political controls, and consequently that political sovereignty has declined . . . The decline in sovereignty of nation-states, however, does not mean that sovereignty as such has declined. (*Empire*, xi)

In rejecting this thesis, however, they do not make clear that the new global form of sovereignty that they posit means that political controls have become more autonomous from the economic relations of capitalist production and exchange. To be sure, "capital has always been oriented toward the production, reproduction, and control of social life" (*Multitude*, 146)—which, for Negri and Hardt, is the defining feature of Empire—but not all social forms that aim toward the production, reproduction, and control of social life are capitalistic. And, indeed, by speaking in terms of Empire instead of capital, they testify not just to the primacy of

---

[3] Michael Hardt and Antonio Negri, *Multitude: War and Democracy in the Age of Empire*, New York: The Penguin Press, 2004, xiv–xv.

the political with regard to the economic but, more drastically, the supersession of the economic altogether. Of course, Negri and Hardt do speak of Empire as the fruition of a process in which "capitalist sovereignty" has finally "become immanent" (i.e., there is no longer a transcending sovereign, as was the case in modernity), but as the section in *Empire* titled "Capitalist Sovereignty, or Administering the Global Society of Control" testifies, it is unclear to what extent this new form of sovereignty deserves to be called "capitalist" at all.

Negri and Hardt's position is, in essence, that there is a "primacy of the political," and this position, especially when it is coupled with their commitment to a "broadly interdisciplinary approach" (*Empire*, xvi), is reminiscent of "critical theory"—the first-generation Frankfurt School theorists, in particular. According to Negri and Hardt, as well as the first generation of critical theorists, capitalism's totalizing impulse strives to transcend the dualities that comprise it. But for Negri and Hardt, Adorno's greatest fear, the "totally administered society," actually establishes itself: "With the appearance of Empire, we are confronted no longer with the local mediations of the universal but with a concrete universal itself" (*Empire*, 19), which signifies the passage beyond Foucault's "disciplinary society" to "the society of control." This position was becoming ever more conspicuous in Negri's work, and it has reached its pinnacle in *Empire* and *Multitude*, in which he and Hardt all but transform what is arguably Marx's central economic category, the "labor theory of value," into a thoroughly political one. Within the context of an unparalleled increase in market intervention by the state, whether in its fascistic (Nazi) or liberal (Keynesian) forms, the evolving relation between the economic and the political is also one with which the Frankfurt School was forced to grapple—in fact, its internal economic debates regarding this issue in the early 1940s largely prompted critical theory's shift from a more orthodox concern with critiquing political economy to its later emphasis on "ideology critique." Thus, although "the basic hypothesis" of *Empire* is that the sovereignty of the state is being usurped by Empire, which is "a series of national and supranational organisms united under a single logic of rule" (*Empire*, xii), critical theory's early debates concerning "state capitalism"—the conflicting positions staked out by Friedrich Pollock's "State Capitalism: Its Possibilities and Limitations" and Franz Neumann's *Behemoth*, in particular—are useful for making sense of Negri and Hardt's claims.

Beyond these convergences, Negri and Hardt's positions, which arise directly out of the autonomist Marxist tradition,[4] would seem to have little in common with those of the critical theorists. Although both traditions

---

[4] See the Introduction.

arose out of western Marxism, which sought to revivify the moment of subjectivity that was lost in orthodox Marxism, and both traditions seem to repudiate the unmediated nature of orthodox Marxism's "base-super-structure" dichotomy, they approach sociopolitical matters in diametrically opposed ways. From the critical theoretic standpoint of a dialectic gone bad, subjectivity tends toward one-dimensionality by virtue of the socio-cultural mediations of capital, which penetrate the workplace to manufac-ture a false consciousness that fails to properly grasp its own exploitation. Conversely, from the autonomist Marxist standpoint, contradictions within the workplace have engendered the development of a subjectivity that is increasingly opposed to the aims of capital, thus leading capital to increas-ingly displace these contradictions into the sociocultural realm, which only radicalizes the larger population. Both theoretically and practically, how-ever, these perspectives, signified by critical theory's "culture industry" and autonomist Marxism's "social factory," actually reflect two sides of the same coin, and this is also manifested in terms of the relation between the-ory and practice. Although critical theory's theoretical pessimism has tended toward quietism and autonomist Marxism's theoretical optimism has tended toward decisionism,[5] these conflicting tendencies are informed by the same underlying phenomenon, the absolutization of the political.

I

In the Preface to *Empire*, Negri and Hardt assert that "the central portion of the book, Parts 2 and 3, tells the story of the passage from modernity to postmodernity, or really from imperialism to Empire"—that is, from the standpoint of "the history of ideas and culture," *or really* from "the stand-point of production" (*Empire*, xvi–xvii). Crucially, however, while the "really" in this excerpt suggests that what underlies the phenomenon of Empire is actually the process of economic globalization, Negri and Hardt qualify this emphasis, stating that production is to be "understood in a very broad sense, ranging from economic production to the production of sub-jectivity" (*Empire*, xvii)—which, it seems, brings us back to the history of ideas and culture. Likewise, they assert, "in the postmodernization of the

---

[5] Admittedly, these are generalizations of two rich traditions that bring together diver-gent perspectives. His *One Dimensional Man* to the contrary notwithstanding, Herbert Marcuse was far more optimistic than Theodor Adorno and Max Horkheimer (who I have in mind here), and, from a practical standpoint, he was anything but quietistic. Conversely, Sergio Bologna is far more pessimistic than Negri, and, by virtue of the complexities of work-ing class composition, sees certain daunting impediments to effective working class action. Nevertheless, as generalizations based upon the inherent tendencies within each tradition, these conclusions, I would argue, are sound.

global economy, the creation of wealth tends ever more toward what we call biopolitical production, the production of social life itself, in which the economic, the political, and the cultural increasingly overlap one another" (*Empire,* xiii). In a very real sense, then, Negri and Hardt's approach to comprehending the complicated processes of globalization, which culminate in "the concept of Empire," mirrors the concept itself: "it is characterized fundamentally by a lack of boundaries" (*Empire,* xiv). And this goes well beyond their laudable desire to approach globalization from an interdisciplinary perspective, i.e., from a perspective that recognizes the mediated nature of the disciplines, for it tends to break them down altogether. One is reminded here of Kierkegaard's lament that "there is no ear for the harmony of spheres of category relations but only for the rattle of money in the cash box,"[6] but, of course, Kierkegaard, succumbing to nostalgia, was bemoaning the collapse of categorial differences within capitalist modernity, while Negri and Hardt, suffused with expectancy, seem to be celebrating it within capitalist postmodernity. Furthermore, not only is the relation between what remains of the disciplines increasingly blurred on their account, but, as a result, so too are the intradisciplinary concepts. This is particularly so within the context of "the economic," for not only is the concept of "production" increasingly unclear, but so too are the concepts of "value" and "labor." Thus, after asserting that "the old distinction between economic and political struggles becomes merely an obstacle to understanding class relations" (*Multitude,* 105), Negri and Hardt go on to declare:

> Exploitation under the hegemony of immaterial labor is no longer primarily the expropriation of value measured by individual or collective labor time but rather the capture of value that is produced by cooperative labor and that becomes increasingly common through its circulation in social networks. The central forms of productive cooperation are no longer created by the capitalist as part of the project to organize labor but rather emerge from the productive energies of labor itself. This is indeed the key characteristic of material labor: to produce communication, social relations, and cooperation. (*Multitude,* 113)

I shall parse the concepts of "production," "labor," and "value" set forth here momentarily. In the meantime, however, I would preliminarily say, in a more general vein, that the tendency to generalize economic concepts, and, more importantly, the phenomena that they represent, arises from, but is ultimately a distortion of, the impulse that led to some of autonomist Marxism's earliest and most invaluable formulations—most

---

[6] Soren Kierkegaard, *The Corsair Affair,* tr. Howard V. Hong and Edna H. Hong, Princeton: Princeton University Press, 1982, 171–72.

notably "the social factory." By rejecting hard and fast distinctions between work time and non-work time, and thus the waged and unwaged, autonomist Marxism captured the nature of capitalism's own homogenizing push, and gave the lie to a good bit of its ideology. If pushed too far, as is the case with Negri's work, however, autonomist Marxism's functional concepts no longer actually capture the mediated nature of the underlying phenomena—which is precisely what capitalist ideology obscures—but rather tends to homogenize the phenomena itself, and therefore becomes no less "ideological." And, indeed, that this is the underlying tendency of capitalism itself, as Negri and Hardt rightly claim, simply makes it all the more inexcusable. As Adorno, in particular, recognized, even theories nominally in the service of emancipation tend to unwittingly collude with the prevailing powers when they idealistically schematize in accordance with prefabricated conceptual categories, for this abstract steamrollering of particulars—even if in the name of an unalloyed singularity—has a tendency to reproduce the given state of affairs.

Perhaps the best example of this tendency is Negri and Hardt's emphasis on "immaterial labor"—namely, "labor that produces an immaterial good, such as a service, a cultural product, knowledge, or communication" (*Empire*, 290)—which, they say, "occupies an increasingly central position in both the schema of capitalist production and the composition of the proletariat" (*Empire*, 53). Now, surely, there is more than a grain of truth in this analysis, but, as an initial matter, it is still not clear what exactly they mean by "immaterial labor." When Negri and Hardt speak of it, they are usually referring to those employed in the cutting edge communication and information technologies, but when they first proffer "concrete evidence" for the "hegemony of immaterial labor" in *Multitude*, they say: "Immaterial labor is central to most of what statistics show are the fastest growing occupations, such as food servers, salespersons, computer engineers, teachers, and health workers" (*Multitude*, 114). Most of these workers, although not producing commodities, are not very far removed—if they are removed at all—from the kind of brute material labor that characterized labor under the regime of "disciplinary governability" (i.e., labor in the factory, which served as a model for society, more generally). Thus, while Negri and Hardt are right to point to the increased influence of highly educated, "high-tech" workers, they exaggerate it, and, moreover, lose sight of the fact that the global decentralization and deregulation of production, which constitutes the so-called postmodernization of capital, has been a boon not simply to those sectors of capital that deal with cutting edge communication and information technologies but also to those less advanced ones that continue to deal primarily in brute material labor. And not only does brute material labor continue to be a weighty presence in the proliferating low wage service sector, but it also continues to thrive in the older manufacturing, retail, and agricultural sectors, often in forms at least as egregious as before.

To be sure, Negri and Hardt qualify their claim in *Multitude*, declaring that "immaterial labor has become *hegemonic in qualitative terms,* and has imposed a tendency on other forms of labor and society itself . . . [It] is today in the same position that industrial labor was 150 years ago" (*Multitude,* 109). But, as George Caffentzis asserts, even if Negri and Hardt were right on the money concerning the preponderance of intellectual labor, their optimism would be misplaced because these workers, as the new aristocracy of labor, are far from emiserated.[7] And, unlike Marx, who pinned his emancipatory hopes on an industrial proletariat that in the 1860s also constituted a relatively small percentage of the overall work force, Negri and Hardt have not performed the necessary empirical analyses to make good their claim that these workers will continually increase as a proportion of the workforce or, if they do, that their experiences will bear out the revolutionary role that Negri and Hardt attribute to them. Consequently, by failing to analyze concretely the prevailing composition of labor, and by virtually ignoring the brute material labor on whose back the more advanced sectors are able to thrive, Negri and Hardt inadvertently give succor to those who still profit from the imposition of this sort of labor by taking it off the radar screen.

So, too, by virtue of their commitment to Deleuze and Guattari's ontology,[8] Negri and Hardt—despite their commitment to the immaterial labor found in the emerging information and communication technologies—strangely argue that "one of the central and most urgent political paradoxes of our time" is that "in our much celebrated age of communication, struggles have become all but incommunicable" (*Empire,* 54). One would think that the homogenized workforce of Empire would pull in the opposite direction—the increasingly homogenized industrial work force that Marx foresaw, which had nowhere near the communicative capacities, surely did—but as postmodernists of a sort, Negri and Hardt are also committed to an unalloyed singularity, and, therefore, "struggles not only fail to communicate to other contexts but also lack even a local communication" (*Empire,* 54). What we need, they speculate, is "a communication of singularities" (*Empire,* 57), but, ever optimistic, they assert that "because

---

[7] George Caffentzis's unpublished paper, "The End of Work or the Renaissance of Slavery," is discussed in Nick Dyer-Witheford's "Empire, Immaterial Labor, the New Combinations, and the Global Worker," in *Rethinking Marxism,* vol. 13, no. 3, Fall/Winter, 2001, 70–80.

[8] See David Sherman, "The Ontological Need: Positing Subjectivity and Resistance in Hardt and Negri's Empire," *Telos* 128, Summer, 2004, 143–70, where I focus on Negri and Hardt's "materialist" ontology, which, I believe, does irreparable harm to many of the positions that they take.

all these struggles are incommunicable, and thus blocked from traveling horizontally in the form of a cycle, they are forced instead to leap vertically and touch immediately on the global level" (*Empire,* 55). The awkward notion of a global labor force that is utterly singularized in its homogeneity aside, there is no incommunicable solidarity that will lead to the toppling of global capital from a thousand singularities, and to assume that there is one again has a detrimental effect: it enables Negri and Hardt to avoid the hard work of ascertaining the precise relationship between various local struggles, which, of course, are neither completely communicable nor incommunicable, as well as what it would take to reconcile them in the face of a global regime that is being imposed on all alike.[9]

As suggested above, the homogenizing push to level a still diverse labor force is driven by Negri and Hardt's higher-order theory of the contours of late capitalism—in particular, what I take to be their break with Marx's value theory, which is precipitated by their interpretation of Marx's distinction between "formal subsumption" and "real subsumption." According to Marx, formal subsumption takes place when capitalist relations are imposed on the labor processes of a social context within which they did not previously obtain. When this occurs, he states, surplus value can not be appropriated relatively but only absolutely, i.e., the increase in value appropriated by capital is the result of an increase in the total number of work hours that it is able to impose. Within an existing capitalist context, this is the result of increasing the working day. Due to worker struggles that reduced the working day within the more advanced capitalist countries, however, capital increasingly was compelled to look elsewhere for sources of absolute surplus value, and the additional hours that it acquired increasingly came from labor in other countries, as the fruit of imperialistic undertakings. Once capitalist social relations are firmly ingrained within the new context, however, value is appropriated relatively—that is, the increase in value appropriated by capital is the result of productivity increases, which are often achieved through technological development. As Marx puts it: "With the production of relative surplus-value the entire real form of production is altered and a specifically capitalist form of production comes into being (at the technological level too)."[10] Now, according to Negri and Hardt, Empire is the result of the implementation of "the specifically capitalist form of production" worldwide. This means that imperialism as a phenomenon, which was a function of formal subsumption, is now superseded, for there are no longer noncapi-

---

[9] This sentiment is shared by Nick Dyer-Witheford. See "Empire, Immaterial Labor, the New Combinations, and the Global Worker," 75.

[10] Karl Marx, *Capital*, Volume 1, tr. Ben Fowkes, London: Penguin Books, 1976, 1024.

talist environments to be subsumed. And with the real subsumption of the globe under capital and with the increased emphasis upon technological development that is part and parcel of it, "the integration of labor into capital becomes more intensive than extensive and society is ever more completely fashioned by capital" (*Empire*, 255).

Under these circumstances, Negri and Hardt argue, there is a metamorphosis of sorts, as both the capitalist expropriation of value and the worker from whom value is expropriated take on entirely different forms. In *The Politics of Subversion*, published in 1989, Negri sets forth in greater detail than *Empire* the theoretical underpinnings of this metamorphosis. He contends that with the movement from formal to real subsumption, there is a corresponding movement from the archetypical worker as a "mass" worker to a "social" one—that is, from a worker engaged in the productive cooperation necessary for mass production to one engaged, first and foremost, in "the production of the social cooperation necessary for work."[11] Although this formulation seems to suggest that "work" is something other than "the production of the social cooperation necessary for it," the fact is that Negri conflates the two. Work is actually nothing other than the production of this social cooperation: "The socialized worker has come to develop the critique of exploitation by means of the critique of communication."[12] That is, value is reposited within communication itself, and thus the expropriation of value is tantamount to the expropriation of communication. Negri's position here bears superficial similarities to Habermas's theory of communicative action, but for present purposes what bears emphasis is that for Negri and Hardt not only does "manual labor tend to become intellectual labor,"[13] but intellectual labor becomes tantamount to communication itself, which means that all human beings are workers to an equal degree: "communication is to the socialized worker what the wage relationship was to the mass worker."[14] Thus, by virtue of its very ubiquity, "work" as a meaningful category drops out of the picture, which Negri concedes when he says that the new social formation "makes it difficult to retain the terminology and conceptual definitions used by Marx: for example, one might ask why a worker should still be described as a 'worker' rather than an 'operator' or a 'social actor'."[15] In this way, Negri and Hardt are positioned not only to hurdle

---

[11] Antonio Negri, *The Politics of Subversion: A Manifesto for the Twenty-First Century*, tr. James Newell, Cambridge: Polity Press, 1989, 80.

[12] Ibid., 57–58.

[13] Ibid., 58.

[14] Ibid., 118.

[15] Ibid., 84.

[16] Ibid., 87–88.

"the rotten dialectic of workerism"[16] but to demand "a social wage and guaranteed income for all," for "the entire multitude produces, and its production is necessary from the standpoint of total social capital" (*Empire*, 403).

Crucially, then, with this position Negri and Hardt bring the autonomist Marxist tradition to its conclusion in two interrelated ways. First, the movement beyond the factory to the social *factory* is itself surpassed by the *social* factory—that is, society no longer simply facilitates the valorization processes of the prior locus of economic productivity, the spatially identifiable place called "the factory," but deconstructs it through assimilation by every social cell, all the while intensifying its nature. Stated differently, autonomist Marxism's prior distinction between social capital and individual capital—i.e., the distinction between capital meant to reproduce nothing less than capitalist social relations at a societal level and capital meant to serve as the foundation for each individual capitalist's value creating processes in pursuit of profits—disappears, as it all becomes a matter of social capital. Second, the contention that capitalism, distilled to its very essence, is about imposing work to reproduce the prevailing set of social relations, based on domination and subordination, is also surpassed: rendered superfluous by technology, work, in the very process of becoming ubiquitous, ceases to exist by virtue of its universalization as communication, and what remains is nothing but the domination and subordination.

Needless to say, in all but name, Negri and Hardt overturn the heart of Marx's theory, the labor theory of value, through this formulation. And, once again, *The Politics of Subversion* sets forth the underlying theoretical arguments in greater detail than *Empire*. Tacitly suggesting that the labor theory of value is no longer adequate, given the culmination of real subsumption and the concomitant rise of the socialized worker, Negri asks "how an adequate theory of value can be reconstructed" within a context in which value has become "reactualized," thereby giving rise to "a new, original accumulation."[17] Stated plainly, the problem that Negri is confronting arises from what, for him, is the ubiquity of work. If communication, by virtue of its reproduction of the underlying social relations of domination and subordination, is work, then the production of value is also ubiquitous, which Negri recognizes when he asserts that value "flows freely" and that "the socialized worker produces value 'naturally'."[18] This seems to end value theory as a useful explanatory tool, but Negri refuses to jettison it: "We must abandon the illusory notion of [value] measure-

---

17 Ibid., 77–78.
18 Ibid., 79.

ment and the mystification of mediation. Notwithstanding this, it is both possible and necessary to construct a theory of value . . . but let us not confuse accountancy with a theory of value nor perpetuate the naturalistic illusion that it is possible to find a foundation."[19] Still, Negri does not construct a value theory, nor could he, given his theoretical commitments: one need not "confuse accountancy with a theory of value" to claim that the mere assertion of an "excessive" value, engendered in the move "from the factory to the ecological machine"[20] (i.e., in the comprehensive socialization of work), obscures rather than clarifies the value question.

Now, to be sure, value theory, as Harry Cleaver states, "always designated primarily the role of labor as undifferentiated capitalist command rather than its role as producer of wealth,"[21] but the roles are interrelated in capitalism, which means that "primarily" cannot be understood as "exclusively," as appears to be the case for Negri and Hardt. Similarly, although exchange value always designated capital's primary concern, it is interrelated with use value in capitalism—as Cleaver states, they express not only "the two-sided contradiction characteristic of class relations in capitalism" but also the "two different class perspectives."[22] However, for Negri and Hardt, use value has, for the most part, ceased to exist: "Use value and other references to values and processes of valorization that were conceived to be outside the capitalist mode of production have progressively vanished" (*Empire*, 386). And, finally, as Stephen Resnick and Richard Wolff state, although Negri and Hardt offer "rich detail and original analysis" with respect to the new corporate forms, their concepts "remain unconnected to surplus-value—that is, to the capitalist class processes."[23] Ultimately, then, command cannot be comprehended as capitalistic if it is not situated within the context of capital's extraction of surplus value from laborers producing use values (however broadly defined) in some determinate work process. And, indeed, given Negri and Hardt's across-the-board theory—with its sweeping characterizations of "productivity," "work," and "value," and its related tendency to see wealth creation as chiefly a function of the administration of fixed capital

---

[19] Ibid., 92.

[20] This is the title of chapter 4, in which Negri tackles the value question. See ibid., 89–101.

[21] Harry Cleaver, "Work, Value and Domination: On the Continuing Relevance of the Marxian Labor Theory of Value in the Crisis of the Keynesian Planner State," https://webspace.utexas.edu/hcleaver/www/offenegri.html.

[22] Harry Cleaver, *Reading* Capital *Politically*, Leeds: AK and Anti/Theses Press, 2000, 99.

[23] Stephen Resnick and Richard Wolff, "*Empire* and Class Analysis," in *Rethinking Marxism*, vol. 13, number 3, Fall/Winter 2001, 61–69.

(technology) rather than the employment of labor[24]—it is unclear whether any aspect of social life remains subject, strictly speaking, to economic considerations.

II

The question of the relation between the economic and the political is a longstanding one, and Negri has tackled it on numerous occasions, generally opting for the primacy of the latter. When asked in 1986 by the French journal *Terminal* whether "the political, as Lenin maintained, is a concentrated form of the economic, and power a concentrated form of value," he said: "Exactly the opposite is true."[25] So, too, in *The Politics of Subversion* he says that "the capitalist elite is a political elite [for whom] the political aspects of social production take on prime significance . . . Just as commodities were once conceived of as being produced by means of control, one can now talk in terms of the production of control by means of control."[26] While hedging their bets a bit, given that the lack of boundaries indigenous to Empire allegedly breaks down disciplinary divisions, Negri and Hardt also give pride of place to the political in *Empire*. Part I is titled "The Political Constitution of the Present," and the concept of Empire is described from the outset not in terms of free market capitalism but rather "global sovereignty," "world order," or "the society of control." And, when Negri and Hardt do speak about multinational corporations, they usually do so from the standpoint of power instead of profit: "The activities of corporations are no longer defined by the imposition of abstract command and the organization of simple theft and unequal exchange. Rather, they directly structure and articulate territories and populations" (*Empire*, 31).

Ironically, Negri and Hardt's argument for the primacy of politics over economics is reminiscent in certain crucial respects of the position taken by the Frankfurt School's Friedrich Pollock, who had argued pretty much the same thing with regard to Nazi Germany. Of course, the institutional structures with which Negri and Hardt are concerned bear little resemblance to the ones that concerned Pollock—indeed, in some ways they are diametrically opposed—but by virtue of the totalitarian politico-capitalistic

---

[24] As early as 1989, Negri asserts: "In the organic composition of capital, the proportion of constant capital has become enormous, while the proportion of variable capital has become correspondingly small." *The Politics of Subversion*, op. cit., 214.

[25] The interview, which appeared as "Vers de nouvelles valeurs?" in *Terminal*, no. 26, December-January 1986, Paris, is reproduced in *The Politics of Subversion*, op. cit. See p. 215.

[26] Antonio Negri, *The Politics of Subversion*, op. cit., 106.

impulse that both sets of critiques discern, Pollock's critique, even if only as a foil, is useful for the purpose of shedding additional light on both the theoretical and practical implications of Negri and Hardt's critique. To be more exact, Pollock's theories on state capitalism, most prominently set forth in his influential essay "State Capitalism: Its Possibilities and Limitations," are a forerunner of Negri and Hardt's theories on what might be called "empire capitalism," as they themselves paradoxically indicate: "The decline of nation-states is in a profound sense the full realization of the relationship between the state and capital" (*Empire*, 236). In other words, according to Negri and Hardt, the impulse toward the politicization of the economic, as manifested by the nation-state, always fell short of the mark inasmuch as each nation-state was constrained by its own particular constitutional principles, which not only limited the rates of profit that could be achieved at the national level, but also limited, as Marx argued, capital's innate drive, the creation of a world market. With the inauguration of Empire, however, the constitutional principles that befit capital are instituted globally, nation-states are correlatively undermined, and "the entire world market tends to be the only coherent domain for the effective application of capitalist management and command" (*Empire*, 254).

At first blush, Pollock's state capitalism would seem to be at odds with Negri and Hardt's empire capitalism in some fairly basic ways. Although Pollock sporadically ruminates on what a democratic form of state capitalism might look like, his analysis is concerned primarily with what he calls "totalitarian state capitalism," which "offers the solution of economic problems at the price of totalitarian oppression,"[27] while Negri and Hardt's analysis of empire capitalism is seemingly concerned with investigating the democratic form of state capitalism raised to an international level: "The first task of Empire," they maintain, "is to enlarge the realm of the consensus that supports its own power," and "juridical positivism and natural right theories, contractualism and institutional realism, formalism and systematism can each describe some aspect of it" (*Empire*, 15–16). Even this basic distinction seemingly understates their differences, however. According to Pollock, whether in its totalitarian or democratic form, state capitalism deposes the market from its controlling function in coordinating production and distribution, thus causing so-called economic laws to disappear, and vests these functions in the state, which sets up pseudo-markets to regulate and expand production and coordinate it with consumption.[28] In contrast, according to Negri and Hardt, empire capi-

---

[27] Friedrich Pollock, "State Capitalism: Its Possibilities and Limitations," in *Critical Theory and Society: A Reader*, eds., Stephen Eric Bronner and Douglas MacKay Kellner, New York: Routledge 1989, 115.

[28] See ibid., 96.

talism does not squelch the operations of the market but rather (in its post-modernization of the economy) sees them through to completion, and it does not centralize production but rather decentralizes it: "Through the decentralization of production and the consolidation of the world market, the international divisions and flows of labor and capital have fractured and multiplied" (*Empire*, 335).

For Negri and Hardt, however, this is only one side of the coin, and the flip side looks a good deal like the totalitarian characterization that Pollock delineates—"totalitarian" understood not so much in brute authoritarian terms, as Pollock means it when he distinguishes "totalitarian" and "democratic" forms of state capitalism, but "totalitarian" in the sense that is indigenous to both forms, namely, as a central authority in which "all conflicts, all crises, and all dissensions effectively push forward the process of integration and by the same measure call for more central authority" (*Empire*, 14). Negri and Hardt acknowledge that "the processes [of Empire] are and will remain contradictory" (*Empire*, 20) in terms of the tension between its simultaneous impulses to centralization and decentralization, but in actuality centralization trumps decentralization: "The decentralization and global dispersal of productive processes and sites," they rightly point out, "provokes a corresponding centralization of the control over production," which consists of the "extensive monitoring of workers from a central, remote location" (there is a "virtual panopticon of network production"), "increasingly centralized management and planning," and lastly "a new centralization of specialized producer services, especially financial services" (*Empire*, 297). And, in turn, this global centralization of production is underwritten by heavy-handed global juridico-economic institutions such as GATT, The World Trade Organization, the International Monetary Fund, and the World Bank, all of which operate at the behest of the first tier of Empire, which is comprised not of multinational corporations (the second tier) but instead assemblages of nation-states—most notably, the G7 (*Empire*, 309–10). Despite constant references to the world market, then, "the market" on Negri and Hardt's account is actually no less rigged than it is on Pollock's: it is not Smith's "invisible hand" that insures the general equilibria (economic and otherwise) of the global system, but the imperial administration and command of Empire itself.

Notwithstanding surface differences, therefore, Negri and Hardt's conclusions dovetail nicely with Pollock's in numerous important ways (although, of course, it would be folly to push this line too hard, given the vastly different sociohistorical constellations under consideration). When Pollock variously contends that under state capitalism "the replacement of the economic means by political means is the last guarantee for the reproduction of economic life," "men meet each other as commander or commanded," and "the profit motive is superseded by the power motive,"[29] there is nothing contained within these descriptions that would give Negri and Hardt a moment's pause if they were attributed to empire capitalism. So, too, although Negri and Hardt's empire gives lip service to "the democratic moment," and we are nominally dealing with "democratic" rather than "totalitarian" empire capitalism, as Negri and Hardt rightly point out "we are [actually] dealing here with the imperial overdetermination of democracy, in which the multitude is captured in flexible and modulating apparatuses of control" (*Empire*, 318). The power of the global juridico-economic institutions to countermand democratic initiatives at the local and national levels when they interfere with "free" trade is a stark example of this. And, indeed, more broadly, perhaps nowhere is the anti-democratic impulse of these "flexible and modulating apparatuses of control" better exemplified than in the jurisprudential sphere. Although Pollock did not deal with such matters, empire capitalism, as described by Negri and Hardt, has the same jurisprudential bent as totalitarian state capitalism, which is just another way of reaffirming that the decentralized, liberalistic, pluralistic side of Empire is invariably trumped by its centralized, illiberal, monolithic side. According to Negri and Hardt, Empire's hegemony over juridical practices, manifested in both domestic and supranational law, are predicated upon the permanent "exception" (*Empire*, 16–17)—i.e., the juridical flexibility to make situation specific findings that reinforce Empire's imperatives (for example, impromptu military and police interventions to maintain control)—rather than the classical rule of law or formal universal norm, which is in accordance with classical democratic theory, and would otherwise preclude such actions. And, of course, the "exception" is what was operative in Nazi Germany, whose leading jurisprudential theorist, Carl Schmitt, presently has a good deal of support among many proponents—and, in fact, (nominal) opponents—of Empire.

As all of this suggests, in discerning the primacy of the political, Negri and Hardt see Empire's integrative powers as no less formidable than Pollock saw the integrative powers of totalitarian state capitalism—indeed, perhaps more so. Pollock, to be sure, contended that he was "unable to discover any inherent economic forces, 'economic laws' of the old or a new type, which could prevent the functioning of state capitalism . . . [for] economic problems in the old sense no longer exist when coordination of all economic activities is effected by conscious plan instead of by the natural laws of the market."[30] Nevertheless, he did concede the possibility that non-economic problems, such as "conflicting interests within the ruling

---

[29] Ibid., 101.
[30] Ibid., 109.

class," could "thwart the construction of a rational general plan" and thus undercut state capitalism in the long run.[31] In other words, as Adorno stated it, Pollock rejected—or, at least, questioned—"the undialectical assumption that a non-antagonistic economy might be possible in an antagonistic society."[32] However bleak, therefore, destabilizing political possibilities remained under totalitarian state capitalism. Negri and Hardt, conversely, seem to take even these limited possibilities away. They assert that "as the concept of national sovereignty is losing its effectiveness, so too is the so-called autonomy of the political": "The decline of any autonomous political sphere signals the decline, too, of any independent space where revolution could emerge in the national political regime. . . . A new type of resistance has to be invented" (*Empire*, 307–308). And "invent" is what Negri and Hardt do, as they move from the sociohistorical to ontological plane to ensure not just the grounds for, but the inevitability of, successful resistance. Yet, much like Pollock, Negri and Hardt's absolutization of the political really leaves no space for meaningful resistance: remaining abjectly on the sociohistorical plane, as does Pollock (not to mention Adorno and Horkheimer, whose depiction of the "administered society" in *Dialectic of Enlightenment* builds on Pollock's politico-economic diagnoses), or shifting triumphantly to the ontological plane, as do Negri and Hardt, are, practically speaking, two sides of the same coin.

As a corrective to the absolutisms that propel both of these analyses, Franz Neumann's *Behemoth*—which is, in part, a reply to Pollock's state capitalism thesis—is worth consideration. In certain theoretical respects, such as the sociocultural mediations of the psychological (which Negri, too, tends to play down), Neumann's analyses lagged behind the cutting edge work that was being done by Adorno, Horkheimer, and Marcuse, but his painstaking empirical analyses in *Behemoth* are an important counterpoise to their more dire diagnoses by calling into question the politico-economic foundations on which they are founded. Going beyond Neumann's renowned claim that "the very term 'state capitalism' is a *contradictio in adiecto*"[33] (which is a semantic quibble in this context because he defines "state capitalism" as a situation in which "the state has become the *sole owner* of the means of production"), what is truly admirable about Neumann's analysis is not just that he balances economic and political considerations instead of cashing out one way or the other, but that he reaches

[31] Ibid., 110.

[32] Letter from Adorno to Horkheimer, June 8, 1941, cited in Rolf Wiggershaus, *The Frankfurt School: Its History, Theories, and Political Significance*, tr. Michael Robertson, Cambridge, MA: MIT Press, 1995, 282.

[33] Franz Neumann, *Behemoth: The Structure and Practice of National Socialism*, New York: Oxford University Press, 1942, 224.

this conclusion by plowing through the data instead of merely doing an end run on it. His conclusion that the German economy "is a monopolistic economy—*and* a command economy" (i.e., "it is a private capitalist economy, regimented by the totalitarian state"), and therefore properly described as "totalitarian monopoly capitalism,"[34] is based on well-documented analyses of general trends with respect to both economic concerns (i.e., the regime's promotion of cartels, industrial organization, price controls and the market, investments and profits, foreign trade and imperialism, and labor policies) and political ones (i.e., the dynamics of the bureaucracy, the party hierarchy, the civil services, the armed forces, and, especially, the working class). On this basis, he rejects the notions that prices and wages are just "administrative," that "the law of value is no longer operative" (as is truly the case for Negri and Hardt when they assert that it is "immeasurable"), and, finally, that the "appropriation of labor is a political act, not economic."[35]

What's more, as a rejoinder to a particular type of theorizing that is actually much more descriptive of Negri and Hardt's approach to social phenomena than Pollock's, its designated target, Neumann declares that the state capitalist theory "violates the principle that the model or ideal type must be derived from reality and must not transcend it."[36] The essence of Neumann's complaint is that while the proponents of state capitalism admitted that Germany still had many of the attributes of the classical capitalist form, they disregarded those attributes in arguing that "reality is rapidly approaching the [state capitalist] model," and therefore also failed to do the empirical work that was required to justifiably predict the model's instantiation even as a future possibility: "They cannot merely point to trends within capitalism in order to show that these trends must necessarily beget a system of power politics without economics, they have to prove their case for each of the systems concerned."[37] Negri and Hardt's conception of Empire violates Neumann's injunctions. The movement to a political ordering akin to the one that they offer in *Empire* may well be a "trend," but currently it more "transcends" reality than is "derived" from it. In some respects the process of globalization is undermining the sovereignty of the nation-state, but Negri and Hardt's report of its demise is severely overstated: The diplomatic events that preceded the American invasion of Iraq evinced good old-fashioned nation-state politicking at its worst, as the always already existing consensus that, in some sense, *is* Empire (and makes up Negri and Hardt's version of the "end of history"

---

[34] Ibid., 261.
[35] Ibid., 222.
[36] Ibid., 224.
[37] Ibid.

thesis) quickly unraveled. So, too, despite the undeniable advance toward some form of globalization, the process is still inchoate, and there are currently no grounds for seeing it in the "smooth," "unstriated" terms that Negri and Hardt do (*Empire*, 332): the present tendency toward more or less cohesive politico-economic blocs of nation-states, such as the European Union and the North American Free Trade alliance, which retain aspects of the competing nation-state model that Negri and Hardt would have done with, might point to a longer term constellation. And, on the flip side, their homogenization of labor, based upon its "immateriality," is highly speculative. Lastly, although it is true that global capitalism is about social control, it is also way too premature to dismiss Neumann's claim that as between patriotism, power, and profits, "profits and more profits are the motive power" for this control.[38]

As Douglas Kellner rightly contends, the problem with using models or ideal types is that "they tend to provide a static model of society rather than a more dynamic Marxian model which would root social trends within existing social relations and struggles," and this is the reason that "in Pollock's theory there are no analyses of the contradictions, tendencies, and struggles that might lead to a society beyond capitalism."[39] Negri and Hardt avail themselves of ideal types far more vigorously than did Pollock, and, like Pollock, "there are no *analyses* of the contradictions, tendencies, and struggles that might lead to a society beyond capitalism." But, unlike Pollock, in their narrative these contradictions, tendencies, and struggles are not theoretically precluded but rather ontologically posited: "Political philosophy forces us to enter the terrain of ontology" (*Empire*, 354), where "the decline and fall of Empire is defined not as a diachronic movement but as a synchronic reality" (*Empire*, 385) and "the social conflicts that constitute the political confront one another directly, without mediations of any sort" (*Empire*, 393). While, as Neumann declares, state capitalist theorists "must admit that their system may very well be the millennium," the empire capitalist theorists all but decree the new one. In either case, however, political paralysis is a real prospect, for there is no determinate basis for action. And although Negri and Hardt say that "empire is defined by crisis, its decline has always already begun, and consequently every line of antagonism leads toward the event and singularity," they virtually admit as much: "It is midnight in a night of specters . . . and nothing manages to illuminate our destiny ahead" (*Empire*, 386).

To reductively afford primacy to the political, in sum, not only undercuts the aim of an interdisciplinary approach that seeks a comprehensive

[38] Ibid., 354.
[39] Douglas Kellner, *Critical Theory, Marxism and Modernity*, Baltimore: The Johns Hopkins University Press, 1989, 62.

theory of society, but also has the affect of undercutting the commitment to the political itself, both theoretically and practically, by leaving it insufficiently mediated, and therefore insufficiently concrete.

III

It was Neumann's considered belief that Pollock's state capitalism thesis could, by giving rise to "utter hopelessness," betoken the end of a genuine critical theory.[40] Neumann is right. Indeed, the attack on this sort of one-sidedness (i.e., theorizing social phenomena exclusively from the politico-cultural perspective of a progressively more hegemonic capitalist class), which begins with Adorno's "totally administered society" and arguably ends with Foucault's rejection of "the repressive hypothesis," is what I take to be one of the crucial insights of the autonomist Marxist tradition. In one of his most important early works, "Marx on Cycle and Crisis," Negri not only points to the possibility of capitalist crises, but, no less significantly, emphasizes the need to theorize this possibility from the working class perspective, which might well be the ultimate condition of this possibility's actual possibility:

> Having said all this, we should remember that so far we have outlined only an initial approach to Marx's analysis of cycle, crisis, and development. We have described them in objective terms, in their capitalist guise. But phenomenology is not aetiology, and capital's viewpoint is not the viewpoint of the working class. Now we have to move from the abstractness of the capitalist possibility of crisis to the actual way in which that crisis takes effect—from the description of an objective possibility to the dialectic of how it comes about.[41]

Negri is right. Phenomenology is not aetiology, and the abstractness of the capitalist possibility of crisis is surely not tantamount to an account of the actual way in which this crisis takes effect, but neither of these insights appears to slow down Negri and Hardt's triumphal neo-Deleuzian ontology in *Empire*. Moreover, not only is there is no description of how to move from what is now the ontological inevitability of the multitude's overthrow of Empire to how it comes about, which is fair enough since there are no hard and fast road maps for such things, but there is not even

---

[40] See William E. Scheuerman, *Between the Norm and the Exception: The Frankfurt School and the Rule of Law*, Cambridge, MA: MIT Press, 1994, 149, drawing on Franz Neumann, Letter to Max Horkheimer, July 23, 1941.

[41] Antonio Negri, "Marx on Cycle and Crisis," in *Revolution Retrieved*, London: Red Notes, 1988, 62.

a theoretical basis for making sense of such a movement, as the "midnight in a night of specters" language cited at the end of the prior section suggests, and as Negri and Hardt openly assert: "It is certainly true that the serpentine struggles we are witnessing today do not provide any clear revolutionary tactics, or maybe they are incomprehensible from the point of view of tactics . . . In the constitution of Empire there is no longer an 'outside' to power and thus no longer any weak links" (*Empire*, 58).

It is this lack with respect to praxis in *Empire* that is arguably one of the central gaps that *Multitude* seeks to fill, as is implied in its preface. Although Negri and Hardt warn that the book does not "propose a concrete program of action," they do say that its "primary aim is to work out the conceptual bases on which a new project of democracy can stand" (*Multitude*, xvi–xvii). A few things are worth noticing here. As an initial matter, democracy moves to the forefront, as "the project of the multitude" not only demands democracy "but provides the means for achieving it" (*Multitude*, xi). Given the wholesale politicization of the economic, in which economic categories all but drop out of the picture, it makes sense that "real" political democracy, one that transcends the modern forms of democracy grounded in representation, would become the "primary aim." And, conversely, it makes sense that the virtual omnipresence of war, which justifies the suspension of democracy, would not only "become the general matrix for all relations of power and techniques of domination" (*Multitude*, 13), but would also assume the role once held by a capitalist dynamic that required ever greater rates of exploitation, and therefore provided the conceptual basis for praxis.

Thus, although Negri and Hardt do not explicitly draw this analogy, and, indeed, declare that we must "try to conceive exploitation as the expropriation of the common, [which] has become the locus of surplus value" (*Multitude*, 150), it is truly war, on their account, that is the emiserating factor that spurs the multitude to overthrow Empire. Their rejection of Marx's notion that "the degree of exploitation corresponds to the quantity of surplus labor time" (*Multitude*, 150), and, more broadly, their failure to tie this in to an escalating dynamic involving such things as worker recalcitrance, falling rates of profit, the increased use of technology, higher unemployment, lower real wages, and the like, shifts the focus from economic to military warfare. And, as already asserted, it also shifts the focus from the fact that longstanding capitalist preoccupations, with the longstanding forms of worker degradation that they engender, are still dominant.

Moreover, in support of a conceptual basis for praxis that did not exist in *Empire* (their Spinozist ontological commitments notwithstanding), Negri and Hardt veer off their unqualified emphasis on non-communicable singularities in *Multitude*: "Once we recognize singularity, the common begins to emerge. Singularities do communicate, and they are able to do so because of the common they share" (*Multitude,* 128). Indeed, they assert, "the contradictory conceptual couple, identity and difference, is not the adequate framework for understanding the organization of the multitude. Instead we are a multiplicity of singular forms of life and at the same time share a common global existence" (*Multitude,* 127). Yet, although "the multitude replaces the contradictory couple identity-difference with the complementary couple commonality-singularity," it is still the case that "in practice the multitude provides a model whereby our expressions of singularity are not reduced or diminished in our communication and collaboration with others in struggle" (*Multitude,* 217–18). This last claim is rather dubious, and seems not only to conflict with their privileging of "hybridization," but also points to the fact that "commonality-singularity" is itself an unreconcilable couple. "Commonality-particularity" is actually the conceptual coupling that Negri and Hardt are moving toward, but once "singularity" is jettisoned, so are their postmodern commitments, and with this coupling the specter of a dialectical analysis opens up—which, of course, they reject. In any case, Negri and Hardt's newfound emphasis on "commonality"[42]—in particular, the "production of the common"—evidences their recognition that the multitude, if understood as "a plane of singularities" (*Empire,* 103), is not up to the task of taking on the "concrete universal" that is Empire (even if, as they assert in *Empire,* these singularities invariably strike at Empire's heart). "What kind of political project can bring the multitude into existence" (*Multitude,* 212), of course, is still an open question, and theoretical difficulties remain (even with this more promising turn toward commonality).

Along these lines, Ernesto Laclau, drawing on the work of Jacques Rancière, maintains that Negri and Hardt's "radical immanentism" is "profoundly metapolitical," and that in their positivistic ontology, with its postulation of "the multitude" as the genuine historical subject that realizes full immanence, "politics becomes unthinkable."[43] Laclau puts the matter in overly stark terms: "*Either* we assert the possibility of a universality which is not politically constructed and mediated, *or* we assert that all universality is precarious and depends on a historical construction out of heterogeneous elements. Hardt and Negri accept the first alternative without hesitation."[44] Conversely, Laclau accepts the second alternative,

---

[42] Unlike "singularity," "commonality" did not even warrant an index reference in *Empire.*

[43] Ernesto Laclau, "Can Immanence Explain Social Struggles?," *Diacritics* 31, no. 4, Winter 2001, 3.

[44] Ibid., 5

which, as he articulates it, places him "on the threshold of the Gramscian conception of hegemony."[45] It seems to me that Laclau is correct in his depiction of the political consequences of Negri and Hardt's ontology, but he is incorrect with respect to the either/or that he offers, as well as the soundness of his own position. The abstract "homogeneity and unity of the multitude,"[46] as Laclau puts it, is only the flip side of the abstract unalloyed singularities that I just discussed, and, either way, there is no basis for what Laclau calls a "political articulation." Accordingly, in *Empire* it is the ontology that does all the work, and while in *Multitude* there is a "brief, practical empirical investigation," which manifests itself as a concrete laundry list of grievances (*Multitude,* 268–85) and reforms (*Multitude,* 289–306), one is left with the impression that this list sits uneasily beside the theory that ostensibly gives rise to it.

Conversely, Laclau's utter rejection of any class analysis, which is in the service of what he calls a "radical democratic politics" in *Hegemony and Socialist Strategy,* is neither "radical" nor, in the final analysis, all that "democratic." Negri and Hardt are absolutely right to continue to theorize the dominance of class in the contemporary political constellation, and, furthermore, they are absolutely right to update old notions such as "the working class" or "proletariat," which are no longer up to the task of adequately describing the new politico-economic realities. What's more, their movement toward a more expansive concept to replace these older categories, given what has been an increasing polarization in both wealth and income (in the United States, at any rate), is absolutely warranted. The problem with Negri and Hardt's account, and what opens it to Laclau's charge, is its ontological scaffolding,[47] which effaces key differentiations. Resnick and Wolff are right to "protest against the omission of the class differences that deserve inclusion in the analysis of the multitude and its capacities for effective unity in opposition to Empire."[48] So, too, they are right to assert that

> Marx went to considerable pains to distinguish within capitalism between productive and unproductive laborers . . . [in order to] present differences that the organization of an anticapitalist workers' movement would have to recognize and accommodate. *Empire*'s theorization of "the multitude" aggregates so as to minimize the issue of class differences within such multitudes. Yet a respect for the diversity of subjectivities within the multitude

---

[45] Ibid.

[46] Ibid., 3.

[47] For a more expansive attack on the ontology, see David Sherman, "The Ontological Need: Positing Subjectivity and Resistance in Hardt and Negri's Empire," *Telos* 128, Summer, 2004, 143–70.

[48] Stephen Resnick and Richard Wolff, "*Empire* and Class Analysis," op. cit., 68.

need not and should not entail neglecting how people diversely participate in the production, appropriation, and distribution of surplus. Different class participations have their distinctive roles to play in shaping the subjectivities, contradictions, and revolutionary possibilities of Empire and of "the multitude."[49]

Consequently, by virtue of its underlying ontology, Laclau is right to say that "what is missing in *Empire* is any coherent theory of subjectivity,"[50] but this need not be the case, for the book's ontology, which is what precludes such a theory, can be stripped away at no cost to Negri and Hardt's many worthwhile empirical insights. And, crucially, by stripping away the ontology, the kinds of differentiations necessary for Laclau's political articulations would arise. Conversely, by rejecting all references to class in his own political theory, it is Laclau who abstracts from the sociohistorical contents of subjectivity, thereby leaving subjectivities that are the very stuff of capitalist ideology to enter his overdetermined marketplace of proliferating agonistic discourses. And, in fact, Rancière's valorization of "the people," which Laclau (at least implicitly) buys into, and arguably supplements Laclau's valorization of "discourse," is well diagnosed by Negri and Hardt—it is an abstract construct that justifies political forms that are "democratic" in name only.

What all of this suggests is that the notion of class must be both "construed and denied."[51] In a neoliberal capitalist society that is plainly exacerbating previously existing class disparities, the notion of class must neither disperse into "just discourse," as if the proliferation of discourses itself reflects a vibrant democracy instead of the overdetermined communicative circuits through which capitalist society reproduces itself, nor must it ossify into an abstract notion such as "the multitude," which overruns the differentiated groups that nevertheless do comprise it. To their credit, Negri and Hardt are not insensitive to this problem, but by contending that the multitude is constituted by incommensurable "singularities," which are no less abstract, they do nothing to ameliorate it. Nevertheless, ameliorate it they must, for to be clear on the sorts of practices that are necessary for the purpose of any liberatory project, it is necessary to be clear on the nature of the subjects who are to undertake these practices. As Adorno asserts, "a simple consideration of history demonstrates just how much the question of theory and praxis depends

[49] Ibid., 68–69.
[50] Ernesto Laclau, "Can Immanence Explain Social Struggles?," op. cit., 8. I argue much the same in David Sherman, "The Ontological Need: Positing Subjectivity and Resistance in Hardt and Negri's Empire," op. cit.
[51] Adorno uses this phrase to describe the way in which we must approach the concept of "universal history." I see it as no less applicable here.

on the question of subject and object,"[52] and it is for this reason that Negri and Hardt, despite basing their thought on a Deleuzian ontology that repudiated it, are concerned with making sense of subjectivity, even if, in the end, the very ontology to which they have hitched their theoretical wagon prevents them from doing so.

---

[52] Theodor W. Adorno, "Marginalia to Theory and Praxis," in *Critical Models: Interventions and Catchwords*, trans. Henry W. Pickford, New York: Columbia University Press, 1998, 259.

PART II

Reading Negri with Marx: Value, Measure, Limit

4

Immeasurable Value?:
An Essay on Marx's Legacy
Dedicated to Sol Yurick

GEORGE C. CAFFENTZIS

The Lawyers have twisted it into such a state of bedevilment that the original merits of the case have long disappeared from the face of the earth. It's about a Will, and the trusts under a Will—or it was, once. It's about nothing but Costs, now. We are always appearing, and disappearing, and swearing, and interrogating, and filing, and cross-filing, and arguing, and sealing, and motioning, and referring, and reporting, and revolving about the Lord Chancellor and all his satellites, and equitably waltzing ourselves off to dusty death, about Costs. That's the big Question. All the rest, by some extraordinary means, has melted away.

"But it was, sir," said I, to bring him back, for he began to rub his head, "about a Will?"

CHARLES DICKENS, *Bleak House* (1853)

Introduction: A Bleak House legacy?

Opposition to capitalism was not invented by Marx. Anticapitalist movements had an enormous presence before his time and they continue to "change the world" long after the collapse of the governments run by self-defined Marxist parties in the former Soviet Union and Eastern Europe.[1] Surely, reading and accepting Marx's work was never a necessary condition for opposing capitalism, but is it still sufficient?

---

[1] The study of anticapitalism in the pre-Marx period is becoming increasingly sophisticated. Two important recent books in this literature are (Federici 2004) and (Linebaugh and Rediker 2001). The first deals with the anticapitalist struggle at the originary moment of capitalism (in the fifteenth, sixteenth and seventeenth century) and the second with the rise of anticapitalist movements in the Atlantic world during the seventeenth and eighteenth centuries. An important collection of immediately pre-Marx communist writings is to be found in (Corcoran 1983).

Whatever the answer to that question, surely Marx's textual legacy stimulates tremendous ambivalence in the anticapitalist movement. For it is hard to imagine a serious analysis and critique of capitalism that would not use at least some of this mountainous legacy, but there is an anxiety in approaching it due to its alleged associations with Stalinism, nineteenth-century capitalism and its political economy, totalitarianism, secular humanism, or any of a thousand other contemporary phantoms haunting one or another person's imagination. Is Marx's textual mountain something of a cursed (though tantalizingly huge) legacy like the one in Dickens' *Bleak House* which literally drives a number of characters insane in their futile efforts to appropriate it through endless legal procedures in a hellish "Court of Chancery"?

The ambivalence expressed in this question cries out for a criterion that would neatly separate the useful parts of Marx's work from the out-dated or even reactionary. There have been a variety of efforts in the past to provide such a criterion. For example, the famous "early" versus "late" Marx debates from the 1950s to the 1970s provided simple temporal dichotomies between acceptable and unacceptable texts—before or after 1848, before or after 1858, before or after 1867 (c.f., the *locus classicus* of this effort being (Althusser 1996)). But they have proven as interminable and indecisive as the "Jarndyce and Jarndyce" case of *Bleak House*.

In this essay, I will investigate whether there is an appropriate criterion to distinguish the useful from eliminable works of Marx. I will do this indirectly via an analysis and critique of Antonio Negri's and his collaborator Michael Hardt's work on these issues, since Negri, to his credit, has enthusiastically addressed the "Marx ambivalence" syndrome thoroughly, positively, and often unseasonably for decades while Michael Hardt has joined him in the last decade in presenting a widely discussed and conceptually simple answer to the "Is there Marx after Marx?" questions. They claim that though much of Marx's work is still vital to the anticapitalist movement, the part of Marx's work that logically depends upon the Law of Value should be rejected while the part that is not dependent on the Law could be usefully introduced into the anticapitalist philosophy of the future. I will call this dichotomy of Marxist texts, Negri and Hardt's "*criterion of viability.*" They justify this criterion on two counts:

(i) the Law of Value is obsolete, i.e., it was applicable, at best, to nineteenth century capitalism, but it has lost all grip on the reality of contemporary postmodern capitalism (e.g., Negri 1984, xv–xvi, 25, 172; Hardt and Negri 1994, 9, 175; Hardt and Negri 2000, 209, 355–359);

(ii) the Law forms the ideological basis of unacceptable socialist and Stalinist reactions to capitalism.

Surely Negri and Hardt are not alone in trying to rid the anticapitalist movement of Marx's rather embarrassing continuity with the "classical tradition" in political economy which is typified by Marx's presumed adherence to the Law of Value. Marx's Labor Theory of Value, with its Law of Value corollary, is continually attacked as being both empirically passé or conceptually incoherent. But Negri and Hardt's critique of the Law of Value (and the LTV) differs from those left-wing Sraffians like Ian Steedman and "analytic Marxists" like G.A. Cohen and Jon Elster who argue that the key question for the anticapitalist movement is simply whether the capitalists can justly divide the productive results of the system (Steedman 1977; Cohen 1988; Elster 1985). If the answer is "no," then that is reason enough to challenge it. Why be saddled with an elaborate and, in the bargain, mythical "value-foundation" for an anticapitalist ideology, especially in an era when "foundationalism" is out of favor as a philosophical/political attitude (Derrida 1994, 170)?

Negri and Hardt differ from such critics in that they claim to find this rejection of the Law of Value in Marx's own work, especially the "Fragment on Machines" in the *Grundrisse* and in the unpublished Part Seven of *Capital I*, ("Results of the Immediate Process of Production"). They claim that Marx—in Cassandra-like moments between 1858 and 1866, especially while writing the midnight notebooks later called the "Grundrisse," (translated as the "Foundation of a Critique of Political Economy") and the "Results"—prophesied that the development of capitalism would undermine the Law of Value . . . *in the future*. Negri and Hardt argue that Marx's "future" is simply now. That is, capitalism came to a point during the late twentieth century when:

(i) science and technology—the products of the "general intellect" and "immaterial labor"—not material labor, dominate the productive metabolism with nature;

(ii) capitalism subsumes under its own control not only the productive process, but all of the allied processes of social reproduction (education, sexuality, communication, demography, etc.), i.e., biopolitics, in the terminology that he (and later Hardt) borrow from Foucault.

They claim that these developments literally "explode" (to use Marx's term in the *Grundrisse's* "Fragment") the older value form and put the Law of Value in crisis.

In this essay I will show why Negri and Hardt's criterion of viability based on the rejection of the Law of Value is not the best way to "save" Marx's work for the anticapitalist movement.[2]

---

[2] The term "anticapitalist movement" that I am using here is broader (both temporally and socially) than the one developed by Alex Callinicos in his *An Anti-Capitalist Manifesto* (Callinicos 2003), where he relegates the referent of the term to the post-Seattle movement against the G-8, WTO, World Bank and IMF.

Part I. Marx on Value and the Law of Value: Prolegomena

A necessary step and, at the same time, an important problem for Negri and Hardt's criterion of viability is simply that what they refer to as the "Law of Value" is *not explicitly defined* in Marx's work. There are many explicitly stated laws (e.g., the law of the tendency of the falling rate of profit, the general law of capitalist accumulation) and many explicitly identified values (e.g., use-value, exchange-value, surplus value) in Marx's texts, but there is little evidence of a "Law of Value." Although Engels seems to have used it often, Marx rarely employs the phrase in *Capital I, II, III* or in the letters and unpublished manuscripts, and, when he does, he uses the phrase loosely and in passing. For example, in the 860 pages of *Capital III* attributed to Marx there are only seven uses of the phrase according to the index and it is difficult to "abstract" a law-like statement of the Law of Value from simply putting all these different uses in Marx's texts side-by-side.

This paucity of use might be surprising, since the phrase was often deployed as if its meaning was obvious by many writers after Marx to describe complex relationships among a set of "hidden variables" below the level of overt economic discourse which is normally dominated by prices, wages, profits, interest rates, and rents expressed in monetary terms. Perhaps that is why Negri seems to be so nonchalant about the phrase; it was so commonly used during his youth in the pages of Italian Communist and Socialist Parties' newspapers and pamphlets that it didn't need explicit definition.

Certainly, even if it does not have a central role in Marx's writings, "the Law of Value" is a widely used technical phrase in the Marxist tradition. The problem with this traditional use is simply that the Law of Value has been given a wide variety of definitions by Marxist economists and politicians. Thus in Leontyev's Soviet-era textbook on political economy, the Law of Value is narrowly defined as claiming that "the value of a commodity is determined by the amount of socially necessary labour expended on its production" (Leontyev 1974). But Fredrik Haffner in his encyclopedia article on "the Law of Value" provides a maximal definition having four different, but related meanings:

(i) a "price theory" version of the law, similar to Leontyev's definition, which claims that the exchange values and production prices of goods are "established according to the labour social necessary for their reproduction;"

(ii) the Law explains the market-price mechanism in quantitative terms;

(iii) the Law explains class relations, alienation, and impoverishment in capitalism;

(iv) "the laws of development of capitalism in history (concentration, theory of crises, etc.) can be incorporated, too, so that the law of value embraces the economic law of motion of capitalist society" (Haffner 1973, 268–69).

If one accepts the "maximal" definition, then most of Marx's typical tenets would be identified with the Law of Value. Consequently, there would be few Marxian "phenomena" to "save" once one applies Negri and Hardt's "everything but the Law of Value" criterion of viability!

Does that mean that we should use the "restricted" Leontyev definition for the purposes of our discussion? The difficulty with making such a decision is simply that the phrase is not in common use outside of the pages of economists who were dealing with a crisis of planning immediately after the Russian Revolution. The Communist Party in the Soviet Union had to make good on its claim that a planned economy is not only possible, but superior to one based on "the anarchy of production." The discussions of a "Law of Value" really took off during the debates about the transition from capitalism to socialism and the nature of economic planning.[3] Questions like, "Is there a law of value that is either fully put into play in socialism (as Leontyev argued) or is capitalism, much less socialism and communism, beyond the law of value (as Stalin insisted)?" were frequently posed (Leontyev 1974, 166; Stalin 1972, 473–75). However, there is no doubt that these debates, which now appear to many as baroque verbal jousting over the corpses of millions of workers, would fill Negri with contempt or despair, inspiring him to say, "Basta!" But unless we are to practice the *ad hominem* fallacy and find concepts guilty by their historical associations, we are still left with the problem: what is the Law of Value and can its rejection be used to differentiate "the quick from the dead" in Marx's work?

In order to best decide what meaning "the Law of Value" might have that can give Negri and Hardt's criterion of viability some plausibility, we must briefly consider the value-discourse Marx validates, since that discourse sets the parameters of the Law's meaning. Marx's work is certainly replete with value-discourse. The key text of the nineteenth century anticapitalist revolution, *Capital I*, not only begins with Value, its first chapter is a detailed, scholastic and, some would say, pedantic disquisition on value (in all its forms and their tensions) which eventually leads to a sort of "dialectical deduction" of money (*the* language of capitalism). Why did Marx require his readers to climb this dialectical purgatorial mountain

---

[3] For acerbic accounts of these debates see (Steele 1992) and (Rutland 1985). However sourly one might depict these debates, they are still important to study for any movement that wants to say more than "Another World is Possible." For without saying more, one is in the position of being a logician instead of a revolutionary.

before they could fly to the paradise of class struggle? Marx was certainly conscious of the heavy demands on his readers. But he brushed them off by proudly inverting Dante's *Pugatorio*: "Segui il tuo corso, e lasci dir le genti" ("Follow your path, and let the people talk.")

It is no accident that Marx begins his major critique of political economy in *Capital I* (1867) with Value. That was the originary axiom of the genre Marx was critiquing, after all. But there are other, contextual reasons as well to account for the attractiveness of the concept of value, for during *Capital's* composition in the 1850s and 1860s, the concept of value transcended the boundaries of political economy into ethical and mathematical discourse, especially in Germany. On the ethical side, "value" marked out a new terrain of volitions and affective dispositions versus the realm of fact and the norms of pure reason, and on the logical and mathematical side, value marked a shift from a substance-abstraction to a function-relational conception of concepts and mathematical ontology.

Value in the ethical region refers to a forceful vector of desire irreducible to either reason, utility, or instinct. But value in this sense is not autonomous, it needs an object to be manifested. Hence, at this time, ethics becomes a field of propositional *attitudes* and behavioral *dispositions*. In effect, the ontological features of economic value became generalized, but the converse movement prevailed as well and political economy became ethicized.

This interplay between ethics and political economy can be illustrated in the comparison between Marx's and his younger contemporary, Friedrich Nietzsche's critical projects. Whereas Marx identified his project in the 1850s and 1860s as a critique of political economy (and hence a critique of the notion of value as enshrined by that discipline), Nietzsche in the 1870s and 1880s defined a parallel project in the *Genealogy of Morals*: "we need a *critique* of moral values, the value of these values themselves must first be called in question" (Nietzsche 1968, 456, Nietzsche's italics). Just as Marx looked on the "the immense collection of commodities" comprising capitalist society to self-reflexively question the value of exchange value and surplus value and to show that a notion like the "value of labor" is a "yellow logarithm" (Marx 1976, 125; Marx 1966, 818), Nietzsche was able to judge value judgments and evaluate the tables of values generated by the Christian good and evil, simply because the whole field of ethics had been "valorized" by the mid- to late nineteenth century. Objects and actions lost their inherent moral characters (or "virtues") and became functions, attitudes, or judgments of value.

Nietzsche recognized this logical revolution in ethics (as Marx did in political economy) and saw the inevitable next step: the self-reflection of the ethical function, attitude, or judgment. This is the conceptual source of Nietzsche's "tremendous new prospect" and existential "vertigo," not some über-relativism of personal preferences (Nietzsche 1968, 456). Moral and aesthetic values were only gradually being distinguished from economic values, and they still shared a strict objectivity with them in Nietzsche's writings. As Robert John Ackermann pointed out: "Nietzsche's values are still related to these objective economic roots in that they are capable of objective assessment of their impact on our interactions with the surrounding world" (Ackermann 1990, 90).

The critique of value in ethics and political economy was also deeply involved in a great development in the mathematics and logic of the later nineteenth century— the transformation of substance into function.[4] The new nineteenth century model of the universal rejects abstraction from thing-like substances. The mathematician Drobisch in 1875, for example, characterized it as "the mathematical function [that] represents a universal law, which, by virtue of the successive values which the variable can assume, contains within itself all the particular cases from which it holds" (quoted in Cassirer 1923, 21). A value arises therefore from a relation to other values determined by a universal principle of serial order. Values are determined not by increasing abstraction from properties (as in the Aristotelian paradigm), but by being engaged in an increasing density of relations and series. Moreover, values are dependent upon variables, laws, sets, and series that can become values of further variables, laws, sets, and series, i.e., they are open to being reflexively *transvalued*. This laid the basis for the many revolutionary mathematical insights of the period including set theory and Hilbert-space theory.

The "value" of mid- to late-nineteenth century mathematics and logic and the "value" of political economy (as Marx analyzes it) are not mere homonyms. In Marx's critique of political economy the notion of value arises not through the stripping of the qualities of the commodity to find an "inherent" property, but through its manifold actual and potential exchange relations with other commodities (especially that prime self-reflexive universal commodity, money).[5] Value discourse, then, allowed Marx to both use the language of the object of his critique, political economy, and to be able to transvalue the values he criticized. In other words, valuation and transvaluation in their political-economic, ethical, and logical

---

[4] This development was described retrospectively by the neo-Kantians like Simmel and Cassirer in the early twentieth century (Simmel 1990; Cassirer 1923).

[5] Similar to the neo-Kantian critique of Marx, Philip Mirowski's main criticism of Marx is that he was not attentive to the transformation of substance to field theories in the physics of his day (Mirowski 1989). He claims that Marx's economics was still "substance" based and that he saw labor as a substance (like caloric) that is stored in the commodity. But this critique is off the mark for two reasons: (i) Marx was quite familiar with the development of field theories in physics and (ii) his notion of "social necessary labor time" was a "field" concept since it can change independent of the local condition of production.

dimensions were the entrée to a set of conceptual revolutions in his era that Marx could hardly resist.

But Marx not only used, criticized, and transvalued value discourse, he employed a specific variant of that discourse, i.e., labor-value, to both analyze capitalism and its science, political economy, as well as to criticize, overturn, and transvalue them. He saw in his use of labor-value discourse a political-philosophical epoché and a scientific invitation to go below the "surface" of capitalist society (to its inferno and pandemonium in the process of production) to solve a number of problems faced by the anti-capitalist movement of the time.

- First (analytic), labor-value discourse allows for an apparently precise and measurable definition of exploitation in capitalist society. This clarity is especially crucial in capitalism because exploitation is formally and legally hidden by the wage form. As Marx frequently points out, it is clear to the serf when s/he is working on his/her land versus on the land of the lord, whereas for the waged worker the moment when the labor-time necessary to create the value of his/her wage is finished and surplus labor-time begins is systematically obscured by the wage form and the general process of valuation.

- Second (critical), labor-value discourse provides a narrative (i.e., the class struggle) that workers can use in an antagonistic way to describe themselves as fundamental actors in the drama of history and the capitalists and landlords as parasitic upon their labor, anxiety, and suffering. It allows the worker to view the totality of capitalist relations from his/her point of view and not from the perspective of the capitalist (Cleaver 2001).[6] For the capitalist perspective as expressed in the "illusions" of the Trinity Formula (Marx 1966, 814–31) and the actual increase of the productivity of labor due to application of scientific knowledge to production (and reproduction) inevitably leads to the view that capital (not labor) is productive and is the legitimate force to determine the future of humanity.

- Third (revolutionary), if labor is the ultimate force of value creation (as the Law of Value claims and gives a measure to), then laborers are valuable and creative in themselves. A revolutionary corollary

---

[6] It is interesting that in the late 1970s Harry Cleaver and Negri were equally interested in reading Marx's texts "politically." They published their results nearly simultaneously (Cleaver in 1977 and Negri in 1979). In doing so, Negri expunged Chapter I of *Capital I* from the roster of "quick" texts of Marxism since it clearly was dependent upon the Law of Value and labor-value discourse. Cleaver rejects this conclusion in his Introduction to *Marx Beyond Marx* and tries to "save" all of Marx's writings (Negri 1984, xxvii).

follows: workers are capable of creating non-capitalist "tables of values" and, indeed, an autonomous world beyond capitalism. This conviction is crucial for the development of a revolutionary alternative to capitalism. Without it, the class struggle becomes a form of "bad infinity," always there, always producing the next step, but never the last step.

This discussion establishes the centrality of Marx's value discourse, but it still leaves open the question of the meaning of the Law of Value. In order to proceed in the spirit of charity, I will assume that the best meaning of "the Law of Value" is the most restricted one, i.e., the value of a commodity is determined by the socially necessary labor-time required for its production.

Part II: Negri's Critique of Marx (from Marx Beyond Marx to Empire); A Transvaluation of the Law of Value

According to the argument of the last section, there are a number of good scientific and political reasons why Marx developed a labor-value discourse (along with an occasional mention of a Law of Value) in the 1850s and 1860s. Does one need to go beyond labor-value discourse in general and the notion of a Law of Value in particular in order to answer the basic questions of the anticapitalist movement today? If the answer is "no," and there are enough texts in the Marxist canon that could survive the result of excising those that rely on the Law of Value, then Negri and Hardt's criterion of viability would create a useful dichotomy. In this section, I shall examine the development of the criterion in Negri and Hardt's writings and in the next I will demonstrate its strengths and weaknesses.

It is important to recognize, however, that Negri first attempted to construct a criterion of viability for Marx's texts long before he began his collaboration with Michael Hardt. He attempted this in his lectures in the École Normale Supérieure on the *Grundrisse* in 1978 which were published in Italian and French the following year. Negri found that Marx's decision to "begin" the *Grundrisse* with Money instead of with Commodity or Value to be a sign that the Law of Value and the other parts of the labor-value apparatus can be excised from Marx's theoretical writings to create a viable (and revolutionary) Marx *beyond* Marx:

> The theory of value, as a theory of categorical synthesis, is a legacy of the classics and of the bourgeois mystification which we can easily do without in order to enter the field of revolution. That was true yesterday for the classics, as the attack of the *Grundrisse* demonstrates; today, one can show

in the theory that is still applicable that it is in this way that we must begin, against all the repeaters of the theory of value, from *Diamat* to Sraffa. (Negri 1983, 23)

In an amazingly "this sided" fiat of interpretation, Negri claims that "there is no logical way [in the *Grundrisse*] which leads from the analysis of commodities to that of value, to that of surplus value; the middle term does not exist; it is—that, yes—a literary fiction, a mystification pure and simple which contains not an ounce of truth" (Negri 1984, 24). This interpretation clearly distinguishes the *Grundrisse* from Marx's later work including, by the way, the *Contributions to a Critique of Political Economy* that was published a year after the last *Grundrisse* notebook was completed and which entirely devotes itself to an analysis of the commodity and value, i.e., engages in literary fictions, according to Negri! Negri has even harsher words for *Capital*:

> The passage from the money-form to commodity-form, from the *Grundrisse* to *Capital*, only adds abstraction and confusion. Despite all the intentions and declarations to the contrary, that which the attack on the problem of commodities determines, it is a more idealist, Hegelian method. (Negri 1984, 39)

Indeed, the polemic against "the abstract void of the discourse on value" and the "law of value" is continued throughout the text with Negri drafting a none too enthusiastic "Marxism of the *Grundrisse*" into his crusade against value discourse. In effect, Negri argues that monetary values are adequate for the definition of the most important concepts of Marxism that are still relevant to contemporary anticapitalist thinking. Though Negri's argument in *Marx Beyond Marx* is based on a rather peculiar hermeneutical method (clearly rejecting any reading that is sympathetic to Marx's intentions and his historical context), the result is not too different from the more mathematical and analytic critiques of the Labor Theory of Value in Steedman, Elster, and Roemer.

The problem with Negri's early criterion (which literally banished any role for labor-value discourse in a viable anticapitalism) is simply that almost all of the Marxist canon would be rejected if the criterion were to be applied scrupulously. Thus the criterion would not be a criterion at all, but simply a broad negation of Marx's whole *opus*.

Some time after the publication of *Marx Beyond Marx*, especially with his collaborations with Hardt in the 1990s, Negri ended his hostility to value discourse *per se* (but not to the law of value which presupposes a *measurable* value). In *Empire*, Negri and Hardt welcome the return of value and living labor as "powerful and ubiquitous" components of postmodern capitalism, with a catch: their notions of value and labor are unrecognizable from a Marxist perspective. Negri and Hardt reject Marx's Labor Theory of Value which is, "really a theory of the measure of value" (Hardt and Negri 2000, 355). The value they cherish and refer to in one of their many sibylline passages (354–61) is both *immeasurable* and *beyond measure.*

(Economic) value is *immeasurable,* in the context of what Hardt and Negri call Empire, because it cannot be measured by labor-time or any other "fixed scale." At best, value can be indexed "on the basis of always contingent and purely conventional elements" imposed by "the monopoly of nuclear arms, the control of money, and the colonization of ether" (Hardt and Negri 2000, 355). In other words, there is no "objectivity" to the economic statistics, the stock market indexes, and the commodity prices that stream forth daily. These numbers *measure* nothing, not because they mismeasure, but because the measuring methods are continually open to revision and are imposed by pure power considerations that can change without warning so that "contingency becomes a necessity and does not descend into disorder" (Hardt and Negri 2000, 356). These numbers and their "enforcers" are the result of "the impossibility of power's calculating and ordering production at a global level."[7]

Value also is *beyond measure* according to Hardt and Negri, because though value is created by living labor, that labor is identified with "general social activity" or "a common power to act" which cannot be regimented by clocks or any other economic and/or political measures. In making this identification, Negri and Hardt seem to willfully ignore the well-known ontological distinction between labor and action from Aristotle's day to the present via Marx (cf. Aristotle 1981, 64–65, 183–85; Arendt 1998 [1958]; McCarthy 1990).

Labor has traditionally been conceptualized as having a beginning-middle-end temporal structure, as being able to be planned and imposed externally while action is spontaneous, creative, unique and cannot be imposed externally. One can force another to labor again and again, but one cannot force another to act even once. In Aristotle's terminology, a master can compel a slave to labor, but action cannot be compelled by masters, for action must be the product of free men participating in the work of the state and constitution. Surely by identifying living labor with action, and communal social action (or *vita activa,* in Hannah Arendt's parlance) at that, Negri and Hardt can easily demonstrate that the values created by that labor are beyond measure, since (i) the very products of

---

[7] Negri's and Hardt's implication being that there was a historical era when power could calculate and order production at a global level. The period of the gold standard is the most likely candidate for such an era, since gold became the common standard of world trade then. One could directly measure the value of a commodity anywhere.

such "labor" could not be foreseen before the action itself, and (ii), real action is not reproducible. They seem to justify their blurring of the distinction in the following words:

> This leads us to a paradox: in the same moment when theory longer sees labor, labor has everywhere become the common substance. The theoretical emptying of the problem of labor corresponds to its maximum pregnancy as the substance of human action across the globe. Although it is obvious that in this totality of reference—given the impossibility of considering labor as actually (or even simply conceptually) transcendent—the law of value is blown apart, it is equally obvious that this immersion in labor constitutes the fundamental problem not only economic and politics but also of philosophy. The world is labor. (Hardt and Negri 1994, 11)

Of course, one must question such a notion of labor *cum* action, for it does not seem to refer to what billions of people across the planet do everyday under the surveillance of bosses vitally concerned about *how much time* the workers are at their job and *how well they do it* (*again and again*). The world might indeed be labor, but if the bulk of labor in the early twenty-first century was as Negri and Hardt describe it—"Labor that has broken open the cages of economic, social, and political discipline and surpassed every regulative dimension of modern capitalism with its state-form now appears as general social activity" (Hardt and Negri 2000, 357)—then surely capitalism, the law of value, and much else would have been a thing of the past! But, indeed, capitalism is quite present and seems to have a future.

In order to critically examine Negri and Hardt's criterion of viability and their substitution of activity for labor, it is important to introduce a basic premise of their critique of Marx's Law of Value: nineteenth-century modern capitalism is logically a different entity than post-1968 postmodern capitalism. Capitalism during Marx's time constituted a *formal* subsumption of society, but after 1968 capitalism has finally consummated a *real* subsumption of society. Their idea of periodizing capitalist history is based on an important distinction Marx made between *formal and real subsumption of labor by capital* in the previously mentioned unpublished section of *Capital I*: "The Results of the Immediate Process of Production" (Marx 1976, 1019–25). Negri and Hardt describe this distinction in the following words:

> Marx uses the term "formal subsumption" to name processes whereby capital incorporates under its own relations of production laboring practices that originated outside its domain. . . . Through the real subsumption, the integration of labor into capital becomes more intensive than extensive and society is ever more completely fashioned by capital. (Hardt and Negri 2000, 255)

The putting-out system for textile manufacturing or share-cropping are fine examples of formal subsumption of labor by capital whereas the development of "post-Fordist" "just-in-time" techniques of production would be examples of real subsumption. For in the putting-out system, merchants would "put out" raw material inputs to cottagers who continued to work with archaic production techniques and collect textile outputs to in turn sell them on the world market. The merchants never tampered with production. Contrast this with "post-Fordist" production that studies all the ways that human psychology (social and individual) can be used to make workers more productive and put the results into practice. Such managers never let the production process rest.

Negri and Hardt expand this distinction between formal and real subsumption into one between capital and society and use it to define different phases of capitalist history (Hardt and Negri 1994, 15). Capitalism, they claim, managed this transformation from formal to real subsumption through the increasing employment of the "General Intellect" and "immaterial labor" in the production process and a regime of control over the reproduction process. The connection of this historical transformation and the Law of Value is straight-forward: the Law might have been appropriate to a period when capital had only formally subsumed society, but with the real subsumption of society the notion that a commodity's value can be measured by "socially necessary labor time" is worthless. Value, in the period of real subsumption, is now created by living immaterial labor coordinated across continents via informatic planning and is increasingly directed at biopolitical objectives. The notion of a discrete amount of socially necessary labor time "pumped" into and "crystallized" in a commodity is completely inappropriate (Caffentzis 1997).

Negri and Hardt provide a paradigm for understanding both capital's post-Cold War tendency towards constituting a new legitimacy (which they term "Empire") based upon a "global" state and a biopolitical regime (released from the constraints of the Law of Value) and the new anticapitalist movement taking shape in the 1990s and resisting this tendency. Their paradigm challenges both traditional Marxism and postmodernism. The failure of the former is simple, for it is that of "Marx as the author of the old competitive capitalism, incapable of coping with the social capitalism of the present age" (Negri 1984, xv). The Law of Value might have been appropriate for the period of formal subsumption, but it is definitely inoperative in the period of real subsumption. Postmodernism as a theory for anticapitalists fails because of its mystification of struggle: "In reality, the operation of real subsumption [which Negri identifies with the 'postmodern condition'] does not eliminate the antagonism, but rather displaces it to a social level. Class struggle does not disappear, but it is transformed into all the moments of everyday life."

Certainly, Negri and Hardt seem to dismiss any of Marx's texts that try to explain the whys and hows of the capitalist "surface structure" (since it is those texts employing labor-value discourse and at least the restricted Law of Value that purport to do so). Consequently, they seem to be unconcerned about the loss of explanatory power in any anticapitalist theory of the future. If value is beyond measure, while the quantities of everyday life (from the prices of basic consumer commodities to stock futures and currency exchange rates) are measured arbitrarily in Humpty-Dumpty style, then either Negri and Hardt's ideal anticapitalist theory is a self-proclaimed failure at quantitative explanation or the very task of quantitative explanation is to be rejected because its object, postmodern capitalism, is lacking any feature worth measuring.

Part III: Critique of Negri and Hardt's Criterion

In order to evaluate Negri and Hardt's criterion of viability, I should begin by noting one of its strengths. It is definitely superior to Negri's *Marx Beyond Marx* criterion of the late 1970s for accepting or rejecting Marxist texts. The latter simply espoused excising the whole value discourse from the "usable" part of Marx's canon and thus threatened to eliminate nearly everything in it. Negri and Hardt's criterion of the 1990s is a sharper tool, for the texts in the Marxist canon that referred to labor and value (if they don't presume the law of value) could escape their new textual razor. Labor and value should continue to play an important role in the anticapitalist movement, according to Negri and Hardt, but the cost of their preservation, however, is that they become something like unmeasurable "things-in-themselves." Much that is qualitative in Marxist theory might survive, but the quantitative aspects should be totally eliminated post-Negri and Hardt.

Is the Negri-Hardt criterion useful? There are at least two reasons why it is not: (1) *quantity* is still a crucial aspect of capitalism, and (2) the notion of *subsumption* has quantitative aspects in Marx's work that would make it impossible to use the notion while neglecting these aspects.

QUANTITY

Capitalism imposes an extremely quantified form of life on its constituents. Indeed, early post-Marx thinkers like Simmel and Weber identified capitalism with the domination of quantitative reasoning in social life while early twentieth-century "avant garde" artists and writers often pictured the resistance to capitalism as a revolt against the rule of the number. Surely, any anticapitalist movement must have a quantitative capacity to deal with such an obvious feature of its antagonist. Marx was committed to creating a theory that could explain capital's quantitative character though he was not a professional mathematician. Even with this limitation, he proved to be surprisingly successful in a number of his mathematical efforts. His most impressive achievement was presaging the linear algebraic approach to social reproduction (in *Capital II*). Of course, his lack of formal training (and the horizon of mathematical technique during his lifetime) led to certain lapses (especially in his mathematical effort to solve the "transformation problem" of converting values into prices of production in *Capital III*.) But Marx's work definitely has served as a "core" for a research program that has generated an enormous amount of mathematical analyses of capitalism and of post-capitalist possibilities (cf., Howard and King 1992a and 1992b).

Marx's assumption of the measurability of value is crucial to the creation of his quantitative analysis of capitalism. The Law of Value, however interpreted, clearly presupposes this measurability as does most of the other quantitative indices Marx uses in *Capital* from surplus value, to the rate of profit, to the rate of exploitation, to organic composition, etc. Negri and Hardt challenge this assumption by claiming that though value exists, it is both outside and beyond measure in contemporary capitalism. By implication then, the quantitative aspects of Marx's work must be rejected by their criterion of viability. Only the qualitative aspects and relations of value and living labor, e.g., the existence of exploitation, in Marx's work would survive Negri and Hardt's razor.

But how does one prove that something is immeasurable? One thing that the history of mathematics teaches is that such proof claims have often proven false. One might go back to one of the first "discoveries" of immeasurability, the "irrationality of square root of 2," to remember the precariousness of such claims. Indeed, the very notion of an "irrational" number expresses the horror of the *initial* confrontation of this anathema among the Pythagoreans. But as Eudoxus and Euclid, in their theory of proportions, pointed out: the "irrational" is perfectly measurable (a.k.a., rational), the problem is simply that the methods of measurement cannot be limited to ratios of whole number units.[8]

Indeed, one can look at the development of the notion of number as the continual confrontation with the "immeasurable" that is then integrated into an enlarged domain of number. The vocabulary of mathematics is littered with terms like "imaginary number," "complex number,"

---

[8] In the early twentieth century there was much discussion about kinds of measurements that parallel this discussion of substance versus field quantities. These included direct versus indirect measurements and extensive versus intensive measurements. Thus the measurement of length would be direct and extensive measurement, while the measurement of temperature would be indirect and intensive (Savage and Ehrilch 1992, 2–3).

"transcendental number," or "a cardinal number of an uncountable set" that are semantic fossils of this transformation of the immeasurable into measurable.

The difficulty in measuring values (including the notion of value based on preferences used in neoclassical economics) is well known and was the source of debate even in the nineteenth century. There was no doubt that labor value was a "field" quantity and not a "substance" quantity then, to use Philip Mirowski's dichotomy (Mirowski 1989). Marx certainly recognized the field aspect of value in his many efforts to point out that value of a commodity produced at point A might be dramatically reduced (or increased) due to changes in the production process at point B, thousands of miles away. The field aspect of value *qua* socially necessary labor time has only intensified as capitalism is globalized, biopoliticized, and organized according to intricate divisions of labor; it is not new. But "field measures" are just as objective as "substance" ones (e.g., temperature of gases versus velocities of individual particles). They are not "immeasurable" simply because their measurement requires indirect and "conventional" methods.[9]

Negri and Hardt base their claim for the immeasurability of value on two grounds—historical and philosophical. Historically, they point to the arbitrariness and conventionality in the measurement of value in contemporary capitalism brought about, paradigmatically, by the unilateral decoupling of the dollar from gold and abrogation of the Bretton Woods accords by President Nixon in August 17, 1971. This led to the explosion of a worldwide currency market that was not restrained by any commodity base (like gold or silver). From then on, Negri and Hardt claim, the economic, political, social and personal weave together so that "in the globality of biopower every fixed measure of value tends to be dissolved, and the imperial horizon of power is revealed finally to be a horizon outside measure" (Hardt and Negri 2000, 384). That is, the post-1971 period of "free floating" currencies is one where there is no economic determinant of the last degree. The prices of commodities, say Negri and Hardt, are based on so many woven together elements that it is impossible to see them as indicators of any one quantity like socially necessary labor time. At best, "the

---

[9] According to the legend, the Pythagoreans both discovered the "irrationality of the square root of two" and kept it hidden, threatening to kill any member of their society that revealed it to outsiders. The proof is very simple and, if one believed that only those entities that can be expressed by ratios of whole numbers are measurable, then the square root of 2 (and infinite other such entities) would be immeasurable. The solution to this problem was devised by Eudoxus and later formalized by Euclid. He specified the definition of same ratio as the following: P/Q is said to be the same as X/Y when, m and n being any (positive) integers whatever, mX is greater than, equal to or less than nY according as mP is greater than, equal to, or less than, nQ (Koslow 1992, 151). In other words, the test for proportional equality is infinite, but determinate.

indexes of command [e.g., currency exchange rates] are defined on the basis of always contingent and purely conventional elements" (Hardt and Negri 2000, 355).

However, Negri and Hardt place too much historical importance on Nixon's abolition of the gold standard in 1971. On the one side, specie-backed monetary systems were always subject to "contingent and purely conventional elements" from debasements to bullion export restrictions, on the other side, the determination of the socially necessary labor time required for the production of a commodity inevitably wove together a wide variety of economic, political, social, and even personal-cultural considerations in determining its value. The post-1971 monetary environment might be more subject to political power than the previous periods, but that does not give us any reason to think that Nixon's fiat caused a historical leap from the finite to the infinite in economic value. After all, one can hardly claim that there are no continuities in economic ratios (e.g., of profitability, exchange rates, and exports) between the pre- and post-1971 periods.

The second source of Negri and Hardt's rejection of the measure of value is the evocation of a philosophical curse. Negri and Hardt identify measurability with all that is intellectually hateful to the rebel soul: "the great Western metaphysical tradition," "a transcendent order," "God," "cosmos," and "epistemological prohibitions," etc. Negri and Hardt apparently believe that any claim to be able to measure a phenomenon delegitimizes it and the social form it is a constituent of: "Even Marx's theory of value pays its dues to this metaphysical tradition: his theory of value is really a theory of the measure of value" (Hardt and Negri 2000, 355).

The curse attached to measurability deepens when Negri and Hardt link it with "the transcendent" and then point out "When political transcendence is still claimed today, it descends immediately into tyranny and barbarism" (Negri and Hardt 2000, 355). A good example of this generality is George W. Bush's evocation of God as the inspirer of the invasion of Iraq and its implication is: if you insist on measuring value, then you are on the way to supporting genocidal "shock and awe" displays!

After such a performance, our authors rightly pause to ask: "Are we thus simply making a nonsensical nihilist claim when we assert that in the ontology of Empire value is outside measure?" Their answer is "No," and then they invoke, contra those reactionary measuring philosophers Aristotle, Hegel and Marx, unnamed Renaissance humanists (perhaps Pico della Mirandola, Machiavelli, Bruno) to support their own transcendental insistence that "no transcendent power or measure will determine the values of our world. Value will be determined only by humanity's own continuous innovation and creation" (Hardt and Negri 2000, 356).

What is the source of Hardt's and Negri's philosophical curses and transcendental assurances? My answer is: Hardt's and Negri's confusion of two distinct kinds of skepticism. For in agreement with Marx's transvaluation of value, one might question the value of value and ask why indeed should the value of a commodity be "the material expression of human labour expended to produce them"? This skepticism towards the "false" objectivity of value, however, is often confused with a skepticism towards the value of objectivity itself. Whatever one might think about the value of objectivity, one should not confuse skepticism with regard to it and skepticism with regard to the value of commodity values. For very different arguments and considerations must apply in support of either. This confusion has a tradition in the history of Marxism that goes back to Georg Lukacs and continues to other contemporary theorists beside Negri and Hardt like John Holloway (Lukacs 1971; Holloway 2002). But it is a confusion just the same and I believe that it lead to Negri and Hardt questioning and even putting a curse on measurement, scientificity, and any other objectifying process.

However, such an approach would inevitably disqualify these two authors from explaining the major phenomena in contemporary capitalism (postmodern or not!)—the most important being, why is the average rate of profit positive? Moreover, their Renaissance insouciance toward measuring in a post-capitalist world would strike anyone who is tempted to think that "another world is possible" with fear and trembling, for he or she might wonder how bread would be baked in the measureless ovens of the future. For bread baking does require knowing how many cups of flour must be mixed with how many cups of water and how many minutes of kneading to make dough, i.e., there is a value to objectivity.

In other words, whatever one thinks of the correctness of Marx's texts dealing with the metrics of capitalism and their relevance to the debates on post-capitalism, they at least entertain the problems that any adequate anticapitalist revolutionary theory must pose. The Negri-Hardt criterion would simply relegate these texts to the "dust bin of history" and leave the anticapitalist movement bereft of the only thoroughly discussed body of thought on these vital matters. Consequently, their criterion decisively fails on this count.

SUBSUMPTION

The second reason for the failure of the criterion is that it undermines the analysis of capitalism that Negri and Hardt themselves present. In other words, their criterion's razor threatens to cut apart their own work. This is due to Negri and Hardt's enormous emphasis on Marx's distinction between formal and real subsumption of labor by capital. They use the term "real subsumption" to refer to social-cultural phenomena otherwise associated with "postmodernism" and with productive phenomena otherwise associated with "post-Fordism." It is their primary Marxian loan word.

This conceptual move is attractive, but it certainly does not fit Marx's historical assumptions. For Marx real subsumption was not a thing of the "future," it was fully present in his time. Indeed, he devised a set of conceptual pairs that parallel each other:

formal subsumption	real subsumption
absolute surplus value	relative surplus value
commodities exchanged at value	commodities exchanged at their price of production
most industries operating with a low organic composition	industries operating with a widely dispersed composition

There are vertical as well as horizontal relations between these columns of pairs. The vertical connections are logical and roughly as follows:

With the *formal subsumption* of labor by capital there is little effort made to increase the productivity of labor and so the productive (and reproductive) routines and techniques used are largely "as is." Consequently, the only way to increase surplus value is by extending the working day (i.e., through *absolute surplus value* creation). Since there is little investment in equipment, the *organic composition* (the ratio of constant capital to variable capital, i.e., investment in machines and plant with respect to the wage bill) is relatively and uniformly low in most industries and human labor (direct application of muscle, bone, and brain) is the prime "input." Consequently, the primary determinant and differential of exchange *value* is direct socially necessary labor-time.

With *real subsumption* there is a "revolutionary" application of science and technology to the productive process making it possible to decrease the necessary part of the working day and to intensify its productive density (hence producing *relative surplus value*). This leads to a great variety of investment possibilities both within and among branches of production, hence there develops an *immense vertical spectrum of organic composition possibilities* (from almost labor-less production in atomic power plants to labor-intensive production in sweat shops and plantations). Since any source of commodities must be owned and invested in by capitalists, they will demand an equal rate of profit as their brethren (in the long run) even if "their" workers produce next to no surplus value. In other words, these capitalists will demand *the price of production* (i.e., the sum of their constant capital and their variable capital plus the product of this sum and the rate of profit) in value terms instead of the actual value of their commodities.

The horizontal relations among the rows of pairs are historical, in the sense that capitalism tends to move from the left to the right element of the pair simultaneously. That is why Marx writes in the *Grundrisse* that the notion of value "explodes" in the period when science and technology takes an increasing role in the production process in many industries (Marx 1973, 705). For in these industries there is no correlation between the labor-time expended there and the price of the commodities sold. But it is not that the value of these commodities is immeasurable. Marx introduces a notion of "price of production" after writing the *Grundrisse* to point out that this situation will not automatically lead to a fundamental breakdown in capitalism. On the contrary, the prices of the commodities produced in many branches of production with relatively little labor have a mathematically determined character: their price of production includes surplus value created in other branches of production of lower organic composition in proportion to the capital invested in the industry.

Consequently, Negri and Hardt's use of Marx's notion of subsumption (formal and real) is fundamentally distorted, because for Marx this notion is logically connected with value phenomena (indeed with the law of value as expressed in the notion of the price of production). A judicious application of the Negri-Hardt criterion would cut off the very Marxian concept that they hoped to save, and hence mangle their own texts. For any such criterion needs to conserve the logical structure of the text it is operating on.

Another consequence of my textual analysis of Marx's work is the recognition that Marx was not prophesying about the deep future when he was writing in the *Grundrisse* about production being dominated by machines and their operators becoming mere appendages. Or, at least, he turned that prophetic vision into an everyday observation by the time he described an "organized system of machines" in *Capital I* (Marx 1976, 503). The moment of real subsumption had already occurred in "modern industry" along with the allied value phenomena: increasing relative surplus value creation, increasing organic composition differentials, and increasing deviation of prices of production from values. These tendencies were common phenomena in the mid-nineteenth century as well as in the beginning of the twenty-first century.

"General Intellect" and "immaterial labor" are not invitations to go beyond capital, as Negri and Hardt claim, but rather have always been part of the work capital has exploited whether it was waged or not; the recent crisis of the "New Economy" (the capitalist expression of Negri and Hardt's "real subsumption" description) has shown that the amount of labor involved in the computer industry does not change the dynamics of capitalist accumulation. Bangalore's high tech workers are more terrifying to U.S. "symbolic analysts" than the Taliban fighters in Kandahar because they are their real competitors in the international labor market. In fact, the Law of Value has been most tyrannical in the current neoliberal period! Any reading of the financial press and economic policy makers' positions statements would give one the impression that the Law of Value, as usually understood, is a truism. Surely what is the prescription for any economic problem but more discipline of labor, more labor flexibility and productivity, a reduction of labor costs, and so on? This is so obvious one must be incredulous in hearing the snide comments academic economists make about the law of value. Of course, if you want your products to compete on the world market you need to reduce the socially necessary labor time required to produce them, by any means necessary.

By applying to Negri and Hardt's theory Marx's observations of what occurs to social perception in the transformation from formal to real subsumption one can understand how Marx would explain why Negri and Hardt might be tempted to reject the Law of Value. When one moves both mentally and socially from the items on the left column of our Table to those on the right a process of occlusion and oblivion prevails: the productive powers of labor seemed to be transferred to those of capital. As Marx writes in *Capital III*:

> Capital thus becomes a very mystic being, since all of labour's social productive forces appear to be due to capital, rather than labour as such, and seem to issue from the womb of capital itself. . . . Not only does it appear so but it is true in fact that the average prices [of production] of commodities differ from their value, thus from the labour realised in them, and the average profit of a particular capital differs from the surplus value which this capital has extracted from the labourers employed by it . . . Normal average profits themselves seem immanent in capital and independent of exploitation. (Marx 1966, 827–29)

Negri and Hardt simply inverted this mysticism of capital to a mysticism of an immeasurable value-creating labor process.

Though Marx clearly believed that over time the second column of phenomena under "real subsumption" in the Table becomes more dominant than the first, *it never becomes a totality as long as capitalism continues to exist because of the crises associated with the Falling Rate of Profit*. That is, if the branches of high organic composition increase without limit, the rate of profit will fall to zero, unless there are countervailing forces that shift the weight back to the column of formal subsumption. The major countervailing force is the creation of new areas of absolute surplus-value creation among populations that are formally out of the capitalist system, either due to their ability to preserve their precapitalist subsistence economy in the face of centuries of capitalist threat or due to their ability to recreate some new form of noncapitalist subsistence in postcolonial or postcapitalist settings.

In conclusion, Negri and Hardt's use of the notion of subsumption detached from the Law of Value in even its more restricted sense is problematic, for the notions of real and formal subsumption in Marx's texts are part of a network of concepts defined in labor-value terms like organic composition, surplus value, price of production. By stripping "subsumption" from "labor-value" discourse Negri and Hardt provide only a distant approximation to Marx's concept to the point that it appears to be a little like the imaginary togas of the French revolutionaries of '89.

Conclusion: A Broken Heart?

"Mr. Kenge," said Allan, appearing enlightened all in a moment. "Excuse me, our time presses. Do I understand that the whole estate is found to have been absorbed in costs?"

"Hem! I believe so," returned Mr. Kenge. "Mr. Vholes, what do *you* say?"

"I believe so," said Mr. Vholes.

"And that thus the [Jarndyce and Jarndyce] suit lapses and melts away?"

"Probably," returned Mr. Kenge. "Mr. Vholes?"

"Probably," said Mr. Vholes.

"My dearest life," whispered Allan, "this will break Richard's heart!"

—CHARLES DICKENS, *Bleak House* (1853)

Negri and Hardt presented a relatively simple criterion for determining what part of Marx's works is still relevant to the struggles of the anticapitalist movement in the twenty-first century. My rejection of their criterion is not only a reflection on the limitation of their effort, however. Their failure, when added to the more than half century-long failure of efforts to devise a satisfactory criterion to determine the "true" Marx, the "scientific" Marx, the "humanistic" Marx, the "subjective" Marx, or the "revolutionary" Marx is evidence for a wider claim that appears on our horizon: no criterion will be able to create a dichotomy among Marx's texts that will isolate the acceptable kernel for today's anticapitalist movement.

Is the result of this essay, then, that Marx's texts cannot be used for the anticapitalist movement or that the cost of "saving" Marx's legacy has used up its value, as the Jarndyce and Jarndyce suit used up the Jarndyce estate in *Bleak House*? Is this a prescription for suffering with a Marxist broken heart? No. It is a call, however, for *defetishizing* the vast collection of texts that come to the anticapitalist movement under the name of Marx or, to use another metaphor, for Marx's texts to be used as a *common* instead of as a *memorial park*. His texts are not "a legacy" to be preserved. Marx set the model for dealing with his texts in the way he related to the texts of the political economists, the philosophers, the chemists, mathematicians, biologists, and physicists of his day. He "borrowed" massively from them without apology and without permission. If an organic chemistry model worked in describing the micro-exchanges that made up the reproduction (and rupture) of capital, Marx used it. If a piece of Hegel's dialectical logic would make the point he wanted to make, he "coquetted" with it. Marx was a shameless bricoleur on the commons of knowledge.

At the moment, unfortunately, Marx's texts are treated like nuggets of always fluctuating political exchange value instead of use values for anti-capitalist thought and action. For example, the century-long discussion of the transformation of values into the prices "problem" revolves around the vindication or the public humiliation of Marx's texts instead of whether this transformation tells the anticapitalist movement anything useful about the structure and vulnerability of capitalism. The struggle over the trans-formation problem has been largely a game of "gotcha" with the bour-geois academics (whenever they are politically threatened) pointing out the logical and mathematical infelicities of *Capital III* and Marxists running to provide ever more weighty mathematical retorts. The animus on all sides of the debate is a struggle of worth (of the preservation of tradition and honor) instead of use.

The key question in this particular matter, however, is: does the trans-formation of values into prices have explanatory power to help in under-standing the structure of capitalism or not? What are the areas of capital's operation that this transformation helps to explain? If there are such areas (e.g., in the examination of "unequal exchange" or of the "energy crisis") then the logical and mathematical difficulties can and will be overcome. For as any student of the history of science knows, there are no interesting theories without logical and mathematical infelicities (quantum mechanics and general relativity theory included).

In general and in conclusion, there is no evidence that the hunt for a criterion to determine the "quick and the dead" in Marx's texts (embed-ded in either their logical structure or historical coherence) will end in suc-cess. Perhaps Marxists, finally liberated from the search for their "legacy," can start to use it.

References

Ackermann, Robert John 1990. *Nietzsche: A Frenzied Look,* Amherst, MA: University of Massachusetts Press.

Althusser, Louis 1996. *For Marx,* London: Verso.

Arendt, Hannah 1998 [1958]. *The Human Condition,* second edition, Chicago: University of Chicago Press.

Aristotle 1981. *The Politics,* revised edition, Harmondsworth: Penguin.

Caffentzis, George 1997. "Why Machines cannot Create Value: Marx's Theory of Machines," in Jim Davis, Thomas Hirschl and Michael Stack, eds., *Cutting Edge: Technology, Information Capitalism and Social Revolution,* London: Verso, 1997.

Callinicos, Alex 2003. *An Anti-Capitalist Manifesto,* Cambridge, UK: Polity Press.

Cassirer, Ernst 1923. *Substance and Function and Einstein's Theory of Relativity,* New York: Dover Publications.

Cleaver, Harry 2001. *Reading Capital Politically,* second edition, Leeds, UK: Anti/Theses.

Cohen, G.A. 1988. *History, Labour, and Freedom,* Oxford: Clarendon Press.

———. 2000. *Karl Marx's Theory of History: A Defense,* expanded edition, Princeton, NJ: Princeton University Press.

Corcoran, Paul E. 1983. *Before Marx: Socialism and Communism in France, 1830–1848,* New York: St. Martin's Press.

Derrida, Jacques 1994. *Specters of Marx: The State of the Debt, the Work of Mourning, and the New International,* New York: Routledge.

Elster, Jon 1985. *Making Sense of Marx,* Cambridge: Cambridge University Press.

Federici, Silvia 2004. *Caliban and the Witches: Women, the Body and Primitive Accumulation,* New York: Autonomedia.

Federici, Silvia and George Caffentzis 2001. "A Brief History of Resistance to Structural Adjustment," in Kevin Danaher, ed., *Democratizing the Global Economy: The Battle Against the World Bank and the IMF,* Monroe, ME: Common Courage Press.

Haffner, Friedrich 1973. "Value, Law of Value," in C.D. Kernig, ed., *Marxism, Communism and Western Society: A Comparative Encyclopedia,* New York: Harder and Herder.

Hardt, Michael and Antonio Negri 1994. *Labor of Dionysus: A Critique of the State-Form,* Minneapolis: University of Minnesota Press.

———. 2000. *Empire,* Cambridge: Harvard University Press.

Holloway, John 2002. *Change the World Without Taking Power: The Meaning of Revolution Today,* London: Pluto Press.

Howard, M.C. and J.F. King 1992a. *A History of Marxian Economics, Vol. 1: 1883-1929.* Princeton, NJ: Princeton University Press.

———. 1992b. *A History of Marxian Economics, Vol. 2: 1929-1990.* Princeton, NJ: Princeton University Press.

Koslow, Arnold 1992. "Quantitativeness in Eudoxus, Newton, Maxwell," in Savage, C. Wade and Philip Ehrlich, eds., *Philosophical and Foundational Issues in Measurement Theory,* Hillsdale, NJ: Lawrence Erlbaum Associates, Publishers.

Leontyev, L. 1974. *Political Economy: A Condensed Course*, New York: International Publishers.

Linebaugh, Peter and Marcus Rediker 2001. *The Many-Headed Hydra*, Boston: Beacon Press.

Lukacs, Georg 1971. *History and Class Consciousness*, Cambridge, MA: MIT Press.

Marx, Karl 1966. *Capital: A Critique of Political Economy, Vol. 3*, Moscow: International Publishers.

———. 1973. *Grundrisse*, translated and introduced by Martin Nichalous, Harmondsworth: Penguin.

———. 1976. *Capital: A Critique of Political Economy, Vol. 1*, translated by Ben Fowkes and introduced by Ernest Mandel, Harmondsworth: Penguin.

McCarthy, George E. 1990. *Marx and the Ancients. Classical Ethics, Social Justice, and the Nineteenth Century Political Economy*, Savage, MD: Rowman and Littlefield Publishers.

Midnight Notes 1992. "The New Enclosures," in Midnight Notes Collective, eds., *Midnight Oil: Work, Energy, War 1973-1992*, New York: Autonomedia.

———. 2001. "The Hammer and . . . or the Sickle: From the Zapatista Uprising to the Battle of Seattle," in Midnight Notes Collective, eds., *Auroras of the Zapatistas: Local and Global Struggles of the Fourth World War*, New York: Autonomedia.

Mirowski, Philip 1989. *More Heat than Light. Economics as Social Physics: Physics as Nature's Economics*, Cambridge: Cambridge University Press.

Negri, Antonio 1984. *Marx Beyond Marx: Lessons on the Grundrisse*, South Hadley, MA: Bergen and Garvey Publishers (reprinted by Autonomedia in New York in 1991).

Nietzsche, Friedrich 1968. *Basic Writings of Nietzsche*, edited and translated by Walter Kaufmann, New York: The Modern Library.

Rutland, Peter 1985. *The Myth of the Plan*, La Salle, Illinois: Open Court.

Salleh, Ariel 1997. *Ecofeminism as Politics: nature, Marx and the postmodern*, London: Zed Books.

Simmel, Georg 1990. *The Philosophy of Money*, second enlarged edition, London and New York: Routledge.

Stalin 1972. *The Essential Stalin: Major Theoretical Writings, 1905–1952*, edited with an introduction by Bruce Franklin, Garden City, NY: Doubleday and Co.

Steele, David Ramsay 1992. *From Marx to Mises: Post-capitalist Society and the Challenge of Economic Calculation*, LaSalle, Illinois: Open Court.

5

Marx Beyond Marx, Marx Before Marx: Negri's Lucretian Critique of the Hegelian Marx

MELINDA COOPER

Lucretius . . . is correct when he maintains that the declination (*clinamen*) breaks the *fati foedera* [bonds of fate], and, since he applies this immediately to consciousness, it can be said of the atom that the declination is that something in its breast that can fight back and resist.

KARL MARX, *Doctoral Dissertation.*

Perhaps we should here recall a minor tradition in the history of the idea of time, but one that is not any less important or suggestive. It is the hypothesis of classical materialism, that of Democritus, Epicurus and Lucretius. It is an entirely ontological hypothesis that, on the basis of a relation between mutation and time, proposes the definition of time as innovation and/or corruption . . . as asymmetry, as displacement.

ANTONIO NEGRI, *The Constitution of Time.*

This article explores the vicissitudes of Negri's reading of Marx, beginning with his early commentary on the *Grundrisse* and extending to later articles and developments in *Empire* and *Kairòs, Alma, Multitude*. I will argue that Negri's attempt to uncover a "Marx beyond Marx" has been concerned, from the beginning, with the question of the limit (the mediation or the measure) in Marx's conception of value, and in particular in those lesser known aspects of Marxian philosophy in which he explores the question of a creation of value "outside of measure." For Negri, the "outside of measure" is precisely the horizon of production in which we have entered, at least since the social movements and anticolonial struggles of the 60s, the U.S. economic crisis of the 70s, the subsequent deregulation of national financial markets and reorganization of labor. In response to these events, Negri's later work has become an inquiry into the nature of exploitation "outside of measure" and of the possibilities of a resistance "beyond measure."

In my approach to this question, I will attempt to understand why the notion of the "beyond measure," for Negri, is intimately associated with the project of "recreating the world" or a "self-recreating world." I will suggest that Negri's counter-reading of Marx leads him to one of Marx's earliest works, his doctoral dissertation on Lucretius's philosophy of creation and the concept of the *clinamen* (Marx 1975i, 25–106; Marx 1975ii, 403–509).

My article takes as its point of departure the following quote from Negri and Hardt's *Empire*:

> The great Western metaphysical tradition has always abhorred the immeasurable. From Aristotle's theory of virtue as measure to Hegel's theory of measure as the key to the passage from existence to essence, the question of measure has been strictly linked to that of transcendent order. Even Marx's theory of value pays its dues to this metaphysical tradition: his theory of value has always been a theory of the measure of value. (2000, 355)

In this highly condensed passage, moving from Aristotle to Hegel to Marx, Negri outlines the crux of his critique of Marx's theory of value. This is a critique that centers on the first book of *Capital*, where Marx develops the notion of the value form as a law of measure establishing the quantitative equivalence of abstract labor, commodities, and exchange value. In what does this law consist? In Negri's words, "Marx poses the relation between labor and value in terms of corresponding quantities: a certain quantity of time of abstract labor equals a quantity of value. According to this law of value, which defines capitalist production, value is expressed in measurable, homogenous units of labor time. Marx eventually links this notion to his analyses of the working day and surplus value" (2004, 145). The law of value, in other words, defines exploitation as a measurable quantity, locating it in the extortion of a surplus of labor above and beyond the expenditure of force necessary for the reproduction of the worker's body. The philosophical sources of Marx's law of value are clear. The first book of *Capital I* refers explicitly to Aristotle's writings on exchange and measure. But ultimately it is Hegel's *Science of Logic*, with its reflections on measure, the limit and quantity that provides Marx with the logical scaffolding for his theory of surplus value.

For a certain tradition of historical materialism, the law of value represents the crowning achievement of Marx's critique of political economy. This law, according to Althusser, represents much more than the possibility of quantifying exploitation. It is also the philosophical lynchpin that allows Marx to conceive of the relationship between capital and labor in the form of a dialectics of contradiction and mediation (Althusser 1979 [1967]). For the materialist tradition represented by Althusser, the law of value thus places Marx squarely within a tradition of dialectical philosophy, however complex his relation to Hegel. Negri's political philosophy, on the other hand, could only be described as a sustained effort to take Marx *beyond* the dialectical Marx of historical materialism, and hence beyond and outside Hegel's philosophy of time as measure. (Ironically of course, Althusser himself will later acknowledge and critique the Hegelian influence in historical materialism, precisely via a return to Lucretius.)[1]

At least since *Marx beyond Marx*, Negri's intervention into the Marxian tradition has been inseparable from a radical critique not only of the law of value but also of the antinomies and mediations of the dialectic. Ultimately, Negri's perspective on Marx bears on the question of *time* and its relation to difference, resistance, and crisis. The law of value, Negri insists, is obsolete as a law of exploitation (although I will later question the historical validity of this affirmation). We can no longer figure the relationship between capital and labor, on the one hand, or crisis and accumulation, on the other, in the mode of the dialectic and its syntheses. For Negri, this means that political philosophy itself must renew and reinvent Marx's methodology in order to deal with the specific conditions of production and resistance in the contemporary moment. As Negri and Hardt write in their latest collaborative work:

> The temporal unity of labor as the basic measure of value today makes no sense. Labor does remain the fundamental source of value in capitalist production, that does not change, but we have to investigate what kind of labor we are dealing with and what its temporalities are. (2004, 145)

Negri has always been interested in a current within Marx's thinking, present right from the beginning, which is concerned with the question of a production outside and beyond measure. This problematic exists as a philosophical direction in Marx's thinking, aligning him with the Epicurean and Lucretian philosophy of time *contra* Hegel (on this point, Negri is in accord with Francine Markovitz's (1974) reading of Marx's early work). But it also has an historico-practical dimension: from his earliest writings, Negri has sought to uncover a nondialectical understanding of revolution in Marx's work, focusing in particular on the seminal *Grundrisse* notes, predating *Capital* by ten years.

In what follows, I will first explore the historico-practical dimension of Negri's critique of the law of value before looking in detail at the philosophical aporias of this critique and the positive project of ontological reconstitution with which Negri's later work is increasingly preoccupied.

---

[1] See note 5.

Taking Marx Beyond Marx—Negri's Historical Critique of the Law of Value

In 1978, Antonio Negri, a former student of the *Ecole Normale Supérieure*, was invited by Althusser to hold a seminar there. In response to the *Capital*-centric school of Althusserian Marxism, Negri's seminars pointed to the *Grundrisse* notebooks (an unfinished work composed ten years before *Capital* and long considered peripheral to Marx's political philosophy) as the point of departure for a new intervention into Marx. It was the lessons from this seminar that would later provide the material for *Marx Beyond Marx*, the text in which Negri first articulates his *historical* critique of the law of value as a law of exploitation. What is perhaps most provocative about Negri's intervention here is his insistence that it was Marx himself who formulated the most radical and prescient of critiques of the law of value, in particular in the so-called "Fragment on the Machines" (between books VI and VII of the *Grundrisse*). Returning to the *Grundrisse* at the end of the seventies, an era of continuing political crisis in Italy and an intense phase of capitalist restructuring worldwide, what Negri claims to uncover here is a "formidable anticipation" of the present, a productive hiatus in Marx's work which would allow us to reinvent Marx for the contemporary era, beyond the manifest failures of orthodox historical materialism ([1979] 1996, Introduction, unpaginated).

In what follows, I will outline the crux of Negri's historical critique of the law of value. It is in relation to three sites of transition that Negri identifies the necessity of moving beyond a theory of value as measure in Marx's work: the first of these is production; the second is the geopolitics of space as it affects the relationship between the nation-state and the world-market; while the third concerns the temporalities of accumulation, crisis, and resistance.

1) It is in the "Fragment on the Machines" that Negri finds the most productive of Marx's reflections on the possible future transformations of labor. In this text, Marx sets himself the task of imagining the possibilities of labor under the conditions of "real subsumption," in other words, under conditions in which "capital has subjugated all conditions of social production to itself" (Marx 1993, 532). What Marx is imagining here is a scenario in which the divisions he himself establishes between productive and unproductive labor, individual and collective labor, base and superstructure, intellectual and manual work have ceased to be operative. As Negri writes in his 1996 introduction to the French edition of *Marx beyond Marx*, this is a scenario which offers a remarkably apt diagnosis of post-Fordism:

This is . . . an extraordinary *theoretical anticipation of advanced capitalist society*, that is of a society in which the function of the worker's labour [le travail ouvrier] (as immediate labour) is no longer more than a secondary element in a process of civil production that is completely subsumed within the organisation of capital; in which productive labour is intellectual, cooperative and immaterial labour. [. . .] We live today in a society that is increasingly characterized by the hegemony of immaterial labour (intellectual, scientific, technological, etc.). The links between the production of goods (itself digitalized) and their distribution (along with the social links that tie together the production and distribution of goods) are immaterial links. This means that in relative terms, immediate labour is increasingly marginal to their constitution and that conversely, they are effectively organized by technological and communicative cooperation. ([1979] 1996, Introduction, unpaginated, my translation)[2]

In his subsequent writings, particularly the collaborative work with Michael Hardt, the terms of Negri's interpretation of the "Fragment on the Machines" will be modified and become considerably more subtle. The Italian autonomists have been criticized for the bias towards the more privileged forms of cognitive labor that characterize the postmodern (a bias that is reflected in their preference for the terms "immaterial production" and "general intellect"). In *Empire*, Negri and Hardt follow feminist theorists who insist that real subsumption is characterized not only by the breakdown of all distinctions between base and superstructure, intellectual and productive labor, but also by the integration of the Keynesian-Fordist reproductive sphere into capitalist relations (hence, the increasingly marketable nature of affective service labor). In *Multitudes*, they acknowledge the biopolitical and ecological dimension of real subsumption, in other words, the tendency of post-Fordist production to invest in the spheres of biological life and the elements. It remains to be seen how, if at all, these revisions will modify the theoretical premises of Negri and Hardt's thesis of "immaterial production."

---

[2] "Il s'agit . . . d'une extraordinaire *anticipation théorique de la société capitaliste avancée*, c'est-à-dire de la société dans laquelle la fonction du travail ouvrier (en tant que travail immédiat) n'est plus qu'un élément secondaire dans la production civile complètement subsumée dans l'organisation du capitalisme, le travail productif, c'est le travail intellectuel, coopératif, immatériel. [. . .] Nous vivons aujourd'hui dans une société de plus en plus caractérisée par l'hégémonie du traval immatériel (intellectuel, scientifique, technologique, etc.). Les liens entre la production des biens (elle-même informatisée) et leur distribution (et les liens sociaux qui relient production et distribution des biens) sont des liens immatériels; ce qui veut dire que le travail immédiat est proportionnellement de plus en plus secondaire dans ce qui les fonde et ils sont par contre effectivement organisés par la coopération technologique et communicationelle".

In any case, perhaps the most enduring and interesting contribution of "The Fragment on the Machines" to Negri's political philosophy lies in its methodological premises rather than the precision of its historical anticipation of the present. What becomes of exploitation and revolution, Marx seems to ask himself here, when the capitalist relation has become so pervasive that it permeates all other social relations; when production and reproduction, base and superstructure become indistinct; and when the categories of political economy can no longer be thought of in the mode of contradiction and mediation? In this passage, it is as if Marx had already posed the methodological problem of (re)thinking exploitation, resistance, and crisis in a context where all dialectical contradiction has been definitively subsumed, where all possible outsides have been integrated into the self-productive dynamic of capitalism itself. It might be assumed that such a scenario could only suggest the final and ultimate triumph of capitalism itself, or else a radically voluntarist perspective on revolution (the one being the dialectical inversion of the other). What Negri uncovers here instead is a Marxian critique of the law of value—one which would invalidate both these scenarios. The key passage on this point can be found in book VII of the *Grundrisse* where Marx envisages the eventual obsolescence of the law of value in the face of the increasingly communicative, immediately collective basis of production:

> [The worker] steps to the side of the production process instead of being its chief actor. In this transformation, it is neither the direct human labor he himself performs, nor the time during which he works, but rather the appropriation of his own general productive power, his understanding of nature and his mastery over it by virtue of his presence as a social body—it is, in a word, the development of the social individual which appears as the great foundation-stone of production and of wealth. The *theft of alien labor time, on which the present wealth is based*, appears a miserable foundation in the face of this new one, created by large-scale industry itself. As soon as labor in the direct form has ceased to be the great well-spring of wealth, labor time ceases and must cease to be its measure, and hence exchange value [must cease to be the measure] of use value. The *surplus labor of the mass* has ceased to be the condition for the development of general wealth, just as the *non-labor of the few*, for the development of the general powers of the human head. With that, production based on exchange value breaks down, and the direct, material production process is stripped of the form of penury and antithesis. (Marx 1993, 705–706)

It is in this passage, where Marx seems to subject his own work to the most radical of critiques, that Negri locates the "summit" of Marx's political philosophy. Taking his cue from Marx, Negri suggests that materialist method must itself undergo a "fundamental metamorphosis" in order to

understand the figures of labor, exploitation, and resistance that characterize the contemporary moment (1984, 147). Labor time remains the generative source of economic value, he claims. But under the conditions of
real subsumption, it is the very temporality of labor that has shifted: work
as the individual expenditure of force has long since been replaced by the
collective productive powers of the common; the linear time of accumulation has given way to the nonlinear generativity of crisis; production, in a
word, *has ceased to be measurable*. The historical demise of the law of value
therefore raises two questions for Negri: how do we rethink the conditions
of exploitation (and thus the nature of surplus value) in a context where
we can no longer appeal to or indict the mediations of the dialectic? And
more importantly, how do we figure the possibilities of resistance outside
the dialectical form of revolution (understood here as an inversion of the
dialectic)?

2) In a second sense, Negri's critique of the law of value bears on the
geopolitical or imperial dimension of the law. In Marxian terms, argues
Negri, the nation-state needs to be understood as one of the many incar-
nations of the law of value—the juridical and spatial overdetermination of
labor which functions to regulate exchange value in terms of the relations
between different spatial territories of the earth (First, Second and Third
World, center and peripheries). In this sense, "*[t]he nation state was a singular organization of the limit*" (Negri and Hardt 2000, 236). The mediating function of this limit, he goes on to argue, became most forcefully
effective in the post World War II era, when the combined forces of the
Bretton Woods accord and the Keynesian social state came together, under
the aegis of U.S. economic power, to form a world imperialism based on
the nation-state. It was in the context of this singular organization of imperial rule, contends Negri, that various anticolonialist theorists (following
Rosa Luxemburg) sought to formulate the law of value as a principle of
spatial exploitation, allowing them to theorize the peripheral nation-state
as the territorial basis for their struggles against First World imperialism.
Luxemburg's work on imperialism locates the self-destructive impulses of
such an imperial order within its very reliance on the spatial dynamic of
expansion and resource extraction (Luxemburg 2003). At some point, she
argued, capitalism would no longer have any outside space to subsume and
would therefore encounter ultimate limits to its expansion. This encounter
with limits had seemed to offer a horizon of imminent crisis in which anti-
imperialist struggle would bring about the ultimate destruction of capitalism itself.

Negri's take on the question is considerably more nuanced. In a
sense, he concedes, the spatial organization of twentieth-century imperialism did come up against the extensive limits imposed by the anti-imperialist struggles of the post World War II era. Postcolonialism then, did

signal the end of a certain form of imperialist relation, centered on the juridical and economic structures of the U.S. as the dominant nation-state. But what we have witnessed in the ensuing period is certainly not the end of the capitalist relation per se, but rather a violent reorganization of imperial rule *in response to anti-imperialist struggle*, a reorganization effected through various strategies of spatial remobilization such as off-shore production, the creation of "free trade" zones, and the emerging transnationalization of juridical and political structures. Negri's perspective on the geopolitical dimension of the law of value can thus be expressed as follows: the imperialist relation, although no less violent, is no longer mediated by that *"singular organization of the limit"* embodied in the First World nation-state of the post World War II era (Negri and Hardt 2000, 332–36). In this sense, the geopolitics of empire (as opposed to imperialism) must be understood to be spatially *immeasurable*. Negri and Hardt go on to suggest that we need another geometry of difference in order to understand the specific segmentations that now organize the space of imperial power. If the Hegelian (and a certain Marxian) conception of world space was founded on the mathematics of integration (difference always being mediated by the limit or the tangent), Negri and Hardt make the claim that only the mathematics of fractal difference can account for the new spatialities of imperial power (a fractal being a difference without tangent or limit, a difference that produces more difference) (2000, 339–40).

3) This brings us to the third and most important aspect of Negri's critique of the law of value—a critique that relates to the temporality of accumulation and crisis. The key text here is Negri's 1967 essay "Keynes and the Capitalist Theory of the State" ([1967] 1994), where he argues that the Keynesian social state should be understood as the attempt to establish the law of value as a political and economic order mediating between the twin catastrophe limits of capitalist accumulation (crises of overproduction and revolution, the two being necessarily entwined according to Negri). Again what characterizes the postmodern era, argues Negri, is the deliberate *self*-dissolution of the nation-state and its mediating function between these two catastrophe limits, a self-dissolution that can only be understood as a response to the catastrophic risk posed by the various social insurgences of the sixties. As Negri writes in his "Twenty Theses on Marx,"

> The characteristics of the current period of capitalist development, as the initial phase of the third industrial revolution, took shape during the 1970s, and in particular between 1971 and 1982. 17 August 1971: Nixon and Kissinger abandon the convertibility of the dollar and gold. A powerful signal of deregulation is thereby sent out to world capitalism. The idea was to

break with the cumulative pressure produced by workers' struggles in the advanced capitalist countries and the liberation struggles of the Third World in the course of the 1960s. . . . (1997, 351, my translation)

Negri's thesis is that the breakdown of Bretton Woods inaugurated a fundamentally new era of accumulation, in which world capitalism, initiated by the U.S., strove to maintain itself *in a state of permanent crisis* (as defined in Keynesian terms). In this era, characterized by the deregulation of financial markets and the adoption of floating exchange rates, financial capital became the means by which capitalism could maintain itself in a relentless state of restructuring, allowing it to both absorb and keep ahead of the ever-present threat of insurgency:

In 1982, crisis is reaffirmed as the permanent form of the cycle in which we have entered; (1997, 353)

In this phase of development, the capitalist state is the crisis-state and is nothing else: it is the state that plans for crisis. (1997, 352)

It is the catastrophic nature of the postmodern state, Negri suggests, which accounts for the peculiar imbrication of social transformation and control in the contemporary moment. Capitalism transforms itself through acts of sporadic self-revolution, Marx insisted. Negri brings two provisos to this argument. In the first place, he wants to argue that capitalism itself only ever "revolutionizes" its modes of production in response to the resistance of those it seeks to exploit. Resistance, crisis, and restructuration are thus necessarily implicated. But Negri also contends that there is a peculiar quality to this co-implication in the postmodern era: where capitalist cycles of boom and bust are typically characterized by periods of relative equilibrium punctuated by sporadic crises, postmodern accumulation takes place in a permanent state of disequilibrium. Hence, the difficulty of distinguishing between the act of resistance and its moment of recuperation: in a context where derivatives trading (futures on futures) predominates over commodities, stocks, and futures *tout court*, capitalism strives to hedge against and trade in all possible contingencies. Its relationship to resistance has become speculative and preemptive (Cooper 2006). In his latest work, Negri thus points to the central role now played by finance capital in preempting the labors of the common:

Money, of course, is not only a general equivalent that facilitates exchange but also the ultimate representation of the common. Financial instruments, such as derivatives, cast this representation of the common into the future. Through financial markets, in other words, money tends to represent not only the present but also the future value of the common. Finance capital bets on the future and functions as a general representation of our common future productive capacities. The profits of finance capital are probably in its purest form the expropriation of the common. (Negri and Hardt 2004, 151)

It follows that the theoretical question posed by postmodern forms of control is how to understand a mode of power which both presumes and mobilizes the immeasurable, while striving to rechannel it into the measurable form of exchange value:

> In stretching out within temporality, power wants to invest the *to-come* as well. Biopolitical domination is thus presented as a future investment whose aim is that of establishing control over present production. (Negri 2003d, 257)

> [Postmodern] exploitation is deflation; it is a thwarting and a reduction to measure of the power of biopolitics open to the *to-come*. (Negri 2003d, 233)

Implicit in these passages is a substantial revision of the theory of surplus value, one where the extortion of value bears on the creation-in-common of an immeasurable future and where control operates through the reimposition of measure in and against the immeasurable.[3]

Thus far, I have outlined Negri's *historical* critique of the law of value, a critique he continues to refine and develop even in his most recent work. But how should we read Negri's assertion that the law of value *has become* obsolete? Is Negri's critique merely to be read in a chronological sense? (The dialectic, on this reading, once represented an effective operation of powers but has since been displaced by more recent formations of power and control). There are certainly elements of Negri's work, even the most recent, which would suggest such a reading. One problem with this historical presentation of Negri's critique is that it tends to reproduce the linear, historical temporality that Negri is purportedly trying to displace (in "Twenty Theses on Marx," Negri accuses Marx of lapsing into a "natural history" of capitalism in which the dialectics of labor and capital seems to unfold according to the circular laws of movement prescribed by the law of value) (1997, 335). Another problem lies in the terms of Negri's own historical analysis: while he most often establishes the crisis of the seventies as the decisive moment in the transformation of capitalist relations, Negri at times wants to

---

[3] I wonder however if Negri needs to reintroduce the notion of measure *a posteriori* in order to account for the peculiar coercive powers of new financial instruments such as derivatives, which seem to operate independently of any notion of measure or fundamental value. Perhaps Negri's critique of the law of value doesn't go far enough on this point.

push his critique of the law of value so far back that it becomes a historical nonsense. Thus in "Twenty Theses on Marx" again, Negri contends that the law of value was *already obsolete* as a description of exploitation at the time of the second industrial revolution, when Marx was writing (1997, 342–43). But at other times again, Negri offers a more interesting perspective on the sense in which we should read his critique of the Hegelian (Marxian) philosophy of time as measure. In these texts, Negri moves beyond the historical critique of the law of value to make the claim that the whole question of time needs to be thought otherwise, "outside and beyond" the mediations of the dialectic. At this point, Negri's critique morphs into a creative counter-philosophy of time. As Yann Moulier Boutang writes in his Introduction to the French edition of *Marx beyond Marx*:

> It seems to me that it [*Marx Beyond Marx*] offers one of the most global responses to the theoretical positions of Louis Althusser, in the sense that it is a positive, reconstructive critique: it takes its point of departure from an already coherent system. ([1979] 1996, unpaginated) [4]

Unlike Yann Moulier Boutang, I don't think Negri fully accomplishes this labor of "reconstruction" in *Marx beyond Marx*. However, this text does signal a turning point in the sense that it enunciates a project to come. It is this creative, philosophical project that occupies Negri in his subsequent work. In the following section of this article, I will be looking in detail at Negri's philosophical work on time, crisis, and resistance, from "The Constitution of Time" to *Kairòs, Alma, Multitudo*. It is in these philosophical texts that Negri fully comes to terms with the temporal problematic that exists only in the form of historical rupture in *Marx beyond Marx*.

Time: From Catastrophe to Constitution

Marx Beyond Marx was composed in an atmosphere of enduring crisis. The crisis of orthodox Marxism; but also the nascent crisis of the Fordist Keynesian model of capitalism and the fragile equilibrium it had established at an international and domestic level over the preceding three decades. What draws Negri to the *Grundrisse* is precisely the parallel between his situation and that of Marx. The *Grundrisse* too were written as a response to the political and financial crises of the mid nineteenth

---

[4] "Il me semble que c'est au fond l'une des réponses les plus globales aux positions théoriques de Louis Althusser, en ce qu'elle est une critique positive de reconstruction: elle part en effet d'un système cohérent en tant que tel".

century—the revolutions that wracked Continental Europe in the late 1840s and the emerging American financial crisis of 1857. As Negri reminds us, the *Grundrisse* "is not a text that can be used only for studying philologically the constitution of *Capital*; it is also a *political text* that conjugates an appreciation of the revolutionary possibilities created by the 'imminent crisis' together with the theoretical will to adequately synthesize the communist actions of the working class faced with this crisis" (1984, 8). In the *Grundrisse* then, Marx conceives of the rhythms of capitalist crisis and reconstruction as inextricably entwined. Indeed, for Negri, the *Grundrisse* is the text where Marx develops his most rigorous and provocative perspective on the temporality of crisis and resistance. What Marx offers us here is a science and methodology of the nonresolvable crisis, a philosophy of time that definitively wrests the moment of negation from any possibility of measure or mediation: "the materialist method . . . cannot be enclosed within any dialectical totality or logical unity" (1984, 12). As early as *Marx beyond Marx*, Negri thus draws a distinction between two conceptions of crisis—crisis proper, understood in Hegelian terms as the continual effort of capital to subsume its own negation; and crisis which resists subsumption, crisis as resistance or *catastrophe* (1984, 85–104). The latter understanding of crisis requires a wholly different philosophy of temporality to that implied in the Hegelian dialectic.

But already here, Negri is interested in much more than the affirmation of the catastrophe event as absolute, nonresolvable crisis. The strategy of the catastrophe, he writes, must ultimately become the source of a constitutive model of labor and time. The refusal of work as an absolute exodus from the dialectical relationship between labor and capital must at some point give rise to new possibilities of collective being and transformation. Resistance needs to become self-constitutive or self-valorizing in order to acquire a positive, creative temporality of its own. "The movement of inversion is powerful, so much so that the form of the transition is not simply antithetical, but rather constitutive of a new subject, and of its potential for total transformation" (1984, 165).

In *Marx beyond Marx*, however, Negri gets only so far in his attempt to realize this "total transformation" of the possibilities of production. What this text offers is the affirmation of an absolute resistance and a practical strategy of irrecuperable exodus—the "refusal of work" as the refusal of all mediation:

> When the capital relation has reached the point where it explodes, the liberated negation is not a synthesis. It knows no formal equivalences whatsoever. *Working-class power is not the reversal of capitalist power, not even formally.* Working-class power is the negation of the power of capital. (1984, 150)

This moment of absolute refusal, however, is not yet sustained by any positive, constitutive philosophy of time. In *Marx beyond Marx*, Negri's attempt to articulate an alternative philosophy of resistance seems to return inescapably and maddeningly to the terms of the dialectic, if only to rework the contradiction as absolute antagonism. Ultimately, then, *Marx beyond Marx* reads as an ambitious but frustrated gesture of rupture. It is this frustration that seems to fuel Negri's subsequent work over the following two decades, where he attempts to elaborate the positive ontology of time and constitution that failed him in his first engagement with the *Grundrisse*. Perhaps the most familiar aspect of Negri's recent philosophical trajectory is to be found in his writings on Spinoza, political constitution, and the multitude. (For a detailed and complementary reading of this particular aspect of Negri's post-Marxian political philosophy, see Michael Goddard in this volume). But what I will argue here is that Negri's later philosophy is equally indebted to the Lucretian philosophy of time, and via Lucretius, to the very early, little-known Marx—the Marx who affirmed that the swerve of the atom or *clinamen* constitutes the ultimate gesture of resistance. In two texts in particular, "The Constitution of Time" ([1981] 2003a) and *Kairòs, Alma Venus, Multitudo* (2003c), it is possible to trace the subsequent vicissitudes of Negri's philosophy of time via a return to the Lucretian Marx.

It is in "The Constitution of Time" ([1981] 2003a), written shortly after *Marx beyond Marx*, that Negri first articulates his own frustration with the philosophical problematic of time, crisis, and resistance raised by his earlier work. This text, which unfolds as a dense reflection on the temporal "aporias" in the work of Marx, restates in philosophical terms the historical-practical problematic that Negri had earlier discovered in the *Grundrisse*. "If social labor covers all the time of life, and invests all of its regions, how can time measure the substantive totality in which it is implicit? . . . When the entire time of life has become the time of production, who measures whom?" (2003a, 29). In other words, when we reach a historical threshold where the whole of social life, the reproduction and circulation of social relations, have been subsumed into the capitalist relation, in what sense can we continue to refer to Marx's law of value (either as a law of exploitation or the basis for resistance)? When social time becomes constitutive of itself (autoconstitutive) at the same time as it becomes subject to the self-valorization of capital (real subsumption), how is it possible to untangle the dense complicities of resistance and control? Where does the law of value find its principle of measurement? Paradoxically, Negri wants to move beyond the Hegelian Marx of Althusser by insisting that the dialectic of labor and capital has *in any case* been realized and thereby exhausted: to affirm that we have entered an era of "real subsumption," after all, is to acknowledge the ultimate realization of the dialectic and hence the final imposition of the law of value as a law of command. At this point, argues Negri, the law of value has become wholly tautological:

> Whenever the passage towards real subsumption occurs . . . time-as-measure, as equivalent, as reversible, etc, manifests its aporias in definitively tautological form. [. . .] When the dialectic is resolved (and we know that under real subsumption that indeed occurs), tautology reigns. Real subsumption means the complete realization of the law of value. (2003a, 27)

The question is—where do we go from here? After all, such an affirmation could be read as the characteristic move of postmodernism. It has led other philosophers to proclaim the end of history (Fukuyama) or the passage from a dialectics of labor and capital to a world of triumphant fetishism in which the "mirror of production" endlessly feeds of its own reflections (Baudrillard). The novelty of Negri's move is to suggest that far from heralding the final triumph of capitalism or the end of history, "real subsumption" marks the threshold beyond which the question of time (crisis and resistance) needs to be formulated otherwise, in nondialectical terms. For Negri then, the notion of "real subsumption," as the point of exhaustion of the Hegelian Marx, opens up an enormously productive aporia in the materialist tradition: "Marx's tautology of time, life and production at the level of real subsumption is both the consummation of the materialist tradition (and the overcoming of its substantial deficiencies) as well as the eruption of a new horizon of reflection on time" (2003a, 35). For Negri, the question then becomes how to think through this new horizon of reflection on time without reducing it to indifferent repetition, the endless end of history proclaimed by the postmodernists. In other words, how is it possible to reintroduce difference (rupture, crisis and resistance) into political philosophy without resurrecting the dialectic? For Negri, the dissolution of the law of value as a law of measure in no way abolishes the antagonistic dimension of resistance (nor for that matter the reality of exploitation). But it nevertheless compels us to rethink the antagonism in nondialectical terms. As Negri comments in his Afterword to "The Constitution of Time," written two decades later: "My concern evidently was to remove any possibility of a dialectical recuperation of the antagonism: to fix the opposition of the temporalities with the aim of breaking with any possible 'synthetic' and 'sublimating' reformist recuperation of the analysis of temporality" (2003b, 131).

Importantly, Negri's ambition is not only to theorize a notion of time as nondialectical difference—to conceive of time as absolute innovation, hysterisis, catastrophe—but also to construct an autoconstitutive ontology of time on the basis of this absolute difference. The paradigm, he admonishes himself, must become "ontological," the philosophy of the catastrophe must become "constitutive" (2003a, 35).

But does "The Constitution of Time" actually accomplish this task? Negri's own critique of this text would suggest that it doesn't. Again, in an Afterword composed two decades later, Negri offers this retrospective appraisal of his earlier work: "the result became hysterical and led to the blockage of the investigation: indeed, how would it have been possible concretely to open once again the radical *difference* of the subjective and constitutive temporality once it was defined in a sort of symmetry with the analytic temporality of capital?" (2003b, 131). In Negri's own judgment then, "The Constitution of Time" merely outlines the project for a philosophy to come, but remains poised there, unable to make the leap into the new horizon of constitutive time. However, the text does offer an important clue as to the direction in which Negri's philosophy of time would later move. It is here, for the first time, that Negri evokes the Lucretian philosophy of the *clinamen* as a creative counter-point to the Aristotelian-Hegelian tradition of time as measure (2003a, 45). And it is this return to Lucretius that enables Negri, in his later work, to articulate a constitutive philosophy of time—a philosophy that not only affirms the power of absolute, non-mediated resistance but also claims to think through the constitutive, world-creating powers of this same resistance. At this point, the philosophical and political inflections of Negri's later work merge together again. The refusal of work gives way to the multitude's strategy of self-valorization, the collective creation of an immeasurable future world. The practical strategy of creating the common comes together with a theory of the multitude as common name and creative resistance.

It is in *Kairòs, Alma Venus, Multitudo*, a text written in the late nineties, that Negri offers the latest and, to date, most interesting development in his philosophy of time. In his introduction to the English translation, Negri offers the following contextualization of this text:

> . . . a large number of the reflections that I have developed in '*Alma Venus*' and in '*Kairòs*' are directly linked to the theoretical outline and the practical experience of living 'with' Marx and 'beyond' Marx (that is, in the area of historical materialism) that has always guided my philosophical and political thinking, for better and for worse. In particular, the reflections here on temporality and its ontological import, are linked to the work published in 1981 on the constitution of time . . . . (2003c, 143)

Negri thus establishes *Kairòs, Alma Venus, Multitudo* as the continuation and response to the productive aporias of his 1981 text "The Constitution of Time." And it is surely not a coincidence that the introduction to this text also acknowledges the inspiration provided by the philosophy of the ancient materialist Lucretius. "Lucretius," as Negri bluntly writes, "was my book during that period" (2003c, 139). At his own prompting then, albeit with a delay of two decades, Negri returns to the philosophy of the *clinamen* as a way of moving both with and beyond the tradition of historical materialism. It is Lucretius who first breaks with the determinism of the ancient materialist tradition (extending from Democritus to Epicurus) by proposing, however surreptitiously, the concept of the *clinamen* as an irreducible swerve interrupting the monotonous, vertical fall of atoms in empty space:

> In classical materialism the theme of innovation is both central and unresolved. From Democritus to Epicurus the atomistic construction of the world is immersed in eternity. As for freedom, it is the conduct of life played out in terms of the metaphor of the cosmos. In this flattening-out, freedom is extinguished and innovation is incomprehensible. Only in Lucretius does freedom strive to break this meaningless metaphor so as to act autonomously in the physical ensemble of atomism, that is to say, to inflict a tear in the eternal. Nevertheless Lucretius poses his *clinamen* only furtively, in a whisper, as though he were trying to annul the violence of the tear that comes from the imperceptible deviation (*clinamen*) that allows the world to be renewed; that permits one to grasp the singular and, along with it, the meaning of freedom. The shower of atoms is traversed by a minuscule—but nonetheless—immense glow: poetry is exalted by it, philosophy humiliated, the problem posed. Modernity will inherit this problem unresolved. (2003d, 186)

It is here that Negri begins to formulate a possible solution to the temporal aporia he has grappled with since *Marx Beyond Marx*: to be effective at all in the conditions of the present, Negri seems to conclude, Spinoza's theory of self-constitutive power needs to be resuscitated by Lucretius' philosophy of time. The imperative that Negri discovers here is that of thinking through Spinoza's philosophy of constitutive power (the potentia of the multitude as *causa sui*, constitutive of its own world) *along with* Lucretius's philosophy of time as *clinamen*.[5] *Kairòs, Alma Venus, Multitudo* thus defines the constitutive power of the multitude as a power to produce a future without common measure in the present, a future that can only be conceived *ex nihilo*, as radical deviation, a future that takes ontological

---

[5] The philosophy of Spinoza, on the other hand, has provided Negri with the principle source of his reflections on the notion of self-constitutive power since the early eighties (power being understood here as *potentia*, power of composition and common notion, rather than *potestas* or power over). But Spinoza, Negri argues here, ultimately fails to deliver a fully catastrophic, radically irreversible theory of time. The *clinamen* escapes him (2003d, 187).

precedence over the repetitions of the present (the future as *clinamen* or *kairòs*). The catastrophic event of resistance here becomes something other than a mere act of absolute antagonism or refusal and affirms itself as the source of another kind of constitution—the self-constitution of the multitude that Negri will theorize in his late work. And it is this constitutive theory of time as catastrophe event that Negri ultimately counterposes to the Hegelian philosophy of time as measure and negation:

> What is the indefinite? It is the idea of a measurable infinite. But the eternal, eternal matter, is not measurable, it is immeasurable. It is so because the eternal always confronts the *to-come*, and this relationship is itself immeasurable. Therefore the indefinite is an illusion. But it becomes an effective illusion when it introduces transcendence as the measure of immanence. In this case, illusion becomes transcendental mystification: it is the continuously repeated attempt to subordinate the present to the infinite, and so to subordinate the present to a measure. (2003d, 182)

Marx Beyond Marx—Lucretius Before Marx

At this point in Negri's philosophical trajectory, we might well ask whether he has not in fact left Marx entirely behind. After all, the most interesting developments in Negri's later work seem to derive as much from Spinozian ontology and the Lucretian philosophy of time (via that other reader of the materialist tradition, Gilles Deleuze) as from his early critique of Marx. Even in his latest work however, Negri never declares himself "over" Marx. As a passage from *Multitude* points out, we are always discovering that Marx was already there before us, just when we feel we've finally gotten beyond him (2004, 149). It is surely significant then that the early Marx was fascinated with the ancient materialist tradition and wrote his doctoral dissertation on the question of "The Difference between the Democritean and Epicurean Philosophy of Nature" (1975a [1838–1839]). Indeed at least one reader of the early philosophical work of Marx, Francine Markovits, has forcefully argued that Marx was here engaged in a quite self-conscious attempt to elaborate a counter-philosophy of time, where the constitutive powers of the *clinamen* would be mobilized against the Hegelian dialectic:

> In fact, the plurality of texts that Marx copies and comments upon in this period, along with his choice of authors, lead us to believe that his purpose was not so much to confirm the pertinence of Hegelianism as to begin the task he had announced in a letter of the 10th of November 1837: that of writing a new metaphysical system and even a new logic. (Markovits 1974, 12; my translation)

Certainly, Marx's early dissertation and notebooks on Lucretius contain his
most eloquent philosophical riposte to the Hegelian philosophy of time. In
the Hegelian tradition, time is always mediated by the quantitative measures of space and can therefore only account for the linear fall of atoms in
space—it is for this reason, contends Marx, that Hegel is unable to respond
to the shock of the *clinamen* and ultimately refigures it in terms of the
dialectic of space and time (Marx 1975a, 48). In Lucretian philosophy,
Marx discovers something that resists the very terms of Hegel's analysis—
the *clinamen* introduces a swerve in the fall of atoms, a movement of
absolute deviation through which time is able to diverge from the mediations of space. The *clinamen* thus allows Marx to refigure resistance in
nondialectical terms, as the affirmation of an absolute and prior difference—a difference without possible mediation:

> Lucretius . . . is correct when he maintains that the declination (*clinamen*)
> breaks the *fati foedera* [bonds of faith], and, since he applies this immedi-
> ately to consciousness, it can be said of the atom that the declination is that
> something in its breast that can fight back and resist. (Marx 1975a, 49)

Marx however (like Negri) is not satisfied with theorizing this purely disruptive notion of resistance. Once we have discovered the *clinamen* as difference without possible mediation, he insists, we need to get *beyond* here
to a positive philosophy of time and constitution—in other words, we need
to discover how the *clinamen* itself can become constitutive of its own
world (Marx 1975a, 51). Here again, Marx finds a precursor in
Lucretius—for in Lucretian philosophy the movement of the *clinamen*
functions precisely as the principle of shock which initiates all being-
together and all possible compositions of bodies, thereby giving rise to the
myriad forms of nature. With Lucretius, Marx discovers the elements of an
ontology in which time (as *clinamen*, *kairòs* or absolute resistance)
becomes constitutive of its own world:

> Lucretius is therefore correct when he says that, if the atoms were not to
> decline, neither their repulsion nor their meeting would have taken place,
> and the world would never have been created. For atoms are *their own sole
> object and can only be related to themselves*, hence speaking in spatial terms,
> they can only *meet*, because every relative existence of these atoms by which
> they would be related to other beings is negated. And this relative existence
> is, as we have seen, their original motion, that of falling in a straight line.
> Hence they meet only by virtue of their declination from the straight line.
> It has nothing to do with merely material fragmentation. (Marx 1975a,
> 51–52)

> *Time*, excluded from the world of essence, becomes for him *the absolute
> form of appearance*. That is to say, time is determined as accidens of the

accidens. The accidens is the change of substance in general. The accidens of the accidens is the change as reflecting in itself, the change as change. This pure form of the world of appearance is time. (Marx 1975a, 63)

Moving beyond Marx, Negri returns to the earliest Marx, or rather to Lucretius. But again, such a return amounts to much more than an exercise in philological rigor. Ultimately, Negri's project can only be fully understood as a philosophical *recreation* of Marx's world, a project that fittingly takes its inspiration from Marx's reflections on the Lucretian cosmos and its powers of self-constitution.[6]

References

Althusser, Louis 1979 [1967]. *For Marx*, trans. Ben Brewster, London: Verso.

———. 2006. *Philosophy of the Encounter: Later Writings, 1978–1987*, edited by Francois Matheron and Oliver Corbet, translated by G.M. Goshgarian, London and New York: Verso.

Badiou, Alain 2003. *Saint Paul: The Foundations of Universalism*, translated by Ray Brassier, Stanford, California: Stanford University Press.

Cooper, Melinda 2006. "Preempting Emergence: The Biological Turn of the War on Terror," *Theory, Culture & Society*, Vol. 23, No. 4, 113–35.

Goshgarian, G.M. 2006. "Translator's Introduction," in Althusser (2006), xiii–xlviii.

Luxemburg, Rosa 2003. *The Accumulation of Capital*, translated by Agnes Schwarzschild, introduction by Tadeusz Kowalik, New York: Routledge.

Markovits, Francine 1974. *Marx dans le jardin d'Epicure*, Paris: Editions de Minuit.

Marx, Karl 1975a. "Difference between the Democritean and Epicurean Philosophy of Nature," trans. Dirk J. and Sally R. Struik. *Karl Marx Frederick Engels: Collected Works. Vol. 1*, London: Lawrence and Wishart, 25–106.

———. 1975b. "Notebooks on Epicurean Philosophy," trans. Richard Dixon.

---

[6] Ironically Negri's turn to Lucretius finds an echo in the later work of Althusser, who in the form of sustained auto-critique, attempts to escape the Hegelian legacy in Marx's philosophy by recovering an Epicurean counter-tradition of "aleatory materialism." Where in his earlier work, Althusser had recuperated the dialectical method of historical materialism while denying Marx's Hegelianism, he subsequently reversed this position and turned the critique against himself. In a series of fragments composed in 1982–83, Althusser (2006) articulates a position which comes remarkably close to that of Negri, in its insistence that the materialist, Lucretian Marx, must be rescued from the historical determinism of the idealist, Hegelian Marx. The differences between Negri's and Althusser's "aleatory materialism" remain considerable however. At a philosophical level, Althusser's is a "punctual" theory of the irruption of contingency in history. Negri, closer to Deleuze, elaborates an ontology of the clinamen, in which turbulence functions as the generative principle of entire worlds. More generally, the "aleatory materialisms" of Negri and Althusser are informed by very different

Karl Marx and Frederick Engels: Collected Works. Vol. 1, London: Lawrence and Wishart, 403–509.

———. 1977. *Capital: A Critique of Political Economy*, trans. Samuel Moore and Edward Aveling, ed. Frederick Engels. Vol. 1. Moscow: Progress Publishers.

———. *Grundrisse: Foundations of the Critique of Political Economy (Rough Draft)*, trans. Martin Nicolaus, Harmondsworth, Middlesex: Penguin Books and New Left Review.

Moulier, Yann 1996. "Présentation," in Negri (1996), unpaginated.

Negri, Antonio 1984. *Marx Beyond Marx: Lessons on the Grundrisse*, translated by Harry Cleaver, Michael Ryan and Maurizio Viano, ed. Jim Fleming, Massachusetts: Bergin and Garvey Publishers.

———. 1994 [1967]. "Keynes and the Capitalist Theory of the State," in *Labor of Dionysus: A Critique of the State-Form*, Minneapolis-London: University of Minnesota Press, 22–51.

———. 1996 [1979]. *Marx au-delà de Marx: Cahiers de travail sur les "Grundrisse,"* trans. Roxanne Silberman, 2nd ed. Paris: Harmattan.

———. 1996. "Introduction," In Negri (1996), unpaginated.

———. 1997. "Vingt Thèses Sur Marx." *Futur Antérieur (Marx après les Marxismes, Vol. II: Marx au Futur)*, 333–72.

———. 2003. *Time for Revolution*, New York and London: Continuum.

———. 2003a. "The Constitution of Time," in Negri (2003), 19–126.

———. 2003b. "Afterword to 'the Constitution of Time'," in Negri (2003), 127–35.

---

political investments and understandings of praxis. As G.M. Goshgarian points out in his perceptive introduction to Althusser's late work, the philosophy of the contingent event allowed Althusser to affirm an untimely commitment to the "dictatorship of the proletariat" at a time when the PCF had decided to formally renounce the idea. As a political gesture, Althusser's turn to Lucretius was highly ambivalent—both the sign of his "hyper-Leninism" and what was perceived to be his anti-party "anarchism" (Goshgarian 2006, xvi–xxxvii). The influence of the later Althusser can be discerned in neo-Leninist philosophies of revolution such as those of Badiou, for whom the 'universal proletariat' becomes the subject of universalism *tout court*. For Badiou, the "event" is the contingent encounter which, for all its indeterminacy, will nevertheless give rise to a universalism of laboring "sons," "coworkers in the enterprise of Truth" (Badiou 2003, 60). Negri too is a neo-Leninist of sorts, although he wants to take "Lenin beyond Lenin," that is to take Lenin beyond the limits of industrial labor and its historical class structures, in order to imagine a "subject" adequate to contemporary conditions of production and resistance (Negri 2007). The multitude, with its transversal, minoritarian affiliations and precarious relation to traditional class categories, would thereby replace the 'universal worker son' as the revolutionary subject of the contemporary era. Whether this move avoids any of the authoritarian or absolutist dangers of Leninist revolution remains debatable. In particular, one might want to ask whether the multitude is immune from the claim to genealogical purity. It is remarkable, for example, that some of the most potent religious movements of the contemporary world take on the organizational form of the multitude rather than the people. This has not prevented them from seeking to impose absolute political truths. In this respect, Negri's philosophy of the event is undoubtedly more attuned to the contemporary formations of the political but will not have escaped the larger problematic of genealogical purity, which can perhaps reproduce itself quite happily beyond the determinations of either the people or the state.

———. 2003c. "Introduction to 'Kairòs, Alma Venus, Multitudo'," in Negri (2003), 139–46.

———. 2003d. "Kairòs, Alma Venus, Multitudo," in Negri (2003), 148–261.

———. 2007. "What to Do Today with *What Is to Be Done?*, or Rather: The Body of the General Intellect," in *Lenin Reloaded: Toward a Politics of Truth*, ed. Sebastian Budgen, Stathis Kouvelakis, and Slavoj Žižek , Durham and London: Duke University Press.

Negri, Antonio, and Michael Hardt 2000. *Empire*, Cambridge, MA and London, England: Harvard University Press.

———. 2004. *Multitude: War and Democracy in the Age of Empire*, New York: The Penguin Press.

6

Empire, Imperialism, and Value: Negri on Capitalist Sovereignty

MAX ROSENKRANTZ

Introduction

Hardt and Negri's *Empire* is the latest in a long line of works in the Marxist tradition that take seriously Marx's contention that capitalist society is "no crystal, but an organism capable of change and constantly engaged in a process of change" (Marx 1867, 93). Such works, by their nature, attempt to do two things. The first is to offer an account of capitalism in its totality. In other words, they attempt to do for their epoch what Marx did for his. Of course, there would be little point in the enterprise if one simply wanted to "re-do Marx." Thus, the first task is inevitably accompanied by a second: to indicate the degree to which Marx's theory requires revision to take account of whatever is new about these new times. For over 35 years Negri (individually and in collaboration with Michael Hardt) has devoted himself assiduously to that task.[1] His is the only body of work to appear in that time that is comparable in stature to such paradigmatic works in this genre as Bernstein's *The Preconditions of Socialism*, Lenin's *Imperialism: The Highest Stage of Capitalism*, Lukacs's *History and Class Consciousness*, and Adorno and Horkheimer's *Dialectic of Enlightenment*.

Empire is a complicated work, operating at many levels. Most salient is its discussion of the eponymous institution of global capitalist sovereignty. Hardt and Negri root the emergence of Empire in changes in production and the market. Empire, they argue is the type of capitalist sovereignty appropriate to the era of "biopolitical production" (roughly, the production of life rather than mere commodities) and the world market. For good

---

[1] In what follows I'll use 'Hardt and Negri' in referring to the works they have written together and 'Negri' to refer to the works he has written individually as well as to his works generally, including those written with Hardt.

measure, *Empire* contains a historical narrative detailing the gestation and creation of its subject.[2]

The levels are inseparable. My entry point will be their analysis of the political institution they designate 'Empire'. I am going to mix defense with criticism. In the first part of the paper I defend Hardt and Negri's analysis of the *form* of capitalist sovereignty. In particular, I endorse their view that Empire has replaced the nation-state. To put the same point in a more pointed fashion, they are correct in holding that capitalist sovereignty is now "one," not "many." In the second part I criticize their characterization of the *content* of capitalist sovereignty. Hardt and Negri's great failing here is that they offer no characterization of its content at all. While they effectively articulate the ensemble of organizations and institutions that constitute Empire, they have nothing helpful to say about the end towards which Empire exerts its power. In this there is an interesting disanalogy with their analysis of the form of Empire. The form of sovereignty changes from many nation-states to one Empire. The content of sovereignty changes from the imposition of work to . . . Nothing!

My defense of *Empire's* theory of the form of capitalist sovereignty proceeds by way of reflection on its rejection of the theory of imperialism, a theory which puts the nation-state at the center of analysis. My critique of *Empire's* theory of the content of capitalist sovereignty proceeds by way of an interrogation of Negri's long standing claim that Marx's "law of value" is in crisis. I'll argue that Negri's abandonment of Marx's value theory is unwarranted and has objectionable political consequences.

1. Empire or Imperialism

The concept of "Empire" is designed—at least in part—to take account of the neo-liberal restructuring that has characterized capitalist development since the mid to late 1970's. Many, especially since the collapse of the U.S.S.R., have seen the march of neo-liberalism as indicative of a triumph of corporations over the state; or, more generally, of the economic over the political. Hardt and Negri disagree. To their eyes the state and capital are no more opposed now than they ever were, and it is simply a mistake to think that the importance of the state to the continued reproduction and

---

[2] This level has attracted the least amount of critical attention, which is unfortunate since Hardt and Negri's claims about, for instance, the relative unimportance of the cold war and the imperial—not imperialist—heritage of the United States are among the most fascinating in the book. The latter claim is dismissed by Panitch and Gindin in their critical review of *Empire* (Panitch and Gindin 2002, 26–29), but their critique is far too slight to be decisive.

expansion of capital has diminished (*Empire*, 300–309). As Hardt and Negri put it,

> Although transnational corporations and global networks of production and circulation have undermined the powers of the nation-state, state functions and constitutional elements have effectively been displaced to other levels and domains. (*Empire*, 307)

Empire is an attempt to describe the results of this process of the displacement of the nation-state by Empire:[3]

> Even the most dominant nation-states should no longer be thought of as supreme and sovereign authorities, either outside or even within their own borders. *The decline in sovereignty of nation states, however does not mean that sovereignty as such has declined.* . . . Our basic hypothesis is that sovereignty has taken a new form, composed of a series of national and supranational organisms united under a single logic of rule. This new global form of sovereignty is what we call Empire. (*Empire*, xi–xii; emphasis in the original)

Switching from worldly developments to textual ones, we can say that the process Hardt and Negri describe is the displacement of *Imperialism: The Highest Stage of Capitalism* by *Empire*.[4] It is therefore no surprise that some of the most vocal criticisms of *Empire* have come from the defenders of *Imperialism*.[5] In the rest of this section I describe the significant differences between the theoretical frameworks that inform the two works. Having done so, I shall argue that *Empire's* articulation of global sovereignty is more cogent than the sundry variations on Lenin that are still so prevalent on the left today.

Imperialism, like *Empire*, was written against the backdrop of war.[6] Lenin's goal in writing *Imperialism* was to show that WW I was a struggle between imperialist states "for the division of the world, for the partition and repartition of colonies, 'spheres of influence' of finance capital etc."

---

[3] In his contribution to this volume, David Sherman rightly points out that Empire is not an "*über* nation-state but . . . the opposite of one" (Sherman 2010, 75). Whether or not the Bush administration's zeal for unilateral action is, in effect, to position the United States as an "*über* nation-state" is an issue which I touch on below.

[4] That is how Hardt and Negri see their work, "This is the alternative implicit in Lenin's work: either world communist revolution or Empire" (*Empire*, 234; italics omitted).

[5] For some representative examples see Foster (2002) and Petras (2002).

[6] Hardt and Negri explain, "This book was begun well after the end of the Persian Gulf War and completed well before the beginning of the war in Kosovo. The reader should thus situate the argument at the midpoint between those two signal events in the construction of Empire" (*Empire*, xvii). *Multitude* is even more centrally concerned with war, as its subtitle makes clear.

(Lenin 1916, 9). According to Lenin, each state enters into this struggle in support of its own national capital. Thus, the German State acts on behalf of German Capital; the U.S. State acts on behalf of U.S. Capital, and so on. The central actors in Lenin's drama are nation-states. He is therefore consistent when he claims, in effect, that the first world exploits the third (Lenin 1916, 10–11, 61, 107).

The signal innovation of Lenin's theory vis à vis Marx's is its abandonment of the concept of class. Lenin replaces class struggle, which was central for Marx, with the struggle between imperialist powers. He replaces capitalist exploitation of the working class—the techniques of which are the subject matter of *Capital*—with the exploitation of the third world by the first. Whereas for Marx the subjects involved in the relations of struggle and exploitation are the same; for Lenin they are not. What is most important is that the working-class is not a term in either relation. To the extent that it appears at all it is as the "labor aristocracy" which has been co-opted by sharing in the "super profits" generated in the third world (Lenin 1916, 13–14, 107–108).[7]

The preceding is obviously a highly compressed account of Lenin's theory. For example, I have omitted any mention of "monopoly capital" and "finance capital," concepts which are central to Lenin's analysis. I have done so because my point here is not to revisit the well-worn subject of the accuracy of Lenin's account as a picture of his times.[8] Rather, I am concerned solely to clarify the issues involved in assessing Hardt and Negri's claim that the era of imperialism is over and the era of Empire is upon us, and those concepts simply have no relevance here.[9] A reading of the literature on this topic indicates that clarification of this sort is in order. Its lack has led too many to assume without argument—or at least without anything approaching an adequate argument—that the United States is now, "Imperialist Power #1."

Two passages from *Empire* will help clarify and focus the issues:

> Many locate the ultimate authority that rules over the processes of globalization and the new world order in the United States. Proponents praise the United States as the world leader and sole superpower, and detractors denounce it as an imperialist oppressor. . . . Our basic hypothesis, that a

---

[7] In light of the absence of any class analysis in Lenin's theory, it is surprising that Hardt and Negri treat it with such deference. For example, on the basis of a single quotation from Cecil Rhodes (Lenin 1916, 79) they credit Lenin with the view that imperialism was a capitalist response to class struggle at home (*Empire*, 232). Yet they surely recognize that the view expressed in the quotation plays no role in Lenin's analysis. My hunch is that the praise of Lenin is designed to get *Empire* a sympathetic hearing from quarters that would ordinarily be hostile. If so, the strategy does not seem to be working.

[8] Those interested can consult Warren (1980, 50–70) and the literature cited there.

[9] One still sees the terms bandied about but they have become empty slogans.

new imperial form of sovereignty has emerged, contradicts both these views. The United States does not, and indeed no nation-state can today, form the center of an imperialist project. (*Empire*, xiii–xiv)

Imperial monarchy is not located in a separate isolable place—and our postmodern Empire has no Rome. (*Empire*, 317)

To those who remain committed to a Leninist framework these remarks seem not merely false, but obviously false. Yet they are obviously false only if one reads Hardt and Negri as denying that the U.S. government plays a singular role in the structure of global sovereignty or if one takes it as axiomatic that when nation-states act on the global political stage they do so solely to benefit their domestic capital at the expense of foreign capital.[10]

The United States—here understood as a state as well as specific administrations—occupies a unique position in *Empire*.[11] To put it somewhat inaccurately, Hardt and Negri argue that it is the executive branch of Empire.[12] It discharged this role most clearly in Gulf War I:

The importance of the Gulf War derives . . . from the fact that it presented the United States as the only power able to manage international justice, not as a function of its own national motives but in the name of global right. Certainly, many powers have falsely claimed to act in the universal interest before, but this new role of the United States is different. Perhaps it is most accurate to say that this claim to universality may also be false, but it is false in a new way. The U.S. world police acts not in imperialist interest but in imperial interest. (*Empire*, 180)

Since not even the most cursory reader could have overlooked the centrality of the U.S. to Hardt and Negri's conception of imperial rule, it is best to see the disagreement as centering around the second point mentioned above: the belief that state action must always be analyzed as in the interests of domestic capital at the expense of foreign capital. It is with respect to this claim that the argumentative gap I identified above is most obvious.

---

[10] For an excellent analysis that shows that the continued existence and efficacy of nation-states is compatible with the existence of Empire see Green (2002, 40–51; cf. *Empire*, xii).

[11] Again Green (2002, 40–51) is very helpful on this point.

[12] It is inaccurate because though Hardt and Negri find the Polybian idea of a mixed constitution useful for articulating the structure of imperial sovereignty, they deny that Empire has either a tripartite (Monarch, Aristocracy, People) or trifunctional (Executive, Judiciary, Legislature) structure (*Empire*, 314–19). In this instance the inaccuracy does not distort

Talk of states acting in the interests of domestic capital has meaning
only if there is a *clash* of interests.[13] In the absence of this, it is more accurate to describe states as acting in the interests of capital *simpliciter*. Yet
inspection of numerous works which take up the Leninist cudgels, either
implicitly or explicitly, reveals something quite interesting: an absence of
any interimperial tensions.[14] To develop this point I shall examine two significant, recent attempts to develop a Leninist analysis of the "new world
order": (1) Peter Gowan's interpretation of "globalization" as a series of
attempts on the part of U.S. administrations since Nixon to insure the continued dominance of U.S. capitalism[15] (Gowan 1999); and (2) David
Harvey's recent attempt to argue that we are witnessing a "new imperialism" (Harvey 2003).[16]

Gowan argues that the movements toward globalization he charts were
initiated by the Nixon administration on behalf of U.S. capital against the
growing threat posed by European and Japanese capital. Yet, he is forced
to concede that Europe is now a willing participant in Nixon's project
(Gowan 1999, 126). Japan, he argues, remains as a legitimate, albeit weak,
opponent of U.S. dominance, but the only evidence produced in favor of
this is Japanese support for a different solution to the Asian financial crisis
of 1997–1998 than the one supported by the United States (Gowan 1999,
106–107). Such cracks and fissures within the global ruling class are no
more incompatible with the existence of a *global* ruling class than are the
disagreements between the more and less sane elements of the Bush
administration incompatible with the existence of that administration.
Gowan has, I believe, mistaken imperial pluralism for imperialist rivalry. He
has mistaken U.S. "imperial interest" for U.S. "imperialist interest."

It is worth commenting here on an episode from the early days of the
United States' bid for dominance. Gowan notes that—contrary to popular
belief—the oil price increase of 1973 was not undertaken as an attack on
the U.S., but with its encouragement. He also notes that it was widely
believed, including by some in the Nixon Administration, that the U.S.
pursued this policy in order to strike a blow against European and Japanese

---

[13] The first Gulf War struck a significant blow against Leninist theories, but by itself it is
not decisive. The Leninist can always argue that it represented an anomalous confluence of
interests between, say, U.S., European and Japanese capital.

[14] Green (2002, 52–63) develops a similar line of argument.

[15] Gowan's work appeared before *Empire*, so obviously it is not an attempt to develop a
Leninist alternative to it. Nevertheless, that fact of publication history does not prevent it
from being the most careful and detailed alternative to *Empire* of which I am aware. That is
why I consider it here. Gowan is also used as a foil by Green (2002, 50–51, 54–55). Green's
analysis is discussed and seemingly endorsed by Bromley (2002, 33–34).

[16] Almost any relatively recent issue of *Monthly Review* and *New Left Review* will provide
further examples of the type of view I am criticizing here.

capital.[17] Whatever the evidence is concerning the intentions of the Nixon administration in pursuing a policy of high oil prices, one cannot identify the significance of that policy with those intentions for the simple reason that the policy failed to realize them (Oppenheim 76–77, 51–57). What it did achieve, however, was a reduction in the wages of workers across the developed world (via inflation) while increasing profits for capital of all nationalities (Caffentzis 1980). In addition, higher oil prices allowed the O.P.E.C. countries the resources to deal with domestic opposition, both through concessions and repression (Moran 1976–77).[18]

David Harvey argues that the second Bush administration's penchant for unilateral action is an attempt to perpetuate U.S. political and economic supremacy—which is threatened by the U.S.'s eroding dominance in the spheres of production and finance—through the use of military force. Seizing control of Iraq is part of a larger attempt to control the Middle East's oil and thus thwart economic, and possibly military, competition from Europe and Asia[19] (Harvey 2003, 24–25, 74–75, 128).

There can be no doubt that the invasion and occupation of Iraq is a war for oil.[20] However, by itself that fact provides no support for Harvey's thesis that the U.S. is pursuing a neoimperialist project. That thesis requires two additional claims: (1) there are any serious tensions between Europe, Japan and the United States; and (2) control of Iraq's oil would or could be used to shore up U.S. economic power at the expense of other nations. As concerns (1), it is of course true that Germany and France were obstreperous in their opposition to the U.S. invasion of Iraq. But in the end Germany did not deny the U.S. military access to bases on its soil and French military forces were soon acting in concert with U.S. forces to depose Aristide. Further, the intelligence services of both countries continued to cooperate with their U.S. counterparts. Japan supported the invasion, as did various other minor European powers. As concerns (2), it is sufficient to point out that

---

[17] Gowan relies here on the evidence presented in Oppenheim (1976–77).

[18] I owe my awareness of the articles by Oppenheim and Moran and their significance to Harry Cleaver.

[19] Harvey's argument is much more baroque than my presentation of it suggests. However, since the complications are largely a matter of the development of a theoretical apparatus that does no work in explaining or supporting the analysis of Bush Administration policy, they can be ignored.

[20] That invasion and the unilateralist bent it manifests pose a problem for *Empire*, but it is not the sort that suggests a vindication of Lenin. The Bush administration is clearly attempting to centralize global decision-making. This runs counter to the thesis of *Empire* that power is—and must be—decentered. That view is put forward in full awareness of the possibilities of unilateral action by the U.S. (*Empire*, 37). *Empire* stands or falls with the Bush administration's ability to realize its ambitions, a prospect that appears increasingly unlikely (Hardt and Negri 2004, 61).

Harvey offers no evidence or explanation as to how the U.S. could or would use its control over Iraqi oil to attack European or Japanese economic power.

The absence of significant interimperial tensions is strong evidence against the continuing relevance of the Leninist framework.[21] Lenin's analysis cannot be reduced to a description of such tensions, however. Recall that Lenin identifies the subject of interimperialist rivalry as the third world. One might argue that the lack of interimperialist tension simply bespeaks the weakness of the other powers vis à vis the United States. All are united in a global imperial structure in which the first world exploits the third. The United States is the dominant partner in an enterprise in which all the developed nations participate. Of course, strictly speaking this is not Lenin's vision of imperialism, in which interimperialist conflict is a necessity, but Kautsky's, in which peaceful imperial coexistence and cooperation is a possibility.[22] However, in the context of my critique—which is to argue against analyses that make the nation-state rather than class central—this difference makes no difference.

The claim that the first world exploits the third has much greater *prima facie* empirical plausibility than the claim that U.S. policy is to be explained in terms of the twists and turns of interimperialist rivalries. Despite Hardt and Negri's claims about the smooth space of *Empire* and the commingling of first and third worlds (*Empire*, 332–36), one cannot deny that material prosperity is distributed unevenly across the globe. Moreover, the period Hardt and Negri celebrate as one of vibrant capitalist development has seen the intensification of these territorial striations (Arrighi 2003, 32–34, 39–40). However, it does not follow from this that they are wrong to posit a single global form of sovereignty.

Theorists of imperialism move too quickly from the obvious facts described above to the conclusion that there are two worlds, and thus multiple sovereignties. This arises from a conflation of two claims. The first,

---

[21] This criticism also applies to Robert Went's otherwise exemplary "Globalization in the Perspective of Imperialism" (Went 2002/2003, 473–97). Went assembles impressive evidence showing that since the early 80s the world has become increasingly integrated politically and economically and that consequently the ability of nation-states to act autonomously in those areas has declined. He does not conclude that these developments have rendered Lenin's concept of imperialism obsolete (see 489); rather he argues that "rivalries [between imperialist powers] are fought out economically rather than militarily" (490). The argument fails for want of an analysis of these rivalries and a demonstration of their significance.

[22] For examples of views according to which this possibility has been realized, see Anderson (2002) and Bromley (2003). Barkawi and Laffey in their generally sympathetic discussion of *Empire* are a bit more hedged, but the logic of their argument points in the direction of a defense of a Kautskian position (Barkawi and Laffey 2002, 123–26). That is strange since it reintroduces the state-centric perspective they praise Hardt and Negri for rejecting (see 110, 118–19).

which I have already conceded, is that the world is not the smooth space Hardt and Negri contend it is. The second is that the wealthier territories (the first world) exploit the poorer ones (the third world) and hence that sovereignty is multiple, not singular. The problem is that the second is neither equivalent to the first, nor a straightforward entailment of it. A great deal of theoretical and empirical work is needed to bridge the gap between the two. Unfortunately that task is rarely acknowledged, still less tackled.

The first world-third world division is better understood as a global wage hierarchy. The workers in territories at the top no more exploit those at the bottom than do, say, longshoremen exploit migrant farm workers. Further support for this way of thinking is to be found in the fact that the U.S. government is as busy imposing neoliberal restructuring at home as it is abroad, with the same dire consequences (falling wages, longer hours, etc.) Neoliberal restructuring is not a quintessentially imperialist maneuver, but a plan of a global capital.[23] The U.S. merely spearheads implementation.

I do not want to suggest that the division between first and third world—or as I would prefer to describe it, the existence of a global wage hierarchy—poses no problems for Hardt and Negri. However it impugns their concept of "the Multitude" not of "Empire." Hardt and Negri's depiction of the multitude as being as "smooth" as the Empire it opposes has struck almost every reader as at best underdeveloped and at worst fanciful.[24] The concept runs roughshod over the economic, national, and racial divisions which run through the global working class. The phenomena which seem so obviously to pose problems for Hardt and Negri are indeed real and do pose genuine problems for them, but they must be located properly. As I have tried to show, that location is "the Multitude" not "Empire," which remains a valid concept for understanding the *form* of capitalist sovereignty. I turn now to the question of *content*.

2. Empire and the Law of Value

In this section I want to interrogate Negri's long-standing contention that the "law of value" is in crisis. Though the claim is found in *Empire*, it is not brought to the fore. Nevertheless, the thought expressed by it is fundamental to the theory elaborated there. I'll begin with a few remarks designed to clarify some of the issues involved in Negri's declaration. I'll then present, without argument, an interpretation of Marx's concept of

---

[23] See Went (2002/2003, 484–88).

[24] Hardt and Negri's recognition of this inadequacy provided the motivation for *Multitude*. My judgment, which I cannot argue for here, is that the inadequacy remains.

value.[25] This approach is justified by the use to which I want to put the interpretation: It will serve as a foil to be used in interpreting the claim that the law of value is in crisis. I'll then turn from interpretation to critique, arguing that Negri's arguments that the law of value is in crisis are neither cogent nor politically salutary. I conclude with a brief, speculative diagnosis of Negri's error.

First a point of terminology. Marx coins the phrase 'Law of value' in Volume III of *Capital*, where it is introduced in connection with certain complications arising in the attempt to analyze the formation of an average rate of profit across industries. However, it is not a phrase that he puts to heavy use, and I think that Negri's understanding of it can be grasped independently of its textual origin. In proclaiming the law of value to be in crisis, Negri is best thought of as rejecting Marx's general notion of value (or "value theory"—I'll use the two phrases interchangeably), at least in its classical formulation.

In the first Chapter of *Capital*, Marx explicates his theory of value under three headings: substance, measure, and form. The substance of value is labor. Its measure, time. Its form, money. For my present purposes the form of value is of no concern. Marx's theory of value has—as he points out—a dual character: viz. a qualitative and a quantitative dimension. Labor also has a dual character: it is concrete and abstract.[26] Concrete labor is labor devoted to the production of a specific use value: a coat, a barrel of oil, a computer program, and so on. Abstract labor is labor with all of these determinations stripped away. Marx finds it necessary to make this distinction because of his insight that under capitalism there is a tendency to reduce all life to work; not work of any particular sort ("concrete labor"), but *work* ("abstract labor"). Put somewhat differently, the content of capitalist domination is work. Marx's concept of domination is thus qualitative (domination through work), but the qualitative dimension cannot be made sense of apart from a quantitative dimension. Capitalism is a system of domination not because its aim is to make everyone work, but because its aim is to make everyone work *endlessly.*[27]

Capitalism is not merely a work based social order, but an *antagonistic* one. Capital and the working class stand in an antagonistic relationship. Marx introduces the distinction between necessary labor and surplus labor

---

[25] The interpretation is based on Cleaver 2001. A more thorough argument for it can be found there.

[26] Marx claims originality in making this distinction (1867, 132).

[27] Marx acknowledges that concrete labor is a "condition of all human existence which is independent of all forms of society" (1867, 133). The implication is that abstract labor is a condition of life under capitalism only. See (Marx 1867, 153–54).

to analyze this antagonism more precisely. Necessary labor time is the amount of abstract labor required for the worker to reproduce herself (i.e., to meet her needs).[28] Surplus labor time is the amount of time the worker works beyond that (Marx 1867, 325).[29] The ratio of surplus to necessary labor is "an exact expression of the degree of exploitation of labor power by capital" (Marx 1867, 326). The working class struggles against exploitation, that is, against the imposition of ever more surplus labor. Capital struggles for precisely the opposite. The point that needs stressing here is that Marx's understanding of capitalist domination and the struggle against it depend upon the quantitative aspect of the theory of value. Without that dimension, one is hard pressed to give any content to talk of "domination," "struggle," and "exploitation."

In light of the preceding discussion, it is surprising that for over 30 years Negri has combined a commitment to the signal importance of class struggle with a pronounced skepticism with regard to Marx's value theory. Negri announces his skepticism as early as "Marx on Cycle and Crisis" (1968, 72) and "Crisis of the Planner State" (1971, 101; 121–22). He reiterates it in works up to and including *Multitude* (150–51).[30] His reasons for skepticism are best understood by unpacking his slogan "Exploitation consists in command" (1982, 225; see also 1978, 172). In effect, Negri argues that exploitation is no longer the extraction of surplus labor, but "command." He regards this not as a refutation of Marx's theory of exploitation but as an updated version of it, one that is appropriate to our present situation.

Though it is difficult to imagine Hardt and Negri writing *Empire* prior to the collapse of the Soviet Union, it would be wrong to think that they accord that event the world historical significance that others do. According to Negri, "our era" was inaugurated not in 1989 or 1991, but during the period running from 1968–1971 (Negri 1996, 159–64).[31] Negri characterizes the era that was brought to an end—one running from 1918–1968—as the era of the "mass worker." During that era factory workers were the linchpin of capitalist development. In exchange for wage

[28] Needs are socially determined and change over time. This complication need not detain us here. For some pertinent discussion see Negri (1978, 71–72, 132).

[29] Marx again acknowledges that surplus labor is found in all societies (1867, 325). Capitalism is distinctive in its "voracious appetite for surplus labor" (1867, 344).

[30] Interestingly, in the two early papers I have cited Negri claims that this view is implicit in Marx (see Negri 1968, 71 and Negri 1971, 96). In his more recent work he describes it as a revision of Marx. The two are not incompatible. In the earlier work Negri is claiming that the logic of Marx's analysis recognizes that the law of value would enter into the crisis Negri describes.

[31] One of Negri's great gifts is his ability to periodize the history of capitalist development effectively. The stretch of text cited, which covers 1848 to the present, is a particularly nice instance.

increases, workers delivered even higher productivity increases. Thus wages did not eat into profits. In Marxian value terms capital pursued a "relative surplus value" strategy (see Marx 1867, Part IV). Increased productivity meant a reduction in necessary labor time (less labor was required to meet workers' needs) and, given no reduction in overall labor time, this entailed an increase in the amount of surplus labor. In other words the rate ("degree") of exploitation increased.[32] The upsurge of labor militancy in this period defeated this strategy, as workers no longer delivered the requisite productivity increases. According to Negri, this historical development threw the law of value into crisis.

Negri does not, of course, think that capitalism has been overcome. Therefore he does not think that the theory of value *en toto* is no longer valid. Rather, his claim is that its quantitative dimension has suffered that fate. This poses a problem since, as we have seen, for Marx, the qualitative and quantitative dimensions of the theory of value are inseparable. I'm now going to turn to an examination of the argument that leads Negri to this theoretical difficulty and how he attempts to resolve it.

Negri engages with the law of value in almost all his works. His comments are neither completely clear nor consistent through time. While an attempt to chart out those twists and turns would be interesting and profitable, it is not what I will be concerned with here. Instead, I will take up his present characterization of the crisis of the law of value: that value is beyond measure (*Empire*, 365; see also Negri 1996, 151).

There is a clear sense in which value in Marx's sense was never measurable. The time that is relevant to the quantification of value is "socially necessary labor time," which is simply not something that could be determined empirically.[33] At points Negri writes as if his objections to the theory of value boil down to this empirical problem. For example, he sometimes seems to argue that the theory of value is appropriate to the era of the mass worker because the deskilled labor of the assembly line comes close to being the abstract homogenous labor that Marx's value theory purports to measure (Negri 1999, 78). While it is true that Negri regards the theory of value as tied to the era of the mass worker, the connection has nothing to do with issues of measurability I have been discussing here.

For Negri, the law of value is obsolete because the distinction between necessary labor and surplus labor can no longer be maintained. This is

---

[32] Loosely speaking, this increase was equal to the difference between productivity increases and wage increases.

[33] The *average* amount of labor time could be, but this would be an average of labors of different levels of skill, complexity, etc. and thus would not be "socially necessary labor time."

because the passage from the era of the mass-worker to the era of the "socialized worker" (to use Negri's old terminology) or the era of Empire and the Multitude (to use his new terminology) has meant the collapse of the distinction between life and work. Negri refers to this development as "the real subsumption of society" (see Negri 1989, 82–85).[34]

The paradigmatic institution of the era of the mass worker is the large factory (General Motors, Fiat, etc.). In a social order structured around factory work there is a clear partition between work and life. Work takes place inside the factory walls; life takes place outside of them. The strategy of working-class opposition in this social order is to *refuse work*. The working-class seeks to reduce the amount of surplus-labor it performs, transforming work-time into life-time. In other words, the struggle against work is the struggle against exploitation.

Negri thinks that the struggle against work—more precisely, against factory work—was largely successful.[35] The defeat of capital within the factory did not mean the defeat of capital *per se*. Instead "work has become diffused throughout society" (Negri 1989, 77). The thesis is notably lacking in either empirical clarification or support. What Negri has in mind is the view—by no means peculiar to him—that an understanding of the dynamics of capitalist development requires an analysis of institutions other than the factory (or, more broadly the work-place): for example, the school and the family. Marx could not conceive of such a task because the picture that guides his analysis is of a world in which factory work is so totalizing as to guarantee its reproduction:

> The individual consumption of the working class is the reconversion of the means of subsistence given by capital in return for labor-power into fresh labor-power which it is then able to exploit. It is the production and reproduction of the capitalist's most indispensable means of production: the worker. The individual consumption of the worker, whether it occurs inside or outside the workshop, inside or outside the labor process, remains an aspect of the production and reproduction of capital. . . . The maintenance and reproduction of the working class remains a necessary condition for the reproduction of capital. *But the capitalist may safely leave this to the worker's drives for self-preservation and propagation.* (Marx 1867, 718; emphasis mine)

---

[34] The terminology derives from Marx's distinction between "formal" and "real subsumption of labor." In formal subsumption Capital simply appropriates the commodities produced by the worker. In real subsumption Capital takes control of the labor process itself (Marx 1867, 1019–34).

[35] He writes that in this struggle "neither side was victorious" (1989, 76). However, capital's victory turns out to be "Pyrrhic": capital succeeds in regaining control of the factory but at the price of displacing the factory as the foundation of capitalist development.

Marx's vision here may well have been too limited for his own day; it is certainly too limited now. As the working class's struggle against work has liberated time from the confines of the factory, capital has worked zealously to make sure that that time is recouped by being devoted to the production of "that most indispensable means of production." To take just one example, higher education is now an integral to the production of labor-power, inculcating as it does traits essential to being a worker: self-discipline, deference to authority, and the like (Henwood 2003, 75–78). Were Marx to write *Capital* today, he would have to take account of "reproductive labor" in addition to "productive labor."

Whereas the labor performed by the mass worker was all too material, the paradigmatic labor of the socialized worker is "immaterial labor." Hardt and Negri define immaterial labor as "labor that produces an immaterial good, such as a service, a cultural product, knowledge or communication" (*Empire*, 290). Immaterial labor is not merely intellectual but affective as well. The concept of "immaterial labor" thus incorporates both productive and reproductive labor (see *Empire*, 293).

The concepts of the real subsumption of society and immaterial labor are brought together in the concept of biopower:[36]

> Biopower is another name for the real subsumption of society under capital, and both are synonymous with the global productive order. . . . Intelligence and affect (or really the brain coextensive with the body), just when they become the primary productive powers make production and life coincide across the terrain on which they operate, because life is nothing other than the production and reproduction of the set of bodies and brains. (*Empire*, 365)

Negri's claims about the hegemony of immaterial labor and the real subsumption of society are two ways of capturing the same social phenomena, namely the replacement of labor with biopower: "Life is no longer produced in the cycles of reproduction that are subordinated to the working day; on the contrary, life is what infuses and dominates all production" (*Empire*, 365). With this, Negri's vision of a world in which there is no distinction between life and work is complete. Yet, far from concluding that the colonization of all life by work makes the quantitative aspect of the theory of value all the more applicable, Negri concludes the opposite. As he puts it, "Subsumption generates a completely enveloping temporal *Umwelt* that dissolves the possibility of measure" (Negri 1981, 42).

---

[36] Negri introduces biopower into his theoretical repertoire in *Empire*, where he and Hardt appropriate it from Foucault.

The argument seems to go as follows: Exploitation, as Marx conceives it, requires a division of the workday into necessary and surplus labor; that is, a division between the time the worker spends working "for himself" and the time he spends working for capital. The real subsumption of society collapses this distinction:

> Clearly profit and the wage continue to exist, but they exist only as quantities regulated by a relation of power—a relation of forces which no longer admits the threefold partition of the working day into necessary labor time, surplus labor time, and free-time or reproduction time. (1982, 224)

A simple example of the sort that Marx is fond of will help clarify this. Consider a worker working 12 hours a day. Suppose that the day is divided into 8 hours of necessary labor and 4 hours of surplus labor. Now suppose the workday is reduced to 10 hours. The worker has changed 2 hours of work-time into 2 hours of free time. This is impossible given the real subsumption of society. Since work is everywhere, the best the worker can do is exchange one form of it for another.[37]

I now want to argue that the real subsumption thesis provides an inadequate basis for the rejection of the labor of value. First, let us grant Negri's claim that immaterial labor is now hegemonic within capitalism.[38] This shows only that intellectual, aesthetic, and emotional activities *can* be turned into work. It does not follow that all such activities *are* work. To take a simple and obvious example, consider the case of a computer programmer who spends part of her day writing code for commercial applications and part writing code for a computer game that will be distributed freely over the internet. It is simply false to characterize both such activities as labor. Of course, both are instances of concrete useful labor but that is not the category that is relevant to Marx's distinction between necessary and surplus labor. That distinction has to do with *abstract* labor. Writing code for commercial applications falls into that category; writing code for a game that will be distributed *gratis* does not.

Negri has given no reason to think that the scenario I have described is not possible. To the contrary, real examples seem to be proliferating. Therefore, he has not established the real subsumption thesis. But without that thesis he has no basis for the claim that "value is without measure." I conclude that Negri has provided no reason for abandoning the theory of value. The importance of retaining it can be seen by examining the political implications of the revised concept of exploitation that this abandonment forces Negri to adopt.

---

[37] This is what Negri is getting at when he writes: "When the entire time of life has become the time of production, who measures whom" (1981, 29; see also 1982, 220).

Earlier I quoted a passage in which Negri proposes to replace the concept of exploitation with that of command. If the proposal is to be anything more than a terminological shift, Negri must give content to the concept of "capitalist command." It cannot be that capitalist command is the imposition of work because that depends upon the quantitative side of Marx's value theory. Thus Negri has no recourse but to talk of command in an unqualified sense:

> Class struggle, pushing the nation-state toward its abolition and thus going beyond the barriers posed by it, proposes the constitution of Empire as the site of analysis and conflict. Without that barrier, then, the situation of struggle is completely open. Capital and labor are opposed in a directly antagonistic form. This is the fundamental condition of every political theory of communism. (*Empire*, 237)[39]

Negri is here implicitly contrasting the "directly antagonistic form" prevailing now with the "indirectly antagonistic form" prevailing earlier. Earlier workers did not confront capital directly, but indirectly in struggles over work. Now they confront capitalist command directly. But again, what is meant by capitalist command? The answer, so far as I can tell, is that nothing more can be said. Capitalist command is the command of the capitalists.[40]

It is no surprise then that in *Empire* Hardt and Negri think that the sole task remaining to the multitude is to break through the carapace of Empire. They write, "With respect to the virtuality of the multitude, however, imperial government appears as an empty shell or parasite" (*Empire*, 360). Throwing off the shackles of *Empire* will liberate the productive powers of the multitude.[41] We are back to the old communist project of

---

[38] The claim is of course controversial, and in my judgment probably wrong. Many critics have objected on the grounds that it ignores the proliferation of employment in sectors that are all too dreary and material: sweat shops, low-wage service jobs, and so on. For a good critique of the concept of "immaterial labor," see Dyer-Witherford (2001). For a fine overview of the condition of the U.S. working class circa 2000, see Henwood (2003, 39–78). Hardt and Negri rightly note that their claim cannot be decided by simple head counting (2004, 107). However, to substantiate their claim they would have to show that immaterial laborers are to Empire what the waged factory workers were to the Keynesian state. I don't see that they do that.

[39] It bears mentioning that Negri has been promising just such a direct confrontation for years.

[40] Hardt and Negri's definition in Multitude of exploitation as "private appropriation" of what is produced in common (2004, 150) is not helpful. It cannot be a reiteration of Marx's analysis according to which capital imposes work via the commodity form because that analysis depends on his theory of value. But they have not told us what else it can mean.

[41] Chapter 4.1 of *Empire*, "Virtualities," is a veritable hymn to the productive power of the multitude.

where taking control of the means of production is an end in itself, not a means for the working class to liberate itself from them.[42]

There are two major problems with this prescription. First, and most obviously, it is redolent of one of the worst aspects of Soviet ideology: its productivist ethos.[43] Indeed, at points *Empire* reminds one of Lenin's argument that the only problem with capitalism is that it is run by the capitalists. Second, the project they commend will be appealing only to those workers for whom productive life is as cheery and vibrant as *Empire* says it is. It goes without saying that most of the working class would be better off having their productivity unshackled from Empire only if that meant that they were unshackled from their productivity.

I want to conclude by offering a brief diagnosis of how Negri has wound up in this blind alley. He is, I believe, a victim of two things. The first is the undue limitation he places on the refusal of work strategy. Though he is one of the thinkers responsible for making the refusal of work central in analyzing class struggle, he sees this strategy as confined to a particular moment in capitalist development: the era of the mass worker (Negri 1996, 162; see also *Empire*, 203–204). The second is his relentless optimism. Negri shares with other autonomists a salutary belief in workers' power. He is distinctive however, in his resolute refusal to recognize defeats and setbacks. Having identified the refusal of work as the defining strategy of the mass worker, he is compelled to pronounce it a success. Having pronounced the quantitative battle over, he has no choice but to reject the conceptual apparatus designed for articulating it. The crisis in the law of value is a way of pronouncing the battle against work won in a society that is still structured around it.

References

Anderson, Perry 2002. "Force and Consent," *New Left Review* 17, 5–30

Arrighi, Giovanni 2003. "Lineages of Empire," in Gopal Balakrishnan, ed., *Debating Empire*. London: Verso, 2003.

Barkawi, Tarak and Laffey, Mark 2002. "Retrieving the Imperial: *Empire* and International Relations," *Millennium: Journal of International Studies* 31, 109–27.

Bromley, Simon 2003. "Reflections on *Empire*, Imperialism and United States Hegemony," *Historical Materialism* 11, 17–68.

Caffentzis, George 1980. "The Work/Energy Crisis and the Apocalypse," in *Midnight Oil: Work, Energy, War 1973–2002*, New York: Autonomedia, 1992.

---

[42] Negri endorses this discredited project at several points (1996, 162 and 1989, 85).

[43] For a good critique of Negri's productivism see Thoburn (2001).

Cleaver, Harry 2001. *Reading Capital Politically*. Second edition. Leeds, UK: Anti/Theses.

Dyer-Witherford, Nick 2001. "Empire, Immaterial Labor, the New Combinations, and the Global Worker," *Rethinking Marxism* 13, 70–80.

Foster, John Bellamy 2002. "The Rediscovery of Imperialism," *Monthly Review* 54, n. 6, 1–16.

Gowan, Peter 1999. *The Global Gamble: Washington's Faustian Bid for World Dominance*, London: Verso.

Green, Peter 2002. "The Passage from Imperialism to Empire: A Commentary on *Empire* by Michael Hardt and Antonio Negri," *Historical Materialism* 10, 29–77.

Hardt, Michael and Antonio Negri 2000. *Empire*, Cambridge: Harvard University Press.

Hardt, Michael and Antonio Negri 2004. *Multitude*, New York: Penguin Press.

Harvey, David 2003. *The New Imperialism*, Oxford: Oxford University Press.

Henwood, Doug 2003. *After The New Economy*, New York: The New Press.

Lenin, V.I. 1916. *Imperialism: The Highest Stage of Capitalism*, New York: International Publishers, 1939.

Marx, Karl 1867. *Capital: A Critique of Political Economy, Vol. 1*, translated by Ben Fowkes, Harmondsworth: Penguin, 1976.

Moran, Theodore 1976/77. "Why Oil Prices Go Up (2) The Future: OPEC Wants Them," *Foreign Policy* 25, 58–77.

Negri, Antonio 1968. "Marx on Cycle and Crisis," in Negri 1988, 43–90.

———. 1971. "Crisis of the Planner State: Communism and Revolutionary Organizations," in Negri 1988, 91–148.

———. 1978. *Marx Beyond Marx: Lessons on the Grundrisse*, translated by Harry Cleaver, Michael Ryan, and Maurizio Viano, New York: Autonomedia, 1991.

———. 1981. "The Constitution of Time," translated by Matteo Mandarini. in *Time For Revolution*, New York: Continuum, 2003, 21–135

———.1982. "Archaeology and Project: The Mass Worker and The Social Worker," in Negri 1988: 199–228.

———. 1988. *Revolution Retrieved: Selected Writings on Marx, Keynes, Capitalist Crisis and New Social Subjects, 1967–1983*. London: Red Notes.

———. 1989. "From the Mass Worker to the Socialized Worker—and Beyond," translated by James Newell, in *The Politics of Subversion*, Cambridge: Basil Blackwell, 75–88.

———. 1996. "Twenty Theses on Marx: Interpretation of the Class Situation Today," in Saree Makdisi, Cesare Casarino, and Rebecca E. Karl, eds., *Marxism Beyond Marxism*. New York: Routledge.

———. 1999. "Value and Affect," *Boundary 2* 26, 77–88.

Oppenheim, V.H. 1976/77. "Why Oil Prices Go Up (1) The Past: We Pushed Them," *Foreign Policy* 25, 24–57.

Panitch, Leo and Gindin, Sam 2002. "Gems and Baubles in *Empire*," *Historical Materialism* 10, 17–43.

Petras, James 2002. "The Fragrance of Imperialism," *Journal of Peasant Studies* 29, 135–60.

Sherman, David 2010. "Metapolitics Now: Negri, Critical Theory, Praxis," this volume 75–98.

Thobrun, Nicholas 2001. "Autonomous Production? On Negri's New Synthesis," *Theory, Culture and Society* 18, 75–96.

Warren, Bill 1980. *Imperialism: Pioneer of Capitalism*. London: Verso.

Went, Robert 2002/2003. "Globalization in the Perspective of Imperialism," *Science and Society* 66, 473–97.

Reading Negri with Spinoza: The Multitude and Its Origins

7

From the *Multitudo* to the Multitude: The Place of Spinoza in the Political Philosophy of Antonio Negri

MICHAEL GODDARD

Introduction

In a 2002 edition of *Multitudes*, the French journal established by Antonio Negri, there appeared a short 'defence and illustration' by him of the book *Empire,* which he co-authored with Michael Hardt.[1] What is striking about this article is its strong emphasis on the importance of Spinoza to this work, a work so focused on the analysis of the political constitution of the present. The following extract from the article underlines very clearly this Spinozian dimension of *Empire:*

> It is clear that the origins of the discourse on the multitude are located in the subversive interpretation of Spinoza's thought. We will never stop insisting on the importance of the Spinozian presupposition. As an entirely Spinozian thematic, we have above all that of the body, and in particular that of the power of the body. (Negri 2002, 41)

This does not mean that Negri's work is an unproblematic application of Spinoza's thought to the present, but rather a complex deployment of some of Spinoza's concepts, or a subversive reading of these concepts, to contest the present and its constitution. In fact an attentive reading of *Empire,* especially of the genealogy of sovereignty presented in the second section (Hardt and Negri, 67–204), reveals a thought in which Spinoza plays as central and exemplary role as Marx. This centrality of Spinoza is even more the case in the sequel to *Empire, Multitude,* the central prob-

---

[1] Antonio Negri, "Pour une définition ontologique de la multitude," *Multitudes 9,* Paris: May/June, 2002, 36–48. Michael Hardt and Antonio Negri, *Empire,* Cambridge; London: Harvard University Press, 2000.

lematic of which revolves around the concept of the common, a problematic that is explicitly derived from the thought of Spinoza.[2]

This essay will trace the development of this Spinozian dimension of Negri's work in order to analyze its role in his current thought. Central to this essay will be a reading of Negri's *The Savage Anomaly,* his full-length analysis of the ontology and politics of Spinoza's thought. I will argue that this work brought about a transformation in Negri's own thought, resulting in the development of a political ontology going far beyond, while still remaining deeply engaged with, the Marxist tradition. Crucial to this work is the affirmation of an entirely immanent and materialist ontology, which for Negri is not only relevant to Spinoza and early modernity but also essential for a contestation of the present. While this project is clearly inspired by Gilles Deleuze's reading of Spinoza and other "minor" or "anomalous" philosophers,[3] it goes further in subverting the history of philosophy through a radical contestation of the principle, transcendent currents of modernity—an approach that is equally evident in *Empire.*[4] This will especially be shown to be the case with the concept of the multitude (*multitudo*) as developed in Negri's reading of Spinoza's *Political Treatise* in the chapter "The Constitution of Reality" (Negri, *The Savage Anomaly,* 183–210). The extension of this reading in Negri's book *Subversive Spinoza* will then be examined, concentrating on the ways in which Negri clarifies and refines Spinoza's conception of the multitude in relation to the political conditions of the present.[5] This reading will be followed by an examination of Negri's more recent work *Kairòs, Alma Venus, Multitudo,* in which his subversive engagement with Spinoza has reached a fruition expressed by a truly original and powerful work that is not only a highly sophisticated political philosophy but also an *Ethics* for the twenty-first century.[6]

There is a very resonant parallel in the development of Spinoza's and Negri's thought. Negri identifies in the development of Spinoza's thought a crucial break between the first two books of the *Ethics* and the last three, corresponding to both a period of political and personal crisis and

---

[2] Michael Hardt and Antonio Negri, *Multitude: War and Democracy in the Age of Empire.* New York: Penguin Press, 2004.

[3] See especially, Gilles Deleuze, *Expressionism in Philosophy: Spinoza,* trans. Martin Joughin, New York: Zone Books; Cambridge, Mass: MIT Press, 1990; and "Spinoza and the Three "Ethics," in *The New Spinoza,* ed. Warren Montag and Ted Stolze, Minneapolis; London: University of Minnesota Press, 1997, 21–34.

[4] See especially, Hardt and Negri, 69–92.

[5] Antonio Negri, *Subversive Spinoza: (Un)Contemporary Variations,* ed. Timothy Murphy, Manchester, New York: Manchester University Press, 2004.

[6] This work has appeared in English as, "Kairòs, Alma Venus, Multitudo," in *Time for Revolution,* trans. Matteo Mandarini, New York; London: Continuum, 2003, 137–261.

Spinoza's turn towards the political expressed through the composition of the *Theologico-Political Treatise*. Similarly, in Negri's work, the turn to Spinoza also constitutes a profound break precipitated by the twin crises of the collapse or, rather, destruction of the Autonomia movement and Negri's imprisonment. However, just as Spinoza's turn to politics was by no means a move away from ontology but rather a deepening of its immanence and productive force, Negri's turn to Spinoza, rather than being a rejection of radical politics, is instead the connection of the most radical elements of Autonomist Marxist thought with a productive ontology capable of going beyond, or rather 'below', the resources of the Marxist tradition. If *Marx Beyond Marx* is Negri's fullest expression of the crisis in his thought and in Marxism more generally, then the books he composed in prison, *The Savage Anomaly* and more obliquely his book *Job ou La Force de l'Esclave,* point to the way beyond this crisis towards a future materialism or communism still engaged with Marxism, but nevertheless beyond its limits. I will conclude that it is therefore impossible to grasp the singularity of Negri's thought in purely Marxist terms, even when it seems most fully engaged with the political constitution of the present, without comprehending its immanent, ontological, and Spinozian dimensions.

Beyond the Crisis in Marxism: Negri's Savage Anomaly

Negri is hardly unique in his turn towards Spinoza in response to the crisis that Marxist thought had been undergoing since the 1960s: one only has only to consider major Structuralist Marxist figures such as Louis Althusser, Etienne Balibar, and Pierre Macherey to realize that this return to Spinoza was a phenomenon intimately associated with the crisis of Marxist thought particularly in the period of the late 60s. As Negri himself put it in the essay, "The 'Return to Spinoza' and the return of Communism":

> The 'return to Spinoza' . . . shows itself to be an event linked to the crisis of Marxism. . . . Within this horizon in which Marxism, like the other ideologies of modernity, no longer knows how to discriminate or orient itself, . . . Spinoza, or rather the ontological anchorage and the productivity of ethics, proposes the possibility of reshaping and defining human action once again. (Negri, *Subversive Spinoza*, 94–95)

This period also saw a renewed interest in Spinoza more generally, with major new interpretations of Spinoza's thought not only by Deleuze but also by Ferdinand Alquié, Alexandre Matheron, Martial Guéroult, and others. Even the relations that Negri draws between Spinoza and Dutch early modernity have been a feature of analyses by Yirmiahu Yovel and especially J. Huizinga, who Negri cites in the opening pages of *The Savage Anomaly*. So the question can legitimately be posed as to whether Negri's particular turn to Spinoza is a singular one or merely echoes these other philosophical and Marxist returns to Spinoza.

The answer to this question is that Negri's book both emerges from a collective tendency and from its very beginnings seeks to go further in its affirmation of Spinoza's political ontology than any of these other approaches that constitute this return to Spinoza. Negri does not turn to Spinoza as a mere supplement to Marxist thought and even less does he undertake this engagement as being of mere epistemological interest as a neglected episode of the history of philosophy, even of materialist philosophy. Instead, Negri fully inhabits Spinoza's thought, especially in its ontological dimensions, always with the goal of constructing this thought as an anomaly both in relation to its time and our own.

From the opening lines of the first chapter, Negri is insistent on the monstrosity of Spinoza's thought: "The chronicles attest, whether approvingly or hostilely, that Spinoza's thought is monstrous. [They] present us with a personage and a body of thought, an image and an evaluation, that evoke a superhuman character. And a double character" (*Savage Anomaly* 3). For Negri, this double character of Spinoza's thought is not merely an external one of conflicting readings, but expresses something fundamental about this thought itself. This is the major heuristic innovation of Negri's reading of Spinoza: in the place of a unified body of work, Negri identifies two Spinozas, the first of whom is fully a part of "the Dutch Utopia," corresponding to Spinoza's earlier work up until Book 2 of the *Ethics*. The second Spinoza is the one who, following the crisis represented by the *Theologico-Political Treatise,* would embark on a 'second foundation' for his thought, radically breaking with his intellectual and cultural milieu. It is this second Spinoza who, according to Negri, is the one that leaps forwards toward the future, toward us, and it is this Spinoza who is able to contribute towards a contemporary conception of the multitude and constituent power. While it may be true, as Michael Hardt points out (Hardt, "Translator's Foreword: The Anatomy of Power," *The Savage Anomaly,* xii), that the theoretical key to Negri's reading of Spinoza is in the distinction between two conceptions of power, *potentia* as constitutive power and *potestas* as a constituted Power of domination, this distinction only emerges through this double, diachronic reading of Spinoza's thought as having a second foundation following a profound rupture: "The doubling of Spinoza's thought . . . is an anomaly so strong and so specific to Spinozian thought that it makes it both close to us, possible for us to grasp, and at the same time irreducible to any of historical ideology's mechanisms of filiation or systemisation" (Negri, *Savage Anomaly,* 5). For this reason it is worth looking at the three phases that Negri identifies in Spinoza's thought, namely the first foundation, associated with the Dutch anomaly, the second phase of the crisis in both Spinoza's thought and his community, and finally the third phase of the second foundation.

The First Foundation and the Dutch Anomaly

At the beginning of his study, Negri emphasizes the situation of seventeenth century Holland as itself anomalous in relation to the rest of Europe. Here in the youngest of republics not only was the "humanist" spirit of the Renaissance fully alive in intellectual, scientific, and artistic experimentation but at the same time there was a very advanced form of capitalism. It is a key point for Negri that the revolutionary humanism of the Renaissance, the "sense of freedom and the love of freedom" (6), continued unabated in Holland, whereas elsewhere in Europe it had been eradicated through monarchist absolutism, a defeat poorly hidden behind the splendor of Baroque aesthetics. One only has to consider the contrast between the Baroque artifice of the Flemish painter Rubens's cherubs and the uncompromising attention to the real and the everyday of Rembrandt or Vermeer to see how the impulse of the Renaissance to grasp the immanence of human life had continued in Holland, whereas elsewhere it had been diverted in a Baroque return to transcendence thinly masking the absolutist recapture of Power. As Negri puts it: "One can perhaps say that the Seventeenth Century never reached Holland" (6). Instead there is a direct and explicit tension between a revolutionary humanism and a savage market capitalism, unmediated, at least to begin with, by absolutist forms of Power.

Negri identifies four currents that are essential to or flow into Spinoza's thought in this first phase, namely Judaism, Renaissance Humanism, Scholasticism, and the philosophy of Descartes. However, even in its beginnings, Spinoza's thought is not determined by these tendencies but rather emerges as an original interference between them, resulting in a productive conception of being and a thought that is at once absolutely immanent, rationalist, and ontological. Rather than Spinoza's thought being determined by these currents, they instead form a backdrop and one that Spinoza will increasingly distinguish himself from as his thought develops. As Negri points out, by Book 1 of the *Ethics* Spinoza is already referring to Descartes's God as an "asylum of the ignorant" and completely rejecting his method in favor of "ontological fullness" (14). Nevertheless, Spinoza's thought in this period is in profound connection with a collectivity of free-thinkers who constitute what Negri calls the Dutch utopia and which maintains the revolutionary principles of the

Renaissance in a manner that would have been impossible elsewhere in Europe.

So what is this "first foundation" that Negri identifies in Spinoza and associates with the "Utopia of Spinoza's Circle"?[7] While Negri engages with Spinoza's earliest works, it is in the *Emendation of the Intellect* that the constitutive ontology of Spinoza's project starts to become apparent. In this work Spinoza aims to develop a method both for understanding the mind and improving it in the direction of rationality and introduces for the first time key concepts such as adequate ideas. Negri sums up the onto-logical force of the project as follows: "The understanding, here, does not know an internal logic that could lead it to the heights of being; the high-est level of being is, for the first time, the being that is present, immediate being . . . The goal, reaching truth and constituting an adequate idea, means making being speak" (34). This is already a highly original and con-stitutive ontology that breaks away from all of the above-mentioned cur-rents that informed Spinoza's thought. However, despite this realist flattening of being, that according to Negri inverts the pantheist philoso-phy of depths into a philosophy of surfaces (34), Spinoza's project imme-diately reaches a limit. On one side this limit is the enclosure in a theoretical asceticism, where the improvement of the intellect or the indi-vidual mind is considered in isolation from the social productivity of being. On the other side it is the limit of the utopia itself, which is incapable of dispensing with idealism: "A strategy of constitution versus a pantheistic utopia. . . . Or instead, is it only the terrific tension of the utopia that, . . . rules the constructive expansivity of the method? Have we not, then, reached the limit, no longer an obstacle to overcome but the actual crisis point of utopian thought?" (35) It is due to this limit that the problems of real constitution posed by this work cannot be resolved, except by resort-ing to idealism and asceticism.

However, this first crisis in Spinoza's thought is only the prelude to the first foundation which Negri discerns as really emerging first in the *Principles of Cartesian Philosophy* and then more rigorously in the first two parts of the *Ethics*. The decisive shift is precisely a rejection of the flight into idealism and a return to ontology but with a "savage" new element: the beginnings of a conception of ontological power: "Suddenly, but with extreme resolve, the theory turns back directly to being and puts in motion a war machine against every possible form of idealism. . . . Being itself is given its own internal necessary tension; there is no abstract, tran-scendental subsumption, there is only the tension of being itself" (43). What Negri is referring to is Spinoza's new concept of *conatus* or the

---

[7] The title of the second chapter of *The Savage Anomaly.*

thing's striving to preserve its own being, which leads necessarily to a productive conception of being as power: "it expresses the first adequate definition of *potentia*, the first materialistic extension of *causa sui* to the modal multiplicity" (43).

In the beginning of the *Ethics,* this ontological tension is presented by much more systematic means involving the complex relations between substance, the attribute, and modal existence expressed through a dizzying array of definitions, propositions, and scholia. Negri's analysis of Spinoza's system, while exceptionally rigorous, more or less conforms to other interpretations such as Deleuze's in emphasizing the nature of his philosophy as a "philosophy of pure affirmation" (47). Nevertheless, despite the complex architecture of Spinoza's system at this point, for Negri it only constitutes a "systematic statement of the absolute ontological and methodological radicality of pantheism" (48). Negri's reading insists on the diachronic nature of the *Ethics* and reads it as a *Bildungsroman*, the work of a life that charts not only the philosopher's development, but also the maturation of being itself. The first book would therefore be the affirmation of existence as essence, power, and totality, and this real and univocal being rather than God is, for Negri, its subject: "The paradox of this Spinozian category of univocal being is that it is constituted by the totality of reality. [Substance] is neither above nor below reality, it is all reality. . . . Absolute being is the surface of the world" (52).

However, the problem of how to pass from the infinity of substance to finite or modal reality is not easily resolved. It is here that the concept of the attribute as a mediation between substance and the world comes in to play. According to Negri, the concept of the attribute attempts to bridge the conceptual gulf between substance and reality, the spontaneity of being and the material organization of the world: the attribute should be a principle of organization of the infinite in the material world. Negri's critique of the attribute is very detailed but the salient point is that the attribute as mediator between substance and the world contradicts the productivity of a system, which rules out both transcendence and mediation in its absolutely immanent and constitutive conception of being. For Negri, the concept of the attribute retains traces of neoplatonic emanation that are entirely incompatible with this system. As such it is another case of a blockage in that it is a concept that can only fail to fulfill its function.

According to Negri, in the second book of the *Ethics,* this problem of the relation between substance and modal existence that the attribute was unable to resolve comes to an absolute point of crisis: "Substance and mode crash against each other and shatter" (62). This is because this part of the *Ethics* has left the realm of metaphysics and concerns the modal realm of reality where substance is expressed under the two attributes of thought and extension. Citing the Scholia to Proposition 3 of Book 2, where Spinoza distinguishes the creative power (*potentia*) of God radically from the mediated power of domination of Kings (*potestas*), Negri asserts that the concept of the attribute is rendered virtually obsolete: "The attributes . . . are reabsorbed on a horizontal field of surfaces. They no longer represent agents of organization but are subordinated . . . in a space where only singularities emerge. And these singularities are not mediated by anything" (63). In other words if reality is not the emanation of substance but substance itself as it is played out in the material world, then there is no place for the mediating concept of the attribute. This is the point at which Spinoza's philosophy truly becomes materialist in that is crosses over from the idealistic claim that "God is all," to the materialist one that "all is God" (64). This entails the privileging of the body in a passage from metaphysics to physics in that modal existence becomes constitutive:

> The object of the idea constituting the human Mind is the Body, or a certain mode of Extension which actually exists, and nothing else" (Spinoza, *Ethics*, Book 2, P13). . . . We have passed from the active existence of the mind to the active existence of the body. . . . The entire thematic of idealistic rationalism . . . is denied. The materialism of the mode is foundational, insofar, at least, as the idea of the mode is constitutive. (Negri 65)

From this one might be tempted to conclude that in this passage from substance to mode, from the metaphysics of substance to the mechanics of bodies that Spinoza had already overcome idealism and definitively broken from the utopia of idealistic, pantheistic reason. For Negri, however, this merely marks the extreme limit of the utopia, in which the metaphysics of substance is given the maximum productive force possible without departing the terrain of idealism altogether. In fact, for Negri, what Spinoza has arrived at is nothing else than the productivity of being as the basis for the mode of production in a real worldly sense: "An extraordinarily complex synthesis, comprehending all the revolutionary coordinates of the century has been compressed into the image of the absolute and its alternatives. This assemblage of the diverse planes of being has been reduced to one single plane of being, and here it has been put into tension" (67). For this tension to break, an absolute rupture from the idealistic utopia, both theoretically and socially is required, and it is this rupture, coinciding with Spinoza's turn to politics, that constitutes the second phase of Negri's analysis of Spinoza.

The Crisis and Interruption of the System

That this rupture is not simply a personal and theoretical one is immediately apparent in Negri's distinction between Spinoza's thought and what he calls Spinozism. For Negri, Spinozism, as the idealistic, bourgeois interpretation of Spinoza's thought, is one with the emergence of bourgeois ideology, the affirmation of the free market and the state and the philosophies that justify them. Starting with Hobbes and passing through Rousseau and Kant to culminate in Hegel, Spinozism is a perversion of Spinoza's thought that rather than abolishing mediation and transcendence insists upon it. This Spinozism is, for Negri, the origin of modern juridical and political thought: "The abrogation of the real world, the duplication of the world in a political and juridical image—this is the effect of this operation, this is the massive and important content of Spinozism as ideology. . . . Spinozism as ideology goes so far as to make it impossible, or at least extremely difficult to imagine a political horizon that is not conceived as a horizon of mediation" (71). In other words, Spinozism consists in the exploitation of the vestiges of idealism in Spinoza's early thought to insist upon mediation and the transcendence of the state and thereby to make human power or *potentia* disappear into a world of *potestas* or domination: "In Spinozism, in the ideology of the market, in the totalitarianism of science, it is impossible to maintain the freedom of *potentia* and its irreducibility to the dialectical process of mediation" (72). The material fullness of being that Spinoza arrived at even before the crisis is emptied out by this bourgeois interpretation and becomes a mere shadow on a dialectical horizon that would remain unchallenged at least up until Marx.

So much for Spinozism. But what of the crisis in Spinoza's thought? This is the point at which the relations between Spinoza and the Baroque again come to the forefront. It must be remembered that, for Negri, the Baroque is the mystified expression, even the ideology, of absolutism, and so to the question, "is Spinoza Baroque?" his definitive answer is no. However, inasmuch as Spinoza confronts the crisis posed by the limits encountered in Book 2 of the *Ethics* as well as the exterior crisis of the development of absolutism and the market, the Baroque is an attraction or temptation that his thought necessarily passes through, a moment of blockage before the reformulation of the system. Essentially the Baroque solution would consist of an acceptance of the unknowability of reality and therefore a retreat from any worldly solution to the relations between substance and modal existence: in other words turning Spinoza's system into an unknowable labyrinth full of irresolvable enigmas. This critique of Baroque complexity for complexity's sake certainly separates Negri's reading of Spinoza profoundly from that of Deleuze. Indeed one could argue that the key difference between these two thinkers is the distance Negri takes from any affirmation of the Baroque, including the thought of Leibniz, instead seeing it as an acquiescence to absolute power, transcendence and dialectical mediation.

Having overcome this Baroque temptation, which in Negri's account seems to last for no longer than a single letter on the infinite! (74–75), and although Negri also detects Baroque resonances in the second half of Book 2 of the *Ethics*, Spinoza's thought enters a radically new phase through a direct engagement with the political. Coinciding biographically with Spinoza's moving from Rijnsburg to Voorburg and hence the end of his utopian circle, Spinoza necessarily confronts the political in order to move from the "destructive" path of the first part of his work which, in its descent from the metaphysical to the world has destroyed along the way every idealist, utopian assumption, to the "constructive path" which will move in the opposite direction from the world to the divine.[8] This requires a practical moment:

> The ethics could not be constituted as a project, in the metaphysics of the mode and reality, were it not inserted into history, into politics, into the phenomenology of a single and collective life. . . . The ontological horizon that the critical development of the first stage of the *Ethics* has produced, must now find a dynamic materiality on which to extend its own force. (84)

This practical moment that necessarily interrupts the *Ethics* between 1665 and 1670 takes the form of the *Theologico-Political Treatise,* which Negri typically reads in great detail. From the first six chapters of the *Theologico-Political Treatise,* Negri extracts two distinct arguments. The diachronic argument essentially boils down to a genealogy from biblical revelation to political institutions, in which from a critique of superstition and mystification emerges the constitutive role of the imagination in the formation of institutions. However, this is coupled with a synchronic argument in which the analysis of the imagination opens up its ontological basis. What this section achieves is no less than the refoundation of Spinoza's thought in the realm of the political. If Spinoza's thought is a political one, this is because:

> Politics itself is metaphysics. . . . Politics is the metaphysics of the imagination, the metaphysics of the human constitution of reality, of the world. . . . It is possible to have adequate ideas that are not exhaustive of reality,

---

[8] The role of the destructive and constructive paths in Negri's reading of Spinoza has been analyzed by Jason Read, "The Antagonistic Ground of Constitutive Power: An Essay on the Thought of Antonio Negri," *Rethinking Marxism,* 11: 2, Summer 1999, 2–8.

but open to and constitutive of reality, which are intensively true; consciousness is constitutive; being is not only something found . . . but also activity, power. (97)

While this is only Negri's presentation of the beginning of this work, it is already clear how absolutely crucial this shift to the political is for Negri's reading of Spinoza, indeed for his own materialist philosophy. By starting from the world, rather than the metaphysical, Spinoza attempts to constitute, via the concept of the imagination, an ontological politics of the human construction of the world. Of course this runs into several problems, not least of which being the maintenance of a separation between the modal world of politics and that of ontology and it can be argued that the *Theologico-Political Treatise* doesn't advance Spinoza's work theoretically on the ontological level. However, its novelty is, for Negri, that the *Theologico-Political Treatise* "is cast on a very large scale and expressed in a constitutive configuration. . . . What we find is a corpulent methodology, founded on the rigour of productive causality, aggressive and indomitable. . . . Within the interruption marked by the *Theological-Political Treatise*, the sense and the definition of being are materialised and deepened" (118). Now the path is opened to the truly constitutive and constructive second foundation of Spinoza's philosophy.

The Second Foundation, the Multitude, and the Constitution of Reality

The constructive path of Negri's reading of Spinoza's later work begins with Book III of the *Ethics,* with Spinoza's famous "geometric" presentation of the body and its affects: "I will consider human actions and appetites just as if it were a question of lines, planes and solids" (Spinoza, *Ethics,* Book 3, Preface). According to Negri, this resort to geometry is misleading as far from a subordination of real bodies to ideal abstractions, it is rather the sign of a profound engagement with the physical world of bodies and affects: "The Spinozian universe is much more physical than geometrical . . . This implies . . . an extreme corporeality of the elements of the scene, so vital a complex of actions and reactions that it transforms this horizon into a horizon of war" (144). For Negri this second foundation is a Copernican revolution that instead of accounting for modal existence through the concept of substance, begins with modal existence in order to construct the idea of substance. In this way it is the body and its affects that becomes foundational rather than substance. Through a refinement of the concept of *conatus*, a truly constitutive level is reached: "We are finally within the constitutive dynamic of being—of the inclusive being

that the human consciousness and human world reveal" (147). It is not
necessary to dwell on Negri's reading of this section of the *Ethics*: it is sufficient to underline the subversive and constitutive dimensions of Spinoza's
physics of the affects, especially his discussion of *conatus, appetites,* and
cupiditas. The latter concept is especially important for Negri as it is not
presented as a possibility or an implication but a veritable power, in the
sense of *potentia,* and it is this form of power, derived from an analysis of
the body and its affects that becomes constitutive in relation to power as
domination or *potestas.*

Negri passes from this second foundation to a crucial reading of
Spinoza's *Political Treatise,* which would elaborate a similar refoundation
of Spinoza's thought as the latter parts of the *Ethics,* except this time on
the terrain of politics. This is a controversial reading, especially considering
that the *Political Treatise* is an unfinished work that many commentators
see as making no significant advances on the earlier *Theologico-Political
Treatise.* Even worse, the point at which the work breaks off is at the beginning of the section on democracy, at the very point that Spinoza has made
a series of exclusions including that of women.[9] Negri does not deny the
incompleteness or even the failure of this project, but nevertheless he
insists on its significance as Spinoza's translation of the second foundation
of the *Ethics,* the constituent power of modal existence, onto an explicitly
political terrain. The *Theological-Political Treatise* already attempted this
expansion but really before Spinoza's thought had reached this level of
immanent, modal constitution. Therefore it is only in the *Political Treatise*
that the political implications of Spinoza's fully developed immanent and
constitutive thought begin to be articulated.

The *Political Treatise* begins as an attack on political philosophy, even
on philosophy in general, that would understand politics on any basis other
than that of an analysis of human passions. Its difference to other contem-
poraneous political philosophies, however, is not to see this limit as a horizon but rather as a condition of emergence. While politicians seem to fare
a little better in Spinoza's account, since he says they have "said it all"
about political forms and endorses their position that politics must be
based on "experience or practice" (187), mere practice is no less deficient
than theory. Rather the problem of practice must be posed radically: if

---

[9] Negri would only specifically address this problematic interruption of the *Political
Treatise* at the precise point at which women are being excluded from democratic power in a
much later essay. See Negri, "Reliqua Desiderantur: A Conjecture for a Definition of
Democracy in the Final Spinoza," *The New Spinoza,* 241. These exclusions, especially of
women, are critiqued in a chapter that also engages with Negri and Balibar's readings of
Spinoza's *Political Treatise* in Moira Gatens and Genevieve Lloyd, *Collective Imaginings:
Spinoza Past and Present,* London; New York: Routledge, 1999, 114–35.

experience is the basis of practice and this experience is essentially that of the passions of the multitude and how they can be governed, then these passions need to be fully comprehended rather than merely being assumed. The multitude is determined being but a constitutive one as Spinoza had already shown in his *Ethics,* so, according to Negri, "true philosophy, as a science of experience and praxis and not their simple description, is the passage to the analysis of the necessity of human freedom, in the collective and progressive rhythm of constitution" (188).

In other words, Negri sees in the *Political Treatise* nothing less than the completion of the *Ethics* in that even the last part of the *Ethics* had tended to view free necessity as a result whereas the *Political Treatise* treats it as a presupposition. Free necessity is the constitutive process at the heart of politics, the dynamism of the multitude that only an engagement with the collective and concrete domain of politics could fully bring out. Crucial for Negri's reading of Spinoza and indeed for his own philosophy is a new conception of the multitude itself. In the political philosophy of this period the multitude was an operative term but a negative one—for example in Hobbes's conception of the war of all against all in the state of nature. However, if nature, including human nature is conceived of as perfection, the multitude becomes a positive rather than a negative condition of politics, indeed its very constitutive element: "The *multitudo* is now no longer a negative condition but the positive premise of the self-constitution of right. . . . This right exists not because of the force of the greater number but because of the constitution of the greatest number" (194). This is really the key to the Spinozian dimension of Negri's thought: this affirmative understanding of the multitude as constituent power is seen by Negri as an alternative model of power whose realization is perhaps only now possible: "The constitutive determination of the horizon of the *multitudo,* then, is given. The multitude has become a productive essence. Civil right is the power of the multitude. Consensus is substituted for the contract, collectivity for that of individuality" (195). For Negri there is no incompatibility between metaphysics or ontology and politics but rather the two spheres reinforce one another in that politics gives to metaphysics a concrete domain of constitution in which otherwise abstract ideas can assume a real dynamism. For this reason the *Political Treatise* must be seen as a success, despite its interruption due to Spinoza's death, in that it leaves behind a project to be continued, in fact that could only be continued through the constitution of new forms of power (*potentia*). As Negri puts it:

> Its immediate political failure is the necessary effect of the triumph of the world, of the *multitudo,* of humanity. The constructive project is now blocked precisely to the extent that the critical power it has developed has moved beyond the historical reality of its times. . . . The project lives: It is

there, taut, ready to be grasped as a message. The temporal dimension, the concept of the future, is formed—an anticipation that the desire and the imagination contain . . . In order to be understood, however, Spinoza needs new real conditions to be given. (209–210)

If Spinoza's project in general and especially in the *Political Treatise* is an arrow aimed at the future, then this explains its re-emergence at precisely the historical point of the late Twentieth Century in which all existent forms of power were being profoundly questioned. In the last section of this essay, we will examine the way Negri's more recent work takes up this challenge and Spinoza's thought becomes an essential dimension of his own philosophical system, especially in the work *Kairòs, Alma Venus, Multitudo.*

"Reliqua Desiderantur," or Negri's Subversive Continuation of Spinoza's Thought

That this reading of Spinoza continued to be an essential component of Negri's thought can clearly be seen from the collection of essays entitled *Subversive Spinoza*. These essays extend Negri's reading of the *Political Treatise* as an essential component of his own political theory and especially of the concept of the multitude, in relation to contemporary problems such as the crisis of Marxism and the end of the cold war. One essay in particular, "Reliqua Desiderantur: A Conjecture for a Definition of the Concept of Democracy in the Final Spinoza," (*Subversive Spinoza* 28–58), reads almost as an attempt at the completion of Spinoza's unfinished political treatise: "there is missing only a final passage that consists in a specific description. . . . Let us imagine that description" (48). For the purposes of this essay what is crucial is the way Negri lays out the concept of the Multitude in Spinoza in such a way as to strongly suggest its applicability to contemporary political conditions.

Negri asserts that the *multitudo,* a term that rarely appears in the earlier *Theologico-Political Treatise* and only once in the *Ethics* (39, 41) is absolutely central to Spinoza's political treatise and indeed constitutes its subject. In this context there are two movements associated with the term. The first 'absolutist' movement tending towards unity is the relatively conventional question of how the *multitudo* can be governed. But the second 'movement' tending towards plurality concerns the power of the *multitudo* itself: clearly, this is the aspect of Spinoza's political thought that most interests Negri. Negri goes on to elucidate three aspects of this power of the *multitudo* in Spinoza. First of all the *multitudo* is a physical power. For Negri, this concept emerges out of the second foundation of Spinoza's thought constituted by the physics of the passions: "A horizon of bare corporeality and savage multiplicity. A world of physical interconnections and combinations, associations and dissociations . . . according to a perfectly horizontal logic" (233). The *multitudo* as physical power is the force capable of refining these associations and compositions in a manner that, in contradistinction to Hegelian dialectics, rules out any mediation whatsoever. The social itself is the direct product of this physical, assembling power of the multitude. Following from this the *multitudo* is also a natural or animal power: this is the transformation from mere *conatus,* or the persevering in being to *cupiditas* or human desire. This is the level at which the *multitudo* begins to emerge as a political subject but a complex and contradictory one tending at once towards plurality and unity, diverse passions, and the singularity of reason. In fact plurality and diversity are presented as primary and constitutive of reason and unity: "reason traverses the natural field on which social life unfolds but does not manage to overcome its violence and dispersion once and for all" (43).

Finally there is the *multitudo* from the point of view of reason. In this regard, Negri insists that for Spinoza, the *multitudo* cannot be organized by anything like a general will or a social contract, by means of which individual rights would be given up in the name of the collective. Instead, the diverse singularities that constitute the *multitudo* must be constructed or composed in a way that respects every singularity: in other words the freedom of the *multitudo* is the positive rather than the negative foundation of democracy, "insofar as it allows individuals to introduce into society as a whole their own values of freedom" (44). These three levels of explication do not mean that for Negri the *multitudo* in Spinoza is an absolutely transparent concept: on the contrary it is an aporetic one, an essential prism through which the relations between absoluteness and freedom, reason and materiality, and singularity and collectivity necessarily pass. However, it is a highly productive aporia and it is especially productive in insisting on an irreducible subjectivity at play in democracy, constituted by the singularities that compose the multitude, or as Negri puts it "a social praxis of singularities that intersect in a mass process." (45) It is these practices of the multitude that will increasingly be the subject of Negri's own political thought.

Spinoza , Multitude, and Empire: The Place of Spinoza in Negri's Recent Work

This thought of the multitude is also an essential component of Negri's most recent works, including *Insurgencies,* as well as his collaborations with Michael Hardt, *Labor of Dionysus, Empire, Commonwealth,* and, of course *Multitude.* Negri's concept of the multitude, however, finds its most complete expression in *Kairòs, Alma Venus, Multitudo.* According to

Negri, this book, or at least its middle section, was born out of the challenge from a friend to construct a counter-history of materialism, or rather a materialist ontology of constituent power (*potentia*) as the other to Power (in the sense of constituted, transcendental power), drawing inspiration especially from the work of Lucretius.[10] However, having drafted this central part of the book, Negri saw the need to preface it with an account both of materialist knowledge and of temporality, expressed through the concepts of "the common" and *kairòs,* the temporality of the event. However, since what was developed in these first two sections ontologically is explicitly linked to the problematics of thinking and living beyond Marx as the horizon of materialism, a political section also seemed necessary to Negri to relate this materialist ontology to processes of real constitution: the possible emergence of a post-Marxist communism to come. This entailed a return to the Spinozian concept of the multitude, but within a completely contemporary political context and one that necessitated a critical redefinition or subversion of the original concept.

Before analyzing the content of this work, it is worth paying attention to the highly Spinozian way it is organized. This series of nine lessons is elaborated according to a geometrical style which, while less complex than that of Spinoza's *Ethics,* is clearly a reprise of its method.[11] Negri begins with the numbered statement of a proposition or problem, follows it through a numbered series of phases (1.1, 1.2, 1.3 . . .) before moving on to the next, related proposition/problem. These series of proposition are arranged in three related 'lessons' that on the next level constitute the three sections of the book. So in total there are four geometrical levels of composition. However, bearing in mind Negri's problematization of the geometrical method in Spinoza, these levels of organization do not prevent more transversal connections taking place between different parts of the book to the extent that the account of the multitude in the last section is indissociable from the ontological account of knowledge and temporality in the first part. In short, the book itself not only concerns itself with the multitude as a subject but is itself a self-referential, theoretical multiplicity, a crystallization of Negri's thought according to the three axes of knowledge/temporality, materialist ontology, and practice that are nevertheless interwoven. Finally the passage in the book from ontology to politics, from the most abstract propositions to the most concrete ones is itself a reprise of Negri's account of Spinoza's thought: as with Spinoza's project, Negri passes from being to modal existence to politics in a trajectory that continually enriches rather than surpasses each individual component of the work.

---

[10] It is from Lucretius that the expression 'Alma Venus' derives.

[11] It also recalls Wittgenstein's *Tractatus Logico-Philosophicus,* itself at least methodologically inspired by Spinoza.

Kairòs, Alma Venus, Multitudo begins with the concept of the common name, which is a direct development of Spinoza's concept of common notions. What Negri adds to this account is a singular theory of temporality under the name of *kairòs,* which is the dimension he had already identified as being relatively underdeveloped in Spinoza's thought. However, this leads more to a recasting of Spinoza's thought rather than its abandonment, since *kairòs* would be directly related to Spinoza's account of the constitutive ontological power of the imagination: "In Spinoza the imagination has the ontological function of recomposing the strata of being. . . . We must therefore return to Spinoza and rediscover in the imagination not the path that enables us to achieve the synthesis of the understanding, but the risk and the love of knowledge, . . . the creative search of the *to-come.* Because being is *kairòs*" (*Time for Revolution,* 156). This is in contrast to the major currents of Modern philosophy from Kant to Heidegger which, while seeming more attuned to problematics of temporality, translate the ontological imagination into a transcendental realm where its power is "drowned in the dialectic" (156). For this reason while Spinoza drops out of Negri's discussion of the Kairòs itself his ontology is an essential backdrop: if the passing moment is capable of actualizing eternity, this is entirely consistent with the second foundation of Spinozian ontology in which modal existence or *conatus* exists in a necessary, constitutive relationship with eternal substance: all Negri is doing at this point is to give Spinoza's conception a more explicit temporal structure. This is confirmed in the final lesson on *kairòs,* in relation to the materialist field, in which Spinoza is invoked once more in his insistence on the constitutive power of the body and its passions: "Spinoza demonstrates that the body is always positive, because it is the form of the affirmative power of being. What would materialism consist in if not in this primacy of the body?" (175). The buried history of materialism is therefore necessarily a history of bodies, but bodies understood from the perspective of the temporality of *kairòs*: the ever-present possibility of actualizing the eternal, a possibility that Negri associates with the proper names Spinoza, Machiavelli, and Marx. Such a history would be a genealogy of the present, radically open to the to-come: in this way *kairòs* is intimately connected to the concept of the multitude.

In the next section of the book, "Alma Venus," Spinoza is invoked again but this time for introducing desire into ontology: "the rhythm of the constitution of the world is sustained—in a confusion of forms—by a living force that unfolds in the world so as to constitute itself as divine" (186). However, on this occasion Negri engages critically with Spinoza, questioning the limits of his system for a full account of materialism. Despite the radicality of Spinoza's reconciliation of eternity with freedom, for Negri this is weakened by Spinoza's asceticism. The concept of beatitude, in particular, is for Negri the trace of a "classical and idealist teleol-ogy," a transcendental idea of the infinite that undermines the radical imma-nence of Spinoza's project. It is this "transcendental poison" that will be developed and finally exhausted throughout the period of modernity and it is only in postmodernity that it has once again become possible to take Spinoza's radical immanence further in a telos rather than a teleology of the common. Nevertheless, despite this apparent criticism, the following sec-tions on poverty and love are highly indebted to the Spinozian physics of the body and its passions and affects. For example, Negri presents poverty as both an "ontological scandal" (199) and as the site for the renewal or innovation of the eternal in a manner that is highly consistent with Spinoza's second foundation of the *Ethics*. Thoroughly rejecting any con-cept of an outside to postmodern biopolitical regimes such as Agamben's concept of "bare life,"[12] Negri posits poverty as being the biopolitical heart of contemporary societies, even of contemporary being in highly Spinozian terms: "The beautiful is lived as joy of the multitude; it is imagination and expression of all wealth in that absolutely singular moment when the poor lean over the edge of time" (203). In this ways the concepts of *kairòs*, the common, and poverty all converge on the figure of the multitude in a man-ner that is both entirely consistent with Spinoza's thought and takes it into new domains. It is at this point that Negri's new account of the multitude can be presented directly in the last section of the book.

Negri defines the concept of the multitude in several ways, beginning with the following: "an ensemble of singularities whose life-tool is the brain and whose productive force is co-operation" (225). However, as with Spinoza's *multitudo*, this is only one of several definitions. Perhaps a clearer one is the one that is presented a few pages later in relation to the plurality of the biopolitical: "The multitude is an irreducible ensemble of singularities, and singularity is the production of new pluralities, of new multitudes" (230). Exactly how these definitions of the multitude are related to Spinoza's concept of the *multitudo* is not made immediately clear by Negri, a problem exacerbated by the fact that references to Spinoza tend to disappear in this section, despite the continued evocation of other names associated with the genealogy of materialist thought from Lucretius to Deleuze and Foucault. If we recall, however, that Spinoza's concept of the *multitudo* involved the three levels of a physical capacity or power, an "animal" transformation from mere physical force to desire, and finally the multitude from the perspective of reason, Negri's transforma-tion of Spinoza's concept becomes clearer. The physical power of the mul-titude in the contemporary world is precisely as an assemblage of

---

[12] Cf. Giorgio Agamben, *Homo Sacer: Sovereign Power and Bare Life,* trans. Daniel Heller-Roazen, Stanford, California: Stanford University Press, 1998.

cooperating bodies and brains and its "animal" or biopolitical power is the capacity to innovate, to bring into being new singularities. It should be evident that Negri is repeating Spinoza's account of the multitude but with a crucial difference: he is only interested in the movement of the power of the multitude, its capacity for self-organization, rather than in the classical problem of how the multitude can be governed that is still a crucial element of Spinoza's concept. This abandonment of the search for the unity of the multitude parallels Negri's rejection of the mystical elements in Spinoza's thought: for Negri, the capacities of the multitude are still expressed through the affects of joy and love but these are strictly material dimensions of what he calls, after Marx, "living labour."[13]

The question can then be posed as to what becomes of Spinoza's third way of approaching the multitude: the multitude from the perspective of reason. This is already partially answered in that Negri shifts the focus from the question of how the multitude can be governed and organized, to one of how the multitude can organize and govern itself. However, he does this through a remarkable subversion of the political concept of the decision. This is not some Schmittian moment in Negri's thought and he explicitly rejects any notion of the decision as the sovereign's decision on the state of exception: "In no case can the decision be defined as a closure of possibilities, as the power of exception; on the contrary, it will have to be acknowledged as the opening of a new horizon of common power" (249). It is only from the perspective of constituted power that the decision appears to reside with the sovereign. In Negri's materialist account, however, it is always the multitude that is the subject of the decision, in a radical reformulation of Machiavelli's political philosophy: "When one speaks of the decision of the prince one is either saying nothing at all (because when this is an individual decision it is necessarily ineffectual), or one is speaking of the entire process of the activity of the multitude that is concentrated on a point of being—like a torrent that discovers a dam that is able to determine its course" (240). Of course this claim requires a good deal of evaluation on an empirical level: if the decision of the sovereign is really determined by the power of the multitude how does one account for decisions that go against the desires of the multitude, for example a decision to go to war? Would one have to distinguish between different multitudes so that, for example, one distinguishes a right-wing, fundamentalist, Republican multitude, in relation to which the apparent decisions of George W. Bush would be a mere focal point? However, this would be to miss Negri's transformation of the concept of the decision from an individual, voluntarist, mental act, to a corporeal transvaluation that takes

---

[13] See especially the section entitled "Multitudo: Living Labour," *Time for Revolution*, 235–47.

place in the collective practices of the bodies and brains of the multitude. For this reason what usually pass as sovereign decisions are in fact no more than secondary responses to decisions/transvaluations that have already taken place, to collective resistances that are always prior, at least in an ontological sense, to the operations of (bio)political Power.

This view of the decision "from below" (248), is really the crux of Negri's deviation from and subversion of Spinoza's concept of the multitude: no longer is it necessary to understand the passions of the multitude from the exterior perspective of reason; rather it is essential to grasp the rationality of the multitude as a biopolitical self-organizing force of innovation and creation and to affirm it. In this way *Kairòs, Alma Venus, Multitudo* not only constitutes a reworking of Spinoza's political philosophy but also a new *Ethics,* in its insistence on taking Spinoza's radical immanence further. It is the rejection of any residual absolutizing tendencies, whether of a political nature as in Spinoza's *Political Treatise,* or of a mystical or ascetic nature as in the *Ethics,* in favor of an ethical affirmation of the power of the multitude that is absolutely materialist and nonteleological

This essay has presented Negri's engagement with Spinoza, not as a mere exercise in the history of philosophy, but in order to bring out what is distinctive about Negri's thought, even in relation to other thinkers of the autonomist Marxist tradition such as Mario Tronti or Paolo Virno.[14] Certainly, Negri is not alone in invoking Spinoza as "the only materialist tradition,"[15] but the level of his engagement with Spinoza's ontology is unique. The only contemporary thinker to approach this level of proximity to Spinoza's thought is Gilles Deleuze and in many ways both *Empire* and *Kairòs, Alma Venus, Multitudo* can be seen as productive, critical engagements with Deleuze's thought, as alternative versions of a contemporary Spinozian political ontology. However, in Negri's insistence on the concept of the multitude rather than on multiplicities, and his insistence on Spinoza's productive ontology, rather than the ontogenesis of becomings, he is more Spinozian even than Deleuze, despite the latter's invocation of Spinoza as the prince or even the Christ of philosophers.

If we return to the citation that began this essay, we can begin to see how even the project of *Empire,* so seemingly located in the present, is completely saturated by a Spinozian ontology in which the ontological full-

---

[14] Cf. Paolo Virno, *A Grammar of the Multitude,* trans. Isobella Bertoletti, James Cascaito, and Andrea Casson, New York: Semiotext(e), 2004, which while acknowledging the Spinozian derivation of the concept of the multitude, substitutes a largely Marxist framework for any engagement with Spinozian ontology.

[15] Cf. Louis Althusser, "The Only Materialist Tradition, Part 1: Spinoza," *The New Spinoza,* 3–19.

ness and constituent power of the multitude, considered as *potentia* is contrasted with the parasitical operations of Empire or constituted power (*potestas*). Even the organization of the book, particularly the two parallel sections entitled "Passages of Sovereignty" (67–204) and "Passages of Production" (219–350), seem to constitute a Spinozian parallelism between thought and extension which, however, tends towards indiscernibility in the final section of the book. Similarly, in the recent series of interviews appearing in English under the title *Negri on Negri,* Negri reiterated this relevance of Spinoza to contemporary political struggles: "We have in our hands the promise of a fearless society. This is what Spinoza said—and what has been rediscovered by feminists, workers and students and all those who hope [. . .] and wish [. . .] something would change" (Negri, *Negri on Negri* 29).

This Spinozian dimension of Negri's thought is expressed most explicitly, however, in *Multitude,* in which this concept is strongly allied with another Spinozian-derived concept, that of the common. In the preface to *Multitude,* the authors link the concepts of the multitude and the common in the following way: "Insofar as the multitude is neither an identity (like the people) nor uniform (like the masses), the internal differences of the multitude must discover *the common* that allows them to communicate and act together. The common we share, in fact, is not so much discovered as it is produced" (Hardt and Negri, *Multitude,* xv). Just as Negri had reworked Spinoza's concept of the multitude from his *Political Treatise,* Hardt and Negri rework Spinoza's concept of common notions from the *Ethics* translating this concept from an epistemological to an immediately political register. In fact it is precisely through this constitutive and productive concept of the common that the authors are able to provide a more precise definition of the multitude, clearly distinguishing it from related concepts such as of the people, the masses, or the working class. In fact, what the common allows for in particular is for a concept of a collective multiplicity irreducible to any unity. This was already the case in Negri's previous engagement with the concept but up to this point it had never been expressed with such clarity. This brings out another Spinozist dimension of *Multitude,* namely the project of producing a work in the register of the common, not only between the two authors but between the authors and their readers. This explains the generosity with which they engage with previous criticisms of *Empire,* for example, as well as the incredibly simple yet clear language in which *Multitude* is written. If *Empire* was already a Spinozist work on a conceptual plane, *Multitude* incorporates a Spinozian approach formally, through the experimentation and development of a common language capable of engaging the maximum number of readers, without sacrificing conceptual complexity. As such, *Multitude* has a strong relationship to *Kairòs, Alma Venus,*

Multitude, as an alternative Spinozian textual procedure that instead of deploying a hermetic, geometric method would be as open and discursive as possible. Nevertheless, both texts, in their own style are texts tending in the direction of the common.

As a final observation that brings us back to the beginning of this essay, one of the most striking conceptual innovations in *Multitude* is the elaboration of a corporeal account of the multitude in terms of the monstrosity of the flesh. The concept of the flesh is used by Hardt and Negri to refer to a contemporary breakdown of corporeal hierarchy in relation to both the individual and the social body. Despite both the Christian and phenomenological resonances of this concept, it again brings us back to Spinoza's project, in which bodies and passions would be described with the same rigor as lines, planes, and solids. While this emphasis on embodiment is hardly unique in contemporary social theory, its presentation in *Multitude* is in a critical relationship with postmodern theories of the body which tend toward models of corporeal organization rather than embracing the monstrous singularity of the flesh that was already signaled in the work of Spinoza: "Spinoza is the one who most clearly anticipates this monstrous nature of the multitude by conceiving of life as a tapestry on which the singular passions weave a common capacity of transformation, from desire to love and from the flesh to the divine body" (194). Not only is Spinoza evoked here in support of this highly original conception of the monstrosity of the multitude, but this monstrosity takes us back to Negri's *Savage Anomaly* with which this essay began. It is on this terrain of monstrosity that the nonlinear but crucial trajectory of Negri's thought over the last thirty years, in its profound relation to Spinoza's philosophy, can perhaps be most powerfully grasped.

8

How Savage Was Spinoza?
Spinoza and the Economic Life of
Seventeenth-Century Holland

GEORGE C. CAFFENTZIS

The said Huygens was, and is still fully occupied in polishing dioptrical glasses. For this purpose he has constructed a machine, in which he can turn tools, and it is indeed sufficiently neat. But I do not yet know what advance he has made thereby, nor, to confess the truth, do I greatly desire to know. For experience has taught me sufficiently that in spherical tools it is safer and better for glasses to be polished with a free hand than by any machine. Of the success of pendulums, and the date of his moving to France I cannot as yet write anything certain. (Spinoza to Oldenburg, November 20, 1665)

This is part of a letter that I will examine in the course of this paper to establish a methodological point concerning the study of Spinoza's philosophy. But before I turn to this task, let me pause for a moment and listen to the voice of the writer. It is self-confident and almost scornful of the efforts of a competitor in the business of lens making. Lens grinding and polishing was an essential high-tech industry of the day, for lenses were something like seventeenth-century computer-chips in that they appeared in many of the most important scientific, mercantile, and military instruments of the day, from telescopes and binoculars to microscopes and spectacles (Wolf 1950). It is not surprising that many in the industry like Christian Huygens would be looking for a way to increase lens-making productivity (and lower the cost of production), hence "the machine."[1]

---

[1] The nature of manufacturing in the Netherlands is discussed at length in (DuPlessis and Howell 1991). They argue that "small commodity production" was still an essential element of manufacturing in the seventeenth century and that full-fledged entrepreneurial capitalism was not yet dominant either politically or economically. Hence the picture they sketch of seventeenth century Netherlands is of an economy still in the process of transition even in the textile trades. On the other side, of course, the Netherlands was at that time the most dynamic player on the world market. This would pose a contradiction indeed for any ruling

193

Spinoza's response is one that we have heard from artisans so frequently in the past few hundred years: better the "free hand" than "the machine." It is also based on the curious mixture of *a priori* and *a posteriori* reasoning that weavers, watchmakers, and other skilled workers have proffered in the face of a new technology. "Experience has taught me" that the free hand is better, but "I do not greatly desire to know" what advances the machine has made. In other words, experience has taught me I need experience no longer! So with the scorn is an apprehension, of course. The said, Huygens, after all, was the son of Constantijn Huygens, Secretary to three Princes of Orange and Lord of Zuylichem; a mathematical and experimental prodigy, the inventor of the micrometer and the pendulum chronometer, and soon to be on his way to an important (and lucrative) post as chief scientific and technological advisor to the French throne at the behest of Colbert while leaving his lens-making factory in the hands of his brother. The competition had capital, brains, and connections. Therefore the undertone of competitive fear is appropriate.[2]

I have opened this paper on Spinoza's philosophy with a piece of microhistory from seventeenth-century high-tech business and industrial espionage for a reason. Spinoza has been taken as the purest of pure philosophers. At best, the images we receive of this most reclusive philosopher is of an excommunicated pariah, neither Jewish nor Christian, a *marrano* of *marranos*, a person so marginalized that he became universal, and an absolute exception to a historical materialism he anticipates (see e.g., Yovel 1989). Synthesizing these images of his life with his abstract quasimathematical efforts to understand God, Nature, and Humanity, the prevailing view of Spinoza as the purest of pure philosophers and the most singular exception of early modern thinkers seems uncontestable.

Expressions of this view are extensive and quite current. Indeed, Spinoza's biographical details are uttered with a certain pride, as if the commentator has finally found someone in the history of philosophy not tainted by ideology. For example, Alasdair MacIntyre writes of Spinoza: "[his] life has least apparent connection with his work. . . . If every fact that we now possess about Spinoza's life were lost to us, his writings would be no more difficult to interpret than they are now, for the difficulties are considerable" (MacIntyre 1967).

Similarly, Alan Donagan in *Spinoza in Context* (1988) devotes only three pages in his more than two hundred page book on, in his words,

---

class. As we shall see, Spinoza's jobs spanned the totality of this contradiction: from import-export merchant to small commodity-producing artisan to industrial/political agent and spy.

  [2] For a general discussion of the tension between artisanal experience and the reality of industrial production see (Sohn-Rethal 1978, chap. 17)

"What Students of Spinoza's Thought Need to Know about his Life, and What They Need Not Know." He summarizes the "necessary" facts of Spinoza's life:

> He was born and reared as a Jew in a community of Marrano immigrants into the Netherlands; he was expelled from the Jewish community for heresy; he did not renounce his cultural heritage, but wished to communicate it to non-Jews; he was a respected, even celebrated, member of the North European community of scientifically-minded philosophers; he refused to become a Christian; and he professed allegiance to the United Provinces of the Netherlands. Generally, his life was of a piece with what he wrote: discoveries about its details—apart from facts about his intellectual exchanges—bear dubiously on disputed questions about what he thought. (Donagan 1988, 10–11)

It is important to note that Donagan does not list the ways in which Spinoza endeavored to survive among the "necessary" facts of his life.

An even more sophisticated and influential recent version of this view is to be found in Antonio Negri's *The Savage Anomaly: The Power of Spinoza's Metaphysics and Politics* which was written in a number of Italian prisons between April 7, 1979 and April 7, 1980.[3] This paper takes its querying title from Negri's book because his view of Spinoza's philosophy as a "savage anomaly" is simply the latest and most passionate contribution to a long commentary tradition that puts Spinoza "outside of history."

I will provide evidence in this paper to show that Negri's exceptional approach to Spinoza is not accurate and that the tradition it extends should be revised. For if one delves into the "details" of Spinoza's life, especially the jobs he did, one would see quite clearly that his curriculum vitae was quite similar to most of the major intellectuals of the seventeenth century (part business man, part industrial spy, and mostly political agent for one or another element of the ruling class of Europe). Moreover, his philosophy had a specific role to play in the political conflicts, industrial intrigues, and class struggles of the epoch. Of course, if one finds "resonances" in his philosophy for the present and if one, like Negri, draws moral support and political cover from his example, then one need not read into his work a teleological message. The use of the intellectual wealth from the past for either edification or strategic conception is a surplus value that is not unique to Spinoza's philosophy.

First, let us consider Negri's claims concerning Spinoza's life and philosophy. According to Negri, one of the most controversial Marxist

---

[3] On Negri's role in autonomia and the background to *The Savage Anomaly* see (Caffentzis 1987).

philosophers of the current generation, Spinoza violates Marx's theory of ideology in order to produce an anticapitalist "philosophy of the future" that would in fact influence Marx's very theory of ideology! For he sees a duplicitous Spinoza; the first being explicable via a theory of ideology and another as an exception to it:

> The first [Spinoza] expresses the highest consciousness that the scientific revolution and the civilization of the Renaissance have produced; the second produces a philosophy of the future. The first is the product of the highest and most extensive development of the cultural history of its time; the second accomplishes a dislocation and projection of the ideas of crisis and revolution. The first is the author of the capitalist order, the second is perhaps the author of a future constitution. (Negri 1991, 4)

> The doubling of Spinoza's thought, that internal leap that dislocates its significance onto diverse horizons, is an anomaly so strong and so specific to Spinozian thought that it makes it both close to us, possible for us to grasp, and at the same time irreducible to any of historical ideology's mechanisms of filiation or systematization. What we are presented with is an absolute exception. (Negri 1991, 5)

The sense of an absolute violation of the rules of historical interpretation that Spinoza's philosophy poses is so strong, Negri claims, it verges on being equivalent to the sacred. "In effect, this definition of his thought that we are proposing comes close to denying that he belongs to history" (Negri 1991, 20). At the very least, Spinoza seems to have leaped over his own historical shadow: "The paradox of Spinoza's thought can be seen in this aspect: his philosophy is presented to us as a postbourgeois philosophy" (Negri 1991, 20).

The rhetorical savagery here is more Negri's than Spinoza's, I'm afraid. Indeed, it seems to violate all of Spinoza's hermeneutical principles as well as his extremely sober assessment of the complex, subtle, and nonteleological conditions of intellectual production. Certainly Negri in *The Savage Anomaly* is savagely anti-Spinozian (and puts the lie to Deleuze's understandable claim that the imprisoned Negri was "authentically and profoundly Spinozian.")

Was Spinoza as "anti-bourgeois" as Negri claims? One way to confront this question is to directly probe Negri's commentary on the development of the *Ethics* in the context of Spinoza's political thought. For he believes that the "interruption" of the *Ethics* in 1665 with Spinoza's beginning of the *Theologico-Political Treatise* was crucial for understanding the structure of the *Ethics*. So also the fact that Spinoza takes up the *Political Treatise* on completing the *Ethics* in 1673 is seen as central in our understanding the intent of Spinoza's metaphysics. And there is no doubt that this alternating motion from metaphysics to politics is an important aspect of Spinoza's work that Negri correctly emphasizes.

However, though Negri plays the game of interpretation on a level that allows for an easy ignition of intellectual pyrotechnics, his performance is ultimately as much at home in the standard world of "the history of ideas" as the work of Cassirer, Lovejoy and Gay. True, Negri contrasts the development of "bourgeois" political thought from Hobbes to Rousseau to Hegel with an "alternative" path from Machiavelli to Spinoza to Marx that "indicates the unity of the human project of liberation against bourgeois mediation" (Negri 1991, 141). Yet I remain skeptical of the continuity of this "project" especially in respect with its mediating link, Spinoza himself. For the bourgeoisie is not a simple essence with one story, even in this period. Consequently, when Negri notes a cleavage between Spinoza and the social contract tradition, one cannot simply presume he is outside of the development of the strategies of class domination in the seventeenth century altogether.

I prefer a more ampliative method in the analysis of Spinoza's work, i.e., one that starts with a precise problem of interpretation and then notes what contextual knowledge is required to solve it. Facts and hypotheses about Spinoza's work and life that are required to adequately interpret key passages of his work will reveal themselves in a spiral, an ever-inclusive rhythm. Exceptionality, especially "absolute" exceptionality, should only be concluded after all such ampliative attempts have failed.

In this paper I argue that knowledge of certain frequently ignored biographical facts is essential in explaining some disputed questions about what Spinoza thought. For without such knowledge it will be quite easy to project onto Spinoza the concerns of our era, confusing both his work and the incisiveness of our own thought in dealing with the struggles of our own period, as Negri has done.

To do this I will further examine a letter Spinoza sent to Henry Oldenburg in 1665, a part of which I quoted as the epigraph of this paper. It is a reply to Oldenburg's (and through Oldenburg, Robert Boyle's) request for an exposition of his philosophy: "Especially do we warmly beseech you to communicate it to us, if you see any light on that most difficult investigation, which turns on the question of our knowing how each part of Nature accords with the whole of it, and in what way it is connected with all the other parts" (Spinoza 1966, 206–207).[4] Spinoza's reply

---

[4] For an insightful analysis of Robert Boyle (and his circle, including Oldenburg) see (Jacob 1977). He summarizes Boyle's general intellectual perspective in the following passage: "Boyle's concern and the concern of some of his colleagues in the Royal Society for empire, trade and the millennium suggests that we cannot accept the stereotype of the Royal

(though delayed by the wind for a week) was relatively prompt, especially given the fact that he was mailing it from The Hague to London, the capitals of two nations warring with each other at the time and the recipient was the employee of the King of England and the crony of the chief member of the English government's Council for Foreign Planations.[5] It has within it one of the most famous expositions of his "difficult" metaphysics:

> Let us now, if you please, imagine that a small worm lives in the blood, whose sight is keen enough to distinguish the particles of blood, lymph, etc., and has reason to observe how each part on collision with another either rebounds, or communicates a part of its own motion, etc. That worm would live in this blood as we live in this part of the universe, and he would consider each particle of blood to be a whole, and not a part. And he could not know how all the parts are controlled by the universal nature of blood, and are forced, as the universal nature of blood demands, to adapt to one another, so as to harmonize with one another in a certain way. (Spinoza 1966, 210–211)

This is a striking image and it has had an important place in Spinoza's exposition of his own thought. Oldenburg, in his reply, wrote that it "gave [him] much pleasure" and in a separate letter to Boyle he mentioned that Spinoza's passage on "the agreement and coherence of the parts of the world with the whole" entertained him. Unfortunately, Oldenburg's reply

---

Society, derived from the accounts of its origins by Wallis and Sprat, that the men whose meetings in London and Oxford in the 1640s and 1650s led to its founding were devoted to pursuing a science divorced from religion and politics-and this may have been Sprat and Wallis' meaning-but their own ideology of science was neither apolitical nor unrelated to religion. Instead it was an aggressive, acquisitive, materialistic, imperialistic ideology justified in the name of the Reformation. This is not to say that those who put it forward were insincere about religion, but theirs was a religion of greed and self-aggrandizement. Given the circumstance, it seemed the best alternative. England was divided by deep religious and political cleavages and challenged by Catholic Europe. The ideology of the Royal Society would compose internal differences by committing every group and individual in the nation to experimental science and its material fruits. Both internal order and pursuit of science, trade, and empire would make England strong enough to face and ultimately overcome the external threat posed by her Catholic enemies" (Jacob 1977, 158–59). At the time of the interchange between Oldenburg and Spinoza, Boyle was writing *A Free Inquiry into the Vulgarly Received Notion of Nature* where he challenged "conception deriving from ancient Greek philosophy, both Neoplatonic and Aristotlean, that there is a governing agency in nature apart from God which cannot be reduced to the mechanical principles of matter and motion" (Ibid., 160).

  [5] For more on the Second Anglo-Dutch War see (Geyl 1964). It should be noted that Oldenburg was imprisoned in 1677 for two months in the Tower of London under suspicion of spying for enemy powers.

of December 8, 1665 was the last correspondence between Spinoza and the secretary of the English Royal Society for another decade; consequently, we cannot know what he would have said to Oldenburg's probing criticism: "I do not follow sufficiently how we can exclude order and symmetry from Nature, as you seem to do. . . ."

Indeed, there is much else about this self-exposition by the purest of philosophers that might trouble someone like Oldenburg. Why are "we" like the worm? Why is "this part of the universe" like the blood? Moreover, why does Spinoza's extended metaphor imply, for Oldenburg, an exclusion of order from Nature? These questions can, of course, be dealt with on the basis of his writing concerning whole and part in other parts of his work. Thus, for example, we can see that by his adamant refusal to identify substance with anything but God *or* Nature (in an inclusive sense) as whole, he then logically loses the temptation to substantialize the part. In so doing, Spinoza's thought is a step toward that "functionalization" of the body and the ego that the neo-Kantians like Simmel saw as the hallmark of modernity (Simmel 1978).

Perhaps Oldenburg's demand for "order and symmetry" arose out of a demand for a more clearly defined hierarchy that would place the relation of part to whole in a moral-political system. But however hard we look in Spinoza's work there is no clue as to the worm in the blood image. Where does it come from? Why does it trigger Oldenburg's anxiety? It is here that my claim for the importance of knowledge concerning Spinoza's place in the economic life of seventeenth-century Holland is relevant. Indeed, if we did not see in his economic activity an essential clue to understanding his work, his work would be decisively refuted!

There were three ways in which Spinoza actually received the money necessary to live in the extremely monetarized Dutch economy of his day. First, from his tenth year until his twenty-third (at least) Spinoza was an apprentice and then a full-fledged merchant and middleman in the import-export trade and money market of Amsterdam. He was an apprentice to his father, Michael, who was a moderately successful "merchant" born in Portugal and involved in, for example, importing raisins from Malaga in Spain and sugar from Brazil. After Michael's death in 1654, Spinoza went into partnership with his brother Gabriel, continuing the import-export trade of their father and taking over "wisselbriefs"—in effect, being collection agents in the frequently forfeiting world of international exchange. One important consequence of Spinoza's *herem* in 1656 was the loss of his access to the complex network of economic relations between Africa, the Iberian Peninsula, the Caribbean, and South America afforded him by being a member of the Jewish community of Amsterdam. This loss meant the end of his part in the mercantile world. We shall see, however, that this personal experience in the world market would be central to his understanding of God *sive* Nature.[6]

The second method by which Spinoza endeavored to live was, as we saw in the beginning of this paper, as an artisan in one of the most competitive industries of the world market: the grinding and polishing of lenses. This work would also give Spinoza an insight into a new microworld of "minute bodies," as Robert Hooke put it in the title of his book *Micrographia* (1665) that was being mapped with the aid of this industry.

The final channel of Spinoza's income flow was via "the pension." His friends and disciples provided him with a modest income, e.g., one of his most devoted followers, the Amsterdam merchant Simon de Vries, arranged for an annuity of five hundred florins (which Spinoza voluntarily decreased to three hundred). Indeed, Spinoza's first biographer, Lucas, claimed that Jan de Witt, the Grand Pensionary of Holland, "had given [Spinoza] a pension of two hundred francs." Whether this is true or not (it is disputed by Herbert Rowen, de Witt's most recent biographer), there is no doubt that Spinoza was supported financially by many influential figures in the ruling circle around de Witt like Hudde (the mayor of Leiden), Burgh (the Treasure General of the United Netherlands), Beuningen (the mayor of Amsterdam) and Boxel (the Pensionary of Gorkum). Summing the annuities, pensions, and lens sales together would most probably have put the mature Spinoza's annual income on par with the 600 guilder annual income of the man who excommunicated him, high rabbi Saul Levi Morteira, received from the Holy Jewish Community of Amsterdam (Levin 1970, 24).

Spinoza at the time of his "worm in the blood" letter was a high-tech artisan, with a "hands-on" experience in world trade, the *guru* of merchants and advisor to the most advanced ruling class in the world. He was neither poor nor lonely, in *our* present meaning of these words. Are these facts "necessary" for a student to understand Spinoza's image? Well, let us see.

The most obvious source of the image, of course, was from the literal explosion of microscopy in the years immediately preceding 1665. Spinoza mentions in a previous letter to Oldenburg a conversation with Huygens who told him "many wonderful things about these microscopes." Perhaps among them were the eels in vinegar described by Hooke (whose book Huygens possessed). But why does Spinoza place his worm *in blood*? Blood was for many in the seventeenth century the locus of union between body and soul. That most famous contemporary student of the blood, William

---

[6] For an imaginative and useful account of Spinoza the young merchant and collection agent in the crux of the world market see (Levin 1970). A good general history of the place of the Netherlands in the world market of the seventeenth century is (van Houtte 1977).

Harvey, argued thus in his last book *De generatione animalium* (1651): "[The] blood is the prime genital Part, whence the *soul* primarily results . . . the *blood* lives and is nourished of it selfe, no way depending upon any other part of the *body*, as elder or worthier than it selfe." Indeed, Dr. John Collop versified Harvey in 1656 thus:

> Thus blood, Sun-like, gives motion, life and sense, Distinct from Blood, who can the Soul aught call?[7]

Harvey's ontological primacy of the blood and its intimate relation to the soul was not new (although it was supported by a careful observation of priority in the ovulation of hens' eggs). Michael Servetus in his *Christianismi Restitutio* (1553) claimed that "The soul itself is the blood" and posited one of the first theories of the circulation of a unitary blood system (and not one divided into two fluids, the veinus and the arterial bloods). He became famous, or rather infamous, because Calvin himself tried him for the heretical implications of his teachings and had him burned at the stake. His name would, undoubtedly, have been remembered in the largely Calvinist Netherlands with some foreboding by the circle of scientific and technological intellectuals opposing Calvin's heirs. The implication that brought Servetus to his death was that if blood and the soul are identified, then the death of the body and the cessation of circulation would mean the death of the soul (Hill 1974a, 169–70).

These implications are, however, exactly what Spinoza claimed in his metaphysical critique of Descartes. They would, undoubtedly, have struck Oldenburg, who was a careful student of Spinoza's differences with Descartes, as significant. The worm therefore is in an active, living fluid that was *both* body *and* mind. Hence we have established one reason for Spinoza's use of the blood in his metaphor.

However, Spinoza's blood fluid was not the magical fluid of Bruno and the iatrochemists. It was an iatromechanical fluid made up of "minute particles" as studied by Hooke and power. The worm apparently sees particles of chyle, lymph, and blood separately dancing and colliding into each other, and therefore it (like us) considers them as wholes. But then again it sees them all flowing together "so mutually adapted" and it considers them parts of the bloody whole. But is the blood whole or parts?

The worm's contradiction is "our" own, Spinoza argues, since it is ignorant of "the universal nature of blood" which controls and forces the parts "to harmonize." The microscopist might pity the worm's ignorance

---

[7] For a discussion of the political significance of the science of blood in the seventeenth century see the spirited debate between Christopher Hill and Gweneth Whitteridge (Hill 1974a, 1974b; Whitteridge 1974).

of the distant violence of the heart's spasms, or the flow to the capillaries, or the return of the fluid to the oxidizing catastrophe of the lungs, etc. Knowledge of these systemic moments resolves the contradiction for the microscopist: the particles of chyle, lymph, and blood are *just parts* since their motion and action is determined by external causes. The non-Spinozistic microscopist, however, is intellectually a worm confusing parts and wholes in a world surrounded by moving and colliding bodies. This is because the relation of the worm to the blood fluid is a finite one, but the relation of the microscopist to the universe is infinite. Thus, Spinoza tells Oldenburg that Oldenburg's master's (Boyle's) corpuscles can have no autonomy, nor, however, do they need an extra-universal God-agent to order them.[8] Here we see another reason for the metaphor, beside the hylozoological: the micrographical blood is a model for a system that is a whole whose parts are only apparently wholes.

Up to now we have seen the source of Spinoza's metaphor in his work as an artisan supplier of the instruments of the modern study of the blood, but there is another layer in the metaphor that would have been understood by Oldenburg which has its roots in another aspect of Spinoza's involvement of the economic life of the Netherlands. This was the period when the notion of the circular flow of economic life was becoming a commonplace. In a notorious book printed in 1651, *Leviathan*, written by a philosopher Spinoza studied scrupulously, Thomas Hobbes, "Mony the Bloud of a Commonwealth" is a section heading. Hobbes writes there:

> By Concoction, I understand the reducing of all commodities, which are not presently consumed, but reserved for Nourishment in time to come, to something of equall value, and withall so portable as not to hinder the motion of men from place to place; to the end a man may have in what

---

[8] A good early (1649–1653) statement of Boyle's conception of the relation between God and the corpuscular universe is following passage from *Some Considerations Concerning the Usefulness of Natural Philosophy*: "methinks we may, without absurdity, conceive, that God . . . having resolved before the creation, to make such a world as this of ours, did divide (at least if he did not create it incoherent) that matter, which he had provided, into an innumerable multitude of very variously figured corpuscles, and both connected these particles into such textures or particular bodies, and placed them in such situations, and put them into such motions, that by the assistance of his ordinary preserving concourse, the phaenomena, which he intended should appear in the universe, must as orderly follow and be exhibited by the bodies necessarily acting according to those impressions or laws, though they understand them not at all, as if each of those creatures had a design of self-preservation, and were furnished with knowledge and industry to prosecute it; and as if there were diffused through the universe an intelligent being, watchful over the pub lick good of it, and careful to administer all things wisely for the good of the particular parts of it, but so far forth as is consistent with the good of the whole" (Jacob 1977, 115).

place soever, such Nourishment as the place affordeth. And this is nothing
else but Gold, and Silver, and Mony...and the same passeth from Man to
Man, within the Common-wealth; and goes round about, Nourishing (as
it passeth) every part thereof; in so much as this Concoction, is as it were
the Sanguification of the Common-wealth: For naturall Bloud is in like
manner made of the fruits of the Earth; and circulating, nourisheth by the
way every Member of the Body of Man. (Hobbes 1985, 300)

This metaphor is not only Hobbes's; it can be found in his rival
Harrington's *Oceana* as well. In fact, innumerable tracts and pamphlets
attest to the metaphorical link of money and blood.[9] Surely it spoke to
Spinoza's experience as the son of a Jewish merchant and a practicing merchant himself *in Amsterdam*. I emphasize "in Amsterdam" because it is
there that elementary connections necessary for the creation and sustenance of a world market were worked out.

The Jewish community's arrival in Amsterdam brought trading ties
with the mortal enemies of the Netherlands: Spain and Portugal, and
through them contact with their world empire in the Americas, Africa, and
Asia. But they also found themselves in an environment that could use
their potential. For the Dutch had begun to form a conception of a high-
tech, world-trade economy not limited by the givens of the "natural economy." Their very success in draining sea-covered land showed the dramatic
power of scientifically applied labor to destroy one of the most hallowed
constants of Nature: the fixity of land. But even more dramatically they
showed how a mastery of the circular flows of trade and the instruments
of exchange can almost paradoxically create wealth from nothing. As a
keen contemporary observer of the Netherlands, English ambassador Sir
William Temple noted in 1672:

'Tis evident to those who have read the most, and travel'd the farthest,
That no Countrey can be found either in this present Age, or upon Record
of any Story, Where so vast a Trade has been managed, as in the narrow
compass of the Four Maritime Provences of this Commonwealth; Nay it is
generally esteemed, that they have more Shipping belongs to them, than
there does to all the rest of Europe, Yet they have no Native Commodities
towards the building of rigging of the smallest Vessel; Their Flax, Hemp,
Pitch, Wood and Iron, coming all from abroad, as Wool does for cloathing
their men, and Corn for feeding them. (Temple 1968, 163)

He, in an almost Spinozistic vein, attempts to explain this capitalist suc-

---

[9] This was not the only metaphoric link between "the Body Natural, and the Body
Politic" relevant to the money-commodity-money flow during this period. In the same year
Spinoza wrote his worm-in-the-blood letter to Oldenburg William Petty published *Verbum
Sapienti* in which he concluded, "For money is but the fat of the body-politic, whereof too
much doth as often hinder its agility, as too little makes it sick" (Hutchison 1988, 36).

cess by the very lack of substantial resources which forced those with capital out to sea and those without to labor or invent "or else to want."

Spinoza developed his philosophy in the context of a direct experience with the world market. Consequently, the metaphor of the worm in the blood reflects the economic dimension of acting in such a market as much as it intersects with physiological and micrographical thought of the seventeenth century. For Spinoza presents an image of perpetual exchange and activity "colliding"—"rebounding"—"communicating," but the power and discipline of operating in a world market force the agent to take a very mediated relation to experience. In order to do business in such a context one cannot attribute wholeness to the units of economic life that "live in this part of the universe." Indeed, this loss of wholeness must be self-reflexively applied.[10]

The most refined and abstracted intellectuality of Spinoza's metaphysics does not demonstrate the supremacy of an ahistorical reason in his thought. But as Simmel points out in his *The Philosophy of Money*, this kind of intellectuality is essentially connected with the rise and totalization of a monetary economy. In a sort of oblique commentary on Spinoza's philosophy, he wrote in 1900:

> Money places the actions and relations of men quite outside of men as human subjects, just as intellectual life—in so far as it is purely intellectual—moves from personal subjectivity into the sphere of objectivity which it only reflects. This obviously implies a relationship of superiority. Just as he who has money is superior to he who has the commodity, so the intellectual person as such has a certain power over the more emotional, impulsive person. (Simmel 1978, 436)

This abstract superiority is redolent in the worm in the blood passage. For

---

[10] Spinoza did not ironically develop this mediational relation to all things, including the self. The whole Dutch economic "miracle" was written in the famous letters of original accumulation's "fire and blood." And this blood was not only that of Africans and Native Americans, as Marx pointed out: "The colonial system ripened, like a hot-house, trade and navigation. The 'societies Monopolia' of Luther were power levers for concentration of capital. The colonies secured a market for the budding manufactures, and, through the monopoly of the market, an increasing accumulation. The treasures captured outside Europe by undisguised looting, enslavement, and murder, floated back to the mother-country and were there turned into capital. Holland, which first fully developed the colonial system, in 1648 stood already in the acme of its commercial greatness. It was 'in almost exclusive possession of the East Indian trade and the commerce between the southeast and northwest of Europe. Its fisheries, marine, manufactures, surpassed those of any other country. The total capital of the Republic was probably more important than that of all the rest of Europe put together.' Gulich forgets to add that by 1648, the people of Holland were more over worked, poorer and more brutally oppressed than those of all the rest of Europe put together" (Marx 1936, 826).

the wise merchant will not get lost in the round of immediate business transactions; s/he will understand that all the emotional depressions and manias that pass through the circulatory system of the world market do not have the final source in any particular (originary) event. It is the system as a whole that is determining the parts and not the (apparent) parts the whole. Hence Spinoza's rejection of what for him would be Oldenburg's emotional demand for "order and symmetry" since "things cannot, except with respect to our imagination, be called beautiful or ugly, ordered or confused." Oldenburg, the Anglicized German, and his imperialist boss, Robert Boyle, still had much to learn about the rigor of the world market!

We have now seen the two-fold meaning of the blood in Spinoza's metaphor, having its roots in the new research on the body as well as the new experience of a world market. But what of the other element of the metaphor or allegory, the worm? It is definitely not the medieval worm that appears in the corpse in the after-hour of death to reveal the vain veil of tears of human existence. Microscopy, on the contrary, revealed for all to see that worms are essential constituents of the living, functioning body. There was, however, a sort of worm in the vicinity of the writer, on his writing desk to be precise. Spinoza had a ring-seal shaped as a snake eating his tail, an *orobarus*, and the inscription of the ring, along with his initials was "Caute" (the Latin word for "Beware"). This piece of jewelry excited much comment and was one of the few "extravagances" Spinoza spared for himself.

What is the relationship between the worm in the blood and the circular, infinite snake on Spinoza's writing desk? The worm has a "keen" sight and reason. It is a sort of spy in the circulatory system. It sees divisions, struggles, and reconciliations among the factions of the blood. It is full of information and intelligence about things other than itself, which it believes to be self-determining wholes. But it is, for all its intelligence, abysmally wrong. It is not *cautious* enough. For not only does the worm not see the circulatory system of the blood it is a part of, it does not see and distinguish the larger system that controls "the laws of the nature of the blood." For "every body, in so far as it exists modified in a certain way, must be considered to be a part of the whole universe, to be in accord with the whole of it, and to be connected with the other parts." Thus, though the worm is stuck with the details of chyle, lymph, and blood particles, Spinoza the orobarus, reflecting on the worm, passes from it, to the blood system, to the human Body, to the infinitely powerful Nature (or God).

However, in seventeenth century discourse "God" ("*sive* Nature," for Spinoza) is a synonym for the State. The multiplicities of theological schemata of the time were used by government officials, or aspiring government officials, as paradigms for the architecture of the State. Indeed, much of the work of seventeenth century intellectuals was the formation and simulated testing of these theological/political models. Spinoza, Hobbes, Descartes, Leibniz and Locke were intelligence agents, (though not *only* in the "cloak and dagger" tradition).[11] That is why they invariably had direct economic relations to state planners or, indeed, they were state planners themselves. Spinoza's worm in the blood image is of the typical intelligence agent in the state machine that views all about it as separate wholes.

But the intelligence agent that observes the worm whose blood it is the worm sees presents another model of the state and intelligence. When Spinoza writes to Oldenburg, "that worm would live in this blood as we live in this part of the universe . . ." he is not being completely honest. Spinoza is not truly a member of the "we;" he has a notion of himself that is not that of the wormy intelligence. His model of the place of the intellectual in the power relations between human bodies and the state (God *sive* Nature) is quite different from the other models Oldenburg is familiar with: the Renaissance magus or the Mechanical Philosopher.

Giordano Bruno was the classic example of the intelligence agent as Renaissance magus whose way of power is through the manipulation of erotic magic and its allied imagery. As Couliano has pointed out, Bruno posed a model of the relationship between the intellectual and the multitude that is strikingly and cynically post-modern:

> All mankind has heard of Machiavelli's *The Prince*, and many politicians have hastened to emulate his example. But only today can we appreciate how much [Bruno's] *De vinculis* [*in genera*] outstrips *The Prince* in depth, in timeliness, in importance—today, when no head of state of the Western world would any longer dream of acting like the Prince but would use, on the other hand, methods of persuasion and manipulation as subtle as those

---

[11] There is a whole field of research that remains to be opened concerning the employment of the seventeenth century intelligentsia, including its paradigm figures, in the intelligence services of England, France and Holland. Certainly the intelligence services of Richelieu and Mazarin were crucial in the formation of the "absolutist state" that employed the talents of the cream of the French intelligentsia. The activities of the English Scoutmaster-General, George Downing, both under Cromwell and in the Restoration were legendary. Downing was especially interested in Holland, England's chief mercantile and military competitor in world trade. "On 27 December 1668, Samuel Pepys recorded in his diary a conversation with Downing in St. James Park. Downing described his operations in Holland, and said that his spies were so skilled that they were able to remove keys from the pockets of the de Witt brothers (then ruling Holland) while they were asleep, open the closet containing secret papers, leave them in Downing's hands for a hours, and then return the papers and the keys without the owners knowing they had been moved" (Haswell 1977, 43). Indeed, Louis XIV had placed one of his agents, Louise de Querouaille, in Charles II's bed and in the process paved the way for the Anglo-French alliance that crushed the de Witt republic in 1672. For more details see (Geyl 1969, 316–18).

the brain trusts are able to place at his or her disposal. In order to understand and show to advantage the timeliness of *De vinculis*, we ought to
know about the activities of those trusts, those ministries of propaganda;
we should be able to glance at the manuals of espionage, from which we
should be able to glean something of what happens outside the corridors
of those organizations whose *ideal* goal is to guarantee order and the common welfare, where it exists. Machiavelli's Prince is the forebear of the
political adventurer, a type that is disappearing. On the other hand, the
magician of [Bruno's] *De vinculis* is the prototype of the impersonal systems of mass media, indirect censorship, global manipulation, and the brain
trusts that exercise their control over the Western masses. (Couliano 1987,
90)

Bruno sold his projected magician-ruler persona, knowledgeable of the
forces of Eros and of the universal, astral language of power-images
throughout Europe, from Venice to the court of Elizabeth I. Bruno writes
in *De Magia* that the key to magician-ruler's success was the ignorance of
the multitude:

> It is all the easier to enchain (*vincire*) people who have less knowledge. In
> them, the soul opens in such a way that it makes room for the passage of
> impressions aroused by the performer's techniques opening wide windows
> which, in others, are always closed. The performer has means at his disposal
> to forge all the chains he wants: hope, compassion, fear, love, hate, indig-
> nation, anger, joy, patience, disdain for life and death, for fortune.
> (Couliano 1987, 94)

But such a model, however analogous to the postmodern world of elec-
tronic political propaganda it appears to be, had two innate difficulties for
political intelligence agents of the mid-seventeenth century like Spinoza.
On the one side, Bruno's magician-ruler had to continually avoid ensnare-
ment by the very powers released by the manipulation of erotic hope and
fear; and on the other, in a period of transition to a market economy there
was a need for a more "rational" approach to political life that would make
it more coherent with the imperatives of the world market, but Bruno's
success depended upon a multitude driven by its passions and not its cost-
benefits.

Thus there was a two-fold possibility of instability, from the peak and
from the base of the hierarchy of magical manipulation. Spinoza identified
this instability in his *Tractatus Theologico-Politicus* as *the* problem of political intelligence in his time:

> . . . we may readily understand how difficult it is, to maintain in the same
> course men prone to every form of credulity. For as the mass of mankind
> remains always at about the same pitch of misery, it never assents long to

any one remedy, but is always best pleased by a novelty which has not yet proved illusive. This element of inconsistency has been the cause of many terrible wars and revolutions. (Spinoza 1951, 5)

This fear of political instability and suspicion of the techniques of imagery and "superstition" that potentiate it is not unique to Spinoza. It was quite common in the mid-seventeenth century and its characteristic discourse was frequently posed in terms of the "passions." For by then the passions, after being the vehicle of political control in the Renaissance magical-state, became the prime obstacle of stability. The political debate among the intelligence agents of states confronting revolution, world war, and economic crisis, from the 1640s to the 1660s, centered on the passions: What was their source? What was the possibility of controlling them? What techniques of repression would work on them? What was their general relation to "reason"? Pascal, Racine, Hobbes, Descartes, Spinoza and many others entered the fray. For the answer to the problem would have great consequences for the formation of state organization in the future.[12]

Negri, in *The Savage Anomaly*, quite rightly points to the period of Spinoza's worm-in-the-blood letter (1664–1665) as crucial to assessing his role in the European intelligence terrain. For it was in this period that Spinoza moves from Rhynsburg to Voorburg and begins to write the *Tractatus Theologico-Politicus*. Indeed, it is in Spinoza's previous letter to Oldenburg in September or October 1665 that Spinoza revealed for the first time that he was turning from the metaphysical deductions of the *Ethics* to the historical-hermeneutical argument of the *Tractatus*. But Negri apocalyptizes this move, for though Spinoza takes a very different path from the Hobbesian one in his analysis of the problem of political stability, Spinoza hardly transforms himself into an anti-bourgeois prophet as a number of Negri's concretely abstract passages claim:

> In English philosophy the immediately political form of the application of capitalistic appropriation is perfectly translated in the contractualistic tradition. The relationship and hierarchization of the contract of union and the contract of subjugation (that is to say, organization and exploitation, of value and surplus value) are just as enigmatic, if considered in purely theoretical terms as is the joyful explosion of the idea of the market in Spinoza . . . it is not very hard to see in [Hobbes'] system the foundation of a science (apologetic, but functionally and technically adequate) for the construction of a capitalistic image of Power (potestas) of the State. In Spinoza it is altogether different: The real Spinoza, not the ideology's version, attacks and supersedes

---

[12] An interesting discussion of "the passion debate" that begins in the seventeenth century and reaches a temporary conclusion in the eighteenth is to be found in (Hirschman 1977).

precisely these connections internal to the Hobbesian definition of Power. (Negri 1991, 70)

This differentiation from the mechanical philosopher Hobbes's system is a primary reason for Negri's claim that we find in Spinoza's thought "something disproportionate and superhuman. A savage development" (Negri 1991, 81). But what exactly was the difference between Spinoza and Hobbes?

For Hobbes, the human body is that of a badly constructed robot, driven by vital springs and forces that cannot be controlled or dampened by some internal extra-physical agent (as in Descartes' model). The Passions are the invisible voluntary motions within the body that precede visible voluntary motion: "These small beginnings of Motion, within the body of Man, before they appear in walking, speaking, striking, and other visible actions, are commonly called ENDEAVOUR" (Hobbes 1985, 118). One is never without passion for "Life it self is motion, and can never be without Desire, nor without Fear, no more than without Sense." So how can Reason, which is the capacity to compute consequences, operate? Certainly, once the Leviathan or "Mortal God" is constituted, the internal motions of the passions face an external force: "For by this Authority, given him by every particular man in the Commonwealth, he hath the use of so much Power and Strength conferred on him, that by terror thereof, he is inabled to form the wills of them all, to Peace at home, and mutuall ayd against their enemies abroad" (Hobbes 1985, 227). Hence the state (in the form of "the God on earth," the Leviathan) must terrorize the bodies of the people (both property owners and workers) into being reasonable. This external terror literally collides with the internal, invisible voluntary motions driving each one in the multitude toward the passionate exteriorization of their desires in a frenzy of violent expropriation. State terror physically dampens passion with an exterior momentum, and leaves open a space for reason to operate. The passions are like a plenum that require terror to create a vacuum for reason:

And when men that think themselves wiser than all others, clamor and demand right Reason for judge; yet seek no more, but that things should be determined, by no other mens reason but their own, it is intolerable in the society of men, as it is in play after trump is turned, to use for trump on every occasion that suite whereof they have most in their hand. For they do nothing else, that will have every of their passions, as it comes to bear sway in them, to be taken for Right Reason, and that in their own controversies; betraying their want of right Reason, by the claym they lay to it. (Hobbes 1985, 112)

The intellectual agent must see the reason in the terror, adjust it, and show the others its inevitability. For once terror does its external dampening of the passions, then reason, which has no Power in it, can come with its adding and subtracting of symbols to beget consequences to the benefit of mankind. But we must remember that Hobbes's animal, the Leviathan, is also a worm in a liquid, but a gigantic one in vast seas called up by the Immortal God in his last direct speech to us in order to awe Job into an unreasoning acceptance of his condition, which then leads to the possibility of Job's new wealth and the recuperation of his felicity. For the frontispiece of *Leviathan* has as its motto, "Non es potestas Super Terram quae Comparetur" (Job 41. 24).

Hobbes' image of the state is of the Leviathan rising from the seas:

> Smoke pours from his nostrils
> like steam from a boiling pot.
> His breath sets coals ablaze;
> flames leap from his mouth.
> Power beats in his neck,
> terror dances before him.
>
> (Mitchell 1991)

Thus we have the "paradox" of Hobbes's political theory and the "miracle" the political agent must help to accomplish. For the paradox is to transform terror into reason, but though this terror has an external source in the State, the state itself must be constituted by the "miraculous" application of reason. Thus we have Spinoza's ironic commentary on Hobbesian philosophy; Spinoza substitutes his little worm-in-the-blood for Hobbes's huge Serpent that makes "the ocean boil." He moves the problematic of the control of the passions from exteriority into the fluid of the passions themselves, the blood.

Spinoza develops for the de Witt faction of mercantile oligarchs, whose power rests on controlling the exchange mechanisms of the world market and an industrial system not quite finished with the transition from small commodity production, a different model of the state and of the intellectual agent in the state than the Hobbesian. He communicated it to Oldenburg (and Boyle) in "the worm in the blood" letter, though with many reservations. Spinoza rejects the Hobbesian model, and at this point we must recognize the truth of Negri's claim that Spinoza offers a radically different model than that of either the Renaissance magus or the mechanical philosopher for the control of the multitude.

After all, the Renaissance conception of the intellectual controlling the masses via images has exactly the instability that Spinoza rejected at the beginning of his political theorizing. But his own model can be sketched out from the letter, for the worm is in me, the worm is of me, *but* I am not the worm. The problem of the passions cannot be solved via some miraculously arrived at reasonable contract among a set of impassioned and crazed machines, as Hobbes suggested. True, for Spinoza, Hobbes's strategy of counteracting passion with passion was correct, but the internally originating passion could not be countered by a miraculously contrived and calibrated external force.

The placing of the worm *in* the blood transforms the process of controlling the passions from the external to the internal fluid. For the blood is the medium of the passions that appear to the worm as separate entities in motion, colliding and recoiling, appearing as whole and irreducible. The key to controlling them is not to create a force outside the system, but to apply a physics of countervailing passions more precisely. For as Spinoza was to write as Proposition 7 of Part IV of the *Ethics*: "An emotion cannot be checked or destroyed except by a contrary emotion which is stronger than the emotion which is to be checked." Hobbes despaired of finding such a contrary emotion within the body (or body politic). Spinoza in the latter and later *Ethics* argued that the emotions or passions can be potentiated by making them the objects of increased intelligence, i.e., by transforming passive emotions to stronger active ones.

The path to this result, which makes intelligence essential to the creation of a stable state, is prefigured in Spinoza's conclusion of the worm-in-the-blood section of the 20 November 1665 letter:

> As regards the human Mind I think it too is a part of Nature: since I state that there exists in Nature an infinite power of thought, which in so far as it is infinite, contains in itself subjectively the whole of Nature, and its thoughts proceed in the same way as Nature, which, to be sure, is its ideatum. Then I declare that the human mind is this same power not in so far as it is infinite, as perceives only the human Body, and in this way I declare that the human Mind is a part of a certain infinite mind. (Spinoza 1966, 212)

Thus, Spinoza suggests the possibility of accessing new (potentially infinite) powers through the self-reflective application of thought. It is on the basis of this path to increasing the powers of countervailing emotions within the body politic that Spinoza argued for the crucial importance of intellectuals like himself: worms in the blood that can intellectually digest themselves.

For the state is neither separated from human bodies (as in Descartes) nor is it identified with them (as in Hobbes). Spinoza dismissed the first as simply silly while the second was totally miraculous and against Nature.[13] Rather the state has different attributes, bodily *sive* intellectual, though

---

[13] The *locus classicus* of Spinoza's critique of Descartes's theory of the passions as "a view which I could scarcely have believed to have been put forward by such a great man" is in the

one unitary being. The bodies are as mad as Hobbes's and the minds are as refined as Descartes's but Spinoza argues that if one applied the intelligence adequately, new powers would emerge in the physical plane that would lead to stability.

The state intellectual must perform his/her job by identifying the body politics' apparent parts (the worms, blood, and bodies) with the whole (through an analysis of the causal context). Hence intelligence is not fact-gathering for Spinoza, it is not spying as the worm does, but contextualizing as the orobarus must. By doing thus did he secure his pensions, annuities, and protection from the multitudinous mob, the cannabilistic assassins, and the Calvinist heretic burners.

In conclusion, we see how knowledge of the three sources of Spinoza's income allows us to understand a significant piece of his philosophical writing. We also see that the type of "history of ideas" approach to Spinoza that Negri uses is bound to make Spinoza appear to be somewhat miraculous. For Negri does not analyze and amplify the tremendous flux of political, economic and social connections Spinoza's work and life was responding to. Consequently, Negri makes Spinoza's philosophy a premature whole that appears to teleologically transcend itself into the future. To properly know Spinoza as Spinoza asked himself to be known would require an enormous and detailed effort. There is much work waiting to be done that would show the actual operation of the remarkable network of spies, intelligence agents, industrial entrepreneurs that we associate with the great figures of "the century of genius" like Spinoza. This work is not only of academic interest. Negri's anxiety to find exceptions before he has tried to adequately conceive connections leads to the generation of political superstitions about the seventeenth century *and* our own. "Caute" should be written over *The Savage Anomaly.*

Before finishing up, however, let us return to our beginning, the trade talk between Spinoza and Oldenburg about Huygens's machine. Does it not reveal a failure in Spinoza's application of his own philosophy, can we really believe that the hand is better than "any machine"? As an artisan, as a merchant, and as an intelligence agent Spinoza was, finally, a failure. Perhaps his major success was in helping develop a philosophy that could explain his failure.

References

Preface to Part V of the *Ethics*. Spinoza's concise self-differentiation from Hobbes is to be found in a 1673 letter to Jelles: "With regard to Politics, the difference between Hobbes and me, about which you inquire, consists in this that I never preserve the natural right intact so that the Supreme Power in a State has no more right over a subject than is proportionate to the power by which it is superior to the subject" (Spinoza 1966, 269). For an interesting commentary on this passage see (Belaiel 1971, 51–52)

Belaiel, Gail 1971. *Spinoza's Philosophy of Law*, The Hague: Mouton.

Caffentzis, C.G. 1987. "A Review of Negri's *Marx Beyond Marx*," *New German Critique*, n. 41 (Spring/Summer), 186–92.

Couliano, Ioan P. 1987. *Eros and Magic in the Renaissance*, Chicago: University of Chicago Press.

Donagan, A. 1989. *Spinoza in Context*, Chicago: University of Chicago Press.

DuPlessis, Robert S. and Howell, Martha C. 1991. "Reconsidering the Early Modern Urban Economy: The cases of Leiden and Lille," *Past and Present*, n. 94, 49–84.

Geyl, Pieter 1964. *The Netherlands in the Seventeenth Century: Part II, 1648–1715*, London: Ernest Benn Ltd.

———. 1969. *Orange and Stuart*, New York: Charles Scribner's Sons.

Haswell, Jock 1977. *Spies and Spymasters: A Concise History of Intelligence*, London: Thames and Hudson.

Hill, Christopher 1974a. "William Harvey and the Idea of Monarchy," in (Webster 1974).

———. 1974b. "William Harvey (No Parliamentarian, No Heretic) and the Idea of Monarchy," in (Webster 1974).

Hirshman, Albert O. 1977. *The Passions and the Interests: Political Arguments for Capitalism before Its Triumph*, Princeton: Princeton University Press.

Hobbes, Thomas 1968. *Leviathan*, ed. C.B. Macpherson, London: Penguin.

Hutchison, Terence 1988. *Before Adam Smith: The Emergence of Political Economy, 1662–1776*, Oxford: Blackwell.

Jacob, J.R. 1979. *Robert Boyle and the English Revolution*, New York: Burt Franklin and Co.

MacIntyre, A. 1967. "Spinoza," in Paul Edwards, ed., *The Encyclopedia of Philosophy*, New York: Macmillan.

Marx, Karl 1936, *Capital: A Critique of Political Economy*, New York: Modern Library.

Simmel, Georg 1978. *The Philosophy of Money*, Boston: Routledge and Kegan Paul.

Sohn-Rethal, Alfred 1978. *Intellectual and Manual Labour*, London: Macmillan.

Spinoza, B. 1966. *The Correspondence of Spinoza*, ed. A. Wolf, New York: Russell and Russell.

Temple, Sir William 1968. *The Works of Sir William Temple, Vol. 1*, New York: Greenwood Press.

van Houtte, J.A. 1977. *An Economic History of the Low Countries, 800–1800*, New York: St. Martin's Press.

Webster, Charles 1974. *The Intellectual Revolution of the Seventeenth Century*, London: Routledge & Kegan Paul.

Whitteridge, Gweneth 1974. "William Harvey: A Royalist and No Parliamentarian," in (Webster 1974).

Wolf, A. 1950. *A History of Science, Technology and Philosophy in the Sixteenth and Seventeenth Centuries*, New York: Harper and Bros.

Yovel, Yirmiyahu 1989. *Spinoza and Other Heretics: The Marrano of Reason*, Princeton: Princeton University Press.

PART IV

Reading Negri Now: Negri's Productive Monstrosity

9

Idiotic Square:
Empire and Its Double

BRIAN KUBARYCZ

The gestural savagery of a multitude is individualized to become the most remarkable manifestation of 'art made by all and not by one'.

JACQUES VILLEGLE

Our analysis has to descend into the jungle of productive and conflictual determinations that the collective biopolitical offers us.

NEGRI AND HARDT

If the traditional task of Marxism has been to assume responsibility for the future, the question asked in *Empire* by Antonio Negri and Michael Hardt will be this: how is it possible to make a significant change within a late Capitalism which has adopted Change and Difference as two of its latest jingles, for which "every difference is an opportunity"? How can one make a difference which makes a real difference? For Negri and Hardt, the production of a "genuine novelty," to use a paradoxical phrase, seem to be a top priority. According to them, such an original insight will require getting beyond Foucault and Deleuze. Consequently, though a major component of their argument is the claim that revolutionary difference is no longer to be found exclusively in the high seriousness of intellectual responsibility, planned progress, and organized class struggle; they also argue it cannot result from either archaeologies of power or rhizomatic intensities. The revolutionary future, Negri and Hardt claim, will rather irrupt violently and monstrously from beneath what had been thought, prior to their own critical event, the most solid social and economic bedrock. Their energetically professed originality, however, will depend upon a specific set of conditions. It will require the staging of a scene of flagrant irresponsibility in an underground theatre in which original sin and its parodic recapitulation are placed on open display. To access and liberate insurgent power, Negri and Hardt will insist, will demand the will to see and speak of what theory has found too contemptible to theorize, to gaze resolutely upon an atrocious surplus which sober critique has heretofore dismissed as beneath its dignity.

The current discussion is informed by two separate disciplines, art theory and anthropology. It may seem an arbitrary detour to traverse fields ostensibly foreign to Marxist political critique. However, this may offer a way to get outside the standard terms of the debate and begin to see *Empire* from a fresh perspective, or at all. Art theory and anthropology are especially useful because, over the last decades, work in these fields, as a result of a traumatic encounter with recent continental philosophy, has entered into a phase of radical skepticism. These disciplines have to begun to assess, and subsequently liquidate, their most basic disciplinary assumptions: the sovereign status of the art object, and the very possibility and desirability of pure theory, of seeing clearly at all. David Carrier, for example, has pointed out in a recent study, *Rosalind Krauss and American Philosophical Art Criticism*, that art criticism in American has begun to abandon what traditionally it has taken for granted, the self-evident value of aesthetic experience. The most striking example of this new iconoclastic attitude is Krauss's own *The Originality of The Avant-Garde and Other Modernist Myths*. Here she performs a highly sophisticated demolition and recoding of concepts that for generations had served as the most basic axioms of art history, in particular "genius" and "original insight." Carrier, though he finds Krauss's individual analyses frequently in error, nevertheless holds her relentless critical audacity in highest esteem. He claims that Krauss, like Hegel and Pater before her, "who got historical details wrong, but [whose] theories remain interesting," must be absolved of her "errors and confusions" so as to make visible "her amazing ingenuity," in particular the force of her critique of high-modernist aesthetics.[1] Here, Carrier, as so many others before him, would seem to remind us that revolutionary insight requires, and conceivably produces, a degree of blindness. Each state would in fact condition the other. To turn ruthless skepticism, such as Krauss's, back upon its own sources, will perhaps allow for the identification of a decisive, and conceivably inevitable, moment of blindness from which *Empire* derives its heuristic power.

Let us continue by expanding upon what Krauss seems to have accomplished. Krauss's major writings of the 1980s launch a frontal assault on the work of her mentor Clement Greenberg, as well as her former associate Michael Fried. These essays lay out the basis for a radically materialist revision of the high-modernist abstract painting championed by Greenberg and Fried, as well as their formalist cult of visual purity. According to

---

[1] David Carrier, *Rosalind Krauss and American Philosophical Art Criticism*, Praeger: Westport, 2002, 5.

Krauss, the realm of autonomous vision to which these critics would have the viewer accede is indeed *not* a domain of cognitive or political freedom, as they have claimed it. Rather, it is a luminous prison, a "scopic regime" in which the subject is dissevered from bodily reality. Krauss seeks to demonstrate that the basic coordinates "subject" and "object," formerly taken for ontological givens within art criticism, are rather secondary effects generated out of a set of conventions and technologies governing the production, distribution, and consumption of art. The aesthetic appreciation characteristic of membership in the modernist empire of light, as well as the belief that the business of art criticism is to provide rules for those privileged works which have greatly occasioned disinterested visual delight; these now appear as wholly contingent upon the immediate repression and subsequent channeling of minute "bio-political" forces. It is this absence of the subject's body, in its concreteness, which makes aesthetic experience possible as well as natural, ennobling, and right. Krauss lays ultimate responsibility for the cultivated taste for modern abstraction at the door of John Ruskin and Roger Frye, whom she depicts as the precursors of Greenberg. Having flatly abandoned this idealist aesthetic, Krauss commences on a project of ruthless institutional self-analysis. Art rejects its interest in the Beautiful, even in beauties of the most rarified kind.

Again, this aesthetic, or anti-aesthetic,[2] approach to *Empire* may seem an arbitrary and unnecessary detour. Yet Negri and Hardt themselves indicate this as an important path to take. It is in the concluding sections of Empire that they identify a primary index of the rise of Empire in the ascendancy of abstract painting over political art. No longer intervening in the overtly political fray, modernist abstraction withdraws from the everyday world and lays claim to an epicene reality of its own. Citing the work of Serge Guilbaut, Negri and Hardt locate the moment after WWII when the center of political and economic power shifts from Europe to the United States. They further point out that this shift arises concurrently with the passage of the torch of aesthetic Enlightenment from Europe to the New World.[3] Guilbaut resituates the work of key American abstract expressionists such as Jackson Pollock and Franz Kline in its historical context. These are the art-historical heroes whose output in the 1940s and 50s made New York, not Paris, the capital of the twentieth century. In particular, Guilbaut traces the shift of powerful critics formerly aligned with Marxist politics, most especially Clement Greenberg, toward the political center. Guilbaut shows how Greenberg vigorously promoted the concepts and sensibilities which allowed for the apotheosis of abstract expressionism

---

[2] See Hal Foster, *The Anti-Aesthetic: Essays on Postmodern Culture*, Seattle: Bay, 1983.

[3] Serge Guilbaut, *How New York Stole the Idea of Modern Art*, trans. Arthur Goldhammer, Chicago: University of Chicago Press, 1983.

and the advent a new gospel of visual presence. This transatlantic shift of powers represented not merely a lateral geopolitical drift, but additionally a decisively vertical ascension. Under the direction of Greenberg, the overtly Marxist and Trotskyist activism which pervaded the American avant-garde in the 1930s began steadily to relinquish any manifest political partisanship, and simultaneously any objective content. Through a Kantian gesture of "transcendental constitution," high art laid out its own higher ground, a realm of disinterested vision. Abstraction abandoned the illusion of space into which the human body could enter, and in its stead presented an exclusive space that permitted access only to the Emersonian transparent eyeball.[4] Freedom, for Clement Greenberg's New York School, no longer indicated the positive power to make changes in the world, but rather a negative escape from the blood, sweat, and muck of the political. Freedom had become a universal concept, a truly inter-, or post-nationalist Idea. For Negri and Hardt, this new cult of universal vision, centered in New York, functions as one of the constitutive moments in the emergence of a postmodern global economy, an Empire which traffics, first and foremost, not in conventional goods and services but disincarnate image-commodities.

> The United States does indeed occupy a privileged position in Empire, but this privilege derives not from the similarities to the old European imperialist powers, but from its differences. These differences can be recognized most clearly by focusing on the properly imperial (not imperialist) foundations of the United State constitution, where by "constitution" we mean both the formal constitution, the written document along with its various amendments and legal apparatuses, and the material constitution, that is, the continuous formation and re-formation of the composition of social forces.[5]

The new abstract art will be a nonrepresentational, and therefore nonpartisan meta-iconography of Empire. Despite the immediate rawness of its energy, this self-referential and totalizing art will represent the triumph of inner Spirit over mere external mechanical technique. Anything falling short of this lofty achievement, or refusing at least to engage in the painterly struggle to suppress particular content and "defeat or suspend its

---

[4] In praise of modernist metal sculpture (specifically that of David Smith), which undoubtedly offers a far greater obstacle than painting to achieving the effect of disembodiment, Greenberg say this: "To render substance entirely optical, and form, whether pictorial, sculptural or architectural, as an integral part of ambient space—this bring anti-illusionism full circle. Instead of the illusion of things, we are no offered the illusion of modalities: namely, that matter is incorporeal, weightless, and exists only optically like a mirage." Cited in Michael Fried, *Art and Objecthood*, Chicago: University of Chicago Press, 1998, 161.

[5] Michael Hardt and Antonio Negri, *Empire*, Cambridge: Harvard, 2000.

own objecthood"[6] will not be considered art. It will become the duty of art criticism to detect and suppress kitsch.

Guilbaut's study will proceed with a quasi-archaeological investigation of Manhattan, one revealing the wide array of artists working outside of Greenberg's stable. This work shows the positive multiplicity of artists whose work was ignored and forgotten because it was tainted with residual (political) content. More recently, a project akin to Guilbaut's has appeared in the work of Thomas Crow, whose *The Rise of The Sixties* outlines the great diversity of artistic insurgencies which arose in resistance to Greenberg's authority.[7] Though often at odds with one another, the minor movements Crow discusses share a deep skepticism regarding the autonomy of art, the image's triumph over its material conditions, and the transcendental subject of aesthetic experience. Appended to Crow's book are timelines, glossaries, and other pragmatic apparatuses. In this manner, Crow's work manifestly rejects the status of pure theory or disinterested appreciation of historical styles and openly announces itself, as well as its subject matter, as pedagogical and partisan tools. This overt instrumentality offers a direct challenge to Greenberg's Kantian insistence that art should do nothing, and freely acknowledge itself as "incapable, objectively, of communicating anything else than a sensation."[8] The 1960s art movements Crow discusses (Situationist International in France, Arte Povera in Italy, Op Art in England, Fluxus in California), precisely because of their dual status as simultaneously regional and international, can be seen to crop up as pockets of local resistance to the hegemony of New York School transcendentalism. These militantly modern communities, loosely associated with the Italian radical Left in which Negri himself participated, offer a particularly valuable perspective on the aesthetic concerns underlying *Empire*. On almost every page Negri and Hardt announce their own staunch skepticism regarding not only Kantian "free beauties," but also with regard to the status of vestiges of indigenous organicism. None of these odd remainders, according to Negri and Hardt's analysis, should be understood as remnants of authentic human experience. Rather, these are the symptoms of Capitalism's flattening of all traditional cultural differences. According to Negri and Hardt, these relics of regionalism and "authentic" indigenous life (for instance, the recently popular California "funk" ceramic) are in fact symptoms of Capitalism itself. They comprise the wide array of artificially produced differences that Empire will seek to reappropriate and circulate in the form of image-commodities.

---

[6] *Art and Objecthood*, op. cit., 151.

[7] Thomas Crow, *The Rise of The Sixties*, New York: Prentice, 1996.

[8] Clement Greenberg, *The Collected Essays and Criticism, Volume 1: Perceptions and Judgments, 1939–1944*, Chicago: Chicago, 1988, 31.

In addition to Guilbaut's and Crow's, a third reappraisal of the Greenberg legacy appears in the work of Rosalind Krauss, to whom we now return. Krauss's *The Originality Of The Avant-Garde And Other Modernist Myths* amounts, again, to a frank declaration of war against her modernist mentors.[9] Holding even the most rarefied Humanist ideals in contempt, Krauss constructs an unapologetically provocative counter-history of modern art, one whose parameters were first staked out by Bataille and Duchamp. Here, drawing upon classical structuralist and psychoanalytic models of critique, she suggests that creative practice, as well as aesthetic sensibilities, are never arbitrary or ahistorical but always take the form of utterances possible exclusively within a strictly delimited field of possibilities. If much of the debate over *Empire* has focused on the validity of its claim of originality, Krauss's work stands as a strong corrective to this tendency. For Krauss, the demand for originality, as well as the complementary outrage over fraud (here Krauss herself will provide a paradigmatic example), are both aesthetic responses motivated by the constraints of an impersonal structural logic. Neither praise nor blame can be spoken, nor can any feeling of endorsement or disapproval be felt, except within a particular ideological system wherein the terms 'original' and 'copy' diacritically determine one another. For example, in the title essay of *Originality*, Krauss analyses William Gilpin's influential writings on the picturesque. Krauss seeks to demystify the spontaneous rush of subjective enthusiasm (the intense feeling of selfhood, place, and "mineness"), which occurs in moments of serendipitous rapport between genuine self and authentic nature. She shows that such Wordsworthian spots of time are in fact the product of a number of conventions, bodily disciplines, and mediating instruments (academic canons, a repertoire of images, as well as cosmeticizing lenses and mirrors, such as Claude Lorrain glasses and mirrors). Beginning with this treatment of Romantic landscape painting (which for Negri and Hardt epitomize Empire's fantasy of "manifest destiny"), *Originality* continues by showing how the same set of expectations which determined the difference between real and false nature, have continued up to the present moment latently to determine aesthetic judgment and the demand for originality which derives from it. The very objective qualities and subjective affects by which original experience and discovery can be recognized (intuition, identity, uniqueness, arrival, anticipatory exhilaration and a feeling of life) are, for Krauss, thoroughly narcissistic and

---

[9] Rosalind Krauss, *The Originality of The Avant-Garde and Other Modernist Myths*, Cambridge: MIT, 1985.

[10] This presentation of Krauss's work may appear to justify certain accusations of unoriginality directed against *Empire*. However, as Krauss indicates, the most compelling recent work, especially that which appeared in the 50s and 60s, has wholly embraced repetition.

nothing but the ongoing retroactive effects of a cultural, linguistic channeling of unconscious drives.[10] In these moment one identifies neither self-evident objective facts nor one's own authentic self, so much as one *mis*recognizes oneself, again, in the place of the other.

This same notion, that repetition conditions original insight, is reiterated by Krauss's colleague Hal Foster, this time in an analysis of breakthroughs in philosophical writing. Of specific interests to Foster are Althusser and Lacan, both of whom enact a systematic "recoding" of the work of a prior master (Marx and Freud, respectively). In each case, the more recent disciple restages the moment of the master's theoretical insight, reading it in terms of a structurally necessary blindness. The goal of these analyses is to recover and defamiliarize the master's discourse. By recovering the master, in his most undomesticated form, such readings disrupt the domesticating discourse of the university and make the master speak in an alarming and authoritative tone once more. Foster states:

> The method of these returns [to Freud and Marx] is similar: to focus on the "constructive omission: crucial to each discourse. The motives are similar too: not only to restore the radical integrity of the discourse but to challenge its status in the present, the received ideas that deform its structure and restrict its efficacy. This is not to claim the final truth of such readings. On the contrary, it is to clarify their contingent strategy, which is to *re*connect with a lost practice in order to *dis*connect from a present way of working felt to be outmoded, misguided, or otherwise oppressive.[11]

Read along these lines, *Empire* ought not to be evaluated in terms of its unqualified uniqueness, but rather in terms of the extent to which it is able to dismantle official history and reenact a rejected and forgotten past, to restage an ancient excess within the present. Here, the criterion of judgment is no longer purity and fidelity but distortion and disfiguration, the ability to make the master speak unheard of pronouncements. If *Empire* were read not as a contemporary "classic," but rather as this sort of audacious act of necromancy,[12] would this detract or rather add to its theoretical or practical value? For such a ritual to be enacted, for such a shocking lugubrious game to be played, what conditions must be met, what actors gathered, what stage set? And finally, what master, or masters, will be summoned to the table?

---

[11] Hal Foster, *The Return of The Real*, Cambridge: MA: MIT Press, 1996, 4–5.

[12] Steven Greenblatt, in his essay "Loudon and London," discusses various cultures in which the high seriousness of religious rite and the frivolity of theatrical performance have yet to be critically separated: "exorcisms integrate feasting, the making of ritual offerings, dancing, the singing of sacred texts, drumming, masking, and the staging of improvised, frequently obscene comedies." *Critical Inquiry*, Winter, 1986, 382.

Negri and Hardt will begin to assemble the players by invoking the specter of Hans Kelsen. The sovereignty of pure vision *per se*, found in Greenberg's modernist aesthetic, finds a juridical analogue in Kelson's *Grundnorm*, which seeks to provide an absolute basis for Kelsen's ideal project of an "organization of Humanity under the United Nations." Kelsen's U.N. offers an objective body dedicated to the infinite task of achieving a Kantian perpetual peace. To provide a sharp contrast to this, Negri and Hardt also summon Foucault and Deleuze to the table. These two philosophers will represent the two most viable alternatives to date to Kelsen's enlightened utopia. Negri and Hardt praise Foucault for his attempt

> to bring the problem of social reproduction and all the elements of the so-called superstructure back to within the material, fundamental structure and define this terrain not only in economic terms but also in cultural, corporeal, and subjective ones. [Which makes it possible to] understand how Foucault's conception of the social whole was perfected and realized when in a subsequent phase of his work he uncovered the emerging outlines of the society of control as a figure of power active throughout the entire biopolitics of society.[13]

Foucault, according to this reading, has managed to articulate a view of society as a wholly material, self-regulating totality. His model avoids all recourse to any contingent exterior, any dialectical other which the system might encounter. Nevertheless, Negri and Hardt take issue with Foucault insofar as he did not, in their opinion, "ever succeed in pulling his thought away from that structuralist epistemology that guided his research from the beginning.[14] "By structuralist epistemology," they continue, "here we mean the reinvention of a functionalist analysis in the realm of the human sciences, a method that effectively sacrifices the dynamic of the system, the creative temporality of its movements, and the ontological substance of cultural and social reproduction." In other words, Foucault's analysis, for Negri and Hardt, reduces society to a mere surveillance mechanism. It keeps its subjects thoroughly disciplined and constantly occupied, thus rendering them docile and devoid of revolutionary potential. This is precisely what Marx suggests in *Capital* when referring to the rationalization of the work process, which converts active labor into a form of contemplation.[15] This form of labor may operate sufficiently well to detain and control its constituent members, to incapacitate their ability to imagine social alternatives. But such a mechanist view of society requires a moment of genuine

---

[13] *Empire*, op. cit., 27.
[14] Ibid., 28.

negativity, some transformative encounter with otherness, which for Negri and Hardt is a fundamental aspect of Empire's infinite capacity for self-discovery and rebirth. Such a society lacks Lack. This view of society allows for a subject for whom an unbroken state of *attention*[16] is imperative. But such a theory can never produce the kind of *absorption*, as opposed to mere *interest*,[17] characteristic of high-modernist aesthetics. It cannot account for the feeling of *conviction* so central to the enlightened view of Empire. Now, this thesis of a Durkheimian Foucault is plausible to the extent that Foucault indeed remains a social scientist investigating a sharply delimited object, perhaps no longer Society itself but rather Power.[18] However, Negri and Hardt's characterization of Foucault requires reading him almost entirely in terms of *Discipline and Punish*, and paying virtually no attention either to the highly nuanced treatment of medical subjects' capacity for fascination or the spectral objects of histological and nosological research (*The Birth of the Clinic*), or to the essential role played by negativity and death within the emergent Sciences of Man (*The Order of Things*).

Further, and perhaps more fundamentally, Negri and Hardt's characterization depends upon a functionalist definition of structuralism that in fact bears little resemblance to the classical structuralism practiced by Levi-Strauss or Greimas. A far more elegant and accurate representation of structuralism appears in Fredric Jameson's staged encounter between Lukacs and Althusser in *The Political Unconscious*. Here structure bears no residual traces of the functionalism which Negri and Hardt's oddly

---

[15] "As a consequence of the rationalization of the work-process the human qualities and idiosyncrasies of the worker appear increasingly as mere sources of error when contrasted with these abstract special laws functioning according rational predictions. Neither objectively nor in his relation to his work does man appear as the authentic master of the process; on the contrary, he is a mechanical part incorporated into a mechanical system. His finds it already pre-existing and self-sufficient, it functions independently of him and he has to conform to its laws whether he likes it or not. As labor is progressively rationalized and mechanized his lack of will is reinforced by the way in which his activity becomes less and less active and more and more contemplative. (As Marx notes, it goes without saying that this 'contemplation' can be more demanding and dehumanizing than 'active' labor. Capital I)." Georg Lukacs, *History and Class Consciousness*, Cambridge, MA: MIT Press, 1997.

[16] See Jonathan Crary's *Suspensions of Perception: Attention, Spectacle and Modern Culture*, Cambridge, MA: MIT Press, 1999.

[17] See Michael Fried's, *Art and Objecthood*, op. cit.

[18] See Paul Q. Hirst's discussion of Durkheim's denial of the privileged status of the subject, which enables his reification of society as the object of an autonomous science. Hirst's manifestly Althusserian reading of *The Rules of Sociological Method* critiques Durkheim's unwarranted faith in the prior givenness of the object, prior to its actual conceptual construction. Paul. Q. Hirst, *Durkheim, Bernard and Epistemology*, Routledge, Kegan and Paul, London, 1975.

impute to Foucault. Rather than any empirically observable interrelation between parts and whole, Jameson presents a model of structure that doggedly rejects all positive science and operates exclusively on the level of the concept. In the *Political Unconscious,* Jameson enacts a dazzlingly brilliant and captivatingly ·elegant interpretive *tour de force*, employing Greimas's semiotic square to reduce and logically map the seemingly arbitrary and uneven development of modernist literature. This virtuoso performance did not escape the notice of Rosalind Krauss. Fascinated by Jameson's own fascination, and perhaps even feeling an anticipatory burst of her own powers of discovery; Krauss, in *The Optical Unconscious*, repeatedly acknowledges her indebtedness to a critical virtuoso of the first order. Making specific reference to Jameson's continuous recourse to this heuristic tool, she marvels, using terms which are unmistakably phallic,[19] at his masterful abandonment to a "graph's idiot[ic] simplicity and extravagant cunning."[20] In Jameson's hands this simple grid, when imposed as an exterior and contingent device, reveals itself to be a powerful and addictive heuristic tool. It serves as the agency out of which arises a series of significant insights, a chain of bursts of interpretive *jouissance.* Here, meaning is produced within texts, erupting in the form a various symptoms, as the results of decisive acts of creative violence. Jameson's Nietzschean will-to-meaning depends upon his unapologetic acceptance of a vicious habit, along with all the attendant consequences. The same might be said of Krauss. However, her work displays a decidedly more downward orientation. Rather than focusing her attention on discovery and insight, Krauss will stress structuralism's powerfully repressive operations. The precise moment in which Jameson, in a veritable act of transcendental deduction, achieves a pellucid insight, transforms itself for Krauss into its dialectical other, a spell of blindness and oblivion. Anagnoresis becomes Sparagmos. In setting forth the conditions for the possibility of a universalizing modernist vision, Krauss's *Optical Unconscious* exposes how high-modernism's field of pure vision depends implicitly and thoroughly upon the production, and continual reproduc-

---

[19] Hegel describes the absurdly contradictory character of the "symbol which signifies signification," and thus opens up the field of meaning, in this manner: "The depth which Spirit brings forth from within—but only as far as its picture-thinking consciousness where it lets it remain—and the ignorance of this consciousness about what it is really saying, are the same conjunction of the high and low which, in the living being, Nature naively expresses when it combines the organ of its highest fulfillment, the organ of generation, with the organ of urination. The infinite judgement, qua infinite, would be the fulfillment which comprehends itself; the consciousness of the infinite judgement that remains at the level of picture-thinking behaves as urination." G.W.F. Hegel, *Phenomenology of Spirit*, trans. Miller, Oxford: Oxford University Press, 1977, 210.

[20] Rosalind Krauss, *The Optical Unconscious*, Cambridge, MA: MIT, 1994, 27.

tion, of an ideological subject. For Krauss, this subject constitutes itself in terms of an imaginary relationship between the self and a series of stand-ins, objects in which the ego identifies a semblance of itself. In rapturous moments of insight, the subject recognizes (or *mis*recognizes) a reflection of its own anticipated inner consistency. Consciousness, here, take the form of a compulsive consumption of images. Jameson himself serves as a particularly compelling example of the logic of this late-capitalist subjectivity. Having laid out the model of vision, Krauss then uses it to explain the captivating power which action and all-over paintings exerted upon modernist abstractions greatest exponents. In these paintings ground collapses into identity with picture surface (Mondrian), or the shape of the canvas rigorously determines the series of nested frames comprising the painting's content (Stella). Each of these options objectifies a distinct aspect, or capability, of the transcendent subject. Krauss continues her argument by interrogating the "natural obviousness" of this perfect coincidence between sensation and cognition. These modernist masterpieces, from the official standpoint, beam forth as inspired objectifications of the cognitive conditions of vision. From another standpoint however, that of Krauss's anti-vision, they harden into monuments to stony obtuseness, examples of vision reified and congealed.[21]

My assertion is that this scopic regime that Krauss brings into naked visibility (at once liberating and addictive, as well as enlightening and stultifying) is nothing other than the formal basis of Negri and Hardt's Global Empire. Empire manifests itself as a perpetual state of intuition and absorption, but bound always to the possibility of reverting into its other. The subject of Empire is constantly bemused, curious, concerned, and cautious. It seeks out cultural others, and understands its own history in terms of its encounters with these alter egos. But even prior to this, Empire manifests itself as a fear of blindness and a repudiation of the dark. Empire's state of constant vigilance, for Negri and Hardt, has come to appear perfectly natural and right. But this is the case only insofar as its violently repressive foundational act is itself forcefully and repeatedly buried.

---

[21] Krauss sardonically exemplifies this moment of gaping absorption and obliviousness to the outside world in the idiot stare of the child who would later produce the sprawling, five-volume disaster which is *Modern Painters*. "And what about little John Ruskin, with his blond curls and his blue sash and shoes to match, but above all else his obedient silence and his fixed stare? Deprived of toys he fondles the light glinting off a bund of keys, is fascinated by the burl of floorboards, counts the bricks in the houses opposite. He becomes the infant fetishist of patchwork. 'The carpet,' he confesses about his playthings, 'and what patterns I could find in bedcovers, dresses, or wall-papers to be examined, were my chief resources.' This, his childish solace, soon becomes his talent." (Krauss, *The Optical Unconscious*, op. cit., 1).

> Now supranational subjects that are legitimated not by right but by con-
> sensus intervene in the name of any type of emergency and superior eth-
> ical principles. What stands behind this intervention is not just a
> permanent state of emergency and exception, but a permanent state of
> emergency and exception justified by the appeal to essential values of jus-
> tice. In other words, the right of the police is legitimated by universal
> values.[22]

Again, Krauss identifies the experience of this visual field, as well as the
"permanent circulation" and "continuous flow" of imaginary goods within
it, to be anything but natural and inevitable. Rather, she sees it as entirely
structurally motivated. Intuition and interiority cannot exist without an
outer darkness, a disavowed vacuity intrinsic to both thought and vision.
This is corrosive interior is the place of the "unthought" and "anti-vision."
Krauss names it the "optical unconscious."

At this point perhaps it has become clear why Negri and Hardt entertain grave reservations about the work of Deleuze and Guattari. If
Foucault's thought, as portrayed by Negri and Hardt, remains entirely
dominated by a concept of totality and mere subjective interest, one
which causes him to reject any exteriority, Deleuze and Guattari, on the
other hand, can only formulate a pre- or anti-oedipal condition of radical flux, a state of distraction devoid of all interiority. Here, in terms even
more radical than those Negri and Hardt attribute to Foucault, the
'scopic regime' is simply not possible. And so there is no possibility of
explaining how Empire could ever arise. While Foucault (again, as Negri
and Hardt cast him) remains far too flat and "modern," Deleuze and
Guattari (correlatively) utterly refuse to perceive any gestalt at all. If
Foucault presents a paranoid consciousness, under constant surveillance
and in a state of continual alert, the authors of *The Anti-Oedipus* offer
instead a schizophrenic body in a state of perpetual centrifugal motion,
adrift in an unlimited flux of intensities and sensations. For Negri and
Hardt,

> Deleuze and Guattari present us with a properly poststructuralist under-
> standing of biopower that renews materialist thought and grounds itself
> solidly in the question of the production of social being. Their work demys-
> tifies structuralism and all the philosophical, sociological, and political con-
> ceptions that make the fixity of the epistemological frame an ineluctable
> point of reference. They focus our attention clearly on the ontological sub-
> stance of social production. Machines produce. . . . Deleuze and Guattari,
> however, seem to be able to conceive positively only continuous movement
> and absolute flows, and thus in their thought, too, the creative elements

---

[22] *Empire*, op. cit., 28.

and the radical ontology of the production of the social remain insubstantial and impotent.[23]

Deleuze and Guattari can think an utterly deterritorialized distributional network of circulating bodies, as well as their sedimentary accumulation. They can think the "decentralization and global dispersal of productive processes and sites, which is characteristic of the postmodernization or informationization of the economy," but they cannot conceive how this "provokes a corresponding centralization of the control over production" (Empire, 297). For Negri and Hardt, Deleuze and Guattari fail, as does Foucault, to theorize, the state of fascination and "feeling good" which converts either discipline or anarchy into Globalism. They do not account, as Krauss would say, for how "the speaker becomes a subject: what structural linguistics calls a 'subject of enunciation,' the one who gives 'I' its (existential) meaning in the act of speaking it" (Optical, 23).[24]

Attempting to situate themselves amid the Panopticon and the Body without Organs, the opening move of Negri and Hardt's *Empire* consists in their cleaving a sublime abyss between these rival theories. On one side of this chasm stands Foucault's paranoid subject of Management, while on the other side babbles Deleuze and Guatarri's schizophrenic Nomad. For Negri and Hardt, one of the most basic and evident problems with these rival theories, which inversely mirror one another, is that each expresses a subjective state which is manifestly pathological. Deleuze and Guattari, according to this model, play Locke or Hume's Empirical Reason against Foucault's Hobbesian Leviathan. Both the extreme positions fail properly to articulate the distinctive mood of Empire, which despite its secondary concern over terrorism and its solicitude with regard to the poor, nevertheless presents itself primarily as anything but sick. As Negri and Hardt unceasingly insist, Empire everywhere presents itself as, or at least plays the part of, a beaming portrait of robust wellness. According to the logic of Empire, what will heal and synthesize the opposed realms of paranoia and schizophrenia is sound Kantian judgment, with its attendant feeling of

---

[23] Ibid.

[24] Krauss, *The Optical Unconscious*, op. cit., 23. Krauss points out this state of complete imbrication within the optical regime does not arise spontaneously, but is rather through an external moral agency or police force—imbued with what Negri and Hardt call "rights of intervention". The transparent visual order is imposed from without through a inaugurating gesture, or series of bodily commands (stand here . . . hold this . . . look there . . .), which mark out the site within which the subject will recognize itself as "I." She states that this gesture comes from outside the subject. It is a primary pointing to the infant by someone or something else, a pointing constituted for example by the look of the mother, a look that names the child to itself, for itself. The child's identity is to be found in the look, just as its terror of identity's loss is prefigured in its withdrawal (24).

energetic life. Experienced from within, the enclave of Global Order, for Negri and Hardt, is constituted neither by extremes of state-regulated or *laissez-faire* economics. Empire, rather, develops and expands through the cultivation of healthy Taste. Further, it is precisely in opposition to the apparent living presence and real plenitude of Empire, that Negri and Hardt will announce the coeval advent of Counter-Empire, an underworld of garbage and hybridity: the orgy of unconstrained proliferation and mass-consumption, of "vicarious experience and faked sensations"[25] which Greenberg taught us to spurn as Kitsch, the multi-media theatrical amalgamations which Fried declared to be the nemesis of genuine art.[26]

The creation, preservation and expansion—in a word, the metabolism—of Empire depends intimately upon a seemingly spontaneous and universal moral instinct, one previously associated with the kind of Kantian reflective judgment occasioned by genuine art. As "free beauties," true works of art must not serve as means toward pragmatic technical ends, nor should they offer any immediate sensuous gratification. Taste, according to Kant's third Critique, is linked to freedom and morality, and art becomes the symbol of morality, in so far as the objects (natural or artificial) which give rise to reflective judgment are able to maintain their sovereign aloofness from any particular creed, code of conduct, or set of interests. Negri and Hardt address this Kantian notion of a "supreme ethical idea" in their discussion of the philosophical contribution of Hans Kelsen in the formation of the United Nations.[27] In Kant, the power of judgment subsumes a given representation under a general concept (including the idea of the finality of nature, or merely its suitability for representation and reflection). The same is the case in Kelsen; the suspension of war and the pursuit of mutual interest between sovereign states entail the prior deduction of a transcendental constitution (*Grundform*), and the development of a dynamic hierarchy in which each member must first sacrifice its "natural" rights in order subsequently to recuperate them on a higher collective and spiritual level. Once imbued with an inner force of its own, this system functions as a self-generating and self-regulating entelechy. Such a system assimilates useful external resources and suppressing hostile elements in a constant state of re-creation. Empire is born again at every instant. This untiring regard, moving out from self and tactfully engaging the other, is precisely what Kant, in "An Answer to The Question

---

[25] Clement Greenberg, *Art and Culture: Critical Essays*, Boston: Beacon, 1989, 10.

[26] "At this point I want to make a claim that I cannot hope to prove or substantiate but that I believe nevertheless to be true: theatre and theatricality are at war today, not simply with modernist painting (or modernist painting and sculpture), but with art as such." *Art and Objecthood*, op. cit., 163.

[27] *Empire*, op. cit., 5.

'What is Enlightenment?'" considers expressive of physical and spiritual wellbeing. Further, in the *Critique of Judgment*, Kant declares that disinterested reflection upon natural ends, as well as art which appears as the product of nature's chosen darlings, is precisely what occasions the subjective quickening of the faculties.

Now, Roland Barthes, in *The Pleasure of The Text*, rehearses the various characteristics of this attitude of common decency and civil courtesy, which may in fact be practiced best in solitude, so that one can most easily commune with one's own inner reading voice. Reading, or *lectio*, for Barthes, is a form of narcissistic self-gratification motivated by getting caught up, losing and re-finding oneself, in a good story.[28] To understand our own thoughts, to converse with another, or even to watch a sleeping person breathe; all these are so many ways to read for signs of life. Speech and writing, as well the capacity for identification and sympathy, arise out of a primary communion with the self. Spoken and written gestures travel out from the lucubrating subject into the lugubrious space of the other, and find a place and meaning in the promise of a return. In sharp contrast to this, Barthes also posits (and this is the whole point of his text) the ideal reader's perfect anti-type,

> who abolishes within himself all barriers, all classes, all exclusions, not by syncretism but by simple discard of that old specter: logical contradiction; who mixes every language, even those said to be incompatible; who silently accepts every charge of illogicality, or incongruity . . . . Such a man would be the mockery of our society: court, school, asylum, polite conversation would cast him out.[29]

Crucial to Barthes' speculations, however, is his assertion that the gentle reader emerges by means of a split which separates it from the snarl of convergences and contradictions which are its other half. The writerly "anti-hero" is not a different person than the responsible reader. It is simply the Human viewed in another, monstrous light at an instant prior to its consolidation into an ego. It is in this paroxysm of genesis that we find the good reader's monstrous double.

As if following this lead, Negri and Hardt propose a materialist model of reading practice which does not suppress the question of the emergence

---

[28] "The pleasure of the text can be defined by *praxis* (without any danger of repression): the time and place of reading: house, countryside, near mealtime, the lamp, family where it should be, i.e., close but not too close (Proust in the lavatory that smelled of orrisroot), etc. Extraordinary ego-reinforcement (by fantasy), the unconscious muffled. This pleasure can be *spoken*: whence criticism." Roland Barthes, *The Pleasure of The Text*, trans. Richard Miller, New York: Noonday, 1975.

[29] Ibid., 3.

of this literate subject.[30] Production in writing and reading are transformed in *Empire* into an oneiric state of subjectless reproduction. This is the Spinozist far side of the print revolution, wherein books write and publish themselves, appropriating bodies as their mere operators.[31] In an uncanny fashion, social and sexual relations exist not between subjects but rather between inorganic things, institutions, and technologies. In this middle space between Foucault's disciplined production and Deleuze's lines of flight, Reproduction, liberated from subjective intentions, responsibilities and ends external to itself, becomes a flood of referrals and copies without original. It is an infinite relay of reflections, but without narcissism, without Self. Yet crucially, it offers a place of suture in which the self can arise as it identifies itself in the chain of signification. Seen awry, from outside the purview of normative subjectivity, Kelsen's corporate reality, the embodiment of Enlightenment, is inverted into a ritual performance, a madness which mistakes itself for pure reason. This ecstacy of communication has nothing to do with McLuhan's global village of saints and scholars, or with Habermas's enlightened socialist utopia. Beneath the official image of Empire, Negri and Hardt reveal instead a wildly proliferating jungle of transnational bureaucracies. Officially, ministries, as well as nongovernmental agencies, take up their designated places and perform their appointed functions within a global hierarchy. The will of the individual is now "incorporated" into the superpersonal Globalist Will. For Negri and Hardt, however, Empire, again, from the very beginning, is a split subject. The apotheosis of Communication arises concurrently with a subterrainian unbiding of the hermeneutic function, translation and interpretation with-

---

[30] "For them, First subjectivity is a constant social process of generation. When the boss hails you on the shop floor, or the high school principal hails you in the school corridor, a subjectivity is formed. The material practices set out for the subject in the context of the institution (be they kneeling down to pray or changing hundreds of diapers) are the production processes of subjectivity. In a reflexive way, then, through its own actions, the subject is acted on, generated. Second, the institutions provide above all a discrete place (the home, the chapel, the classroom, the shop floor) where the production of subjectivity is enacted. The various institutions of modern society should be viewed as an archipelago of factories of subjectivity." *Empire*, op. cit., 195–96.

[31] "But, it will be urged, it is impossible that solely from the laws of nature considered as extended substance, we should be able to deduce the causes of buildings, pictures, and things of that kind, which are produced only by human art; nor would the human body, unless it were determined and led by the mind, be capable of building a single temple. However, I have just pointed out that the objectors cannot fix the limits of the body's power, or say what can be concluded from a consideration of its sole nature, where they have experience of many things being accomplished solely by the laws of nature, which they would never have believed possible except under the direction of the mind: such are the actions performed by somnambulists while asleep, and wondered it by their performers when awake." Benedict de Spinoza, *The Ethics*, trans. R.H.M. Elwes, New York: Dover, 1955, 133.

out beginning or end. Empire, here, reenacts a primal struggle between Christ (the gospel as presence and grace) and Hermes Trismegistus (alchemy as unrestricted translation and transformation).

It is in this light that Negri and Hardt, despite key misgivings, see fit to praise the theorization of high-tech communication as it is found in the work of a group of recent Italian scholars (Virno, Agamben, Lazzaretto, etc.). They congratulate these theorists for having succeeded in "grasping it in a pure form, refining it on the ideal plane," as "immaterial labor, massified intellectual labor, the labor of the 'general intellect.'"[32] This new communication culture is akin to that anticipated in the 60s by Thomas Pynchon, in his novel *The Crying of Lot 49*. In this simultaneously whacky and creepy postmodern farce, Pynchon, with great accuracy, though with none of the high tone of Negri and Hardt, depicts the underground Postal Service of Thurn und Taxis as a sovereign agency of transmission. The role of courier is depicted as ascendant over that of sender, receiver, and message. The mediator reigns supreme. Writing, under the aegis of the posthorn, no longer reflects the lucid thought of any self-determined subject, but rather appears as uncannily drawn into existence by the impersonal Agency of The Letter. In this manner Pynchon's novel parodies the secular kabbalism of Kafka's *The Trial*. In each, the concept of an origin, or an original is gradually replaced by that of reified Transmission, the free circulation of signs and signals devoid of any reference to a subject. Enjoying Pynchon's novel depends upon a will-to-forget, one which disregards the basic truths of classical Poetics, Linguistics, and Communication. To surrender to the seductive allure of Simulation is to become immersed within an indefinite flux of signs. It is to descend into Barthesian bliss. So grandiose and unfathomable is this play of signs that to make sense of it demands the pure positing of an Other (Foucault's Power?) projected beyond the blank screen of pure Simulation. Confronted by the manifold forces which threaten to dissolve the ego, the responsible reader will project an author. And the insistant historian, rather than admit reality can not be reduced to a unified world-picture, will posit a plot (no matter how diabolical) determining the course of History. Paranoia is the last resort taken before its structural complement, schizophrenia, sets in.

Negri and Hardt praise Fredric Jameson for the way he "explains wonderfully in the context of contemporary film, conspiracy theories are a crude but effective mechanism for approximating the functioning of the totality."[33] But this kind of totalizing thought is not unique to contemporary film. The same motif can be identified at least as far back as the sixth

---

[32] *Empire*, op. cit., 29.
[33] *Empire*, op. cit., 323.

century. Procopius's *Secret History* depicts the apparent order of Justinian's world empire as a grand illusion, an incoherent global economy of devalued signs of power. In Procopius, the official portrait of Justinian himself becomes an empty sign which merely signifies order and control. Behind this visage of the Emperor, as if a dangerous supplement were preferable to a throughgoing crisis of meaning, Procopius projects the obscene figure of the Empress Theodora. Formerly a trashy actress, Theodora is reknowned for her outrageous behavior, in particular her vivid stage performance of the violation of Leda by the Swan, the mythic origin of Greek culture. Theodora is Procopius's monstrous fantasy of the diabolical forces which "really" undergird the Holy Roman Empire. Commerce, here, becomes an "abominable and voluptuous act."

Almost concurrent with the underground theatre depicted in Procopius, the writings of Augustine provide a remedy to this unbounded economy of signs. They provide a foundational and paradigmatic example of responsible literacy in Western culture, indicating the conditions under which suture may take place. Understanding this orthodox mode of reading will aid a discussion of ideology insofar as Augustine's writings mark a foundational moment in Western culture in which reading becomes equivalent to moral praxis. Augustine stresses the necessity of teaching not only proper readings, but also proper methods and attitudes of reading *per se*. The forms of subjectivity, of attention and absorption, which Augustine outlines in this key text, serve as the foundation on which a reader can begin to read like a true Christian. The clear identification and deliberate transmission of these skills and attitudes becomes the most essential task of pastoral care, as they provide a basis from which leaders can begin the conscious organization of the *vulgus* into a universal catholic Church. Perhaps not so oddly, Ernesto Laclau and Chantal Mouffe, in the Hegemony and Socialist Strategy make an analogous claim with regard to the organization of a revolutionary class:

> Since Kautsky, Marxism knew that the socialist determination of the working class does not arise spontaneously but depends upon the political mediation of intellectuals. Such mediation, however, was not conceived as articulation—that is to say, as a political construction from dissimilar elements. It had an epistemological basis: socialist intellectuals read in the working class its objective destiny.[34]

In *On Christian Doctrine*, Augustine offers a broadly defined program of scriptural exegesis. It is governed by a classical ethic of steering a middle

---

[34] Ernesto Laclau and Chantal Mouffe, *Hegemony and Socialist Strategy*, London: Verso, 1985, 85.

course between two poles, each of which respectively may well recall Negri and Hardt's characterization of Foucault and Deleuze. Augustine seeks to invalidate two sorts of extravagant and heretical interpretation: monolithic literalism and extravagant Alexandrianism.[35] Through an act

---

[35] The first of these options, the literalist, is epitomized by Cyprian, Bishop of Carthage. In his epistle from the year 250, "On The Unity of The Catholic Church," Cyprian denounces in the harshest terms bishops who have left the Church under pagan persecution, and then sought to resume office once the threat is gone. In support of this staunch donatist position, Cyprian adopts a literalist mode of reading scriptural. For him the Church is an indissoluble monolithic institution, one that cannot be fragmented. Or, if we do choose, through apostacy, to "rend the seemless garment of Christ," we do so at the greatest peril. True, Cyprian employs a metaphor here, but everywhere in his writings it is clear that he reads the scripture, with regard to both past and future facts, absolutely literally. The opposite extreme of interpretation, which might be called Alexandrian, can be represented by another donatist, Tychonius. Tychonius, in his "Seven Rules For Seeking And Finding The Meaning of Scripture" proposes a method of reading scripture based entirely in the recognition of rhetorical and poetical tropes within the biblical text. Herein the Bible is taken for pure code, and the ostensible of goal of Tychonius's method will be to decipher the exact moment of Christ's return. Augustine, however, correctly surmises how this hermeneutic in fact opens the possibility not only of an extremely broad array of meanings but in fact their unrestricted proliferation. In response to the dangers inherent in Tychonius, Augustine writes De Doctrina Christiana, hoping to close off the radical apperture in the other. What Augustine finds in Tychonius, however, is not exactly his inclusion of artfulness, or craft into the labor of reading. For, in fact, Augustine incorporates Tychonius's basic tropology into his own hermeneutic. What is problematic in Tychonius is not his skill in rhetoric, but rather his lack of a theory of the subject, one that would limit the uncontrolled multiplication of possible readings. Now, for all that this brief sketch depicts the literalist Cyprian and figurativist Tychonius as diametrically opposed, the two also share, in addition to their donatist stance, an overtly apocalyptic tone resulting from their belief in the immanent end of the world. Cyrpian's recalcitrant puritanism and Tychonius's hermeneutic fervor inversely mirror each other; each is symptomatic of cosomological anxiety. Augustine's De Doctrina Christiana works in concert with his City of God in a broad therapeutic program devoted to suspending this anxiety. Augustine's seeks to domesticate whatever is alien in the Apocalypse, to read its great and terrible images of chimerical beasts and cosmic catastrophes, not as realistic depictions of the end, but rather as emblems of psychological states. This method of taming monstrosity, however, of humanizing the Apocalypse, requires a return to the primacy of literal reading. As is well known, Augustine's four-tiered exegetical model is grounded in the literal level. Yet this very ground is constituted by a more fundamental operation, a grounding of the ground. Augustinian reading, then, begins with the liberation of the text from any prior external reference, from history, or what linguists call "motivation." The literal meaning, for Augustine, is not what actually happened, but rather what the established text actually says. Literal meaning is the lucidity of inner sense. It is a matter of internal reference, conditioned upon the text's autonomy and self-identity, which is confirmed insofar as the text is found to be in accordance with the rules of grammar and common sense, or critically established so that such is made to be the case. Augustine both destroys and preserves the notion of literal meaning. This privileging of the Word itself over the history it relates, and over any specific meaning, recapitulates the major theme of Augustine's *Confessions*, the conversion of the Multitude into the One.

that both cancels and preserves each of these extremes, Augustine, like Marx theorizing abstract Labor in the *Grundrisse*, achieves a passage from manifold instances of textual practice to an abstract concept of Reading itself. This entails a shift from literalism to Literality, from text to Textuality. All interpretation, including so-called literal readings, is now understood as conditioned by a primary *allegoresis*, an operation which establishes the text, first and foremost, as a series of legible signs which may or may not point to a historical reality. This is precisely what Laclau and Mouffe name through the psychoanalytic term "overdetermination," which was strategically adopted by Althusser. "For Freud, overdetermination is no ordinary process of 'fusion' or 'merger'—which would at most be a metaphor established by analogy with the physical world, compatible with any form of multi-causality; on the contrary, it is a very precise type of fusion entailing a symbolic dimension and a plurality of meanings," these authors assert. "The symbolic—i.e., overdetermined—character of social relations therefore implies that they lack an ultimate literality which would reduce them to necessary moments of an immanent law."[36] Such a positing of text *qua* Text, as first and foremost pure symbol, permits the reader to contemplate even most obscene biblical tales of rape and incest in a state of innocent absorption, as hieroglyphs whose images bear no natural relation to their actual significance. Images, like those in dreams, are understood as mere letters, as code for spiritual meaning. Reading, in Augustine, becomes a therapeutic act in which the scandalous surface of the text, a jumble of tessera, is gathered into a meaningful unity. Properly established and read texts however, will yield the effect of a voice expressive of a living presence.[37] Voice may be modulated through the use of various figures of speech, but voice remains an expression of the One and not the Many. In the *Confessions*, Augustine provides a paradigmatic example of this act of consolidation in the image of Ambrose. Augustine describes observing his master, who sits contemplating a text in his study:

---

[36] *Hegemony and Socialist Strategy*, op. cit., 97–98.

[37] Laclau and Mouffe again discuss the possibility of reconstructing a whole from fragments, with respect to post-Kantian poetics, which stress intuition, spontaneity and synthesis. "In the type of theorization we wish to analyze, the elements on which articulatory practices operate were originally specified as fragments of a lost structural or organic totality. In the eighteenth century, the German Romantic generation took the experience of fragmentation and division as the starting-point of its theoretical reflection. . . . It was well known that the Romantics conceived this experience of dissociation as strictly linked to functional differentiation and the division of society into classes, to the growing complexity of the bureaucratic State establishing relations of exteriority with the other spheres of social life.

Given that the elements to be rearticulated were specified as *fragments* of a lost unity, it was clear that any recomposition would have an *artificial* character, as opposed to the natural organic unity peculiar to Greek culture." Ibid. 93–94.

When he was not with [the crowds of other men], and this was but a little while, he either refreshed his body with needed food or his mind with reading. When her read, his eyes moved down the pages and his heart sought out the meaning, while his voice and tongue remained silent. Often when we were present—for no one was forbidden entry, and it was not his custom to have whoever came announced to him—we saw him reading to himself, and never otherwise. After sitting for a long time in silence—who would dare to annoy a man so occupied?—we would go away.[38]

In this passage the proverbially golden-throated Ambrose dazzles Augustine not with a display of rhetorical *copia*, but rather silence. As he observes this unselfconscious exhibition of private vigilance, we see Augustine seeing Ambrose see, reading him read. This is the absorption of pure theory, unperturbed and removed from the theatre of public life. In beholding his master as dead to the world, yet powerfully animated, Augustine discovers the fact of human interiority. This becomes the condition of all orthodox interpretation, the reader's secure establishment with the inner sanctum of the Spirit. Augustine's identification and internationalization of this image of Ambrose, installs a moment of narcissism at the center of an entire ideological order known as the Human. The lucid reader, thus enshrined, is at liberty to wander through a variety of perilous texts without danger of delusion. But these relative freedoms always hinge upon the possibility of returning to the position of security and obviousness, the transcendence of the Letter.

In modern times we find the same set of existential coordinates in place in Marcel Proust. This time, however, the veil of orthodox allegory has worn thin. Rosalind Krauss, in a text that locates the genesis of Cubism in Picasso's loss of personal desire and surrender to the "motivation of the sign," cites Proust's description of this epicene scrutiny of text.

On waking I prepared to reply to Henri van Blarenberghe. But before doing it, I wanted to glance at Le Figaro, to proceed to this abominable and voluptuous act that is called reading the newspaper thank to which all the unhappinesses and disasters of the universe during the last 24 hours, the battles that have cost the lives of 50,000 men, the crimes, the strikes, the bankruptcies, the fires, the poisonings and suicides, the divorces, the painful residue of the emotions of the statesman and the actor, transmitted during our morning feast for our personal use to us who aren't even interested in them, excellently enter into relation, in a particularly exciting and tonic manner, with the recommended ingestion of several throatfuls of *café au lait*.[39]

---

[38] Augustine, *The Confessions*, trans. New York: Penguin, 1961.
[39] Cited in William Rubin, *Picasso and Braque: A Symposium*, New York: The Museum of Modern Art, 1992, 272–73.

Again, the literate subject finds narcissistic pleasure in collecting and recognizing itself in the activity of its own literacy. In opposition to Augustine, however, Proust's account of the pleasure of reading emphasizes not the production of meaning so much as the fact that literacy is at every moment conditioned by multiple accounts of atrocity. Pleasure is taken, and a subject formed, at the site of bliss. For Proust, the subject of Enlightenment, the supercilious critical reader, appears as an effect generated out of scanning the most tasteless concoctions and incongruous juxtapositions of yellow journalism. Negri and Hardt describe this same phenomenon on a more global level: "Empire is born not of its own will but rather it is called into being and constituted on the basis of its capacity to resolve conflicts" (Empire, 15). Schooled in scandal, the Subject of Empire comes into being precisely by compulsively consuming and neutralizing difference, multiplicity.

Now, none of this would come as a surprise to anthropologist Michael Taussig. An avowed disciple of Walter Benjamin, Taussig operates as a veritable writing machine, producing anything but conscious and responsible academic prose. In defiance of expository form, Taussig's texts arise out of a wild eclipse of reason, which he calls "Holy Torpor." In this state, the subject, outside the sanctum of the Augustinian Good, is transfigured into an extravagant, savage, polyglot performer. Incessantly yammering, yet no longer subject to the "significance" of the Letter, the body relinquishes the state of alertness which would allow it to function as the docile instrument of a unified authority.

> People were becoming possessed in turns. A young man in wet red shorts was on his back, shoulders heaving, stomach thrown forwards, herbs and medicines over his bare chest, honey in the form of the cross on his forehead, inner elbows, and knees, so as to make him less violent. He trembled for what seemed like half an hour then got up and almost fell off the cliff as another man took his place.
>
> It was the mixture of routine and sensationalism that [the liberal reformer] Mission found disturbing.
>
> As the next man lay down, someone fished out a bunch of needles wound together with red, blue and yellow ribbons. People drew hard on the tobaccos to concentrate the power as rum and Cinzano were poured over his now inert figure. After a short spell of quivering the man uttered a high-pitched cry so startling it was like his entire being had become ejected into voice. He was given a red robe with a gold border for he had become possessed by Santa Barbara and his companions set to work impaling his cheeks and thighs with the needles. Thus embodied and pinioned, blood streaming with the national colors, Santa Barbara proffered blessings and advice there in the cave cut in the windswept mountain.[40]

---

[40] Michael Taussig, *The Magic of The State*, New York: Routledge, 1996, 68–9.

Even in a professional setting, to witness Taussig read is to experience, raw and unedited, the trace of his wild encounters in the jungles of Columbia. Taussig's vertiginous and mesmerizing performances, which prompt both boredom and awe, forcefully confront the audience with the scandal of a pulsing, struggling, subtheoretical body. Here the viewer is forced to confront the negative image of Augustine watching Ambrose read in silence. Taussig's discursive pastiches, hybrids of oral and written communication, parody the Augustinian authentic voice and stand as antimonuments to the triumph of the Many over the One.

In Taussig's *The Magic Of The State*, for example, the bourgeois state, when viewed from the far side of labor relations, convulses into a macabre dance. This is the lurid underworld of Capital, seen in all its base materialism, heedless of all respectable health and hygiene. Far in excess of the outlines of shamanism, necromancy, and alchemy offered by classic anthropology, Taussig's texts present extended descriptions of drunken orgies, drug cartels, and cult worship. Taussig conjures an apocalyptic vision.

> [H]ordes of people . . . stomachs roped in by national colors and red bathing costumes, red of warring and the Indian, clustered by their shrines becoming possessed some screaming others in trance, people flipping out, people flipping in, get the enemy, become purified, the sacred billowing forth in waves of ecstasy and decay through vacant-eyed stares in mud under imperiled skies, stench of rotten refuse wet newspaper plastic bags juice cartons red plastic containers of gunpowder soda cans cigarette wrappers talcum powder rotting fruit and food heaped high on the shrines vaporizing in tropical heat. Roots running like knotted varicose veins along the earth, trees dripping overhead.[41]

Nothing could offer a greater contrast to the Italian "operaista" critics, whom Negri and Hardt find too captivated by the sterile sex appeal of "immaterial" technologies. Nor does Taussig gaze patronizingly down into the unified cradle of civilization. Rather, he descends beneath all authorized histories, into the jungle of impossible self-contradiction of cultural production's primal scene, the site of much Laclau and Mouffe will call a primordial antagonism.[42] He relates a narrative told by a sorcerer.

> Most of the people who came to him for cure are suffering, he said, from psychosomatic illnesses. Few are afflicted with an invading spirit. As an example of the latter he cited the case of the wife of a captain of the National Guard. She was possessed by the spirit of a dead man who was in love with her and, invisible as he was, would copulate with her in front of

---

[41] Ibid. 64.
[42] *Hegemony and Socialist Strategy*, op. cit., 122.

the captain! The captain was amazed. His own wife fucking herself, so it appeared, on being fucked by the spirit within her. *Contorsiones extrañas*, was how [he] put it in his clinical manner.[43]

In a complete reversal of perspectives, these lowest levels of society are no longer seen in the spiritualizing terms of Augustinian interpretation. Here we find not bedrock or primal elements but rather pure contradiction. Rather than reiterations of an acceptable bourgeois norm, meaning here plunges precipitously into coarse literalism and obscenity. Allegory, debased, is nothing but an infinite chain of illicit couplings—bestiality without shame or interest in redemption. In Negri and Hardt,

> the poor have become productive. Even the prostituted body, the destitute person, the hunger of the multitude—all forms of the poor have become productive. And the poor have therefore become even more important: the life of the poor invests the planet and envelops it with its desire for creativity and freedom. The poor is the condition of every production.[44]

In contrast to this, Classic analyses in cultural anthropology have retained their respectability. In their search for meaning, function and unity (the *arche*) in earlier cultures, these analyses have remained within the familiar enclave of Enlightenment. It is true that in his *General Theory of Magic*, Marcel Mauss, the protégé of Durkheim, accepts a certain irrational remainder at the heart of all cultural practice. But this remainder remains ideal, a merely conceptual impossibility. Mauss's invocation of Kantian *a priori* synthetic judgments serves always to bind multitudes within cohesive and meaningful totalities. Taussig's resolutely materialist dialectic of magic, on the other hand, offers a corrosive alternative. It does not promote symbolic closure but instead displays culture as located over a site of irresolvable conflict—the colonial experience of the "space of death." Taussig, for example, examines conflicting historical accounts of colonialist repression. These narratives come from proponents of slavery as well as liberal reformers, both of whom seek to identify a motive for violence. Just as Negri and Hardt reject Foucault and Deleuze with a single gesture, Taussig finds both oppressors and oppressed to be

> wrong and wrong in mutually dependent ways, with neither statement alone expressing what was going on in conquest and its associated debt-peonage, as if each man represented but one of the outer poles defining the limits of the field within which conquest and debt-peonage functioned. It was not even that this subordination of the Indian was achieved by a blend-

---

[43] Ibid. 74.
[44] *Empire*, op. cit., 158.

ing of force and fraud, or of arms and persuasion, or of conquest through barter and barter through conquest. All that way of thinking is merely truism that preserves the separateness of the domains even while blending them; violence and ideology, power and knowledge, force and discourse, economy and superstructure . . . when we put the two languages together it is not the blending of force with . . . the art of verbal persuasion that results, but a quite different conception in which the body of the Indian, in the process of conquest, in its debt-peonage and in its being tortured, dissolves those domains so that violence and ideology, power and knowledge, become one—as with terror itself.[45]

Classical anthropology fails to access the real forces of cultural production because it consistently attempts to explain magic in terms of a totalizing narrative of the intellectual development of the race (Frazer), or in terms of a total society as the coherent object of social science (Durkheim). Even in Mauss, the rational interpretation of primitive magic and religious ritual inevitably terminates when the analyst reaches an unaccountable "residue," some nonsensical formula, or Letter, which is the vessel of abstract power. The force of *Mana*, like the cunning of Reason, or the categorical imperative, operates heutonomously, and for the ultimate good of the organic community.

To make sense of Taussig, while refusing to dismiss or domesticate the alterity of the text; in other words, to read him ethically; requires the contingent imposition of a structuralist model. In place of adopting a functionalism of the sort that Negri and Hardt impute to Foucault, one must instead construct the complete ground within which lucidity figures as only one position within a complete, expanded field. For Jameson, such analysis requires identifying the basic conflict, or fundamental fantasy, underlying a cultural system, as well as the act of *pensée sauvage* through which such crises are worked through. In a similar fashion, though in a more activist tone, Negri and Hardt insist upon locating the split, the site of the fundamental act of repression and subsequent sublimation, whereas official culture "destroys its relations with the past and declares the immanence of the new paradigm of the world and life." According to this view, Empire's beaming visage is in fact a mask. Empire lives on by perpetually suppressing its own crimes and wretchedness. It sustains its morale by constantly formulating compromises, drafting treaties, and establishing a level field in an effort to come to terms with the contradictions inherent in its own history. Yet it is Empire's very attempt to liquidate all irregularities, to establish world order, which cause these various contradictions to return in an increasingly bewildering and virulent array of cultural symptoms. For,

---

[45] Michael Taussig, *Shamanism, Colonialism and the Wildman: A Study in Terror and Healing*, Chicago: University of Chicago Press, 1987, 29.

how could such a radical overturning not incite strong antagonism? How could this revolution not determine a counter-revolution? There was indeed a counter-revolution in the proper sense of the term: a cultural, philosophical, social and political initiative that, since it could neither return to the past nor destroy the new forces, sought to dominate and expropriate the force of the emerging movements and dynamics.[46]

This labor of primary repression and subsequent re-appropriation is graphically objectified in Rosalind Krauss's reading of Rodin. In Krauss's hands this quintessential modern master transforms into a sublime failure. Ostensibly Rodin's greatest achievement, the *Gates of Hell*, according to Krauss's analysis, was in fact created not by the artist himself but rather the State. For Rodin had bequeathed his studio and its muddle of contents to the French government. In need of an artist whose work might serve as a monument to the national genius, the State posthumously assembled a masterpiece out of what until that time had been little more than colossal wreckage. This fabrication, along with Rodin's monument to Balzac, furnishes Krauss with an example of a strained limit-term, one marking a total break with the premodernist past.[47] After Rodin, sculptural creation, for Krauss, becomes "essentially nomadic," liberated from its cultural roots. Modern sculpture "reaches down to absorb the pedestal into itself and away from the actual place; and the representation of its own materials or the process of its construction, the sculpture depicts its own autonomy."[48] Though key primitivist sculptures (Brancusi) may appear to derive from aboriginal works, their meanings must be understood as essentially severed

---

[46] *Empire*, op. cit., 74.

[47] The retroactive construction of a myth of origin is something which Krauss observes in the enormous array of "authentic copies" which have flooded Europe and America, including the vast shambles which is the actual Rodin legacy to the French nation. Krauss strenuously argues that most of these piece should be viewed as outright counterfeits, "re-assembled" by a posterity eager to recognize its own naissance in the guise of an heroic precursor. So irresistible is the mystic allure of this mythical origin, in fact, that it is quite often the master himself who becomes its greatest devotee, and thereby its most industrious one. It is in stark opposition to this cult of absolute originality, then, that Krauss proposes a counter-culture of copy and simulation. "What would it look like not to repress the concept of the copy? What would it look like to produce a work that acted out the discourse of reproductions without originals, that discourse which could only operate in Mondrian's work as the inevitable subversion of this purpose, the residue of representationality that he could not sufficiently purge from the domain of his painting? The answer to this, or at least one answer, is that it would look like a certain kind of play with the notions of photographic reproduction that begins with the silkscreen canvases of Robert Rauschenberg and has recently flowered in the work of a group of younger artists whose production has been identified by the critical term *pictures*." Rosalind Krauss, *The Originality of The Avant-Garde and Other Modernist Myths*, op. cit., 168.

[48] *Originality of the Avant-Garde*, op. cit., 280.

from all prior historical forms. Such art should not be viewed simply as or stylist residues or returns to the simplicity of the past, for their significance has nothing to do with the genuinely archaic. Instead, their meaning is determined, as Gramsci might put it, by the way they participate in the complex cultural articulation which is the present. Negri and Hardt, too, would suggest such "authenticity" is only apparent. "This [neo-aboriginality] can easily devolve into a kind of primordialism that fixes and romanticizes social relations and identities. What needs to be addressed, instead, is precisely the production of locality, that is, the social machines that create and recreate the identities and differences that are understood as the local."[49]

The great cultural maelstrom found in Taussig's *Magic of the State* may at first appear to be comprised of authentic relics and genuine traces of both Catholic, Indigenous and Revolutionary societies. Yet these bits of cultural rubbish function like works of modern sculpture for Krauss. They are, at best, decontextualized citations, within a larger hegemonic articulation, cut off from any genuine tradition. For Taussig, the official ceremonies of the state, which operate according to this same logic and arise is this same contemporary context, become garish scenes of necromancy. They take the form of tasteless conjugations of cultural detritus. The official cult of Bolivar, as a most poignant example, occurs on a site marked by failure and centered upon a rescued crumb of snot.

> A boat named *The Constitution* was sent along the coast. Simon Camacho, part of the delegation, met with the young French consul and physician Prospero Reverend, who had been in Santa Marta since 1828 and had attended the Liberator in his last days and kept as a relic all the years a small piece of dried of bronchial mucus retrieved from the Liberator's lung at postmortem, "what a somewhat oblong shape," commented Camacho, "porous and similar to the tiny bones to be found in the spines of fish."
>
> It was with boundless appreciation that Prospero Reverend hung onto this dried mucus wrapped in the same paper it was put into at autopsy twelve years before. He planned to send it to France in case he died far from his family. Thus from hand to familial hand and through those hands from nation to nation, the anticipation if not fear of death serves to transfer the mucus of the man coughing to death in exile. Could there be a bond more intimate between nations than that established by the exchange of oddly shaped mucoid ignominy excavated from the corpse? And by what strange logic of taboo and transgression, by what strange mixture of medical license and ritual lore, could an act of such perfectly base materialism come so naturally to glorify the state of the whole?[50]

---

[49] *Empire*, op. cit., 45.
[50] *The Magic of the State*, op. cit., 100.

Now, both Krauss and Jameson have shown, with regard to the maze of capitalist surplus, that what at first appears empirically unmanageable can nevertheless be made to make sense. The contingent imposition of a motivating device, the semantic square, will reveal a deep structure. The same operation can be performed on Taussig's representation of South American democracy, *The Magic of the State*. The term 'republic', if such were attempted, could function as the first term within a coherent *combinatoire*. It names a horizontally organized fraternal network bound together through principles of reason, private ownership, and free exchange of commodities. In a contrary relation to this first term is 'church', a hierarchically structured paternal organization bound by revealed dogma, collective ownership, and mediated exchange. These contrary terms form the complex axis of a square. The neutral axis, or axis of contradiction, represents underground entities which though they mirror those of the complex, are nevertheless radically liberated from the organic conditions named by their official counterparts. These neutral terms appear as analogous to the terms 'not-figure' and 'not-ground' in Krauss's analysis of abstract painting. Through them the sense certainty of "empirical vision," or the naturally given reality, is "cancelled, in favor of something understood as the precondition for the very emergence of the perceptual object to vision." As opposed to 'republic', then, 'not-republic' will represent organs of government, which, like part-objects, have gained a radical independence from the social whole—as Negri and Hardt put it, "not bodies but functions." In their devotionalism and mysticism of rank, these entities will appear as the cancellation and preservation, or the uncanny "mirror restatements," of their diagonal other, the Church. The 'militia' is the quasi-spiritual "neutralization" of the republic. Taussig identifies these groups as "park rangers," "National Guard," and "guerilla fighters. In Negri and Hardt, they are appear as

> "mafias," particularly those involved in the drug trade. The actual repression of these groups may not be as important as criminalizing their activities and managing social alarm at their very existence in order to facilitate their control. Even though controlling "ethnic terrorists" and "drug mafias" may represent the center of the wide spectrum of police control on the part of the imperial power, this activity is nonetheless normal, that is, systemic. The "just war" is effectively supported by the "moral police," just as the validity of imperial right and its legitimate functioning is supported by the necessary and continuous exercise of police power.[51]

Meanwhile, the simultaneous projection of the opposite terms of the neutral axis, generates 'cults', wherein religion operates free of ecclesiastic

---

[51] *Empire*, op. cit. 37–38.

dogma and discipline. Here, the distinction between individual personality and institutional role is preserved, while the notions of identity and hierarchy are neutralized, permitting multiples personas to circulate freely and possess various bodies. As suggested, within this *combinatoire*, the apotheosized figure of Bolivar, like Mauss's Mana, serves as a utopian point of synthesis. In the Liberator, republican liberal reason and ecclesiastical mystical hierarchy complete one another, in Hegelian fashion, within the myth of the State. And yet from another perspective, the equestrian image of Bolivar, which signifies the perfect merger of Church and Government, appears nowhere more often than on a mass-produced handbill, a "magical image obtainable for a few cents in perfumeries and marketplaces across the republic, the image of what we might call meta-death" (Magic, 102). The base-metal currency of Counter-Empire not only provides the stuff of underground economies, but like miasma, also percolates upward to taint even the highest ranks of official culture. Empire and Counter-Empire are not opposed entities so much as the same body seen from two different perspectives. Capital and the State, viewed from the dregs up, appear grotesquely disfigured. The official ceremonies of government become a perverse theatrical reenactment, at once comic and horrifying, of a primal scene of sexual excess, none more revolting than the obsequies of the Liberator himself. The state-sponsored inauguration of the cult of The Liberator Bolivar appears as nothing less than an obscene act of congress.

> The central feature of this state-making apparatus was the huge phallus, the catafalque, created to receive the Liberator's remains. Standing about fifty feet high, its prepuce of soft tasseled drapes flowed down to severe steps on which stood three "Indian" men around a bare-bosomed woman crouching at the foot of the erection. . . . .—the culmination where death engorged the primal organ of statehood sprouting from Indianness, shooting forth silver stars cascading veils and palls of purple velvet with gold arabesques.[52]

As Negri and Hardt suggest, the healthy luster of Capital, when viewed from the perspective of the multitude, is defaced, transfigured into the morbid pallor of "a vampire regime of accumulated dead labor" (Empire, 63). Empire becomes an outrageous invocation of its monstrous *semblable*. It reveals its true *unheimlich*, aneconomic face in the form of orgy of unbounded power.

To surrender fully to this feeling of simultaneous euphoria and horror, to think the possibility of the perfect identity of disgust and joy, is in

---

[52] Ibid., 106.

Fredric Jameson's *Postmodernism*, the quintessential affect, or sensibility, of postmodern critical interpretation.[53] The ceremony of Empire, viewed in terms of the Multitude, is drowned in its own tasteless excess, and transformed into the counter-discourse of Greenberg's abstract aesthetics. Counter-Empire, or what Negri and Hardt call the "Empire of corruption," is founded on a pornographic theatricality, unmitigated Kitsch.

Negri and Hardt's sudden and surprising turn to *The World as Will and Representation*, proceeds from this inverted worldview. Precisely because Schopenhauer viewed the modern State as nothing other than a colossal accumulation of rubbish, he "reacted . . . violently against Hegel, calling him an 'intellectual Caliban' to indicate the barbarity of this thought."[54]For Schopenhauer, Hegelian Spirit manifests its most essential truth not in the guise of the actively watchful Mover's eye, but in the throws of convulsive disgust. As Negri and Hardt say, the "construction of Empire and its global networks is a response to the various struggles against the modern machines of power, and specifically to class struggle driven by the multitude's desire for liberation." If it is true, as Negri and Hardt insist, that the "multitude [has] called Empire into being," this has been accomplished precisely by making the sovereign sick.[55] Here Negri and Hardt share Gramsci's skepticism with regard to Hegelian notions of development or progress. In neither set of writings can History any longer be seen as a programmatic unfolding of Human potential. Still, whereas for Gramsci political actors are continuously called into being through ever-shifting articulations within a hegemonic totality, for Negri and Hardt these moments of subjective epigenesis are far more convulsive. History, for them, does not take the form of a directionless and gradual drift, but instead an endless account of its seizures. Consciousness has become syncope, while Revolution, as Laclau and Mouffe put it, has become "subversion, and it manifests itself as symbolization, metaphorization, paradox, which deform and question the literal character of every necessity."[56]

What remains to address in Negri and Hardt's work, however, is the constitutive blindness, a fantasy of originality, which conditions their entire book. It is difficult to miss how everything unfolds in *Empire* as if the book were inscribing itself. Also, everything arises so as to avoid all mention of the Freudian Unconscious. In their enthusiastic effort to theorize the subject of Empire "*for the first time*," is it possible that Negri and Hardt belatedly, and disingenuously, rehearse formulas that were already codified long

---

[53] Fredric Jameson, *Postmodernism, or, The Cultural Logic of Late Capitalism*, Durham: Duke, 1995.
[54] *Empire*, op. cit., 28.
[55] Ibid., 43.
[56] *Hegemony and Socialist Strategy*, op. cit., 114.

ago? They flatten Foucault and Deleuze down to two cardstock carica-
tures. Propping these figures up on either side of Hans Kelsen, who occupies the "complex" position, the oedipal norm between two pathological
extremes, Negri and Hardt proceed to sit down, four-square, at a table laid
out by the very structuralist movement they claim finally to have overcome. Isn't the readymade "neutral" position they assume the very chair
of the analyst who discovers the secret of the Letter by recognizing it in all
its materiality? How can we fail to see *Empire* reenacting a scene of lure-
and-capture before our eyes, offering a textbook example of how, in the
very moment of seizing the victory, the player is mastered by the game? To
what extent is it possible that the authors' unmistakably euphoric tone is
genuine? How many exclamation points can they deploy before the reader
begins to see in their text an example of what Greenberg called "vicarious
experience and faked sensations"? And yet Negri and Hardt seem wholly
absorbed by the originality of their insight; they seem truly to be playing
in earnest. We are reminded of the state-sponsored event which provided
the occasion for Rosalind Krauss's essay debunking the myth of originality
as the essence of modernist art. During a visit to the National Gallery in
Washington, she attended what had been billed as "the largest Rodin exhibition, ever." Included in this show was a "brand new cast of *The Gates of
Hell*, so absolutely recent that visitors to the exhibition were able to sit
down in a little theatre provided for the occasion to view a just completed
movie of the casting and finishing of the new version."[57] Here we see yet
another burlesque, at once both preposterously solemn and alarmingly far-
cical. "Sitting in the little theatre, watching the newest *Gates* being cast,
watching this violation, we want to call out 'Fraud.'"[58] To be fair to all parties, it must be granted that Krauss's feeling of horror, along with her will-
to-denounce, do not spring from nowhere but are themselves powerfully
motivated by impersonal structures and discourses which she has treated in
her own work, forces from which, most likely, none of us can ever escape.
Still, in the light of the questions posed above, it seems wise to refrain from
too precipitously hailing *Empire* as a contemporary classic. Rather, we
might see it as a particularly striking example of what James A. Secord has
taught us to identify, and indeed value, as the latest reading "sensation."

---

[57] *Originality of the Avant-Garde*, op. cit., 151.

[58] Ibid., 157.

[59] James A. Secord. *Victorian Sensation: The Extraordinary Publication, Reception, and
Secret Authorship of* Vestiges of the Natural History of Creation, Chicago: University of
Chicago Press, 2003.

10

Things to Come: Monstrosity and Futurity

STEVE DeCAROLI and MARGRET GREBOWICZ

The new world of monsters is where humanity has to grasp its future.

MICHAEL HARDT and ANTONIO NEGRI[1]

I. Letter 17

On July 20, 1664, Spinoza composed a short letter to Pieter Balling, an activist Mennonite and a former classmate of Spinoza's during his years in Amsterdam. The letter was written to console Balling on the recent death of his young son, but also to advise him on how to understand the "omens" he had witnessed prior to the death. We learn that while his son was still alive and in good health Balling was awakened from his sleep by the sound of groans that were identical to those that would later be uttered by his son on his deathbed. Spinoza's initial evaluation of the incident is unequivocal: "I am inclined to think that these were not real groans but only your imagination; for you say that when you sat up and listened intently you did not hear them as clearly as before. . . . Surely this shows that these groans were no more than mere imagination."[2] Balling's suspicion that the sounds foreshadowed the fate awaiting his son seems to have been dismissed, for it is quite clear that "none of the effects of the imagination which are due to corporeal causes can ever be omens of things to come"[3] because the cause of an imaginary effect is not, nor can it ever be, derived from a future event. But Spinoza's remarks do not end here.

---

[1] Michael Hardt and Antonio Negri, *Multitude: War and Democracy in the Age of Empire*, New York: Penguin Press, 2004, 196.

[2] Benedict Spinoza, "Letter 17," *The Letters*, trans. Samuel Shirley, Cambridge, MA: Hackett Publishing Company, 1995, 125.

[3] Ibid., 126.

Instead, having left unaddressed those effects of the imagination that may arise from *incorporeal* causes, that is to say, from the mind, he adds, "the effects of the imagination . . . which have their origin in the constitution of the mind *can* be omens of some future event because the mind can have a confused awareness beforehand of something that is to come."[4] A close reading of the letter confirms that, while Spinoza flatly denies the reality of Balling's groans, he does not discount the possibility that they could nevertheless be omens. We find, in fact, that after explaining how it is possible for an imaginary image to appear real—by appealing to his own racialized hallucination of seeing in the early morning the "image of a black, scabby, Brazilian"[5] that he had encountered in a dream—he goes on to contrast his experience with that of Balling, stating that, "since the cause was quite different, your case was an omen, while mine was not."[6]

What is, of course, so striking about this passage is that it preserves the possibility of omens, albeit under a different explanatory principle than the one used by Balling and, in doing so, exposes two significant questions: one concerning the real, the other concerning the future. In the first instance, we must grasp why some varieties of imaginary awareness, specifically those that cannot be explained away as either hallucinations or dreams, appear to us to be real and not as imaginary at all. Here we must discover the ground upon which Spinoza maintains the dissimilarity between Balling's experience of groans and his own encounter with the Brazilian. It is primarily an ontological question. In the second case, we seek to know how it is possible that, under certain conditions, the mind, and particularly the imagination, can give us an awareness of the future. In this case, the question directly addresses the possibility of omens, of knowing the future, and is therefore ultimately an epistemological question. Both questions are distinct and can be answered independently, but by treating them side-by-side we are able to come to a more complete understanding of Spinoza's position. In both cases, the remainder of Spinoza's letter invites a complicated reading.

II. Transindividualism

At the end of a recent essay, Warren Montag takes up the challenge of analyzing Spinoza's letter to Balling. His analysis centers on a well-known but opaque passage that immediately follows the discussion of omens quote above. Taking as an example a father who deeply loves his son, Spinoza

---

[4] Ibid., 126. Emphasis added.
[5] Ibid., 125.
[6] Ibid., 126.

speaks of the two as being, "as it were, one and the same,"[7] and further claims that "since the soul of the father participates ideally in the things that follow from the essence of the son, he can . . . sometimes imagine something from what follows on the essence of the son as vividly as if he had it in front of him."[8] Despite the imprecision of the language, and beyond any simple form of hallucination, we have here a statement that begins to address the question of why some forms of imaginary awareness strike us as decidedly un-imagined. The formulation of any adequate response to this question must, it seems, ultimately come to terms with what Spinoza means when he says that the father "participates" in those things—presumably affects and desires—that follow from the son's essence. The entire task hinges on this point.

Montag's analysis of the passage invites us to read the text broadly; placing it within the philosophical framework of Spinoza's other writings, particularly the *Ethics*, which Spinoza was then composing in Voorburg. In the letter, Spinoza goes to some length to show that the vivacity of the father's imaginary images depends upon his participation with those things that "follow from the essence of the son."[9] While the text is admittedly vague, it is not difficult to see that the passage calls into question the ontological separation between discrete individuals. After all, Spinoza says as much when he characterizes the father and son as "one and the same."[10] Accordingly, for Montag, the passage represents an early formulation of a theory of "transindividualism," a term borrowed from Ètienne Balibar, which designates an affective unity in which "each participates in the affect or desire that marks their composition as a single individual."[11] The father experiences the son's feelings and desires not as a spectator who imagines what it must be like to be in the place of the son, but as a participant in a shared essence that resides neither in the son nor the father, but between them. Since, for Spinoza, the essence of a thing is constituted by the desire, that is, the striving, a thing has for the preservation of its own being (*conatus*),[12] then, as Montag rightly asks, if "I share a desire with another person, do I share

---

[7] Ibid., 126.

[8] Ibid., 127.

[9] Ibid., 127.

[10] Ibid., 126.

[11] Warren Montag, "Who's Afraid of the Multitude? Between the Individual and the State," *The South Atlantic Quarterly* 104, no. 4, Fall 2005, 670. See also, Ètienne Balibar, "Potentia multitudinis quae una veluti mente ducitur," in *Ethik, Recht und Politik bei Spinoza*, ed. M. Senn and M. Walther, Zurich: Schultheiss, 2001.

[12] Benedict de Spinoza, *Ethics* III P7, trans. R.H.M. Elwes, New York: Dover Publications, 1955, 136. "The endeavour, wherewith everything endeavours to persist in its own being, is nothing else but the actual essence of the thing in question."

the *conatus*"[13] as well? What, in other words, "would allow us to be thought of as separate individuals, rather than as part of a singular thing whose *conatus* is expressed in both of us?"[14]

If we bear this in mind, it is reasonable to assume that, according to Spinoza, the sounds Balling heard were in fact expressions of his own transindividual desire, that is to say, a desire that constitutes the essence not of himself alone, but of himself and his son together. The error in Balling's judgment, therefore, was not in supposing the sounds to be omens, but in assuming them to be real, in an objective sense, when in fact they were products of the mind—the product of a shared affective relationship with his son. Balling's error was in attributing independent reality to that which is imaginary. This much Spinoza makes clear. But it is crucial to emphasize that simply being imaginary does not entail being "false" or trivial. In fact, Spinoza's letter suggests just the opposite.

Whereas Spinoza's imaginary experience of the Brazilian was caused by the spilling over of dreams into daytime consciousness—an effect of the imagination which, like a hallucination, is trivial—the cause of Balling's encounter with imaginary sounds was altogether different. Here, as we have seen, a powerful effect of the imagination was produced by the affective union between father and son, and so, in this case, the imagination proceeds in a more meaningful manner, not only because it purportedly bears a relation to the future, but because it embodies a novel approach to conceptualizing our relationship with others. Consequently, despite the fact that both encounters are imaginary, the two events have different causes and therefore have profoundly different significances. One is trivial, the other perhaps even prophetic.

Even though Balling's imaginary encounter is more significance than a mere hallucination, Spinoza nevertheless draws our attention to a critical error in Balling's assessment of his experience, namely, his failure to recognize its proper cause. Balling assumes a system of representation. He assumes that the sounds he imagines *represent* the groans of his son. But, as we have seen, this is impossible. The groans of his son have not yet occurred. Therefore, since the effects of the imagination are not representational, because they span no temporal distances and are not caused by future events, neither are they prophetic in any traditional sense. By assuming the sounds to be independent of his mind, i.e., caused by his son's future actions, Balling attributes to them an independent reality they do not possess and, in doing so, falls into an error that is far more significant that it seems. To mistake an imaginary sound for a real one is, relatively

---

[13] Warren Montag, "Who's Afraid of the Multitude? Between the Individual and the State," op. cit. 669.

[14] Ibid., 669.

speaking, of small consequence, but what if, instead of mistaking imaginary sounds for real sounds, one were to mistake an imaginary god for a real one? The danger is self-evident. Though there may be no real, independent gods, the mind has the capacity to not only imagine them, but also to believe in them as if they were not imaginary at all. This is the danger Spinoza illustrates in his critique of Balling. It is not a question of whether the future is knowable, but whether, in claiming to know the future, we also assume that the future already exists, fully formed and independent of us.

Thus, the same error that Spinoza isolates in Balling's mistaken assumption that the groans are "real," appears whenever we presume the permanence of things that are in fact the products of the mind—and here we include the church, the state, the future, etc. In having a tendency to believe its own creations, the imagination is hazardous, especially since this tendency is typically an effect of social life, of sharing relations with others such that, as an entire society, we externalize our fictions and burden ourselves with them. Whenever we assume the reality of a mental image we reify the future, we make solid what is ephemeral, in short, we assume we have discovered something when in fact we have created it. This is the larger lesson of letter 17 and is precisely why this short correspondence remains philosophically relevant. Against the ontological backdrop of transindividualism we can make out the shape of a new ontology of the subject—a subject that for Spinoza, at least in his unfinished *Political Treatise*, as well as for Hardt and Negri, goes by the name multitude. The anthropomorphic conception of the individual, coupled with the affective distance we assume to exist between individual subjects, between a father and his son, or between an individual and a community, is precisely that which Spinoza's philosophical ontology set out to dismantles—and it is for this reason that it is possible to read within Spinoza's letter powerful political implications. Spinoza asks us to resist the illusion of the real (of real gods, or real states, etc.) because at its center is the most damaging illusion of all, the illusion of an independent, self-possess individual—the autonomous subject. And, of courses, it is precisely *this* illusion that Spinoza's theory of multitude ruptures.

In imagining consciousness to be free from the interventions of the world we are artificially shielded from knowing ourselves as effects, rather than as causes, which in turn prevents us from grasping the extent of our sociality. Accordingly, what is most compelling about Montag's reading of letter 17 is that within transindividualism he locates a political potential, what he speaks of as the "danger" of the multitude. Transindividuality, he tells us, materializes as a political force characterized not by the collective solidarity of separate individuals coming together, for instance, to overthrow the established rule of law, but rather by an affective union whereby the multitude promises to overcome not the law, but the ideological conception of the "juridical individual"[15] itself. Indeed, "from the point of view of law, there is no collective action in the strict sense, merely the simultaneous actions of separate individuals only apparently united into some collective entity."[16] The multitude, therefore, seeks not to transform the law, but to transform our most basic assumptions about desire and subjectivity. "Neither a mere juxtaposition of separate individuals nor a collective entity that draws its legitimacy and function from its source in the voluntary consent of such individuals," Montag writes,

> the multitude precisely has no juridical legitimation or political form. It is that excess or remainder that is irreducible to the antinomies of legal and political thought, overdetermining both political theory and practice, the permanent excess of force over law, and a force that no state can monopolize precisely because it is the force no one can alienate or transfer insofar as it is necessary to life itself.[17]

A potential to literally strive together, to constitute a *conatus*-in-common, lies buried within Spinoza's correspondence and it is this insight that compels Montag's reading. Omens do appear, but they appear as a consequence of desire being released from its confinement within the juridical individual—the liberal subject for whom desires belongs as a piece of property. The power of the multitude, which is also its danger, is presented here as the potential to form a commonality between individuals based on affect and desire, rather than on conventional political interests which invariably preserve the illusion of possessive individualism—the most powerful legacy of modern political thought and practice since Hobbes.

The appearance of transindividualism, then, this symbiotic union among individuals, defines a critical threshold, at which the distinction between reality and imagination, which is so decisive for philosophical ontology, threatens to vanish. The relation between the imagined and the real marks the boundary at which the omen appears, and where any analysis of the real must confront its object as mode of creation and belief, rather than of transcendence or correspondence. It is as if the problem of determining the border between the real and imaginary, which forces itself upon us each time we encounter a tangible apparition that seems out of place, were in fact the problem of desire itself. The desires and affects of individuals having been superimposed so completely, forces the very meaning of individuality to break down, and with it the antinomy of individual and community. When the distinction vanishes and the affects of two individu-

---

[15] Ibid., 670.
[16] Ibid., 659.
[17] Ibid., 663.

als collapse upon each other, the difference between the real and the imaginary, between the objective and the subjective, fades away, and in its place a relation appears for which we seem to lack even an adequate name. Multitude has recently been the word most frequently used to name this form of being, but one could equally employ the word "monster." Either way, what is essential is that we recognize within this reformulation of the ontology of the subject not only a powerful political gesture, but also an equally powerful danger.

III. *The Productive Imagination*

Thus far we have seen that, for Spinoza, the omen is neither real (because it is produced in the imagination, not through physical causes), nor a sign of the real (because it does not point toward, or represent, anything in the future). Both these positions require a faith in the independence of reality, a real beyond production, which Spinoza seeks to demystify. But the question nevertheless remains; what exactly is the relationship of the imagination to the future? And why does it deserve to be called by the name omen? To answer these questions we must address more closely the productive power of the imagination, and for this we turn to the pages of Antonio Negri's *Savage Anomaly*, where letter 17 is examined for what it reveals to us about the imagination's constitutive power. In Negri's reading, the omen that Spinoza preserves is distinctly *productive* not in the sense that it formulates true claims about the future, but in its capacity, through the work of the imagination, to actively produce the future and its relations.

In Negri's account, Spinoza's letter reveals first and foremost the centrality of the imagination. If certain omens are possible, if in some cases we are granted a glimpse into the future, it is because the imagination is capable of presenting this world to us, not as a dim fantasy but, "firmly and vividly, as if such a thing were present."[18] Drawing on Spinoza's assertion that "there is almost nothing we can understand without the imagination instantly forming an image,"[19] Negri insists on the imagination's ubiquitousness. "If the effects of the imagination derive from the soul," he writes, "in what way does the imagination participate in the constitution of the soul?"[20] and more importantly, "to what degree does the imagination participate, with the soul, in the constitution of the world?"[21] The

---

[18] Benedict Spinoza, "Letter 17," op. cit., 126.

[19] Ibid., 126.

[20] Antonio Negri, *The Savage Anomaly: The Power of Spinoza's Metaphysics and Politics*, trans. Michael Hardt, Minneapolis: University of Minnesota Press, 1991, 87.

[21] Ibid.

importance of this letter, then, lies in the conduit it builds between the imagination and the world. In the case of the mind, the closer we investigate its imaginary effects, the more convinced we become that the gap between image and reality has evaporated. The omen, that which opens us to the future, is preserved by Spinoza because, insofar as it has its origin in the constitution of the mind, the omen is a product of the futurity we have always already fashioned through our ways of thinking, our habits of discourse, and our patterns of social commerce. The mind, as it were, lies always ahead of itself, constituting that for the sake of which we live.

But, of course, these habits are never formulated in isolation. Instead, they arise from social participation, from sharing affects and desire with others in precisely the manner Spinoza's loving father participates in the essence of his son. The social, for Spinoza, is a mutual participation in the essence of others, a multitude whose commonality is not grounded in ideas, but in feelings and desires. There is no essence of the social beyond this commonality, nothing independent toward which an omen may point. Thus, the "confused awareness" we may have of things to come is a consequence, not of predicting or calculating, but of anticipating by extending our essence throughout the entire social body. Here the omen and the habit are one in the same.

In *Multitude*, Hardt and Negri employ the notion of habit, drawn from the tradition of American pragmatism, in their explanation of the production of the common. "Habit is the common in practice," they write, "the common that we continually produce and the common that serves as the basis for our actions."[22] The notion of habit, they argue, permits the displacement of traditional philosophical conceptions of subjectivity, moving it away from discussions premised on the inviolability of an inner self toward an understanding of the constitution of social life. Located halfway between a fixed immutable nature and spontaneous individual freedom, "habits constitute our social nature"[23] which we both take for granted and cannot survive without. "Habits are thus never really individual or personal," but, "only arise on the basis of social conduct, communication, acting in common."[24] And despite the ordinary understanding that habits are little more than the repetition of past behaviors, Hardt and Negri insist, along with Dewey, that habits are fundamentally, and creatively, oriented toward the future. "Habits are not really obstacles to creation but, on the contrary, are the common basis on which all creation takes place. Habits

---

[22] Michael Hardt and Antonio Negri, *Multitude: War and Democracy in the Age of Empire*, New York: Penguin Press, 2004, 197.
[23] Ibid., 197.
[24] Ibid.

form a nature that is both produced and productive, created and creative—an ontology of social practice in common."[25]

By prioritizing neither the individual nor the social, the pragmatic notion of habit neatly characterizes the multitude—a collective social subject, unified by its manifestation of common desires in the form of evolving, nonchaotic social relations. The social body itself, what Hardt and Negri term the "flesh" of the multitude, is nothing more or less than the collection of these forces. There is simply no sociality beyond the forces that are put into play. Like the omen of letter 17, there is no referent beyond the presentation; there is nothing objective toward which the omen points as a sign, just as there is nothing natural or divine upon which the social world rests. What remain are the effects of habit, which are equally the effects of social imagination, and the creation of a world which becomes "real" the moment we misrecognize our own constituent power (*potentia*) and mistake the effects of the imagination for the truths of a transcendent power (*potestas*). In other words, we actively produce the reality of our own kings, our own gods, and our own monsters along with every plane of transcendence, and it is through the imagination, and our misunderstanding of it, that transcendence becomes possible. For Negri, in order to be properly understood, every transcendent concept must be thought through the material beings, and the immanent processes of subjectivization, that produced the very Power under which they then subsume themselves. As Negri writes, "the problem consists of the special nature of the effects of the prophetic imagination, of the paradox of an essential nothingness that produces historical being and certainty."[26] In mistaking the constituent power of the imagination for an independent reality we lapse into precisely the same error as Balling. His error, we will recall, was not in accepting the possibility of a knowable future, but in misattributing to that future the quality of being "real" and predetermined. Balling made the mistake of attributing transcendence to the future—a form of the theological illusion in which the potentiality of the present is forever subordinated to, and placed in the service of, the actuality attributed to the future. This is why teleology is contrary to every form of freedom, and is why when teleology expectations are disrupted, the agent of this disruption—the atheist, the revolutionary, the half-man—is invariably monstrous.

In his remarks concerning the discussion of prophecy in the first three chapters of the *Theologico-Political Treatise*, Negri writes, "The horizon of prophecy, then, cannot be anything other than the horizon of mere imag-

---

[25] Ibid., 198.
[26] Antonio Negri, *The Savage Anomaly: The Power of Spinoza's Metaphysics and Politics,* op. cit., 94.

ination." Yet the pronouncements of the prophets are taken to be the word of God. "It comes about, nonetheless," he continues, "that the prophetic imagination is believed to be an expression of the '*directo Dei*.'"[27] The attribution of transcendence to the effects of the imagination (here the law of God) is for Spinoza, as it is for Negri, at the core of all dogma—the transformation of habits into commandments—and this transformation, which keeps hidden, also marks the divergence of ethics and morality. "All that one needs in order to moralize," Gilles Deleuze writes of Spinoza, "is to fail to understand. It is clear that we have only to misunderstand a law [a habit, or way of life] for it to appear to us in the form of a moral 'You must'."[28]

To see the power of this misunderstanding at work, we need only look to Negri's discussion a few pages earlier where he describes the force that the imagination exerts to create the world, leaving open only the manner in which we choose to approach this creation: to approach it ethically, as the immanent construction of our imagination, or morally, as an independent, transcendent reality. In the passage, Negri recounts Spinoza's confrontation with the problem of God who "appears as king and legislator." This conception is delusional, yet, he writes, "this corrupt imagination effectively constructs the world!"[29] The imagination, he continues,

> is as strong as tradition, it is as vast as Power, it is as destructive as war— and it is the servant of all this, so that human unhappiness and ignorance, superstition and slavery, misery and death are grafted onto the imaginative faculty itself, which, on the other hand, constructs the unique horizon of a human society and a positive, historical determination of being.[30]

The imagination, then, can be either positive or destructive. It can either yield new and more empowering ways of life or generate the superstitions of transcendent authority. The fact remains the same: what holds for human sociality is always the effect of the productive imagination. What can alter is our willingness to assume responsibility for this creative potential by refusing the externalization of our capacity for social production.

> Distinguishing the truth and recognizing the human capacity to construct both the truth and the freedom of life, apart from all the calamities that the imagination determines in the world, become the first steps in a logical

---

[27] Ibid., 93.

[28] Gilles Deleuze, *Spinoza: Practical Philosophy*, trans. Robert Hurley, San Francisco: City Lights Books, 1988, 23.

[29] Antonio Negri, *The Savage Anomaly: The Power of Spinoza's Metaphysics and Politics*, op. cit. 89.

[30] Ibid., 89.

reform that is trying to found an ethical reform. And a political reform, too? Yes, necessarily.[31]

IV. Political Monsters

For late-seventeenth-century writers, the appearance of monsters—in the form of prodigious births—was accompanied by heightened political anxiety built upon the imagination's predilection for superstition. For most, the monstrous birth was a sign (from *monstro*, to point out, to indicate) of God's power (*potestas*), thereby providing a rationale for the externalization of desires and fears. Here, huddled around the idols of their own imagination, we find the faithful, the fearful, whose imaginations are willing to accept the inconsistencies of a life lived in obedience. After all, Spinoza writes, "faith does not demand that dogmas should be true but that they should be pious; that is, they should lead the spirit to obey."[32]

But for those writers who denied monsters, for those who knew them to be acts of nature, not of god, the monstrous posed a threat of an entirely different magnitude, namely, the potential to "move multitudes against the crown and church.[33] For these "men of reason," the monstrous is not a vengeful act of God, but a disruptive effect of the imagination. And, as Hardt and Negri have written, in this historical context "the monster is not an accident but the ever present possibility that can destroy the natural order of authority in all domains, from the family to the kingdom."[34] It became necessary, therefore, to exclude the monstrous from the scientific and political orders not because it was false, but because it threatened to expose the inconsistencies upon which privilege was based. The monster, in other words, is dangerous because it threatens to unleash the imagination against the state. In his 1663, *A Discourse Concerning Prodigies*, John Spencer sounds the warning:

> How mean a regard shall the issues of the severest debates, and the commands of Authority find, if every pitiful Prodigy-monger have credit enough with the People to blast them, by telling them that heaven frowns

---

[31] Ibid.

[32] Benedict de Spinoza, *Theological-Political Treatise* XVI. Quoted in Antonio Negri, *The Savage Anomaly: The Power of Spinoza's Metaphysics and Politics*, op. cit., 176.

[33] Lorraine Daston and Katharine Park, *Wonders and the Order of Nature, 1150–1750*, New York: Zone Books, 1998, 335.

[34] Michael Hardt and Antonio Negri, *Multitude: War and Democracy in the Age of Empire*, op.cit., 195. For other contemporary discussions of monstrosity see, Antonio Negri, "Il mostro politico. Nuda vita e potenza," *Il desiderio del mostro: Dal circo al laboratorio alla politica*, ed. Ubaldo Fadini, Antonio Negri, and Charles T, Wolfe, Roma: manifestolibri, 2001.

upon the laws, and God writes his displeasure against them in black and visible Characters when some sad accident befalls the complyers with them.[35]

What writers such as Spencer brought to the early modern discourse on monsters was a new sense of the urgent political dangers that accompany any unregulated mixing of wonder and fear. As with omens, prodigious births easily took hold of the imagination, drawing it in the direction of superstition and illusion. The monstrous, in the hands of the right actors, was revolutionary. Consequently, following a line of argument offered by Lorraine Daston and Katherine Park, the state embarked on a comprehensive strategy "to decouple wonder from fear."[36] Domesticated in this way, wonder would be directed toward the contemplation of nature instead of toward the wrath of God that accidents of nature seemed to foretell. To experience admiration in the presence of the monstrous, instead of fear, "became the self-conscious mark of the natural philosopher," and we might add, the principal concern of modern statecraft as well.

It is of little surprise that the political philosophers of the late seventeenth and early eighteenth centuries parallel so closely the scientific methodologies of the day. The elimination of the subversive potential of wonder and the exaltation of the light of reason were, of course, powerful tools of demystification, but along with these trends we witness the diminishment of political imagination. Stripped of their wonder, monsters become tame. No longer are they allowed to justify forbidden political or social desires. No longer can they be harnessed, intentionally or otherwise, to draw collective attention to social transformation. But the sober explanations of monstrosity offered by science, which were clearly valuable in eliminating common superstitions, were far less effective in ridding the world of their own political superstitions—those other monstrosities that have taken the form not of natural accidents, but of political order and its own, more secular, '*directo Dei*.' It is, after all, Hobbes who applies the name Leviathan to the state and its head, to "the Multitude . . . united in one Person,"—a comparison by no means original with him.[37]

At the end of the seventeenth century, the category of the monster, along with that of the miracle, is attacked by philosophers who see in it

---

[35] John Spencer, *A Discourse Concerning Prodigies* [1663], 2nd ed., London: J. Field, 1665, sig. a3r. Quoted in Lorraine Daston and Katharine Park, *Wonders and the Order of Nature, 1150–1750*, op. cit., 335.

[36] Lorraine Daston and Katharine Park, *Wonders and the Order of Nature*, op. cit., 336.

[37] See John M. Steadman, "Leviathan in Renaissance Etymology," *Journal of the History of Ideas* 28, no. 4, 1967, 575–76.

the imagination's poor attempt to explain that which is currently unexplainable through science. And the most extreme opponents of imagination will go so far as to claim that the church and revelation itself are just as imaginary as the omen or the prodigy. Spinoza is, of course, one such figure. But, as we had seen, in the case of letter 17, Spinoza's criticism is not directed against the use of the imagination per se, but against the tendency to turn the effects of the imagination into independent truths. These are the dogmas, mythologies, and ideologies that Spinoza's writings oppose. And it is in retracing this same path that Negri takes us back to the early seventeenth century when the imagination was still a powerful faculty. But he does so not to reclaim the imagination's capacity to believe in omens and superstitions or its power to make manifest transcendent truths or political theologies. Rather, Negri follows Spinoza in leaving open the possibility that the imagination can have a creative effect on the future without being theological. The imagination can envision a different future and in this alone it is enormously powerful. As we have seen in regard to Spinoza's letter 17, the imagination can never foretell the future, but it can assist us in envisioning one. There is a revolutionary potential within the monstrous imagination, despite its tendency to externalize this power as a theological illusion, and insofar as it is capable of challenging social closure, the monstrous holds out the promise of new forms of life that refuse to reference a transcendent order—both political and ontological.

For monsters to appear, then, two elements are necessary: a presumed natural order and an abnormality that places the naturalness of this order in doubt. There is first of all the state, the artificial sovereign, together with the naturalized habits of social life, whose strength depends on the capacity of the subjected masses to believe in, and thereby constitute, the natural legitimacy of its power. It is against the background of the illusion of a natural order—the teleological structure of all transcendent authority—that the abnormality of the monstrous can be identified. And secondly, there is the appearance of an abnormality that troubles this order from within; the monstrous individual whose very being upsets the consistency that law and sovereignty depend upon. In being outside of the normal order, the atheist, the hermaphrodite, the ascetic, etc., open a space within the obedience of the masses for a contrary possibility to show itself, and by disrupting social consistency, reveal an imposed order resting at the heart of what was taken to be a natural one. Thus, when, on July 27, 1656, Spinoza was issued the harshest writ of *cherem* ever pronounced by the Sephardic community of Amsterdam for his "monstrous deeds" and "abominable heresies," we know that it was against the audacity of disobedience that they were written.[38]

Out of place, and conforming to no existing class, the monster is known only through comparison with an order that precedes it. Only against the background of the pervasive illusions of thought—natural order and the theological illusion of finality—is the monstrous made visible. Its deformed flesh shows that the world is not as regular as our theological illusions suggest, and that there are no durable absolutes—despite every attempt by transcendent authority to preserve the illusion that order is real and that this order is organized in relation to a stable, i.e., moral, notion of the good life. As Hardt and Negri both attest, "Spinoza shows us how today . . . we can recognize these monstrous metamorphoses of the flesh as not only a danger but also a possibility, the possibility to create an alternative society."

At issue, finally, is how the inert facts of hallucinatory omens or physical deformity, enlisted in the service of narrow world views and ideologies, become evidentiary such that counterfactual forms of existence are systematically obscured, destroyed, or demonized in the interest of preserving both the orderliness of the status quo and the desires that have been so thoroughly coordinated with it. We produce our own consistency and in doing so we limit the ways in which facts can become meaningful to us. In establishing these limitations we produce a situation that can only be violent at its edges. So when a person whose very existence is counterfactual— the gay, the Communist, the monster—they will always be confronted with violence. To become a monster today, as Hardt and Negri insist we must, is to remain unconvinced of the reality of our omens, to remain always aware of the potential for establishing yet another theological illusion. By not fitting into the given order of things, by calling into question the seemingly transparent notion that facts speak for themselves, monstrous life promises to preserve the power of the imagination to shape new futures, without transforming these futures into moral laws, that is, into facts which are always already a type of evidence. At its heart, then, monstrosity sunders fact from evidence. It is a matter of remaining unconvinced of any single theory or system of order. Monsters are those who, in being who they are, place this system of order, be it scientific or political or religious, in doubt without succumbing to a rational skepticism that must assume a breach between knowing and being. As we have seen, for Spinoza, as for Negri, there is no such skepticism, no such divide, because imagination is productive not of adequate or inadequate representations of a reality, but of social life itself. Here there is simply no theory of correspondence upon which skepticism can take hold. "Politics is the metaphysics of the imagination," Negri writes,

---

[38] Michael Hardt and Antonio Negri, *Multitude: War and Democracy in the Age of Empire*, op. cit., 194.

the metaphysics of the human constitution of reality, the world. The truth lives in the world of the imagination; it is possible to have adequate ideas that are not exhaustive of reality but open to and constitutive of reality, which are intensively true; consciousness is constitutive; being is not only something found (not only a possession) but also activity, power; . . . Imaginative activity reaches the level of an ontological statute, certainly not to confirm the truth of prophecy but to consolidate the truth of the world and the positivity, the productivity, the sociability of human action. . . . This is the interruption in the system, but above all this shows the enormous Modernity of Spinoza's thought."[39]

V. Social Flesh

Monstrosity today, however, requires more than a particular deployment of the imagination. Various rich and often inconsistent discussions of embodiment and materiality appear throughout Hardt and Negri's work, inviting us to see the living, fleshy monsters among us. Is the multitude—monstrous, queer[40] social flesh—imaginable? We learn that its monstrous constitution makes the multitude unrepresentable, or perhaps that its monstrosity results, at least in part, from this unrepresentability. "The people is always represented as a unity, whilst the multitude is not representable, because it is monstrous *vis à vis* the teleological and transcendental rationalisms of modernity. In contrast with the concept of the people, the concept of multitude is a singular multiplicity, a concrete universal. The people constituted a social body; the multitude does not, because the multitude is the flesh of life."[41] Flesh is not a body. Neither is it a particular kind of collection of bodies. And yet, Hardt and Negri articulate certain characteristics of the multitude with particular attention to the changes in the actual bodies of the people who make up this collectivity. It takes new kinds of bodies to make up social flesh.

In *Empire*, for instance, Hardt and Negri explore the notion of a resistant, hybrid body that challenges hegemonic conceptions of gender and sexual norms, as formulated in the work of Donna Haraway:[42]

---

[39] Antonio Negri, *The Savage Anomaly: The Power of Spinoza's Metaphysics and Politics*, op. cit., 96–97.

[40] Michael Hardt and Antonio Negri, *Multitude: War and Democracy in the Age of Empire*, op. cit., 192–93.

[41] Antonio Negri, "Approximations: Towards an ontological definition of multitude," trans. Arianna Bove. *Multitudes numero 9 'Pour une définition ontologique de la multitude'*, http://www.nadir.org/nadir/initiativ/agp/space/multitude.htm

[42] For a more extensive study of the relationship between Hardt and Negri and Haraway, see Margret Grebowicz, "Relocating the Non-Place: Reading Negri With/Against Haraway," *International Studies in Philosophy*, vol. 38, no. 2, 2007.

The new barbarians destroy with an affirmative violence and trace new paths of life through their own material existence. These barbaric deployments work on human relations in general, but we can recognize them today first and foremost in corporeal relations and configurations of gender and sexuality. Conventional norms of corporeal and sexual relations between and within genders are increasingly open to challenge and transformation. Bodies themselves transform and mutate to create new posthuman bodies. The first condition of this corporeal transformation is the recognition that human nature is in no way separate from nature as a whole, that there are no fixed and necessary boundaries between the human and the animal, the human and the machine, the male and the female, and so forth; it is the recognition that nature itself is an artificial terrain open to ever new mutations, mixtures, and hybridizations.[43]

The fusion of human and machine, they write, "is a fundamental episode at the center of the reconstitution of the multitude and its power."[44] The new nature of productive labor is "immaterial," but "somatic,"[45] and it is this "soma" which manifests the new power relations of Empire, and which the new materialism must mobilize.

However, they continue, "hybridity itself is an empty gesture." The hybrid body "must also be able to create a new life," "the infinite paths of the barbarians must form a new mode of life."[46] This is a move we encounter throughout *Empire*—the charge that postmodern forms of resistance break down boundaries and create hybridities, but fall short of the important project because they fail to effect a new form of life. They remain alienated from praxis and from "the common productive experience of the multitude."[47] In Derrida's work, hybridity, or the breakdown of binary oppositions, is presented in positive terms, as more than critique, or rather, critique itself is presented as affirmation. But Hardt and Negri present themselves as going beyond this to a hybridity which is not only affirmative, but productive, materially creative. They refer to Haraway's contribution, but gesture towards a new project, as in the following passage:

> Once we recognize our posthuman bodies and minds, once we see ourselves for the simians and cyborgs we are, we then need to expose the *vis viva*, the creative powers that animate us as they do all of nature and actualize our potentialities. This is humanism after the death of man: what

[43] Michael Hardt and Antonio Negri, *Empire*, Ibid., 215.
[44] Ibid., 405.
[45] Ibid., 27–29.
[46] Ibid., 216.
[47] Ibid., 217.

Foucault calls 'le travail de soi sur soi,' the continuous constituent project to create and recreate ourselves and our world.[48]

In fact, this gesture is present in Derrida's exploration of the monstrous. "But a monster is not just that, it is not just this chimerical figure that in some way grafts one animal onto another, one living being onto another. A monster is always alive, let us not forget. Monsters are living beings."[49] Hardt and Negri build on this: monsters are living, but not natural. Social flesh is monstrous because its malformations are not the result of nature. "In the previous era modern social bodies and modern social order maintained, at least ideologically, despite constant innovation, a natural character. . . Every reference to life today. . . has to point to an artificial life, a social life."[50] Hybridity and life, metamorphosis and barbarism, and the oxymoronic formulation, "artificial life." What is this new body? Who are these people who come together to form the unrepresentable social flesh? Can we imagine them?

VI. Feminist Monstrosity

A quick scan of the history of teratology shows an ongoing and complex relationship between monstrosity and procreation. Unlike monsters, gods and founding heroes in mythology are not "of woman born." On the contrary, as Rosi Braidotti tells us, one of the signs of a god's divinity is "his ability, through subterfuges such as immaculate conceptions and other tricks, to short-circuit the orifice through which most human beings pop into the spatio-temporal realm of existence."[51] Monstrous births, on the other hand, especially by the time of the Baroque, result from specific "immoral" sexual practices by the mother, so that "all sexual practices other than those leading to healthy reproduction are suspected to be conducive to monstrous events." Not only immoral intercourse, but specific foods, weather conditions, and the woman's wanton imagination could result in monsters. The mother had the power of producing a monstrous child if she thought about evil things during intercourse, dreamed intensely, or even looked at an "evil-looking" creature.[52] Well into the nineteenth cen-

---

[48] Ibid., 92.

[49] Jacques Derrida, "Passages—From Traumatism to Promise," in *Points . . . . Interviews 1974-1994*, ed. Elizabeth Weber, Stanford: Stanford University Press 1995, 386.

[50] Michael Hardt and Antonio Negri, *Multitude: War and Democracy in the Age of Empire*, op cit., 192-93.

[51] Rosi Braidotti, "Mothers, Monsters, and Machines," in *Nomadic Subjects*, New York: Columbia University Press, 1994, 84.

[52] Ibid., 85-86.

tury, the first famous conjoined twins in modern history, Chang and Eng Bunker (the original "Siamese twins") were denied entry into France because officials feared that pregnant women who so much as witnessed their traveling act would themselves bear conjoined twins.[53] "It is as if the mother, as a desiring agent, has the power to undo the work of legitimate procreation through the sheer force of her imagination."[54] Since, according to this logic, the monstrous birth is the direct result of the exercise of this power, it is understood that the power ought not to be exercised.[55]

For this reason, perhaps, the relationship between women and the monstrous is refigured in the postmodern political imagination so that monstrosity is something for feminism to embrace. Donna Haraway's "A Cyborg Manifesto" relies on such a revaluation. The cyborg is not a goddess and its origins are not innocent. It is the "illegitimate offspring of militarism and patriarchal capitalism, not to mention state socialism. But illegitimate offspring are often exceedingly unfaithful to their origins."[56]The cyborg instantiates a break from the horizons of nature and man, thus offering a figure for feminism which once and for all severs the bond with a female embodiment figured as "given, organic, necessary."[57] The essence of woman, Haraway writes, "breaks up at the same moment that the networks of connection among people on the planet are unprecedentedly multiple, pregnant, and complex. 'Advanced capitalism' is inadequate to convey the structure of this historical moment. In the 'Western' sense, the end of man is at stake."[58] She describes the liberatory character of monsters in the following passage:

> Monsters have always defined the limits of community in Western imaginations. The centaurs and Amazons of ancient Greece established the limits of the centered polis of the Greek male human by their disruption of marriage and boundary pollutions of the warrior with animality and woman. Unseparated twins and hermaphrodites were the confused human material in early modern France who grounded the discourses on the natural and supernatural, medical and legal, portents and diseases—all crucial to establishing modern identity. The evolutionary and behavioral sciences

[53] http://zygote.swarthmore.edu/cleave4b.html

[54] Rosi Braidotti, "Mothers, Monsters, and Machines," op.cit., 86.

[55] This tradition continues in contemporary, rural communities in Europe, where girls and young women are often warned not to look too long and hard at "ugly" animals (like toads) and gargoyles.

[56] Donna Haraway, "A Cyborg Manifesto: Science, Technology, and Socialist-Feminism in the Late Twentieth Century," in *Simians, Cyborgs, and Women: The Reinvention of Nature,* New York: Routledge, 1991, 151.

[57] Ibid., 180.

[58] Ibid., 160.

of monkeys and apes have marked the multiple boundaries of late twenti-eth century industrial identities. Cyborg monsters in feminist science fic-tion define quite different political possibilities and limits proposed by the mundane fiction of Man and Woman.[59]

While the monstrous may have been embraced in feminist literature, however, the liberatory status of technology remains contested.[60] Gena Corea, along with other feminist critics of emerging reproductive tech-nologies, argues that technologies allow for a seamless continuation of patriarchal control over women's bodies, resulting in a social order in which biological mothers are replaced with "mother machines."[61] Braidotti shares this position, and offers a different vision of monstrosity:

> The test-tube babies of today mark the long-term triumph of the alchemists' dream of dominating nature through their self-inseminating, masturbatory practices. What is happening with the new reproductive tech-nologies today is the final chapter in a long history of fantasy of self-gen-eration by and for the men themselves—men of science, but men of the male kind, capable of producing new monsters and fascinated by their power.[62]

In these accounts, which have been criticized for being too binaristic and tele-ological,[63] technology *is* domination, not because there is anything inherently patriarchal about technology itself, but because its meaning is determined entirely, exhaustively, by its function in patriarchal social organization.

For Haraway, in contrast, technology offers the possibility of unstable meanings. The technological world is one in which nature is irrecuperable and meaning cannot anchor itself. It remains under constant threat of slip-page and contamination. Thus, we can never guarantee that a technology will be either oppressive or liberatory—these values remain always con-testable. Different technologies have different political belongings and the same technologies can have different political belongings at different times. Along with cyborg identities, then, feminism must formulate new epistemologies that would allow for responsible knowledge claims. Our knowledge claims and our technologies must become responsible, we must

---

[59] Ibid., 180.

[60] For an excellent survey of feminist debate in this area, see chapter 4 of Jana Sawicki, *Disciplining Foucault: Feminism, Power, and the Body*, New York and London: Routledge 1991.

[61] Gena Corea, *The Mother Machine: Reproductive Technologies from Artificial Insemination to Artificial Wombs*, New York: Harper and Row, 1985.

[62] Rosi Braidotti, "Mothers, Monsters, and Machines," op. cit., 79.

[63] See chapter 4 of Jana Sawicki, *Disciplining Foucault: Feminism, Power, and the Body*, op. cit.

become accountable for their political belongings, rather than insulating them from the realm of values (knowledge for its own sake). Haraway writes that we must formulate methods by which to read technology in terms of its social effects and to distinguish between "its promising and its destructive monsters."[64]

But is such a distinction possible? Consider the case of Cecil Jacobsen, whose groundbreaking research on male pregnancy in primates could have revolutionized gender relations (and might still do so). He and Roy Hertz planted a fertilized baboon egg in the abdominal cavity of a male baboon, which proceeded to carry the fetus "to term" (it was removed surgically at 4 months, but the doctors reported that the baboon could easily have carried it to the full seven). Jacobsen is the only scientist on record to have experimented with male pregnancy in primates.[65] What made him famous, however, was his inseminating of possibly up to 75 women[66] with his own sperm, in the course of working at a fertility clinic in the 1980s, an act which resulted in a five year prison term and his license being revoked in 1991. Here, two related acts by the same person appear to have contradictory political belongings. The baboon experiment is readable as feminist (although Corea might not read it so), while the "Babymaker" (as Jacobsen was called) experiment is an arguably violent act of domination of women's bodies by not only a man, but a patriarchal institution and ideology (even, we suspect, for Haraway). This case serves as a good point of departure for exploring the difficulties of distinguishing between productive and destructive monsters, and illustrates why feminist work on a viable notion of responsible knowledge is necessary. As Braidotti writes, "No area of contemporary technological development is more crucial to the construction of gender than the new reproductive technologies."[67] Indeed, while for most of us, technologies of the internet, of contact lenses and deodorants, even of alternative fuel sources have a much more direct impact on daily life than, say, in vitro gestation (also known as "test tube babies" or IVG), it is IVG which has far greater potential to affect women's lives positively and negatively.

---

[64] Donna Haraway, "Situated Knowledges: The Science Question in Feminism and the Privilege of Partial Perspective," in *Simians, Cyborgs, and Women: The Reinvention of Nature*, New York: Routledge, 1991, 190. See also Grebowicz, Margret and Emily Zakin, "On Promising and Destructive Monsters: Reading Lyotard's 'She'," in *Gender after Lyotard*, ed. Margret Grebowicz, Albany: SUNY Press, 2007.

[65] Dick Teresi and Kathleen McAuliffe, "Male Pregnancy," in *Sex/Machine: Readings in Culture, Gender, and Technology*, ed. Patrick D. Hopkins, Bloomington and Indianapolis: Indiana University Press, 1998, 177.

[66] Only 7 of the women Jacobsen treated underwent paternity tests, all of which showed that he was the biological father.

[67] Rosi Braidotti, "Mothers, Monsters, and Machines," op. cit., 79.

VII. *Artificial Life*

The "new monsters" produced by the "men of science" are no longer the babies produced in the test tubes, but the new bodies which result from technological mediation of reproduction. For Haraway, the concern is not with the offspring, but with the relationship of the "adult" cyborg to nature, and thus, to politics—the political subject as cyborg. If we follow Foucault in his description of the monstrous as that which is unclassifiable not only naturally, but also in "civil, canon, or religious law,"[68] then today's monstrous bodies are not the ones emerging from the test tubes, but the bodies into which contemporary reproductive technologies transform ours. In the case of reproductive technologies, the laws of science remain intact, but legal norms are challenged to the core.

For example, in the case of Davis vs. Davis (1992), we see a divorced couple fighting for custody of seven frozen embryos stored in the fertility clinic at which they had been patients in happier times. Mary Sue Davis first wanted the embryos implanted in her uterus, but Junior Davis objected. He wanted to wait until he had decided whether or not to have children outside the bounds of marriage. The Tennessee courts ruled in Junior's favor. After both parties remarried, their positions shifted and they reappeared in court. This time, Mary Sue wished to donate the embryos to a childless couple, but Junior preferred to see them "discarded."[69] Are the embryos persons, or are they the property of the "parents"? Are Mary Sue's and Junior's interests in the embryos the same, and if not, how are they different? How do the possible decisions in this case compromise either of their rights to "procreational autonomy"? The courts ruled in Junior's favor again (by which time the case had traveled to the Supreme Court of the State of Tennessee), and the opinion concludes that "the party wishing to avoid procreation should prevail, assuming that the other party has a reasonable possibility of achieving parenthood by means other than the use of the pre-embryos in question."[70]

The questions above would resonate quite differently in the situation of "natural" procreation, with the fetuses in Mary Sue's uterus and not in a fertility clinic. We can imagine that the Supreme Court's decision would have been different, as well—presumably, Mary Sue would not have had to terminate a pregnancy because of her ex-husband's wish to "avoid procreation." This example illustrates that the difficulties of thinking through

---

[68] Michel Foucault, *Abnormal: Lectures at the College de France 1974–1975*, ed. Valerio Marchetti and Antonella Salomoni, New York: Picador, 2003, 63.

[69] Supreme Court of the State of Tennessee, "Opinion in the Matter of Davis vs. Davis" in *Sex/Machine: Readings in Culture, Gender, and Technology*, op. cit., 216.

[70] Ibid., 232.

these new technologies do not stem from IVF being "miraculous," or breaking with scientific laws, but with the enormous challenges they pose to civil law. The threat stems not from the question *how will these technologies affect the natural order,* but *how will they affect the social order?* Thus, the movement by which natural life is transformed into artificial life is the same movement that makes this life irreducibly social.

> The living social flesh that is not a body can easily appear monstrous. For many, these multitudes that are not peoples or nations or even communities are one more instance of the insecurity and chaos that has resulted from the collapse of the modern social order. They are social catastrophes of postmodernity, similar in their minds to the horrible results of genetic engineering gone wrong or the terrifying consequences of industrial, nuclear, or ecological disasters. The unformed and the unordered are horrifying. The monstrosity of the flesh is not a return to nature but a result of society, an artificial life.[71]

The metamorphosis of society provokes new dilemmas. Biological engineering threatens to result in eugenics, and even a "race of slaves," humans whose sole purpose is to provide a reserve supply of organs. Who will decide on these matters, what tribunal will rule in these cases? Negri states that ethics committees are ineffective in the face of the new dilemmas and that the multitude must decide democratically, with decisions "taken in a collective and practical way." "We must decide which monster we want," which future we want.[72] It seems that, like Haraway, Negri focuses on this decision as a crucial political task, and on the power to decide democratically as central to the ontology of the modern political subject.

This focus on decision, however, seems inconsistent with his call for somatic resistance. The very force of the imperative ("we must") is lost once we do, in fact, decide. As Derrida writes, "as soon as one perceives a monster in a monster, one begins to domesticate it."[73] Returning to the notion of undecideability, we propose that the monster is creative and productive at least in part because it produces the imperative to decide, to act, and that this imperative, *rather than its fulfillment,* is at stake in Hardt and Negri's conception of multitude. We may begin to formulate Hardt and Negri's departure from Haraway in the following terms: while Haraway looks to promising monsters and formulates a particular version of stand-

---

[71] Michael Hardt and Antonio Negri, *Multitude: War and Democracy in the Age of Empire,* op. cit., 193.

[72] Antonio Negri, *Negri on Negri: In Conversation with Anne Dufourmantelle,* trans. Malcolm B. DeBevoise, New York and London: Routledge, 2004, 116–18.

[73] Jacques Derrida, "Passages—From Traumatism to Promise," in *Points. . . . Interviews 1974–1994,* op. cit., 386.

point epistemology in order to facilitate distinguishing them from the destructive ones, Hardt and Negri exploit the ambivalence, the ambiguity between the promising and the destructive, the incessant return of a real danger which keeps the monstrous in fact monstrous.

As much as Hardt and Negri's project relies on the insights of Foucault, this should not be conflated with a Foucauldian position (although the connections are rich and worth exploring at greater length). From the Foucauldian perspective,

> Disciplinary technologies are not primarily repressive mechanisms. In other words, they do not operate primarily through violence against or seizure of women's bodies or bodily processes, but rather by producing new objects and subjects of knowledge, by inciting and channeling desires, generating and focusing individual and group energies, and establishing bodily norms and techniques for observing, monitoring, and controlling bodily movements, processes, and capacities. Disciplinary technologies control the body through techniques that simultaneously render it more useful, more powerful, and more docile.[74]

Thus, the aim of the new reproductive technologies is to "enhance the utility of women's bodies for multiple shifting needs."[75] In Foucault's terms, the political belonging of a practice depends entirely on whether it disciplines the body to be more docile or less so, and the task for feminists is to "resist those forces that aim to enlist such practices in the service of docility and gender normalization and struggle to define them differently."[76] For Negri, however, resistance is neither a matter of redefining practices, nor of establishing new practices. Negri's model of resistance requires a new body, and it is on the level of the body, and not of practices, that the irresolvable ambiguity between oppression and liberation is productive.

VIII. The Future

In *Empire*, the resistant body is described as "a body that is *completely incapable of submitting to command*." Here Hardt and Negri appear to represent the resistant body as altogether undisciplinable, in contrast to the Foucauldian position. What is significant for our analysis is the idea that resistance is not a matter of (disciplinary) practices, but of (undisciplinable) bodies. "It needs a body that is incapable of adapting to family

---

[74] Jana Sawicki, *Disciplining Foucault: Feminism, Power, and the Body*, op. cit., 83.
[75] Ibid.
[76] Ibid., 89.

life, to factory discipline, to the regulations of a traditional sex life, and so forth. (If you find your body refusing these "normal" modes of life, don't despair—realize your gift!)"[77] To put it in terms of the body/soma distinction: resistance needs not a body (understood as the body capable of being regulated), but a soma (the body which refuses regulation). The soma is the body as resistance itself, not as a site of resistant practices.[78]

Lee Mingwei and Virgil Wong are two contemporary artists whose installation, *POP! The First Human Male Pregnancy* (1999)[79], is a website devoted to chronicling the "real-life" pregnancy of Mingwei, the first man to have been implanted with an embryo. Visitors to the website are invited to "monitor Mr. Lee's vitals, learn about the science of male pregnancy, participate in online chats about the social implications of pregnant men, and leave messages for him." From the reactions, it is clear that the visitors to the site do not know that they are participating in a work of art. Mingwei and Wong are part of the group PaperVeins, which describes itself as focused on the "creation, curation, exhibition, and study of contemporary art about the human body in medicine and technology." [80] The work forces us to confront a "real life" pregnant man, not just male pregnancy as an idea or thought experiment. The website includes his pregnancy journal, ultrasound images, and film footage, which, we are told, is being compiled for later use in a documentary film. His being raced ("Asian") particularizes Mingwei even more, so that he is precisely not the all-American boy next door, the norm of maleness. *POP!* does much more than show us the spectrum of public opinions on the topic of male pregnancy. It forces us to deal with a living monster, whom it is impossible to stabilize and categorize as either promising or destructive. The force of this work lies in its never releasing us from the ambiguity, not just on the level of ideas, but on the visceral, experiential level.

There is an essential difference between the monsters of the past, the conjoined twins and "Elephant" men, bodies which today would be classified as "disabled," and the man whom Lee Mingwei performs. The disabled body, which until very recently was read as monstrous, is becoming less and less somatic in the Negrian sense. The political organization and mobilization of disabled people, who are increasingly visible, has resulted in legal subject-status for them. The people whom Hardt and Negri describe as "unformed and unordered" are not those with congenital birth defects. The existence of the latter does not challenge legal norms, thanks

---

[77] Michael Hardt and Antonio Negri, *Empire*, op. cit., 216.
[78] This idea is present in the work of Jean-François Lyotard, as well. See Grebowicz, "Relocating the Non-Place," op. cit.
[79] www.malepregnancy.com, www.leemingwei.com.
[80] www.paperveins.org

to contemporary discourses and practices of normalization and diversification. This double movement— normalization of the disabled body and consciousness on one hand, and diversification of the fully-abled masses, whose consciousness about disability is being "raised" and whose bodies are being moved aside to make room for handicapped ramps and parking spaces—works to integrate the disabled person as fully as possible into civil society. [81] The pregnant Mingwei, on the other hand, remains profoundly "unformed and unordered" and thus belongs nowhere. Spending more time on the website and "getting to know him better" does nothing to relieve our discomfort. His is the body completely incapable of integration into social life and work, of submitting to command—at least at this historical moment. *It is resistant as a body, in its corporeal opacity, its matter, but not in its "nature."* Artificial life has irretrievably distanced this body from nature. It is no longer regulated body, but soma, its materiality and singularity produced by an irremediable mediation by technology. This is immanence understood as artificial life.

"The future can only be anticipated in the form of an absolute danger. It is that which breaks absolutely with constituted normality and can only be proclaimed, presented, as a sort of monstrosity."[82] So writes Derrida in 1967. The imagination which constitutes sociality and the body refigured as social flesh, somatic, artificial, and undisciplinable—these are Hardt and Negri's answers to thinking and living against Empire. But could their scope not be extended to other discourses? We propose that the political monsters found in these works are relevant to other "social justice" discourses in which the ontology of the resistant subject is at stake. Haraway is right that "the past is the contested zone,"[83] in the sense that work in feminist and queer theory consists largely of revising natural and social histories which are used to justify and legitimate contemporary male supremacy. But what is the source of the contesting? Hardt and Negri offer the possibility of relations to the future that produce a space in which to contest, to "be against." The extendibility of these concepts beyond the discourse of Empire points to the fecundity of Hardt and Negri's texts. These relations, the productive imagination and the body as resistant in itself, indicate new ways of being political, the coming of new political beings.

---

[81] This does not mean that normalization of disability is not problematic, or that discourses of diversification are not perpetuating patterns of oppression and privilege. In fact, Hardt and Negri would argue that these discourses are instrumental in the passage to *Empire*.

[82] Jaques Derrida, *Of Grammatology*, trans. Gayatri Spivak, Baltimore: John Hopkins University Press, [1976] 1994, 5.

[83] This is the subtitle of a chapter in *Simians, Cyborgs, and Women*, "Animal Sociology and the Body Politic: The Past is the Contested Zone."

Contributors

George Caffentzis is a Professor of Philosophy at the University of Southern Maine and a member of the Midnight Notes Collective. He is author and editor of many books and articles on social and political theory including *Clipped Coins, Abused Words and Civil Government: John Locke's Philosophy of Money*.

Melinda Cooper graduated from the University of Paris VIII in 2001. She has published widely in journals including *Angelaki: Journal of the Theoretical Humanities, Theory & Event*, and *Theory, Culture and Society*. Her book *Life As Surplus: Biotechnology and Capitalism in the Neoliberal Era* was published by Washington University Press in 2008.

Steven deCaroli is Associate Professor of Philosophy and Director of the Philosophy Program at Goucher College. He is the co-editor of *Giorgio Agamben: Sovereignty and Life* (Stanford, 2007). He has published articles and book chapters on Hegel, Herder, Winckelmann, Arendt, and Agamben.

Michael Goddard is Professor of English, Cultural and Media Studies at the University of Lodz, Poland. He has published on Polish and international cinema, Deleuze's aesthetic theories, and radical Italian thought. He is currently preparing a book on the cinema of Raul Ruiz and conducting research into East European postmodern audiovisual cultures.

Margret Grebowicz is Assistant professor of Philosophy at Goucher College. She is the editor of *Gender after Lyotard* (SUNY, 2007) and the co-editor of *Still Seeking an Attitude: Critical Reflections on the Work of June Jordan* (Lexington, 2005). She has published articles and book chapters on Derrida, Levinas, Negri, Haraway, and Feyerabend.

Brian Kubarycz received a Ph.D. in Creative Writing from the University of Utah, where he currently teaches Intellectual Traditions and The Honors Program. He is a practicing painter and fiction writer, with work appearing in *The Quarterly* and *Unsaid*.

Pierre Lamarche is Associate Professor of Philosophy at Utah Valley University. He is the author of articles on Bataille, Heidegger, Benjamin, and Proust.

Max Rosenkrantz is Assistant Professor of Philosophy at California State University, Long Beach.

David Sherman is Associate Professor of Philosophy at the University of Montana at Missoula. He is the author of *Sartre and Adorno: The Dialectics of Subjectivity* (SUNY, 2007) and co-editor of *The Blackwell Guide to Continental Philosophy* (Blackwell, 2003). Journals in which his articles have appeared include *Philosophy Today*, *Philosophy & Social Criticism*, *Telos*, *Philosophical Forum*, and *Philosophy and Literature*.

Steve Wright is in the Caulfield School of Information Technology, Monash University. He is the author of *Storming Heaven: Class Composition and Struggle in Italian Autonomist Marxism* (Pluto Press, 2002).

Index